T0383421

THE LAND OF
THE WHITE HORSE

David Miles

THE LAND OF
THE WHITE HORSE

Visions of England

In memory of:
Alan Saville (1946–2016)
and Martin Dyer (1948–2017)
A band of brothers on the M5

Frontispiece: Photograph by Angus Haywood looking
out from the White Horse to Dragon Hill and beyond.

First published in the United Kingdom in 2019 by
Thames & Hudson Ltd, 181A High Holborn,
London WC1V 7QX

The Land of the White Horse © 2019
Thames & Hudson Ltd, London

Text © 2019 David Miles

Designed by Karolina Prymaka

British Library Cataloguing-in-Publication Data
A catalogue record for this book is available from
the British Library

ISBN 978-0-500-51993-6

Printed and bound in China by Reliance Printing (Shenzhen)
Co. Ltd

To find out about all our publications, please visit
www.thamesandhudson.com. There you can subscribe
to our e-newsletter, browse or download our current
catalogue and buy any titles that are in print.

CONTENTS

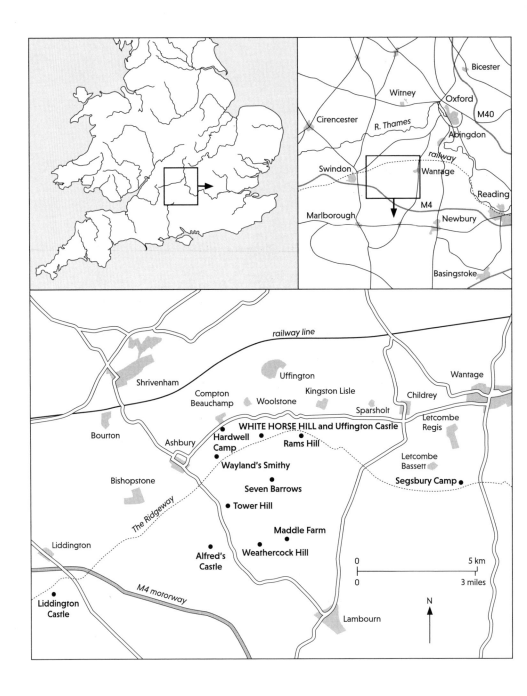

Location map of White Horse Hill within the Berkshire Downs, with modern features, towns and villages and prehistoric sites (in **bold**) in the area.

INTRODUCTION

Before the gods that made the gods
Had seen their sunrise pass,
The White Horse of the White Horse Vale
Was cut out of the grass.

G. K. Chesterton, 1911

Once upon a time someone felt the need to carve the figure of a giant horse into the steep scarp of the chalk downs of southern Britain. This happened long ago, in the time of dreams, way beyond human memory. People then forgot who had made the Horse and why, but nevertheless, they adopted it for themselves, trying to make sense of this strange image on the skyline. Every few years they gathered together in huge numbers to scour the lines of the white coat, to keep the Horse gleaming, and to celebrate with country sports and strong drink: a fine act of remembrance for the ancestors. In the surrounding villages people made up stories, patched from scraps of the past. Over the centuries the stories changed, as gods became heroes and heroes became villains. Sometimes the lords celebrated the Horse, proud of its presence on their land and their lordship. At other times they feared the wrath of the mob. Perhaps the Horse was best ignored and allowed to fade away.

Against the odds the White Horse at Uffington survived and now it is an icon of the English countryside. I am well aware that 'icon' is an overused term, but, in this case, it is an appropriate one. This Horse is unusual, a sleek, segmented, abstract figure about 120 m (395 ft) long, carved into the green turf. It looks out over the heartland of England.

There are other hill figures in Britain – mostly horses that stand rigidly to attention. This one is different: unrestrained, leaping freely across the hillside. The fragmented limbs and sinuous shape convey fluidity and movement. Turn away and the figure could disappear over the western horizon. The Uffington White Horse is also the first of the hill figures, the only one that we know to be ancient. It is the sire (or dam, if you prefer) of the others.

In the twelfth century a medieval scribe included the White Horse, along with Stonehenge and the Giant's Causeway, as one of the 'Wonders of Britain'. For several centuries antiquarians, travellers and local people speculated about the age of the Horse, who created it and why. Was it a memorial to Alfred the Great's victory over the heathen Danish invaders, an emblem of the first Anglo-Saxon settlers or a prehistoric banner, announcing the territory of an ancient British tribe? Or was the Horse an actor in an elaborate prehistoric ritual, drawing the sun across the sky?

One of the pleasures of a project such as the one I describe here is to be immersed in the local: to experience the detailed sounds and smell of a particular patch of land, its fleeting light and weather. At the same time I have tried not to be parochial. We are all part of a wide, interconnected world and always have been. So to understand the role of horses in human civilization, I have deliberately roamed off the downland to the Americas and the steppes of Asia. These are the places where horses and horse-powered societies evolved, to transform much of the world. No man is an island, even if he or she lives on one.

The distinctive image of the Uffington White Horse is constantly reproduced: on book covers, record sleeves and pottery, and by artists and photographers. It is an emblem of the local administrative authority (Vale of White Horse District Council, now part of Oxfordshire), the North Wessex Downs Area of Outstanding Natural Beauty (AONB), the Berkshire Archaeological Society, and even theatre groups and the All Party Parliamentary Archaeology Group. At the village school, the Uffington children wear the Horse on their uniform, and the well-known image flashes by on the side of vans belonging to local businesses – the plumber, the builder, the landscape gardener.

So the White Horse is still a badge of identity. Sometimes it has represented a stolid Englishness, like the flag of St George, the patron saint who is said to have slain the dragon on the distinctive hill just below the Horse. As a supposed symbol of Anglo-Christian nationalism, and the work of Alfred the Great, Victorians held the White Horse in huge esteem – the most important ancient site in the country. Now its known age adds to its fascination. The joy of the White Horse lies in its fluidity and changing identity – like Britishness itself. The ancient Greek philosopher Heraclitus of Ephesus said that nobody steps into the same river twice, or as Plato interpreted this: everything changes; nothing remains still. This idea, in some respects, is true of the Horse: a figure whose form has remained remarkably fixed over millennia, yet which constantly metamorphoses in the human imagination.

A local brewer's beer mat with the White Horse image – this badge
of identity is frequently adopted by local businesses, organizations
and the local authority.

The White Horse remains enigmatic, mysterious, even an embarrassment. The distinguished Cambridge archaeologist Grahame Clark wrote: 'This noble animal, it is well to remember, can only have survived through frequent scouring of the chalk, a very symbol of continuity between the prehistoric past and the present day.'[1] More recently, students of archaeology can search for the Horse in vain in academic textbooks and specialist works on prehistory. The Horse has gone missing. Often there is no mention of Britain's largest prehistoric image. The uniqueness of the figure, like some odd geological erratic, leaves it out in the cold, difficult to fit into the standard narratives of prehistory.

Our team of archaeologists and scientific specialists involved with the White Horse project described in Chapter 6 gathered in an attempt to investigate this enigma, but also to explore the surrounding chalkland and understand how people had lived there since the end of the Ice Age: how they had cleared the forests and created the hillforts, fields, downland pasture and copses that are so familiar today. This is one of England's best-loved and most familiar landscapes, but not always well understood. We need to appreciate the role of geology, climate, plants and animals, as well as humans, in its evolution. So our team took to the skies in aeroplanes, and used geophysics to see what lay beneath the surface, to explore the fourth dimension of time and unravel how the past is still with us in the present – and how we might continue to care for both the Horse and its setting.

Historians and protectors of the landscape are sometimes nostalgic for an idealized past into which modernity is an infringement. Yet the land has always been contested – from the slaughtered victims of a raid, buried in the Wayland's Smithy tomb more than five thousand years ago, to the confiscated monastic lands and enclosures of more recent centuries. And never more so than today, with conflicts over subsidized industrial farming, the drastic decline of wildlife, coal-fired power stations and the arrival of the installations of wind and solar power. Our aim on White Horse Hill was to understand the past not airbrush it or somehow return to what has gone. If we could hear the voices of those who cared for the

An image of White Horse Hill from Thomas Hughes's famous novel *Tom Brown's School Days*. The sheep safely graze on the downland scarp below the White Horse, guarded by a somnolent shepherd and his dog. In the Manger the ploughman cultivates the bottom-land.

Horse they would speak ancient Gallic, Latin, early forms of German, French Norman, the English of Chaucer, Shakespeare and the Berkshire dialect recorded by Thomas Hughes in *Tom Brown's School Days*. Recently I have heard Californian and Estuarine English and Japanese. The White Horse itself remains a silent witness, an enigmatic presence in the present. It is a palimpsest on which much has been lost, but where slight traces remain, providing vital information.

This is an evocative landscape that inspires artists, poets and writers. To many, this chalkland typifies England; patriots have gone to war and died for it. Their fading names are inscribed on memorials in churchyards and stones at the crossroads. Today, some people are so attached to this landscape that they ask that their ashes should be scattered on the hill.

White Horse Hill is a place of imagination: a reminder of mankind's ability to mark the earth for good or ill. Often we erase the traces of the past, in a society addicted to throwaway impermanence; often we do not know what we have lost until it is too late. The Horse is a symbol of

continuity and enchantment, a place where the different pasts remain present. Like the Earth itself, the hill figure is both fragile and persistent. For generations people have come together to work to ensure its survival. We can speculate why, and I have done so in these pages. I do not claim to provide the answers. The White Horse remains a wonder: a myth for modern times.

CHAPTER ONE

THE BOURN IDENTITY

How little do we know of the business of the earth,
not to speak of the universe; of time,
not to speak of eternity.
Edward Thomas, 1909b

TUESDAY, 24 JANUARY 2017: WALKING IN THE RAIN

Drops drip. They spangle the surface of the River Lambourn with widening concentric rings. An impeccably white egret stalks, slowly, in the rain. It stabs shifting targets in the shallow water. As we watch from a low bridge, the egret flaps its wings and slowly rises like a 'seraphic soul'.[1]

On a bleak January day the egret is a startling question mark. This exotic stranger would look at home on the banks of the Nile or the shores of a tropical island. Twenty years ago, when I spent several months tramping this downland landscape on the shifting border between Oxfordshire and Berkshire for an archaeological research project, I never saw such a creature. Now they are relatively common. This was the first of several egrets we were to see in the next few days, stepping carefully and elegantly in the bright chalk streams of North Wessex. England has warmed sufficiently to provide a home even in winter for this distinctive immigrant.

I walk beside my wife, continuing upstream along the trail marked on the Ordnance Survey map as the Lambourn Valley Way. On the headlands of the ploughed fields fragments of chalk lie like confetti. In the rain, nodules of flint glisten blackly. Like the egret I walk head downwards, the habit of an archaeological lifetime – scanning the soil for traces of Roman pottery or prehistoric worked flint. I don't see any, only, disguised among the chalk, a white fragment of a clay pipe. Had some farm labourer, struggling with the plough, bitten the end off, cursed and left the fragments on the ground?

Gypsy women also had a fondness for clay pipes. Thomas Hughes (1822–1896), Uffington's upright Christian author of the English public school classic *Tom Brown's School Days*,[2] rather disapproved of such unfeminine

Edward Thomas, the nature writer and poet of the Downs, photographed
at his home in Steep (Hampshire) in 1914, three years before his death
in France on the Western Front.

habits. He didn't include the women's pipe-smoking competition in his
White Horse scouring games of 1857. Edward Thomas (1878–1917), the great
walker and poet of the South Country, was a connoisseur of clay pipes.
In one poem, he has a Gypsy woman ask: 'Then just a half a pipeful of
tobacco can you spare?'[3] During the Great War he sees clay pipes as memorials of generations of unknown soldiers:

The one I smoked, the other a soldier
Of Blenheim, Ramillies and Malplaquet
Perhaps....[4]

The North Wessex Downs and the Vale of the White Horse are studded
with the memorials of the Great War in which Thomas and many local
young men died. They dug trenches in the same chalk deposits that stretch

from Berkshire, Wiltshire and Kent beyond the White Cliffs and the Channel to Arras and Vimy Ridge in France. Local stones list the names of the youthful dead; their bones lie in foreign fields.

We continue upstream. Within minutes two red kites (*Milvus milvus*) are tacking overhead. They seem to be checking us out, distinctive with their forked tails, russet colour and massive, bent wings. The naturalists of the chalk downs, a century or more ago, made no mention of these impressive birds. Not surprisingly. Like the egrets they are newcomers, or at least recent returners. The *Reader's Digest Book of British Birds,* which I acquired in 1974, shows a red kite glowering from the page. 'Even now', it tells us, 'there are only about a score of pairs, confined to their remote stronghold in the hill-country of central Wales.' Like ancient Britons seeking a retreat from Rome, the kites clung on in central Wales – even if they did not thrive in that barren, sheep-sheared fastness. Then in 1989 they were reintroduced into the Chilterns, 50 km (30 miles) to the east of where we stood by the River Lambourn. For several years motorists on the M40 motorway, from London to Oxford, exclaimed in delight as these great birds soared languidly above the road where it cut through the Chiltern scarp and exposed the ancient calcareous seabed.

The ancestors of the red kites above us probably patrolled the foetid alleys and shambles of medieval London, the city's garbage collectors, until changing human habits almost drove them to extinction. Now they are back, apparently thriving over the North Wessex Downs in search of small, scuttling creatures, rabbits and carrion. The 'detested kite' of Shakespeare's *King Lear* is no longer an urban scrounger. The red kite and the little egret are both reminders of the constant change that takes place in the landscape around us. It is us – human beings – that are now the major change agents.

But we should not console ourselves with the idea that the new arrivals compensate for the losses. The poets and observers of the downlands in the nineteenth and early twentieth centuries, such as Richard Jefferies, W. H. Hudson and Edward Thomas, relished the huge number and variety of birds. Over months of walking on the Downs we have seen small gaggles of linnets, flitting ahead of us, but no goldfinches, fieldfares, yellowhammers or kestrels. Most of all I miss the sight of the tumbling fall of the lapwing (or peewit), which was once so common in these parts that local people collected its eggs as an Easter treat. Now, partly because of the collectors, but mainly due to habitat loss, the lapwing is a rare sight. And the great bustard, the iconic bird of the Downs, present in large flocks in the eighteenth century, had been shot to extinction by the time Thomas strode the chalklands.[5] With big open views and limited shelter, the Downs are traditional hunting country.

Now, with so many of the fields soaked in herbicides and pesticides, the distant hum of traffic has replaced the thrumming of insects. Arable weeds, old grassland and corn stubble no longer provide the habitats and foodstuffs on which the birds of the open country thrived. Even in the mid-nineteenth century, Thomas Hughes complained about the advance of the plough and the loss of meadow. 'Farmers', he is reported to have said, 'would plough up their fathers' graves to grow turnips.' But farmers respond to pressures and incentives, to the environment in which they find themselves. It is for all of us to decide our priorities.

The rain falls relentlessly, a constant mizzle; we head into the workaday village of Lambourn, named after its river. Its importance a thousand years ago, as the centre of a large Anglo-Saxon estate, is reflected still in its impressive church of St Michael. This area is remarkable for the series of Anglo-Saxon land charters that describe local estate boundaries with great precision (see p. 51). In 1032 St Michael's Church is recorded as a minster – in other words, a church of regional importance before the English parish system was fully established. The building that dominates the village centre today was remodelled by the Normans and many generations since have added their flourishes.

North of the village the waters of the Lambourn seep out of the chalk. The precise position of the source varies. Winterbournes appear in the dry valleys only at the wettest times of year and where, exactly, varies. As we walk northwards along the routeway formed by the river, now reduced to a stream, the water finally disappears, sucked beneath the chalk hill.

The slopes above are marked by a group of prehistoric mounds known, with no regard for numerical accuracy, as the Seven Barrows. There are certainly more than thirty of them. Most are round barrows constructed to mark graves in the centuries before and after 2000 BC in the Early Bronze Age. The builders may have been attracted by the presence of an ancient long barrow – the work, about six thousand years ago, of the first farmers and the most ancient burial ground in this area of the North Wessex Downs: 'Blessed are the dead that the rain rains upon'.[6] They began the clearance of the woodland around the river's source and created open spaces in which their animals could graze and where they could cultivate patches of wheat and barley. By creating the long barrow to contain the bones of their ancestors they laid claim to this land: a marker near a source of water in the dry expanse of chalk. This, the first permanent human construction, marked a place in the natural landscape that would have been

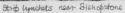
Strip lynchets near Bishopstone

Wayland's Smithy

Entrance to the tomb

visible to travellers taking the route, as we were doing, from the Kennet Valley and up the Lambourn towards the highest point of the Downs, which overlooks the Thames Valley and the expanse of England beyond.

But the water source could be a destination in its own right. There is something magical about springs as they bubble from the ground. Ancient people acknowledged this by building shrines. Several times I have walked to the source of the River Seine in Burgundy, sited in a similar chalk topography to that at Lambourn. French archaeologists unearthed a temple complex there, the focus of a Lourdes-like health cult. Pilgrims immersed themselves in a large wooden tank filled by the curative spring waters. Primitive wooden statues were preserved in the boggy ground. Models or *ex-votos* of body parts, dating to the first century AD, ensured that the gods knew exactly which bits needed healing. I have bought nearly identical *ex-votos* of arms, legs, eyes, even images of young soldiers, at shops and churches in Greece, Italy and Mexico. Fears and hopes persist.

In 1933 excavators at the source of the Seine discovered the more Classical bronze image of the goddess of the river herself, the lady to whom the suppliants appealed. Her name is Sequana (the ancient name

Walking the Ridgeway: from the combe near Bishopstone,
past Wayland's Smithy, the great Neolithic chambered tomb, and towards
Uffington Castle on the horizon, painted by Philip Hughes.

y rises to Uffington Castle

of the River Seine) and she stands, elegantly draped, in a boat the prow of which is in the form of a duck's head, and a feathered tail fans the stern. Gauls came here for centuries to seek cures. Now a few kilometres over the hill there is an abbey dedicated to Saint Seine: it seems the Celtic river goddess has been sanctified, Christianized and given a different sex. Water sources are places in the landscape that retain their power, even if the stories change.

At Seven Barrows there are no facilities for pilgrims, searchers for miracle cures. There is though, nearby, Britain's finest medical facility for horses and other fastidiously maintained premises devoted to the equine cult. The Lambourn Downs are home to that beautifully elegant, highly strung creature, the thoroughbred racehorse. This is racing central. The White Horse marks their territory, although he has seen his kind change: from shaggy pot-bellied British ponies to sleek, fine-limbed Arabians more like his own idealized shape. Today, the pampered athletes are safely tucked up in their luxury accommodation.

Beyond Seven Barrows the gallops stretch across the open, exposed slope of the Downs. The footpath of the Lambourn Way follows the route that would take us to the back of the hillfort of Uffington Castle, delivering us along a holloway that itself was first laid out in the Late Bronze Age. But not today. The rain is getting heavier. We take a less exposed route, avoiding the worst of the peevish winter wind, down the valley that leads towards the village of Ashbury. A slight earthwork on the left of the road marks all that remains of Ashdown Park's medieval pale – the ditch and bank, originally topped with a palisade, that retained the deer and discouraged poachers, both two and four legged. Across the Vale another Anglo-Saxon charter records a *wolfhager* – a fence for keeping out wolves. The wolves are long gone, and the herd of fallow deer that graze here now must have sought shelter from the weather.

Just beyond the pale and scarcely visible in the sleeting rain, is the perfect doll's house: the hunting lodge built for the 1st Earl of Craven around 1662.[7] The house has a distinct Dutch feel about it, which seems strange in this isolated spot on the top of the Downs. But then the latest edition of Pevsner's *Berkshire*[8] reminds the historically forgetful, which includes me, that the Earl of Craven was the protector of Charles I's sister Elizabeth, the romantically named 'Winter Queen' (1596–1662). The house may have been built as a place of retreat for her – after years of exile in The Hague – as a place of safety against the plague; the building's architect, William Winde, was a member of her Dutch household. Nevertheless, death claimed her before the lodge was completed. Today the National Trust rents it to a member of the Rock aristocracy, Pete Townshend of The Who. He was well-known for smashing guitars in the 1960s and singing 'I hope I die before I get old'. Presumably he has changed his mind. Talking about my generation, I am the same age as him and now find that age is relative. Mr Townshend had certainly mellowed when the pair of us used to stand around, looking spare, in Annabelinda's, the dress shop de jour for Boho chic in Oxford while our wives tried on velvet and silk dresses.

Today, my wife, who loathes rain, is looking less elegant and would prefer not to stand around peering at seventeenth-century piles. We shuffle down the valley past the scatter of sarsen stone boulders that dot the valley floor. This is the stuff of prehistoric megaliths: the builders of Stonehenge and Avebury and the great chambered tomb of Wayland's Smithy, which crouches on the Ridgeway above us, used the dense, hard Tertiary sandstone to make monuments that could endure the wear of millennia.

The sarsen stones are incredibly resistant, ideal if you want your monument to last. The megaliths were erected by ancient pre-Christian Britons, hence in effect they are 'pagan stones', or alien foreigners in the soft chalk. The usual explanation of the name 'sarsen' is that it derives from 'Saracen' – the well-known Islamic opposition to medieval crusaders in the Holy Land. John Aubrey, the seventeenth-century antiquary, questioned this attractive, if romantic idea. He suggested that the name came from Anglo-Saxon *sar-stan*, or 'troublesome', stones. He could be right – these heavy blocks, littering the downland valleys, must have been a nuisance to the English farmers who were long past wanting to build henges and megalithic tombs. The boulders are also known to downland farmers as 'grey wethers' because from above they look like a flock of sheep.

We walk down the downland scarp into the village of Ashbury, another spring-line settlement with thatched roofs and cob walls. In 1086, at the time of William the Conqueror's Domesday survey, this was the only manor in Berkshire to be held by Glastonbury Abbey. From Ashbury, the Icknield Way takes us to the foot of White Horse Hill. Above the Manger, an enormous natural bowl in the chalk scarp, lies our objective: the Uffington White Horse, Britain's oldest and most spectacular hill carving. And we can't see a thing. The Horse is lost, invisible under a grey, soggy pillow of cloud that smothers the hill. The road behind us has turned into a torrent, carrying pebbles of chalk, flakes of flint and streaks of silt. The flowing water guides us down into the village of Woolstone and the pub, named after the White Horse, a thatched gingerbread cottage of a building that has a welcoming log fire and rooms. The real White Horse can wait until tomorrow. After all, it has been there nearly three thousand years.

WEDNESDAY, 25 JANUARY 2017: THE LAND OF THE RISING SUN

The next morning we get up in the dark. As we leave the pub and climb back up the hill there is light in the east. The sky is clear. Thank God for changeable English weather. By the time we are on the upper slopes the sun appears over the hindquarters of the Horse. From this angle, the figure is flattened and foreshortened, an abstract pattern of white lines etched in the turf, but the low sun is a searchlight scanning over the hillside, illuminating the figure. Is this theatrical effect an accident or, more likely, did the makers of the Horse place it precisely to appear out of the morning sunlight, silhouetted against the sky on the highest point of the Downs, where the chalk scarp is most pronounced? If so, the audience for this drama should stand to the north, in the Vale that stretches beyond the foot of the scarp. Today, however, the lie of the land and the slimness of the Horse's limbs and body means that the view from the north in most places is less than perfect. It is not easy to distinguish the whole form from a distance. Were the makers of the Horse careless? Were they more concerned about the making of the Horse and its presence than creating the kind of clear cinematic image that we take for granted as normal?

The form of the Uffington Horse, in all its sinuous elegance, appeared with great clarity in the twentieth century when humans took to the skies. Aerial photographers, perched in flying machines made of not much more than balsa wood, paper and gutta-percha, produced startling images. With great foresight the naturalist W. H. Hudson (1841–1922) predicted that one day humans might achieve the bird's-eye view. Like many people I first came across Hudson's marvellous book *Green Mansions* (1904), a novel set in his native Argentina. It was only later that I realized that Guillermo Enrique moved to England, became William Henry and produced a series of classics about the English countryside just as modernity began to transform it. In *Nature in Downland* (1900) he wrote: 'the sight dwells with pleasure on the downs, because they are in appearance easy to walk upon, and in a sense are being walked upon when looked at'. He asks the question 'Why should a wide horizon have so great a fascination for us, wingless walkers on the level ground?' He speculates prophetically about this sense 'pointing to a time when we shall be able with the aid of perfected machines, or better still, by means of some mysterious undeveloped faculty within us, to rise from earth and float hither and thither at will through the boundless fields of air'.[9] That desire for the power of flight, Hudson writes, comes to him most on these green hills that stand naked to the sky.

It required no great imagination to see the White Horse as an image created for observers in the heavens. So much so that when all-too-real and malevolent observers, the German Luftwaffe, appeared over England in the Second World War the chalk figures were camouflaged and covered over in case they provided landmarks to enemy navigators. It would be interesting to know why this decision was made. I spent many hours flying over this area at low altitudes in the 1970s, and while I found the River Thames and its tributaries a convenient guide I never looked at a chalk hill figure and thought, 'Ah, now I know where I am!'[10] Nevertheless, I am thankful for

One of the earliest aerial photographs of the White Horse, taken by Major G. W. Allen in 1933. The hillfort, Uffington Castle, with its western entrance and blocked eastern entrance, stands out clearly. The Ridgeway is immediately behind.

UFFINGTON 3.   31. 7. 33

the decision to hide the White Horse. It provided the key for the project to investigate the White Horse that I was trying to get off the ground.

Back in the present, as the sun rose ahead of us, the light and low shadows emphasized the ancient earthworks on the hill. The youthful Richard Jefferies (1848–1887), the prolific local nature writer, refers in 'A Strange Story', published in the *North Wiltshire Herald*, to 'yonder camp-crowned hill'. His two characters ponder why the White Horse, the fosse and ramparts of the ancient camp, and the time-worn barrow 'should have power to render as naught the wide abyss of a thousand years' and call up 'deeds half-hidden in the mist of years'; while today we hear the call of birds, see rooks overhead and a hare in the fern.[11] We walk uphill past a low mound that lies alongside the track. When I first checked this feature in the Oxfordshire County archive (the Sites and Monuments Record, now known as the Historic Environment Record) it was thought to be a 'pillow mound' – in other words, a medieval structure built to house breeding rabbits, then a valuable source of meat and fur. Our team's research would show that the mound was full of bodies: not those of bunnies, however, but of headless Romano-Britons placed in a tumulus that was already ancient. White Horse Hill is a place where the living inter the dead.

The top of the hill is marked by the most impressive earthworks, the massive bulk of the hillfort known as Uffington Castle. There is a string of these hillforts along the edge of the chalk scarp running in both directions from Uffington along the Ridgeway. They remain prominent in the landscape today because of the sheer scale of earth-moving carried out by the British builders between two thousand and three thousand years ago. The name 'hillfort' belies their variety of uses. Archaeologists continue to enjoy themselves arguing about their functions and purposes: to what extent were they meant to be defensive places of security or principally designed to impress the neighbours?

What a view from the White Horse!

The Victorian Poet Laureate Alfred, Lord Tennyson (1809–1982), grew up in a chalk landscape, the Lincolnshire Wolds (in English, the place names 'Wolds' and 'Downs' both refer to chalklands). In 'The Lady of Shalott', he imagined King Arthur's Camelot, but with his native countryside in mind:

On either side the river lie
Long fields of barley and of rye
That clothe the wold and meet the sky.

I like that precise use of the word 'meet'. But beauty is in the eye of the beholder, according to the cliché. The eminent artist and landscape designer, William Sawrey Gilpin (1762–1843), dismissing the hills of the South Downs, declared 'Chalk spoils any landscape.' He was the pioneer of the Picturesque and preferred the rugged outcrops of the Lake District and the Highlands.

For me, the White Horse view ranks among my favourites, not simply for its beauty but because of its associations: the stories and memories; the layers of geology and history that echo the past and break through into the present; the sound of the wind and the changing patterns of the sky.

I was born in the Pennines and I like high places that look over big panoramas. As an archaeologist, however, I spent many years in the Thames Valley. I found the broad flatlands, gnawed by gravel pits, slightly depressing. I wrote in a catalogue to an art exhibition:

Fortunately the Berkshire Downs were nearby. Here was a landscape that offered freedom and exhilaration. At least mentally. In reality there is too much barbed wire, too many blocked-off and ploughed-up footpaths. The Ridgeway, though, is a liminal place. This ancient track runs along the crest of a great geological wave. The contour map says you are no more than a thousand feet high; your brain and your stomach do not believe it. The sky feels too close and the valley floor too far below. Walking along the Ridgeway is close to flying, or perhaps diving into clear water. Because in reality we are striding over an ancient seabed, on the remains of incalculable numbers of creatures whose remains, precipitated through warm cretaceous waters, have formed the rock on which we stand. But 'rock' is hardly an appropriate word for chalk; it is too easily carved, eroded and liquidized into slurry. When the tectonic plates of Africa shunted into Europe the alps reared up under the violent impact; the shock trembled across Europe, causing the English chalk to rear up to the northeast like a tsunami. White Horse Hill is Big Sur, where the wave is frozen in its most dramatic form. Twelve thousand years ago, as ice-hardened chalk began to thaw, massive mudslides skidded over the scarp, scouring out hollows and chutes. Springs emerged from beneath the porous chalk beds, creating natural amphitheatres and flowing into the valleys of the Ock and the Thames. This is a malleable and changeable landscape.[12]

Richard Jefferies often thought of the sea in these hills: 'There is something oceanic in their magnitude, their ease, their solitude – above all,

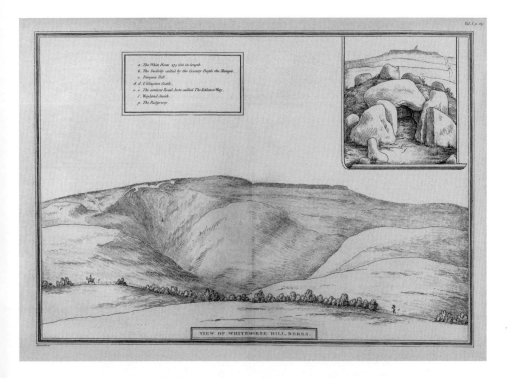

A view of White Horse Hill from the topographical survey *Magna Britannia* (1806),
by Daniel and Samuel Lysons, with a realistic portrayal of the hill figure
on the crest. The inset image is of Wayland's Smithy.

in their liquid forms, that ... flowing on and on, make a type of infinity.'[13]
Looking south from the ramparts of Uffington Castle, the dip slope tips
gently towards the Lambourn valley. England is often said to be a crowded
country. It doesn't seem so from here. There are endless large arable fields
dotted with clumps of beech in which deer seek refuge. The popular image
of the Downs is of green sward where sheep safely graze. In fact, over centuries, the land has been in a state of flux. The local saying is: 'down corn and
up horn'; at times, as in the World Wars, the demand for cereals brought
back the plough. In recent years the illogic of the Common Agricultural
Policy has subsidized mega-fields of cereals growing in this poor flinty soil
saturated with chemical fertilizers and an alien patchwork of startling
yellow oilseed rape in the Vale. Mostly, it is only on the inaccessible steep
scarps of the chalk or on protected ancient monuments that the old turf
remains. Here is a fascinating world teaming with life and drama.

In the ancient turf the careful plant-hunter may find the rare frog
orchid, pyramidal and common-spotted orchids and the small blue but-
terfly perched on the kidney vetch, the food supply of its larva. Peer into

the species-rich grassland on the steep slopes of Dragon Hill and there is a hidden world. Here be monsters! Like the rare black oil beetle (*Meloe proscarabaeus*), which fears no predators because it tastes disgusting. This amazing creature passes through a number of totally different transformations (in the jargon known as hypermetamorphosis) from tiny egg, to larva to grub before the beetle emerges. At the larval stage, with long legs and claws it perches on vegetation and waits its chance to hitch a ride on the right species of bee – get the wrong one and they die. Most do. Those who choose correctly arrive in their new larder, the bee's nest, where they can feed on the brood and food store, then, as a fat grub, on the brood cells. The beetle that emerges is a large, cumbersome, wingless beast that cannot move very far. Only at the larval stage, with its bee transport, can it travel any distance. No wonder the oil beetles are rare.[14]

Dragon Hill is a strange, flat-topped pyramid of chalk where St George is said to have slain the dragon, whose acrid blood soaked into the ground and killed the turf. The hill is probably a natural feature, although it may have been modified and sculpted. Streams emerge beneath the steep scarp, and along the spring line there are villages like Wanborough, to the southwest. Now virtually a suburb of Swindon, originally it was a Roman settlement alongside the Ermin Way, the Roman road that still slices through the countryside with an alien directness as if cut by a blade. From Wanborough, spaced about a kilometre or two apart where the springs emerge, there are villages and hamlets: Hinton Parva, Bishopstone, Idstone, Ashbury, Compton Beauchamp, Woolstone, Kingston Lisle, Sparsholt, Childrey, East and West Challow and then the principal market town of the southern vale, Wantage, alongside the Letcombe Brook. These springs not only provided water to drink, they also powered the village mills, often mentioned in Domesday Book, and fed the watercress beds, for example at Letcombe Bassett ('Cresscombe' in Thomas Hardy's novel *Jude the Obscure*).

These are the villages, with their inhabitants, that the great working-class folklorist Alfred Williams (1877–1930) described on the eve of the First World War. The villages are some of the most ancient in the world, Williams declared with a degree of patriotic inaccuracy. His people, sons and daughters of the soil, he writes, are 'rough and plain, frank and hearty, honest and homely; there was no need to ... dress them up in fictitious finery; I am proud of every single one of them'.[15] Today more local people work in the Honda car factory in Swindon than on the land.

The places mostly have Old English names: Wantage, like Lambourn, is named for its watercourse, Waneting being the Old English name for

Letcombe Brook. Idstone is first mentioned in 1199 and means Eadwine's *tūn* or farm (nothing to do with stones). Old English names are easy to misinterpret. Woolstone, for example, the small village where we spent the night, seems to make sense in modern English, but early forms of the name (it appears in Domesday Book) show that it actually means 'Wulfric's farm or estate'. Before that the land was known as Æscesbyrig (or Æscesburh), the Old English names for Uffington Castle, then in 960 it was one of fifteen villages given to the wealthy English nobleman called Wulfric.

The village to the east of Woolstone, Compton Beauchamp, is mentioned in a document of 1122 as 'Compton by the Whytehorse', one of the earliest references to the hill figure. The name 'Compton' – originally 'Cumtune' – means 'valley farm' (*cumb-tūn*), which is exactly what it still is today. In 2017 fire ripped through the picturesque thatched roofs of its cottages.

The landscape of the Vale is dotted with villages. Most sit along a network of streams that are tributaries of the River Ock, which itself flows into the Thames at Abingdon. As just described, the village names are mostly Old English, given by Anglo-Saxon speakers after Britain had fallen off the edge of the Roman Empire in the fifth century AD. This does not mean the Vale was first colonized by the English, as historians used to claim. The Vale was already a prosperous and productive area for the Romano-Britons who established their roads, towns and villas there. And even they were not the first. A clue lies in the river and stream names: some of them are pre-English, being Celtic or even earlier – names like Ock (from the Celtic word for salmon), Thames, Kennet and Humber (a stripling branch of Letcombe Brook, not the one that flows into the North Sea, spanned by what was once the world's longest suspension bridge). Not surprisingly the historical records show that the Vale of the White Horse, so well supplied with water, was prosperous farmland, much of it belonging to the wealthy Abingdon Abbey. The impressive and idiosyncratic church at Uffington, with its octagonal tower, stands out in the morning mist: the Cathedral of the Vale.

In the middle distance, on the north side of the Vale, the land rises. This feature is known as the Corallian Ridge – geologically a band of Corallian limestone, a hard resistant rock that emerged as a coral reef from a warm Jurassic sea. The earliest churches and the castle tower in Oxford are built of the stuff. From Highworth and Faringdon in the west past Longworth and Kingston Bagpuize, the ridge villages look both southwards into the Vale of the White Horse and north into the Thames Valley. Their parishes, like those of the downland scarp villages, are regular long, thin rectangles linking water, meadow, woods, ploughlands and grazing. They were designed to provide each community with a share of the local resources. Beyond the Corallian Ridge, in the far distance, the Cotswolds are visible, straddling Oxfordshire and Gloucestershire. To the east we can just see the Chilterns, the extension of the chalk hills beyond the River Thames, in the county of Buckinghamshire.

From White Horse Hill this looks like the unchanging heartland of England. In reality it is a land that shifts and morphs. The patchwork quilt of fields is mostly a creation of the eighteenth century, followed shortly by the canal and passenger railway line. The once coal-fired Didcot Power Station, the twentieth-century dragon, visible to the northeast, is shrinking – only three of its cooling towers now remain. It can still be seen from six counties but may soon disappear altogether, as concerns mount about global warming. Wind farms have already emerged in the Vale, slowly scything, blithely, through the air, and solar panels are beginning to multiply.

BROCKLAND

As the sun strokes over the sinuous body of the Horse and the flanks of the chalk hill, we head back down towards the pub for breakfast. At the mouth of the Manger there is a reminder that this is not just a human territory, a cultural landscape formed by and for people. By the narrow, twisting road lies the solid, still body of a badger. During the night he lost an argument with a car, which must have swept round the bend demanding its right of way.

Badgers can be victims of habit, resolutely lumbering along their nocturnal paths. The poet Adam Thorpe (and author of *Ulverton*, an evocative novel that explores a Wiltshire downland village and its people through time) wrote:

> It's the road that crosses the badger, you say –
> his ancestry deep, the behaviour tied
> to custom; the ancient setts concealed from the day,
> each night's an echo of the previous night
>
> where we are the ones who interfere:
> he just stands his ground. Were a car to appear,
> all death and dazzle, he wouldn't swerve or wait:
> his commitment's grown in his blood, like fate.[16]

Like us, badgers split off from their ancestral species a few million years ago. Like us they came down from the trees. We spread out of Africa. They spread from China. We grew big brains and, moving north, learnt to tailor clothes, make shoes and build shelters. Badgers grew bulky, evolved thick pelts and learnt to live sociably in burrows (but not how to cross roads).

About 12,000 years ago humans walked towards Britain, before the melting glacial water separated the peninsula from the Continent. Behind us, in the darkness, the badger shuffled and snuffled, feasting on worms. Like us they thrived in the new land. Today, only Sweden has a higher badger population than the British Isles. They particularly like the Vale of the White Horse area with its well-watered, wooded combes and softish geology, ideal for burrows. The densest population known is in Wytham Woods overlooking Oxford. This might be partly down to university zoologists spreading an enticing bait of peanuts and honey to bring the reticent badgers out into the open.

In spite of high badger numbers most people in the UK have never seen one, and archaeologists don't often find their bones in ancient settlements. However, they did appear at Britain's most famous Mesolithic site at Star Carr in Yorkshire, along with wolf and beaver. W. H. Hudson, the great naturalist and recorder of the Downs, thought that badgers would outlast foxes. Both now turn up in towns, but foxes seem to be more successful at exploiting human fast-food outlets and rubbish bins.

Our badger met its end trying to cross the B4507 road, better known as the Icknield Way, which runs along the foot of the steepest part of the escarpment linking the villages between Wanborough and Wantage. The road cuts across the end of the Manger; below, the ground falls steeply into the hollow known as Woolstone Wells. This is a difficult place to enter, overgrown with nettles, guarded by fallen, mossy tree trunks. The ground is boggy because, in this dark, secret place, springs gush out from beneath the chalk. This is the source of the River Ock, right below the White Horse. In spite of poking around I have yet to find any trace of a prehistoric or Roman shrine. However, this cleft is home to badgers who have mined into the hillside, creating groins and mounds like First World War entrenchments. They may have lived here for several thousand years. The ancient Britons, speaking a Celtic tongue, gave the name 'brock' to the badger. Unusually, the British word passed into English.[17]

Many so-called 'naturalists' in the nineteenth and twentieth centuries took hunting for granted. Edward Thomas hated the cruelty and the waste of life. In 'The Combe', he described a deep valley like this one:

The Combe was ever dark, ancient and dark...
But far more ancient and dark
The Combe looks since they killed the badger there,
Dug him out and gave him to the hounds,
The most ancient Briton of English beasts.[18]

Humans in cars are not their only problem. In 1976 the UK Ministry of Agriculture, Fisheries and Food was busy culling badgers with bureaucratic efficiency and cyanide gas, hoping to control bovine tuberculosis. The men from the ministry were anxious to know if the gas was fully penetrating what they assumed were relatively simple burrows. So they turned 'archaeologist'. A team of seven was given a couple of days to excavate a 'typical' sett in the then county of Avon, but the sett kept going. Eventually the now enlarged team revealed a tunnel network 310 m (1,017 ft) in length with 57 chambers and 16 entrances. Another sett explored in 1990 was over twice as big. As badger numbers expand they extend their homes using some basic architectural principles. Badgers seem better than us at providing cheap, sustainable housing.

Badgers establish territories that also have outlying setts as places of refuge. They mark their borders with latrines, probably to discourage rival males from entering. It's a simple concept, so scientists have invented a suitably complicated jargon for it – the anti-kleptogamy hypothesis (AKH). 'Kleptogamy' means stealing sex. Territoriality seems to be a male badger obsession. Interestingly, males and females fall victim to cars in equal proportions, mainly in the mating season. So boundaries may be a male obsession, but females, it seems, are out at night searching for the best partners. It is not only humans who have social lives, and create territories, homes, pathways and night-time assignations.

Later I tell the National Trust ranger about poor old Mr Brock. He is not exactly distraught. 'Oh, there's loads of them around here. And they eat the hedgehogs and predate the ground nesting birds.' I have a feeling he is more on the side of the lapwings, which as I say I haven't seen for years in this part of the world, and the skylark that, blessedly, this morning flies overhead.

CHAPTER TWO

ALTERING THE EARTH: THE PROSPECT FROM THE RIDGEWAY

The hill road wet with rain
In the sun would not gleam
Like a winding stream
If we trod it not again.

Edward Thomas, 'Roads', 1916

IN SACRED CIRCLES

There is scarcely an acre of the British countryside that has not been altered by human activity in the past six thousand years. The Ridgeway, running past White Horse Hill, provides one of the finest transects across the countryside, a textbook illustration of the making of the English landscape.[1]

About ten thousand years ago, as the climate warmed and the glaciers retreated, sea levels rose and the British Isles were colonized by woodland. People exploited the land by hunting, fishing and gathering wild plants. At the same time, communities in the Near East – today's Syria, Iraq, Israel and eastern Turkey – developed a more complex interrelationship with plants and animals. Instead of simply gathering seeds and leaves, digging up roots and tubers or hunting animals they began the process of domestication. The species involved in the new farming enterprise began to live together and depend upon each other. The ideas and techniques spread and so did the farmers themselves, who tended to multiply faster thanks to their more energy-demanding and productive lifestyle. As human farmers increased in numbers and expanded so did domesticated animal species, which, in western Asia, first included dogs, sheep, goats, cattle and pigs as well as the plants selected for their productivity, notably wheat, barley and pulses. Horses were to come later.

Over a period of about four thousand years, farming spread across Europe into Greece and Bulgaria, along the great river valleys, and leap-frogged around the Mediterranean. Eventually, some bold souls took their sheep and cattle across the narrow stretch of water that, from about 6500 BC, separated the Continent – the northwestern tip of Eurasia – from the archipelago of mild but misty, rainy islands known to geographers as the British Isles, but which today some prefer to distinguish as England, Wales, Scotland and Ireland.[2]

Once farming took root in Britain the habit caught on relatively rapidly – from the southeast in about 4000 BC or a little earlier, it spread to northern Scotland and Ireland over the next three centuries. The forests of oak, ash, lime and hazel gradually succumbed to the sound of stone axes creating clearings; the voracious pigs, cattle and sheep opened the countryside to grasslands, habitats for newcomers from the Asian steppes such as crows, and eventually made it a land fit for horses.

The British farmers created a new landscape and a distinctive culture, first building large circular enclosures, known to archaeologists as causewayed camps because they were designed with many entrances piercing through their earthwork banks and ditches. These seem to have been places for ceremonies, for the bones of the dead, and for festivals and feasts, convenient for exchanging genes. Scattered humans and their animals needed to come together for the good of the species. One of the best-known causewayed camps in Britain straddles the top of Windmill Hill, north of Avebury. Today its shallow earthworks are just visible in the light of the setting sun, if you know where to look.

These people also constructed impressive monuments specifically to contain the remains of the dead, or at least those considered most worthy, perhaps the communities' founding ancestors. Some of these long barrows or chambered tombs, with great sarsen stone sentinels at their entrances, still dominate the British and Irish countryside and are the earliest man-made structures, places to mark the evolving landscape. One of the most impressive is also in the Avebury region at West Kennet, capping the ridge south of the River Kennet. The monuments remind us that over one hundred generations have laboured to create the landscape we see today. Such structures began to appear two or three centuries after the arrival of farming.

As the communities grew in size and developed wider relationships, a new type of place appeared. The most impressive – archaeologists call them henges after the 'hanging stones' of Stonehenge – required massive inputs of labour. Using tools of stone, wood, bone and antler, communities came together to hack out massive ditches, throw up banks of earth and, sometimes, erect huge stones in circles or avenues. Recent isotopic research suggests that people gathered seasonally from far and wide at Durrington Walls, just north of Stonehenge, to create a pilgrimage centre of religious and political importance, and to feast on the pigs and cattle that they brought with them from the West Country, southwest Wales and perhaps even Scotland.[3] Long-distance tracks must have crossed the land.

Such social gatherings were probably lubricated by alcohol. Early farmers in the Near East learnt the trick of fermentation, or producing nourishing yeasts, and sterilizing liquids. Early farmers celebrated with beer and drank from pottery vessels. The first vats were inhabited by the yeast *Saccaromyces cerevisiae*, one of the first organisms to be genetically sequenced. Unfortunately, modern science does not tell us where the first brewers found this miracle of human civilization. But yeasts, like other domesticates, have evolved during their relationship with humans – Britons became especially fond of the yeast genus *Brettanomyces*, which produces that warm bitter generally loathed by Americans and Australians, who don't know any better. Humans also evolved to grow more alcohol tolerant. Some of the party-goers at Stonehenge, like Native Americans, may have found the stuff literally lethal until their liver enzymes learnt to process alcohol more efficiently.

About 20 km (12 miles) north of Stonehenge and close to the Ridgeway is the great henge of Avebury. Unlike the White Horse – visible for miles and recorded as a medieval Wonder – the great henge of Avebury lay unnoticed for generations in the folds of the Wiltshire countryside until a youthful John Aubrey (1626–1697), an Oxford scholar and student of the Middle Temple, found himself in the area. For a royalist family like the Aubreys in the English Civil War, these were uncertain times. Oxford, King Charles I's HQ, fell to the Parliamentary forces in June 1646. On Christmas Eve 1648, John (aged twenty-two at the time) was summoned from Oxford to Wiltshire to look after his seriously ill father's 'country business'. John was unusual for his generation in having a keen interest in matters antiquarian. He records: 'Salisbury plaines and Stonehenge I had knowne from eight years old: but I never sawe the country round Marlborough till Christmas 1648.'

At that time he was invited by a group of well-connected Royalist friends to take part in a hunt that:

met with their pack of hounds at the Greywethers. These Downes look as if they were sowen with great Stones, very thick and in a dusky evening they look like a flock of Sheep: from whence they take their name: one might fancy it to have been the scene where the Giants fought with great stones against the Gods.

Twas here that our game began and the chase led us (at length) through the village of Aubury, into the closes there: where I was wonderfully surprised at the sight of these vast stones, of which I had never heard before, as also the mighty graffe [ditch] about it. I observed in the enclosure some segments of rude circles made with these stones, whence I concluded they had been in the old time complete.

Later in life (between 1665 and 1693) Aubrey would publish plans of Avebury and Stonehenge in his *Monumenta Britannica, or A Miscellany of British Antiquities*[4] in the section devoted to Druid temples. Aubrey did not have a high opinion of his British ancestors. According to him they 'received the knowledge of husbandrie from the Romans' and 'lived sluttishley in poor houses, where they ate a great deale of beefe and mutton

John Aubrey's plan of Avebury, which he made using a simple surveying device known as a plane table. Aubrey was one of the first to recognize the importance of Avebury and to make it more widely known.

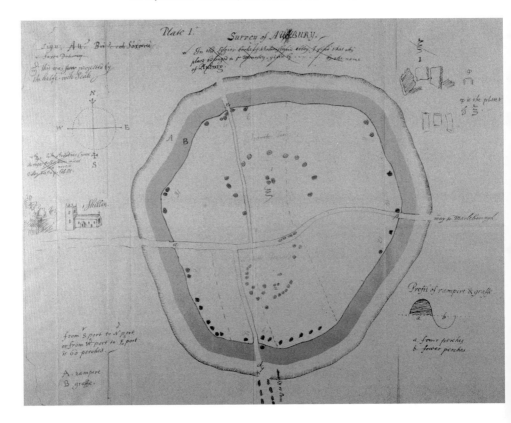

and drank good Ale'. He did, however, propose that megalithic monuments were made by ancient Britons before written history.

As Aubrey admitted, 'This searching after Antiquities is a wearisome task.' He was 'surprised by age' in 1697 and buried in Oxford's fine parish church St Mary Magdalene's on the High Street. His books and papers are a treasure of the Bodleian Library, a stone's throw away. He was the man that put Avebury and Stonehenge on the map and showed the British that they lived in an old country, a land of layers.[5]

Aubrey compared the great henge at Avebury to Stonehenge as like a cathedral to a church. I am inclined to agree. With its sweeping, roughly circular earthwork about 420 m (1,380 ft) across, it encloses about 11.5 hectares (28 acres). Like most henge monuments, there is an interior ditch and exterior bank, originally over 15 m (50 ft) from top to bottom. If the earthwork isn't impressive enough, the interior contains several monumental settings of stone. The Outer Circle follows the interior line of the ditch

Aerial photograph of Avebury, with the village in the middle and roads crossing through it. The great circular earthwork, consisting of a ditch and exterior bank, is clearly visible.

and includes as many as one hundred huge sarsen blocks up to 40 tonnes in weight. The largest are placed to flank the southern and northern entrances into the henge. The whole monument seems to be designed to enforce an almost theatrical experience, or perhaps more appropriately, a ritual procession through a series of carefully choreographed spaces.[6]

And to add to its attractions, the Avebury henge has a public house inside it – probably the only such fortunate coincidence in Britain. The Red Lion, thatched and with a black-and-white half-timbered wing, looks like a clichéd olde worlde English inn, but it began life as a farmhouse in about 1600. On a mild day in late June I sat outside with my wife at a wooden table. I sipped at my pint of Avebury Well Water, fortunately a local beer only named for the nearby well, now capped off and made into a table. Just as well. For an inscription says the well-shaft is 26 m (86 ft) deep and, once upon a time, an unfortunate villager plunged down it to his death.

Edward Thomas stayed in Avebury in October 1914, a few weeks before he succumbed to the 'powerful urge to write poetry'[7] for which he is now increasingly appreciated. Eight months later Thomas, at the relatively advanced age of thirty-seven, joined the Artists Rifles – followed three months later by the poet Wilfred Owen – decisions that sealed both their fates. Thomas was familiar with the Avebury area having often cycled and walked the surrounding Downs, and used his experiences in his book *The Icknield Way*. Here was his 'spiritual epicentre'. To Thomas, Avebury was 'a village of obscure paths and roads that dwindle into paths'.[8]

ALONG THE RIDGEWAY

The official start of the Ridgeway long-distance path is just over 3 km (2 miles) to the southeast, from the car park on Overton Hill by the busy A4. A drab spot. Instead, we began from the Red Lion, crossing the road to follow one of the 'obscure paths' that headed towards the high Ridgeway and the Uffington White Horse. On the Ordnance Survey map this lane is itself marked as Green Street or the Wessex Ridgeway, but its older, more interesting name in the Anglo-Saxon charters is the Herepath, which in Old English means the 'army-path'.

Although the Avebury henge was built by antler-pick-wielding Neolithic farmers four thousand years ago, it is often assumed the name 'Avebury' was given by the early English to the prehistoric henge. However, it is more likely that Avebury was the defended Anglo-Saxon settlement in the west of the modern village, around the church. A thirteenth-century document refers to the henge as the *waledich* (wall-ditch) and even as late as the nineteenth century the henge was known as the Wall-dyke. Avebury probably means the 'fortification by the Avon' – the name of a small winterbourne from the British word *afan* (a stream or water). The regular layout of Avebury village resembles the fortified places, or 'burhs', that appeared as defences against the Danes in the late ninth and early tenth centuries. Their topography still dominates the street pattern of Oxford and Wallingford on the Thames.[9] The Herepath probably provided access to the Ridgeway for Anglo-Saxon forces to patrol the Downs, where they might come into conflict with invading Danes who used the Ridgeway as a route from their bases in the Thames Valley.

The Ridgeway is usually marked on modern maps as an 'ancient trackway', but this ancient trackway is not so simple. There is no arguing about most Roman roads: the builders left records, official itineraries that recorded the distances between towns. Local authorities were also required to erect milestones with informative inscriptions, some of which survive. The roads themselves are archaeologically testable – they were constructed, paved and edged with drainage ditches, which means we can locate them. Supposed prehistoric trackways are more difficult. Occasionally we find them made of horizontal timbers or hurdles, like the Neolithic tracks of the Somerset Levels that crossed boggy ground. Only a small number are known with metalled surfaces; most early routes were probably a green swathe of turf or bare, trodden chalk.

Like the White Horse, the Ridgeway has been subject to much speculation and theories about its age. We can start with a letter written in 1738 by the Oxford don, Francis Wise (1695–1767), discussed in detail later, in which he set out his views on the antiquities around the White Horse. Wise described the land as 'containing large tracts of down and sheep pasture where the great western road passes at this day, being called the Rudge or Ridgeway'.[10] He implies that this is more than a track for local farmers and shepherds.

Our next informant, Sir Richard Colt-Hoare (1758–1838), was the kind of wealthy aristocrat who could have stepped out of the pages of Jane Austen. Scion of a banking family, his grandfather, known modestly as 'Henry the Magnificent', gave Richard a house in Lincoln's Inn Fields in London and an allowance of £2,000 a year when he came of age. This made him not quite such a good catch as the nice but dim Mr Bingley in *Pride and Prejudice*, who was worth £5,000 a year. However, more was to come. Richard shot up the ranks of Georgian society when he inherited the magnificent pile of Stourhead in Wiltshire, one of England's finest country houses and estates. Sir Richard's portrait in Stourhead (by an unknown but competent artist in the Gainsborough manner) shows a young man with a sensitive face, beautifully dressed in a red damask coat and a white cravat. He was now almost, if not quite, in Mr Darcy's league.

Sadly, Colt-Hoare's wife died in childbirth two years after their wedding. Abandoning his baby son to the care of nurses and governesses (the son turned out to be a wrong'un), Richard sought solace in the Grand Tour and journeys around Britain, which he meticulously recorded. He also became a noted antiquarian, organizing the first documented excavations at Stonehenge with William Cunnington, and digging doggedly into almost four hundred Bronze Age barrows on Salisbury Plain. Modern archaeologists are divided between those who admire his antiquarian energy and others who see his diggings as obsessively destructive.

However, to return to the Ridgeway. In 1815 Sir Richard rode along it and produced the first itinerary: 'these ridgeways were the roads made use of by the earliest inhabitants of Britain as lines of communication between their different towns and villages. They generally followed the highest ridges of land on which we also find their habitations: they were not paved with stone and gravel as in later times by the Romans but their basis was the firm and verdant turf.' He rode on past Wayland's Smithy, Uffington Castle and inevitably commented on the Ashdown battlefield, where Alfred was victorious against the Danes in AD 871 (p. 64). From the top of the down, near White Horse Hill, he records 'the eye was constantly amused by an extensive prospect over a rich vale extending to Oxford on the left, with numerous church turrets peeping forth amid dense foliage with which the country is overspread. The scenery at the right exhibited an open and cultivated extent of land. A few barrows occurred occasionally alongside the trackway but I did not see other marks of ancient population.' This description could still apply today – with the addition of a few modern intrusions into the Vale. The following day, Sir Richard continued on to Streatley. 'This ridgeway', he concludes, 'is a curious fragment of British antiquity: and its whole course is most singularly preserved ... to every lover of antiquity, or of fine prospects I strongly recommend this delightful ride.'[11]

Sir Richard opened the floodgates. Thousands of walkers and riders have since taken his advice, nowadays often accompanied by television crews. I took part in two programmes myself. In the first the presenter, at the suggestion of her startlingly imaginative producer, was mounted on a white horse. For the second, an even more desperate producer dressed his presenter (a well-known model) in clinging black leathers and provided her with a growling Harley Davidson motorbike. I played the native guide and fortunately was not required to dress as Sir Richard Colt-Hoare – I don't have the calves for it.

By the later nineteenth century the Ridgeway was a fixture of 'ancient Britain'. In 1885 the Ordnance Survey (normally sticklers for accuracy) labelled the Ridgeway as a 'British Trackway' and since 1889 the name 'Ridgeway' appears in the Gothic script reserved for pre-Roman antiquities. In the 1920s the Ridgeway was given a boost in the popular imagination by the books of Alfred Watkins, who invented and promoted 'ley lines': *Early British Trackways* appeared in 1922, followed by *The Old Straight Track* (1925) and *The Ley Hunter's Manual* (1927). This stuff was essentially archaeological nonsense, yet it successfully lodged ley lines and straight tracks in British topographical mythology. However, more rigorous archaeologists also argued that the Ridgeway was ancient – Harold Peake drove along it in a dog cart and pronounced the routeway to be Early Bronze Age in origin. He studied Anglo-Saxon charters and established that the Icknield Way was a separate track running, usually, below the Ridgeway on ground that was dry in the summer. Stuart Piggott also agreed with the Bronze Age dating.

Piggott's mentor, O. G. S. Crawford (1886–1957), the founder of the journal *Antiquity*, is one of the great figures of twentieth-century British archaeology. He was born and brought up in Newbury, and in 1900 went to the public school, Marlborough College, about 8 km (5 miles) east of Avebury, which was still a bastion of muscular Christianity in the tradition of Rugby School. Crawford loathed the place: he called it 'a detestable house of torture'. A later pupil, John Betjeman, was not much happier and William Golding, Nobel Prize-winning author, grew up in the college's shadow. *Lord of the Flies* suggests he didn't think much of public schoolboys either. The youthful Crawford did, however, appreciate the downland landscape, which he enjoyed on what were probably not very vigorous cross-country runs. Some of his outings involved pounding along the Ridgeway, which he would later populate with prehistoric traders carrying flint axes from the Grime's Graves mines in Norfolk, and jet and amber from the east coast, to the great ritual centres at Avebury and Stonehenge.

THE AGE OF THE RIDGEWAY

Many of the ideas about the origin and purpose of the Ridgeway were speculative. So what can we say about its age? The earliest recorded mention is in Anglo-Saxon estate charters recording land boundaries in the tenth century AD – for example, the bounds of Woolstone and Compton Beauchamp cross the *hryawaeg* ('ridgeway' in Old English) near Uffington Castle. The charters at Blewbury also mention it. The name occurs a number of times in the bounds of Wessex estates, but not always on the same line as the present track.

John Steane, then of the Oxfordshire County Museum, wrote an interesting, Crawford-like article published in 1983 in *Antiquity* asking: 'How old is the Berkshire Ridgeway?'[12] He examined maps of the eighteenth and nineteenth centuries to establish whether the routeway was fixed and static, and compared the first large-scale map of Berkshire, by John Rocque of 1761, with the 1840s tithe maps and the six-inch to the mile Ordnance Survey (OS) map of 1883. These showed that between 1761 and 1844 there had been changes to the route. It had been constrained and formalized, probably by the Enclosure Acts of that period. Landowners had banks and hedges constructed alongside the track, particularly in areas of arable farming, and the Ridgeway became a standard width of 1 chain (20 m/22 yd).[13] This served both to protect the route from the plough and the crops in the fields from passing flocks.

Other forms of evidence have since come into play, notably the aerial photography of cropmarks, soil marks and the more recent technique of Lidar. I have in front of me an OS map that shows the Ridgeway heading northeast beyond the Avebury henge. Onto the map have been inscribed the results of a huge effort to plot the traces of prehistoric and Roman fields by surveyors and aerial investigators of the Royal Commission on the Historical Monuments of England (RCHME)[14] – revealing an extensive and intricate patchwork, which indicates the enormous endeavours of farmers to transform the landscape between two thousand and three thousand years ago.

Most of these fields were set out and used from about 1200 BC to the fourth or fifth centuries AD. My old mentor and friend, the archaeologist Professor Peter Fowler, gets quite curmudgeonly about people who call the Ridgeway 'Britain's oldest road' and suchlike. He intensively studied Overton and Fyfield Downs and their prehistoric and Romano-British fields and pointed out that the Ridgeway can be seen to cut across or overlie these field systems. In other words, the line that we see today appeared after about AD 500, so the route of the Ridgeway near Avebury is not 'ancient British'.[15] The caption of the RCHME map makes this clear. It states that the Ridgeway is marked for locational purposes, but it was 'not part of the "ancient landscape"'.[16] A similar phenomenon can be seen in other areas, notably between the hillforts of Uffington Castle and Segsbury.[17]

I do not wish to be a spoilsport and suggest that the Ridgeway was simply a medieval track, formalized in the late eighteenth century. It would make sense for prehistoric people to develop trackways along the top of the Downs – for local use or possibly to provide long-distance access between the south coast in Dorset and the east coast in Norfolk. Britain was extensively forested in the Mesolithic (around 7000–4000 BC);

Neolithic farmers began to make inroads into this and certainly by 2000 BC areas such as the Thames Valley and Salisbury Plain were extensively cleared. The chalk ridge offered an elevated and relatively dry routeway, easier to navigate than the boggy ground where springs emerged and had to be crossed. The Icknield Way probably provided a summer route when the ground springs retreated.

It is possible that the first Ridgeway tracks were not man-made at all but the result of millions of hooves, driven by seasonal imperatives, hard-wired to search for fresh pasture. Before Britain became a series of islands (about 6500 BC) the North Sea basin was a well-watered, relatively sheltered lowland. Animals could migrate from here onto the higher summer pasture of what we today call the Downs and the Wolds. It doesn't necessarily make sense to pursue the herds across the high ground. Far better to imitate the actions of the crocodile and TV crews in the Masai Mara game reserve in Kenya, who lie in wait for the migrating wildebeest herds that turn up predictably each year at the same stretch of river crossing. And that is probably what human hunters also did in the late Ice Age.

Tim Allen, my colleague at Oxford Archaeology, was observing a pipeline trench being dug across the Goring Gap, the narrows where the River Thames now cuts through the chalk separating the Chilterns to the east from the North Wessex Downs to the west. Tim saw that ten thousand years ago a network of shallow, braided channels meandered across the valley bottom. The present, constrained course of the Thames is the result of modern canalization. A low island of gravel provided a stepping stone between the water channels where human hunters camped while lying in wait for the migrating herds of reindeer or horse. They passed their time preparing for action, making beautiful, but deadly, spear points of flint. The horses must have made relatively easy prey as they laboured through the water. If these herds had created well-worn trails it would be logical for the first farmers to utilize them for their flocks of sheep, newcomers that also needed summer grazing.

By coincidence Peter Fowler and I both later found ourselves living in the same part of southwest France, in the Cévennes, now a UNESCO World Heritage site, and a landscape created by transhumance – the movement of large flocks of sheep from the Mediterranean lowlands into the high summer pastures. It was Peter who first drew my attention to the broad trackways, or *drailles*, along which the *troupeaux* pass in an annual ritual in June, led by older ewes wearing iron bells and decorated with brightly coloured pom-poms of wool. In the autumn the flocks retrace their steps to the warmer lowlands.

In places the tracks are well marked; sometimes they bifurcate and branch, following fingers of dry land down into the valleys and river crossings. The flocks avoid tracks that have become too boggy or worn. No one knows how long the *drailles* have been in existence, but the one I can see on the skyline as I write passes along a narrow ridge by a line of prehistoric megalithic tombs. Are the monuments there because of the topography – silhouetted against the skyline? Or because the builders erected them alongside an existing routeway, rather like the tombs alongside Roman roads? We do not know the answer. But we do know that such trails are formed by ritual cycles of animal movements and, unless physically restricted, they tend to form braided channels like an uncontrolled river.

The fact is, the age of the downland Ridgeway remains uncertain. New light was shed on it during our White Horse Hill project, to which I will return in Chapter 6. I like to think that the present-day long-distance National Trail is the latest manifestation of a very ancient network of paths. But we cannot guarantee that at any point we are walking in prehistoric footsteps.

However, we do know from historical records that before the canals and the railways transformed the movement of goods, the Ridgeway and the Icknield Way were part of an ancient system of drove roads that were used to bring sheep from Wales and the West Country. Today the downland village of East Ilsley, about 10 km (6 miles) west of the Thames crossing to London, is skirted by the busy A34. In 1620 in the reign of King James I it became the site of a sheep market, which grew to be the second largest in England. It was held every Wednesday from Hocktide (the second week after Easter) to St James' Tide (25 July) and on the Feast of the Assumption (15 August). By the mid-eighteenth century, 80,000 sheep were penned there in one day, and the average yearly sales were 400,000. Dealers and graziers came to East Ilsley from all over the country. The village was at a crossroads of downland routes and had a good water supply. One of the routes led down to the Thames crossing and is still known as Halfpenny Lane, possibly a reference to the price charged per head for resting the sheep overnight in a secure pound.[18]

BACK ON TRACK

From the pub in Avebury my wife and I walk along the tarmacked section of Green Street, past Avebury's Nonconformist chapel, first built about 1670. The village's thriving Puritan community did not necessarily appreciate the prehistoric standing stones. The villagers were intolerant of the work of earlier religions, as some hard-eyed fanatics are today. The iconoclastic

Puritans were probably one of main reasons that only fragments of the two interior stone circles survive. The road passes through the northeastern entrance of the henge. A small wooden gate gives us access onto the huge bank. Four large beech trees grow out of it, from which flutter red, yellow, white and blue ribbons. Henges and barrows nowadays attract nature-loving neo-pagans who insist on furnishing nature with extra decoration. One of them is sitting beneath the trees, beating out a rhythm on a set of steel drums. 'I put out a hat to collect a few bob when the National Trust guys aren't about,' he tells me. Today there are no characteristic green jumpers in sight. From this viewpoint it is possible to appreciate the circumference of Britain's largest henge and how it encircles the village. From the inside, the great circle seems to capture its own universe: the chalk bank wrapped around the giant stones, with the big sky above.

We return to the tarmacked road, which leads through a darkened tunnel of beech, sycamore, oak and elder, past tumbledown buildings. As we emerge from the gloom and into the light the road turns white. The local authority tarmac layers have given up and we are back on a path created by the feet of generations of walkers and animals. The surface is rutted and flecked with nodules of black flint. A poster by the wayside tells us of the activities of the environmentally aware, green farmers of the Marlborough Downs. The fields are mostly arable, planted with cereals, but strips have been left to be colonized by wild geraniums, flecked with blue flowers, and by nettles.

'Tall Nettles', Thomas's deceptively simple little poem of two four-line stanzas, is one of my favourites. The first verse goes:

Tall nettles cover up, as they have done
These many springs, the rusty harrow, the plough
Long worn out, and the roller made of stone:
Only the elm butt tops the nettles now.

It perfectly illustrates Thomas's belief that 'Anything, however small, may make a poem; nothing, however great, is certain to.'[19] This bit of scruffy field-edge was just the type of unromantic landscape to inspire the quiet voice of the emergent poet. The poem uses both the present and the past tenses in the opening line, and the imagery of nature recolonizing the works of Man, which Thomas reveals rather like an archaeologist probing beneath the surface, creating a sense of time past and time present. Edward Thomas is not usually seen as a modernist like T. S. Eliot, but I think there are hints of what was to come. The final lines perhaps also invoke the future:

I like the dust on the nettles, never lost
Except to prove the sweetness of a shower.[20]

Nearly twenty years later the painter Eric Ravilious would also create art out of barbed wire, bits of old farm machinery and clapped out abandoned motorcars left on the Downs.

Walking along this path is a journey through time. Looking back, we see the Avebury ramparts, crouched low, sullen, rough and brooding – not at all like their proud, shaven interior bathed in light. To the side is a semi-derelict barn, its windows gaping and with what is left of an aluminium roof. A cockerel crows in mid-afternoon and, in the distance, another answers. A skylark sings its heart out and collared doves moan mournfully. Then an aircraft passes overhead. Thomas would probably have resented the intrusion of modern pandemonium (though he was one of the first to mention aircraft in a poem).[21] His poem 'Good-Night' contrasts the song of the skylark on the Downs with the sound of the city: 'In vain: the noise of man, beast and machine prevails.'[22]

Our aircraft passes, leaving a white trail as a memory in the sky, and the sound of beasts, not machines, is heard. Several Holstein cows are grazing in an old paddock belonging to Manor Farm. Perhaps they are responsible for the large, ripe manure heap over which swallows scythe. Rooks caw in the trees and flocks of sparrows twitter among the steaming cattle. Once as common as muck and taken for granted, sparrows are now becoming a rare sight. Thomas, who loved birds, and other admirers of the Downs like Richard Jefferies and W. H. Hudson, would be sad at the monstrous decline in the numbers of farmland birds since the late nineteenth century. Even when I began first to walk here in the early 1970s, skylarks, fieldfares, peewits or lapwings and kestrels, as well as bees and butterflies, were much more common before the blight of insecticides poisoned the land. As a child in Yorkshire my Uncle James took me for walks up Castle Hill. Yellowhammers flitted in the hedges. They call 'a little bit of bread and no cheese', said James. I haven't seen or heard one in years. At least the Marlborough farmers are doing their bit. Over the next few miles we can see their shaggy hedgerows, left unflailed, and unploughed field margins, which provide some cover in a much denatured landscape.[23]

Beyond the manure heap, where life is thriving, the white way begins to rise towards the high Downs. On the skyline a group of Bronze Age barrows is silhouetted against the sky. These distinctive oval mounds, burial places nearly four thousand years ago, provided Anglo-Saxon charter surveyors with prominent landmarks, man-made features that echoed the

Photograph by Fay Godwin of the Ridgeway Path leading into the distance, with the ramparts of Uffington Castle on the skyline to the northeast.

smooth rounded contours of the landscape itself. Unfortunately, many of them have succumbed to the plough, as generations of farmers sliced into them with steel blades, paring them until they eventually disappeared. Ironically, the wheat or barley plants remember. The quarry ditches of the lost barrows survive below ground, cut into the chalk. Here the soil is deeper and moister. The cereals sink their roots into it and so grow taller and take longer to ripen. As the fields turn yellow, green circles can briefly be seen, especially from the air. These cropmarks are a fleeting reminder of times past: of the people who once worked this land and were laid to rest here.

There is another reminder that this landscape was made by people, apart from the barrows. Sometimes their actions have unintended consequences. One plant thrives along hard-trodden paths. Flat, rosette-shaped circlets of leaves belong to the plantains (*Plantago lanceolata*) – which originally spread with the first farmers. As revealed in scientists' diagrams showing the frequency of different pollens found, as the forest trees and scrub declined and open farmland spread, grasses and plantains thrived. Prehistoric tracks would have acted as corridors for this innocuous plant, just as English railways helped to spread Oxford ragwort (*Senecio squalidus*, a native of Mediterranean volcanic slopes) in the nineteenth century. Once European farmers had crossed into Britain and exploited almost every corner, they would look for New Worlds to cultivate. They inadvertently took the plantains to North America, where the natives, experts on local plants, noticed the persistent newcomer and accurately called it 'White Man's Footstep'.

Today, the 'footstep plant' marks the modern Ridgeway, along the high chalk ridge from the Norfolk coast near the Wash, curving southwestwards past Luton airport, the transit point for a million holidaymakers, through the beech-covered Chiltern Hills, by the White Horse to Avebury. Beyond, the paths connect with Salisbury Plain and the River Avon, which flows past Stonehenge, and the soaring spire of Salisbury Cathedral. Prehistoric travellers could have followed the Avon to the Solent and Hengistbury Head or taken the chalk ridge southwest to the coast at Poole Harbour – both places where prehistoric Britons met traders from the Continent. The Ridgeway invites you to head towards the horizon. Kenneth Grahame, the author of one of the most English of books, *The Wind in the Willows*, walked the Ridgeway regularly. He wrote 'Out on that almost trackless expanse of billowy Downs such a track is in some sort humanly companionable: it really seems to lead you by the hand.'[24]

We head northeast towards the White Horse. At the Ridgeway proper we go by Fyfield Down, where the valley is littered with sarsen stones, those dense sandstone blocks that we also saw by Ashdown House. This was probably John Aubrey's fanciful battlefield of gods and giants – and the source of the hard-wearing megaliths that stand prominently within the Avebury henge and front the massive nearby Neolithic chambered tomb of West Kennet. One of the Fyfield Down sarsen stones is polished, corrugated and grooved, probably by early farmers sharpening their stone axe blades as they set about removing the endless cover of trees. The French have a name for such stones – they call them *polissoirs*.

By the middle of the second millennium BC the great ritual sites, such as Avebury, had fallen out of use. Both the landscape and society were changing. New, impressive monuments, known to archaeologists as hillforts, dominate the hilltops of the Downs. Some of the most impressive lie ahead, along the Ridgeway as we walk northeast. But first we ascend Hackpen Hill, where the scarp tips steeply to the west. You could pass without noticing, but just over the edge, on the slope, is another White Horse. This one was cut in the nineteenth century. Archaeologist and writer Jacquetta Hawkes called it and its brethren 'a link with antiquity because they were sired by the White Horse at Uffington'.[25] That's one way of putting it. However, the Hackpen Horse is a skinny runt and when we pass, a couple of real horses are showing scant respect for it. Steaming piles of their ordure are providing a fertile seedbed ready for weeds to colonize the grubby figure. It needs a damn good scouring! The Hackpen Horse is one of the many hill figures that multiplied in the eighteenth and nineteenth centuries – new landmarks, like the planted clumps of beech, which provide such a characteristic silhouette on the open, smooth downland curves.

The first of the hillforts now comes into view. Unlike the henges, these have external ditches and are more obviously designed for defence, with entrances to control those who approached, originally topped by wooden palisades. From them, watchful guards could scan the valley below and the routeways along the downland crest. Barbury Castle (Pl. xii), Liddington Castle, Alfred's Castle, Uffington Castle and Segsbury Camp all declare the power and authority of Iron Age British tribes – even if their modern names are misleading. These are nothing to do with medieval castles.

Before we can reach White Horse Hill it is first necessary to confront modern reality. The Ridgeway route descends near Badbury (sometimes claimed as the site of King Arthur's battle of Baden), to confront the ceaseless din of traffic rushing along the M4 motorway. At this point the modern road runs alongside the dead-straight Roman road known as Ermin Way. Nearly two millennia ago, a tired traveller from Silchester (Calleva Atrebatum) would probably have been feeling relieved. After a journey of about 55 km (34 miles), the small town and imperial posting station of Durocornovium was almost in sight. Today the charms of Swindon lie nearby – the M4 sweeps westwards away from the Roman road in order to skirt around it.

For most people the motorway probably seems like a permanent and inevitable fixture of the landscape, but I watched it being built. In 1970 I was one of the first archaeologists to be employed to observe the construction of a motorway – the M5 through Somerset and Gloucestershire. As bulldozers cut a swathe through the countryside, a small team of us followed, living and working from a clapped-out, old caravan.

Unfortunately, there was no such team working on the M4 construction in Wiltshire, which was taking place at the same time. A message got through to me in Gloucestershire that something of interest had turned up in the engineering works near Swindon. A couple of us headed out to take a look. South of Swindon and below Badbury there was a massive scar in the landscape. The construction boss took us to the works. There, in the raw line of the un-made motorway, the severed stubs of Roman masonry were visible, the truncated sections of walls, shattered mosaics and a surviving fragment of a bath-house. 'You're too late, I'm afraid. We uncovered this stuff a couple of weeks ago and held off putting the machines in. We told the museum,' said the engineer 'but no one came to look, so eventually we had to carry on with the job.' The big D9s had moved in the day before our arrival and bulldozed the Roman remains.

It was a dismal site. This must once have been one of the largest villas in Roman Britain – its buildings stretched for about 400 m (440 yd) along the line of the motorway – and perhaps five or six mosaics had disappeared without so much as a photograph or plan. I know the motorways of England by their ghosts, the ancient settlements they have severed. But this was the worst loss.

Beyond the M4, the Ridgeway runs relatively straight on the top of the steep scarp, which tips sharply to our left. Below huddle the spring-line villages, like knots on a string. Deep, ancient holloways, shaded by thick hedges, connect the villages to the Ridgeway: 'Landmarks that speak of habit rather than of suddenness.'[26] The hooves of sheep and the nailed boots of shepherds etched these tracks into the soft, steep chalk in the routine rituals of movement between the well-watered Vale and the downland grazing. Today, many are tarmacked and mainly used by tourists or locals walking their dogs. Farmworkers are becoming as scarce as farmland birds.

A distinct clump of beech trees marks the location of Wayland's Smithy, the megalithic long barrow which is the oldest human construction visible in the landscape (Pl. ii). Sir Walter Scott (1771–1832), the wildly popular poet and novelist, was a friend of the Hughes family of Uffington. They may have told him about the local legend, that a horse left overnight outside the tomb would be shod by morning by the Anglo-Saxon smith-god Wayland (or Weland, see p. 206). Scott included the story in his Elizabethan romance *Kenilworth* (1821). Thanks to radiocarbon dating and some very clever Bayesian statistics we now know that Wayland's Smithy was first built about 3600 BC. The people whose bones lie in the earliest burial chamber were victims of a raid, pierced by flint-tipped arrows – probably the aggressors were after the community's herds and their women. Early farming was not always bucolic, and scattered populations struggled for survival. The tomb was later rebuilt, about 3400 BC, on a massive scale. The builders seem to have copied the design of the West Kennet tomb, by the Ridgeway south of Avebury, which, at that time, was almost a century old.[27]

An illustration of Uffington Castle, and the rolling downland landscape (top)
and the chambered tomb of Wayland's Smithy (below), from *A Letter to Dr Mead
concerning some antiquities in Berkshire* (1738).

From Wayland's Smithy we can see the ramparts of Uffington Castle on
the horizon to the northeast, commanding the highest point on the skyline
about twenty minutes' walk away. There is no sign of the White Horse.
It can be an elusive beast. We have to skirt the ramparts and walk over
the ground disturbed by shallow chalk quarries. Only at the last minute
do the attenuated, abstract lines become visible like a puzzling series of
white paths. This is a figure designed to be seen from the north, from the
Vale and the low hills beyond.

CHAPTER THREE

LANDMARKS AND BOUNDARIES

...the pious King [Alfred], that there might
never be wanting a sign and a memorial to the countryside,
carved out on the northern side of the chalk hill, under the
camp, where it is almost precipitous, the great Saxon white
horse, which he who will may see from the railway,
and which gives its name to the vale, over which it has
looked these thousand years and more.

Thomas Hughes, 1857

HILL FIGURES AND GEOGLYPHS

In 1949 Morris Marples published a minor masterpiece of English land-scape writing: a generally unappreciated but well-researched and clearly written book entitled *White Horses and Other Hill Figures*.[1] He began with these words: 'The cutting of the figures in the turf is an obscure and little regarded art. Few people would recognize any art at all in the removal of sods from a hillside in such a way as to form the crude outline of a giant or a horse.'

Marples debated what to call this activity: 'turf cutting', perhaps. Yet in Ireland this describes simply cutting peat for fuel. Should we call them 'chalk figures'? Most are certainly a distinctive feature of the chalk down-lands of southern England. On the other hand, the famous Red Horse of Tysoe in Northamptonshire (now disappeared), as its name implies, did not exploit the geology of chalk. Marples used the term 'hill figures' in his book title, perhaps in deference to the distinguished archaeologist and Egyptologist Sir William Flinders Petrie who wrote a monograph in 1926 entitled *The Hill Figures of England* (see p. 87).[2]

Typically, Marples was not trying to impress so he rejected coining some neologism or academic jargon derived from Latin or Greek, such as 'caespiticidy' or 'colotomy'. He had, half-humorously, occasionally ventured to use 'leucippotomy' for the cutting of white horses and 'gigantotomy' for the cutting of giants – such as the priapic figure at Cerne Abbas. However, he felt that there was a need for a single term.

There are impressive figures made with marks in the Earth's surface in other parts of the world that depend upon neither chalk geology nor steep slopes. Some years ago one of my favourite authors called in to visit my neighbour in Oxford. She was the world-famous science fiction novelist Ursula K. Le Guin. It was only then that I learnt that the K stood for 'Kroeber' – her father was the well-known American archaeologist Alfred Kroeber. In 1926, flying over southern Peru, Alfred Kroeber saw wonderful things – the fantastic patterns, now known as the Nazca Lines, which formed large-scale images of animals such as a condor, killer whale and hummingbird, and abstract and geometric shapes and lines radiating for up to several kilometres from central points. These images were made by removing the stones and pebbles from the ground on a bone-dry plateau.

These spectacular figures and patterns were the creation of people of the Nazca culture (200 BC–AD 600), who also built pyramids and plazas at their great ceremonial centre at Cahuachi. The Nazca had great sensitivity to their natural environment, incorporating the topography into their architecture. Unfortunately, their achievements first came to popular attention when a confidence trickster and subsequently best-selling author, Erich von Däniken, published *Chariots of the Gods* in 1968 (the English translation appeared in 1969). He argued that the Nazca Lines represented an airfield 'built according to instructions from an aircraft', so the 'gods' could land there. Conventional, stuffy old archaeologists, according to von Däniken, just would not accept that aircraft could have existed in antiquity.

Recent studies by conventional (or proper) archaeologists have suggested that the Nazca people observed the constellations in the heavens and represented them in their designs. Other explanations relate the lines to the flow of watercourses beneath the surface of the desert. At any rate, the patterns indicate the sacred geography of the Nazca people, ritual pathways along which processions may have passed. All this calls to mind the ritual monuments in the prehistoric landscape at Stonehenge, Avebury and many other Neolithic/Bronze Age sites in Britain.

The point of this discussion, however, is that American archaeologists studying the patterns and figures of animals cut into or formed on the earth came up with the name 'geoglyphs'. Morris Marples might have shuddered slightly at this academic jargon, derived from Greek, but it is at least short, all-embracing and reasonably understandable: it means 'earth pictures'.

So what is the origin of the English hill figures or geoglyphs? Marples documented seventeen horses, eleven of them placed relatively close together in Wessex (mostly Wiltshire and old Berkshire, now Oxfordshire). Further north we also have the Kilburn Horse (North Yorkshire) and in Scotland the Mormond Horse (Aberdeenshire).

Most of the Wessex animals were created in the later eighteenth and nineteenth centuries – we will return to those in a later chapter. Marples appreciated, correctly, that the 'strange, delightful and intriguing' figure on the North Wessex Downs (the Uffington Horse) 'which has excited so much controversy and about which so little is known' was the prototype. He suggested that on the basis of style 'the Uffington horse dates from the very early Iron Age or later Bronze Age'. He was largely ignored by archaeologists. The other Wessex horses were its offspring, as were the northern outliers.

DOCUMENTING THE LANDSCAPE

In some societies writing originated between four thousand and five thousand years ago. In Mesopotamia, Egypt and Crete, literate scribes kept records of agricultural productivity, the contents of storehouses, the worship of gods, the descent of royal houses, kingly victories and the foundations of cities and temples. On the dark, northwestern tip of Europe, Britain lagged behind. Writing came with the Romans: accounts of military successes by the likes of Julius Caesar and Tacitus, and brief messages telegraphed on tombstones, dedicatory tablets, milestones and coins. There are little notes to the gods: curse tablets that say things like 'the person who stole my cloak, may his bowels rot'. Remarkably preserved letters on wooden tablets in the military rubbish dump at the fort of Vindolanda, adjacent to Hadrian's Wall, are both vivid and banal – invites to tiffin, requests for new socks. There are also itineraries that list the main Romano-British towns (all roads lead to Londinium), but few other places.

The first Germanic-speaking immigrants of the fifth century AD were illiterate and pagan, but that changed thanks to the influence of Irish and Italian monks who persuaded the kings of Kent, Northumberland and Wessex to join the European family of Christendom. The Anglo-Saxons developed one of the finest bureaucracies in Europe; the countryside and its occupants were well documented and effectively taxed – a prize for the Norman victors of 1066. William the Conqueror commissioned Domesday Book to record the changes of ownership and productivity in his new kingdom. With such a well-organized fiscal system he could successfully fleece his English flocks.

THE ANGLO-SAXON CHARTERS AND CHRONICLE

It was this monkish fondness for written records, to ensure the legal security of either their own property or that of their royal patrons and supporters, that has bequeathed a detailed picture of much of the English countryside a thousand years ago – at least where the records have survived the ravages of time, damp, fire and iconoclasts. Much of the land around the White Horse belonged to successive kings, and to well-endowed local abbeys such as Abingdon or ones further afield such as Glastonbury. These powerful organizations documented their land ownership and estates in written charters. There were no maps: the charters are itineraries that describe the bounds of the estate.

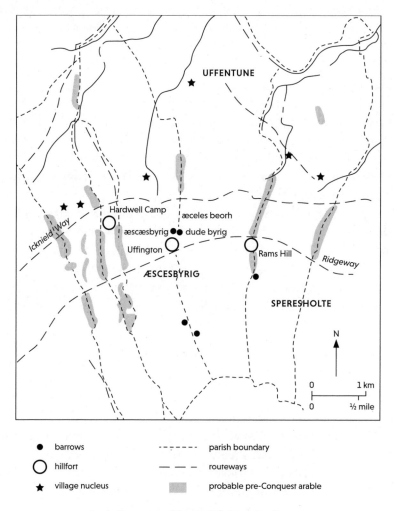

Anglo-Saxon estate boundaries extrapolated
from charters around Uffington Castle, with selected place names.

Anglo-Saxon charters are both fascinating and frustrating. About sixteen hundred of them survive, of varying value. For example, individuals are named in them but it is not always clear who these people were. Southern England seems to be littered with men called Aethelwulf, of varrying rank and status, in the ninth century, including a West Saxon ealdorman, a thegn and several Mercian ealdormen. To add to the confusion, at this time England was divided into rival kingdoms. North Berkshire and the Thames Valley were frontier territory, shifting between the two great rivals, Mercia and Wessex. Another factor to take into account: do not necessarily trust a monk. Some were expert (or, fortunately, not very expert) at the art of forgery. For example, Abingdon Abbey possessed a charter in which land of King Eagbert, at Marcham-in-the-Vale, was made over to them in AD 835. F. M. Stenton, the distinguished historian of Anglo-Saxon England and a scholar who studied both charters and the history of Abingdon Abbey, recognized it as a post-Norman Conquest forgery. Abingdon's monks were trying to do a land grab, exploiting their literacy and the historical ignorance of their victims. Fortunately, modern historians are sharper at spotting false witness lists or anachronistic language than some Anglo-Normans. At least monasteries generally took care of the charters that they held in their archives, hence many have survived. Aristocratic households were more remiss, letting mice, candles and floods attack their documents.

In spite of his long reign (871–899), relatively few charters survive bearing the name of King Alfred. One, of particular interest for us, is dated to AD 856 and is a grant by King Aethelwulf of land at Æscesbyrig, in Woolstone (the village just below the White Horse with the eponymous pub) to his thegn Ealdred. Alfred's name appears as a witness along with that of his brother Aethelred, though both were just boys at the time. Close study of the long list of witnesses and their titles reveals this to be another forgery – yet still of interest because it was probably manufactured in the tenth century at a time of major upheaval for both the Church and aristocracy in Wessex. Reinventing the past was a serious business and it has been possible to cull genuine information from earlier charters and from another vital document: the Anglo-Saxon Chronicle.

'The Anglo-Saxon Chronicle is the most important source for the political history of the period', according to its editor Dorothy Whitelock.[3] It consists of a series of manuscripts that have survived (or have been copied) since the tenth or eleventh century, which record the annals of England, beginning with a brief account of the Romans in Britain and the early events of Christianity. The Chronicle records the arrival of Hengist and Horsa in three ships 'at the place Ebbsfleet',[4] invited by Vortigern, king of the Britons. The Chronicle's early history of England is of dubious accuracy and may be partly mythical. However, the entries become increasingly reliable, even if the scribes limit them largely to the military activities of royal houses.

SHIRES, HUNDREDS AND ESTATES OF THE UFFINGTON AREA

A series of practical and local Anglo-Saxon charters describe the estate boundaries, including those of Uffington and its neighbours, in considerable detail. These were analysed by Margaret Gelling (1924–2009) in her pioneering study *The Place-Names of Berkshire*. She emphasized that a 'high proportion of boundaries of these Old English Surveys can be shown to have remained in existence to the present day'.[5] In many cases, the characteristic long, thin parishes such as Ashbury, Compton Beauchamp, Woolstone, Uffington and Kingston Lisle conform substantially to the bounds in Domesday Book in 1086 and the earlier Old English estate boundaries of the ninth and tenth centuries. There have been alterations and subdivisions of earlier holdings, but we can often reconstruct the old land divisions.

The charters that describe these estate boundaries within Shrivenham Hundred survived for centuries in the abbeys at Abingdon, Winchester and Glastonbury. The Hundred divisions were an administrative system of land division in existence before the Norman Conquest. Shires were formed around selected burh centres (defended places, such as Oxford) to serve the military requirements of the kingdom in the period of Danish aggression. Within these shires, Hundred units were formed (and often regrouped) to act as a means of defence and tax assessment. Each unit ideally contained one hundred hides of land.[6]

It seems that in the Anglo-Saxon period the parishes of Woolstone and Uffington were a single land unit known as Æscesbyrig. It used to be thought that this was the name of the village of Ashbury, but in fact it refers to the hillfort at Uffington Castle – a high, prominent landmark, though there is no evidence that it was occupied at this time.

An Abingdon charter of AD 955 (which survives as a later copy in the Abingdon Chronicle) says, in Latin, that King Eadred grants eight hides at Compton [Beauchamp] – next to the hill known as Æscesdun.[7] The prominent prehistoric earthwork of Uffington Castle, or Æscesbyrig, marked the centre of a substantial Anglo-Saxon estate, according to the Anglo-Saxon Chronicle, as did another nearby hillfort, Blewburton Hill at Blewbury (about 24 km/15 miles to the east).[8] Both hillforts now sit on parish boundaries but originally were landmarks centrally positioned in the larger

estates. Although these estates were first recorded in Anglo-Saxon charters, the land units themselves may go back much earlier, beyond the
Roman period to the time when the hillforts themselves dominated the
landscape, not only physically but also politically and socially, and when
field systems were first laid out on the Downs.

In the mid-tenth century the large estate centred on Æscesbyrig was
divided. From it were formed the two smaller landholdings given the
names 'Woolstone' and 'Uffington' – Wulfric's *tūn* and Uffa's *tūn*. Wulfric
was a powerful Anglo-Saxon thegn who in AD 960 had property across
southern England, including eight villages in Berkshire, five in Sussex
and two in Hampshire. Uffa was an Anglo-Saxon landholder who was
otherwise unrecorded. Because these two villages took the names of
tenth-century lords does not mean that they were founded by them
nor that the lords lived there. What we can assume is that the estates,
settlements, fields and boundaries were already ancient. The charters tell
us about the shifting ownership of well-established assets. The annual
routines of the countryside continued regardless of thegns, lords, abbots
and kings. This continuity of land use is relevant to the survival of the
White Horse, though the motivation of individual landowners also plays
an important part.

THE UFFINGTON BOUNDARY

The charters give a fascinating insight into the features of the landscape
that were important or distinctive to the Anglo-Saxons who managed and
worked the land. Lacking maps, people remembered the bounds from a
series of prominent features – natural ones, such as streams or trees, and
man-made features, such as banks, ditches, roads, field edges or prehistoric monuments. For example, there is a long description of the bounds of
Uffington in the mid-tenth century that can still be followed in the landscape today.[9]

The description begins in the northeast of the parish: to give a flavour
of the Old English it says: '*Ærest of huyres mere andlang pære lace in to pære
blache lace.*' In translation: 'First at the crosswise pool, along the stream to
the black stream.' The boundary continues past a 'tongue of land' along
Bula's ditch to a thorn stump. After these rather ordinary features the
charter takes us to the '*halige stowe*' (holy place). This is a term that often
refers to a Christian church, though we know of none in this area. However,
this is the point of the Uffington boundary where it meets the neighbouring estate of Fawler. Archaeologists love the name 'Fawler' because it often
derives from *fagan flore* (variegated floor) – in other words, it records the

presence of a Roman mosaic pavement. Early forms of this particular Fawler, however, indicate that the derivation is from *flage flore* (flagstone floor) – still probably the site of a Roman building.[10] Perhaps the locals, digging into the ground, found this building, derelict for several centuries, and assumed that it was a church because it was made of stone, unlike the timber, wattle and thatch houses in their own villages.[11]

The boundary continues: past the Icknield Way and Ægelsweard's boundary to the north gate of Raven's Camp (*hremmesbyriges*). This is the outer entrance to the prehistoric enclosure now known as Rams Hill.[12] Usually, this Old English name would be modified to Ramsbury, but here the fortification element has been dropped. And the raven has changed species, as often happens with this Old English word *hremmes*. Later English speakers, having forgotten the language of their ancestors, assumed that the word meant 'ram'. English people today regularly make the same mistake, assuming that a place name means what it sounds like in modern English. We easily forget that languages change. King Alfred, the great English king, would sound foreign to a modern English speaker, as do the thousand-year-old charters quoted above.

The Uffington boundary runs on through the camp (burh) of Rams Hill and out of the south gate and across *hodes hlæw*: Hod's tumulus. Burial mounds are often called *beorg* (barrows) in southern England, but here the word *hlæw*, surviving today as 'low', is used, as it is in the great epic poem *Beowulf*. The boundary description then passes northwards, along the western side of the estate. It continues past a series of tumuli (all referred to by *hlæw*): the stone tumulus, the hound's tumulus and the hawk's tumulus, which is still visible and known today as Idlebush Barrow. Beyond, the boundary is marked by the 'long ditch', which Margaret Gelling suggested was a natural feature. However, excavations indicate that this may be a prehistoric or Romano-British field division. Surprisingly, there is no mention of crossing the Ridgeway. Instead, the long ditch leads directly to *Æscesbyriges sudgeate*, the south gate of Uffington Castle, and then out of the north gate. As we will see later, these two gates are significant features that we investigated during our fieldwork and excavation of Uffington Castle.

Just beyond the hillfort the boundary is marked by 'Dudda's camp' – using the word *byrig*. This is probably a mistake on the part of the scribe, because there is a prehistoric burial mound (*beorg*) at this spot The boundary then climbs up *eceles beorh*, now known as Dragon Hill. The Anglo-Saxon name is interesting. Margaret Gelling and I discussed it at length. In another charter – that of East Woolstone (in other words, the same boundary on the western side of the Uffington estate, but working from north to south) – the hill is referred to as *æceles beorgae*. Both these forms in Old English could derive from Latin *ecclesia*, meaning the site of a Christian church, probably of the Roman period. Was there a church on or near Dragon Hill? If so, it has never have been found. It is also possible that *eceles beorh* could refer to a personal name.

To return to the western boundary of Uffington, below Dragon Hill it crosses the Icknield Way, then into the meadows, the millstream and marshes of the Vale and back to the crosswise pool where it started.

This is just one of a series of charters that describe the bounds of Uffington and its neighbours in the tenth century. What is fascinating for anyone exploring the landscape is how many ancient earthworks and burial mounds are utilized as landmarks on the open Downs by the Anglo-Saxon surveyors. Most of them are given specific names. Of particular interest is the great megalithic long barrow known as Wayland's Smithy, which was over four thousand years old when the scribes recorded the bounds of Compton Beauchamp in AD 955. This charter starts on the *hricg weye* – 'the Ridgeway' – heads north, across the Icknield Way and into the centre of the Vale. It returns, heading south, then on the Downs turns north again, back to the Ridgeway, which it meets *eastan Welandes smiddan* (east of Wayland's Smithy). The great tomb was obviously a well-known landmark and had already, in the tenth century, been given the name of the lame Anglo-Saxon smith-god. The Anglo-Saxons, pagans who in the seventh century converted to Christianity, were mythologizing the landscape, creating stories around it that fitted into their beliefs, and gave them cultural ownership.

But where is the White Horse? Its name does not occur in any of the Anglo-Saxon charters. So did it not exist at this time? Anyone studying the past has to be aware of the old maxim 'absence of evidence is not evidence of absence'. The charters that describe the western boundary of Uffington, where it reaches the highest point on the Downs and descends into the Vale, have a wealth of marker features within a few metres of each other and all precisely on the boundary line – the entrances of the hillfort, a barrow, Dragon Hill and the edge of the Manger (known as 'the ring-pit'). The White Horse itself lies nearby to the east and would be redundant as a landmark for those whose job was simply to define their boundary. These were practical people with a specific task. They were not writing histories nor tourist guides. Wayland's Smithy is mentioned because there are no distinctive features at the point where the western boundary of Compton Beauchamp meets the Ridgeway. There is an echo of the existence of the White Horse in the name of this megalithic tomb. Weland was the

Germanic smith-god and associated, as mentioned above, with the myth that during the night he would shoe the horses left outside the tomb for him (see also p. 206). The White Horse itself is only a few minutes' gallop along the Ridgeway. Perhaps its presence suggested the story.

THE WHITE HORSE IN EARLY DOCUMENTS

The charters provide us with useful landmarks – they locate streams, pools, roads, ditches and trees in the countryside of a thousand years ago – but no definite evidence for the existence of the White Horse. So can we be certain that the Horse is of considerable age? The clearest evidence for this is in documents that post-date the Norman Conquest. These were included in the cartularies of Abingdon Abbey, probably in the late eleventh and twelfth centuries.[13] Again they define land boundaries, yet do refer to the White Horse and White Horse Hill. There is a later document of 1273[14] that contains the name 'le Whitehors', and others of the fourteenth century that document the White Horse and the Vale of the White

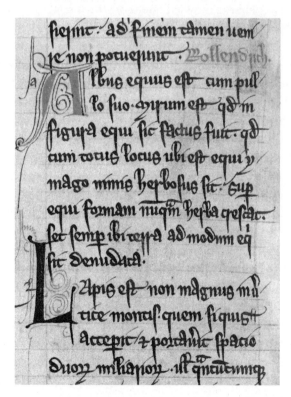

The twelfth-century manuscript of the 'Wonders of Britain'
listing the White Horse ('*Albus equus*', with large capital A)
as a wonder where the 'grass never grows'.

Horse.[15] In 1307, for example, Compton Beauchamp occurs as Compton sub Album Equum (Compton-under-the-White-Horse), and in 1348 there is Bishopstone super Album Equum.

The first report we have of the White Horse as a feature rather than simply as a place name occurs in a document which was itself included in a later twelfth-century chronicle of Ralph de Diceto, Dean of London. The Horse is listed as one of the thirty-five 'Wonders of Britain', alongside Stonehenge and the Rollright Stones. The scribe regards it as a wonder because no grass grew on its surface, which suggests that, at the time, there was no historical memory of its creation. This manuscript (*De Mirabilibus Britanniae*) tells us that: 'Fifth is the White Horse with its foal. It is wonderful that it was so made in the figure of a horse that over the whole place where that image of the horse is, no grass may grow and Grass never grows over the shape of the horse but always there the earth is bare to the full extent of the horse.'[16] The white figure was, of course, no miracle; it depended upon scouring, but the scribe seems unaware of any regular programme of repairs, acknowledgment of which might, in any case, bring the wonder down to earth.

The date of the original document is unclear, although it may pre-date the earliest Abingdon cartulary references. As noted, Ralph de Diceto included a copy of this list of wonders in his *Historical Works* begun in 1180. There is likely to have been more than one copy of the 'Wonders of Britain' – another is held in Corpus Christi College, Cambridge, written in 'Charter Hand' of the fourteenth century. This also deals with the 'Wonders of Britain' and elevates the White Horse to second after Stonehenge. The original manuscripts used by Diceto could be older than the surviving copies. Diana Woolner, a folkore specialist who challenged theories about the dating of the White Horse, suggests that Diceto's sources dated to around 1100, on the basis of the place names he uses.[17]

After the fourteenth-century references there is a gap of a couple of centuries before William Camden (1551–1623) makes an off-hand reference to it in his *Britannia* (1586) when he writes, in Latin: 'Which they call the Vale of the White Horse after some shape or other of a white horse picture on a whitish hill.' Perhaps Camden did not actually see the horse himself, or, if he did, it wasn't looking at its best. Clearly, he was not impressed. However, we need to remember the context. Camden was the greatest Elizabethan antiquary, but he was not interested specifically in the White

Images of a dragon and horse on the fourteenth-century St Birinus bell
of the Abbey Church of St Peter and St Paul, Dorchester-on-Thames,
not far from White Horse Hill.

Horse's origins. That had never been a matter of debate. His concern was to undermine the monkish superstition that promoted the miraculous qualities of the hill figure.

Camden's contemporary, the poet Michael Drayton (1563–1631), author of *Poly-Olbion* (1612), an ambitious celebration of English topography, thought more highly of the White Horse. He referred to it as 'the Wonder of the West', but made no mention of who made it or when.[18]

THE DORCHESTER BELL AND SHELDON TAPESTRY

Another fascinating piece of evidence relating to the Horse is of a very different type. This is the tenor bell that hangs in the western tower of the Abbey Church of St Peter and St Paul at Dorchester-on-Thames (about 30 km/19 miles east of White Horse Hill). The church itself is a fortunate survivor. It could have gone the same way as many of the other abbey churches, such as Abingdon's, when King Henry VIII dissolved the monasteries between 1536 and 1541 and in so doing perpetrated one of the greatest acts of vandalism and theft in English history. However, he was persuaded that the people of Dorchester needed a parish church, so, though the monastic buildings were razed to the ground, the church was retained. And we still have its tenor bell.

The bell was made in the foundry at Wokingham, Berkshire, in the fourteenth century and on it are two unusual images: one is the stretched out figure of a horse, its head to the right and its tail forming a continuous line with its back; the other is an image of a dragon. The two symbols together suggest that here we may have a reference to the White Horse and Dragon Hill. If so, this is the earliest known image of the White Horse – not very

accurate, but still conveying some of its distinctive characteristics, and Christianized as a symbol of good triumphing over evil.

The images on the bell were created at a time when the cult of St George was at its height. The popularity of this mounted warrior saint flourished with the Crusades, and his feast day on 23 April was officially adopted in 1222. Warlike monarchs, such as Edward III and Henry V, promoted the saint to both rival St Denis in France and replace the pacific Edward the Confessor as England's patron saint. George was glamorous, and in the late fourteenth and fifteenth centuries large numbers of religious guilds adopted him and performed colourful rites and processions on his feast day. In cities and towns such as Norwich, York, Stratford-upon-Avon, Leicester, Chester and Canterbury images of the saint and his dragon were paraded by people in fancy dress. In England his popularity grew until the Reformation, which rejected the idea that saints could intercede with God. The fun was briefly resurrected under Queen Mary, but suppressed as Puritanism gained authority under Queen Elizabeth I. As a result, England is in the curious position of having a national saint that is officially ignored, with no holiday on his feast day. In the meantime, ironically, the Catholic Church abolished the cult of St George in the 1960s.[19]

Another inaccurate representation, but a very significant one that certainly represents the White Horse, appears on the late sixteenth-century Sheldon Tapestry recently held in the Victoria and Albert Museum, London, but soon to return to the Bodleian Library in Oxford (Pl. xiii). Ralph Sheldon (*c.* 1537–1613) commissioned a group of tapestries in about 1590 from his own tapestry works in Warwickshire. These provided a panorama across southern England and probably reflected the tremendous interest created by the publication in 1579 of Christopher Saxton's county maps of England, the first of their kind. Ralph Sheldon intended the tapestries for his new house at Weston, Warwickshire, which features on the tapestry along with other important houses, towns, roads and topographical features. The presence of the White Horse, marked in the correct location (but depicted as a natural-looking beast, facing southwards), suggests that it must have been a well-known landmark at the time. Ralph's grandson, also Ralph, was an enthusiastic antiquary and passed the tapestries to the Bodleian Library, hence they have survived as a remarkable image of Shakespeare's England, a time of increasing population, where wealthy landowners prospered.

ATTITUDES TO THE PAST: MYTH OR HISTORY?

So we have a motley collection of charters, manuscripts and images that confirm that the White Horse has stood out on the escarpment of the Downs, resisting the ravages of time, curated by local people for over a thousand years. If about AD 1100 the Horse was regarded as a mystery, and almost magical, then its origins lay almost certainly beyond the scope of historical memory at that period. So how far back do we have to go to discover who made it, when and why? There is no shortage of theories. Human beings are curious animals, and inevitably speculate about the past, creating myths, legends, stories and songs, passing on or reinventing memories.

In the thirteenth century the owners of White Horse Hill, the monks of Abingdon Abbey, made an important discovery, digging not far from their monastery at the nunnery of St Helens. They turned up a metal pin with a distinctive head – a cross inside a circle. This, they declared, with more enthusiasm than accuracy, was formed from a nail of the True Cross, a revered relic that became known as the Black Cross of Abingdon. For the monks this glamorous object forged a link with St Helen, the mother of the Roman emperor Constantine and discoverer of the True Cross in Jerusalem. Archaeologists have somewhat spoilt the story. The Black Cross, which the monks illustrated in their chronicle, closely resembles what is now known as a disc-headed pin, a type of clothes pin found in archaeological excavations of other seventh-century monastic sites, such as St Hilda's, Whitby, the site of the important synod that met on the North Yorkshire coast to unify the British and English Churches in AD 664. If the Black Cross legend is tarnished, archaeologists have at least produced an equally interesting story: that Christianity and monasticism in Abingdon go back to the seventh century. Medieval monks appreciated the worldly fact that the past is powerful – it bestows respectability, establishes credentials and the right to authority – but the medieval Church did not encourage a spirit of enquiry. That developed later.

The great explosion of creativity from the late fourteenth century, which we call the Renaissance, brought with it new attitudes towards the study of the past, spreading out like ripples from Florence, Venice, Milan and Ferrara in Italy to France, Germany and northern Europe. At the same time, the European discovery of the Americas was revealing previously unsuspected human societies, people with very different ways of life, religions and attitudes to land and property. Renaissance scholars were able to make the conceptual leap from just reading about the folk memories of the Roman and Greek Classical past to actually seeking evidence for themselves. Michele Mercati (1541–1593), superintendent of the Vatican's botanical garden, combined the study of ancient authorities with the collection of ethnographic objects from America and with fieldwork in the Italian countryside, where he found and recognized ancient stone tools. Mercati's three-pronged approach formed the basis of modern archaeology.

Such ideas did not suddenly appear fully formed. In England, the reigning Renaissance prince and arch bully-boy, Henry VIII (1491–1547), encouraged the study of antiquities, while dissolving the main repositories of historical knowledge, the monasteries, and seizing their land. Henry employed

John Leland (*c.* 1506–1552), who, equipped with a royal commission, gained entry to abbeys, priories and friaries to seek out old manuscripts. Leland travelled the length of Tudor England, undertaking journeys 'which in their antiquarian excitements, overwhelming possibilities and distressing witnesses of destruction eventually robbed him of his sanity'.[20] Fortunately, Leland left a wealth of information in his *Itinerary*. It includes a reference to the Vale of the White Horse, but no more. At the same time, the Tudor dynasty warmed itself at the fireside of British mythology that cast a glow of legitimacy over their Welsh ancestry. Henry's elder brother, not long for this life – he died in 1502 – was named Arthur in honour of that great Celtic mythical hero, opponent of the Anglo-Saxons.

Attitudes to the past were, however, becoming more rational. William Camden defended the new approach, writing: 'In the study of Antiquity ... there is sweet food of the mind well befitting such as are of honest and noble disposition.' Camden's *Britannia* contained the first English archaeological illustration, including a drawing of Stonehenge and illustrations of ancient British coins, which would come to feature in the lengthy debate about the origins of the White Horse. As we have seen, he only refers in passing to the White Horse itself. A map by Christopher Saxton (*c.* 1543–*c.* 1610) included in the 1637 edition of *Britannia* accurately locates both White Horse Hill and the Vale of the White Horse.

Antiquaries also became figures of fun, and were satirized and ridiculed as maggoty-headed collectors of bric-a-brac. John Earle, later a respectable Bishop of Salisbury, wrote an amusing but affectionate description while a young man at Oxford. 'The Antiquary' is number 9 in his sketches of 78 characters:

> He is a man strangely thrifty of Time past, and an enemy indeed to his Maw, whence he fetches out many things when they are now all rotten and stinking. He is one that hath that unnatural disease to be enamour'd of old age and wrinkles, and loves all things (as Dutchmen doe Cheese) the better for being mouldy and worme-eaten.... Beggars cozen him with musty things they have rak'd from dunghills.... His grave do's not fright him, for he has bene us'd to Sepulchres, and he likes Death the better because it gathers him to his Fathers.[21]

This is reminiscent of the joke told by the writer Agatha Christie, often repeated (at least by archaeologists): it was good to be married to an archaeologist (her husband was Sir Max Mallowan) because the older she became the more he liked her.

The fact is, early antiquaries in Britain were slow to shed much new light on the past. Dr Samuel Johnson was sceptical of their efforts: 'All that is really known of the ancient state of Britain is contained in a few pages. We can know no more than what old writers have told us!'[22] These were not the words of some grumpy old reactionary, rather the contemporary educated view in the later eighteenth century.

To be fair, there had been elements of progress, especially in the field-work of John Aubrey (see p. 32) and the distinguished antiquarian William Stukeley (1687–1765)[23] at Stonehenge and Avebury, but decline set in around 1730. Between 1656 and 1691 Aubrey wrote *The Natural History of Wiltshire*. He began with a complaint about his fellow countrymen because 'twas held a strange presumption for a man to attempt an innovation in learning'. It was considered 'not to be good manners [for a person] to be more knowing than his neighbours and forefathers'. He goes on: 'There is no nation abounds with greater varietie of soiles, plants and mineralls than ours; and therefore it very well deserves to be surveyed.' This is exactly what Aubrey did, examining everything from weather, rivers, minerals and fossils to plants, animals and agriculture. He tells us, 'The wheat and bread of [Wiltshire] is but indifferent; that of the Vale of the White Horse is excellent.' Aubrey is often eccentric, misguided and is, of course, writing before the scientific revolution that began in the nineteenth century, but he is admirably inquisitive and broad-minded, and willing to look at the evidence for himself.

Aubrey had views about more than the quality of bread in the Vale. Because of its riches, he proposed, the area had been taken into the pos-session of the first Saxon kings Hengist and Horsa. These are the invaders of Britain who, according to the Anglo-Saxon Chronicle, arrived in Kent about AD 450 – both their names mean 'horse'. As the White Horse was their standard when they conquered Britain (so it was said), it made sense to Aubrey that the hill figure or geoglyph should commemorate the *Adventus Saxonum*, the arrival of the English in their new land. He was, however, willing to consider other explanations. Antiquaries were, by then, aware of pre-Roman, British coins. Aubrey described one found at Colchester (Camulodunum) and noted that the reverse featured a horse (as did many others), which put him in mind of the White Horse. In other words, the style of the hill figure bore a close resemblance to that on coins about two thousand years old.

Nevertheless, the Anglo-Saxon White Horse was the one that persisted in the popular mythology of the seventeenth and eighteenth centuries. This was the common view when Daniel Defoe (1660–1731), creator of

Robinson Crusoe and *Moll Flanders*, rode by the site in the 1720s. Defoe's most remarkable statement is that the Horse consisted of 'a trench cut on the side of a high green hill, this trench is cut into the shape of a horse and not ill-shap'd I assure you. The trench is about two yards wide on the top, about a yard deep, and filled almost up with chalk, so that at a distance, for it is seen many miles off, you see the exact shape of a white horse.'[24]

Defoe was a good reporter (when he felt in the mood), and in this case his sources were accurate. Our excavations would confirm the Horse was, indeed, made with a chalk-filled trench. Most other sources suggested the hill figure was simply etched into the natural chalk by removing the turf and cleaning the surface.

THE BATTLE OF THE REVERENDS

The antiquarian period drifted towards its end with a magnificent spat between academic rivals, at a time when academe was largely lethargic and of dubious competence. The Reverend Francis Wise of Trinity College, Oxford, was at least energetic in university politics and place-making. In 1719 he became Bodley's sub-librarian; in 1726 keeper of the University Archives as well as holding assorted church livings; and finally in 1748 he gained the desirable sinecure of Radcliffe librarian, in the architect James Crabb's fine new rotunda built with £40,000 left for the purpose by Dr Radcliffe. The new building, it was said, was 'little cumbered by books and almost entirely unencumbered by readers'. Not surprisingly, Wise held on to this undemanding post until his death in 1767. His scarcely arduous duties left him time for other things. In 1722 he had published 'an unscholarly' text of Asser's *Life of King Alfred*. This roused his interest in the Battle of Ashdown, where in AD 871 Prince Alfred and his brother King Aethelred fought, according to the Anglo-Saxon Chronicle, 'against the whole army of the Danes'. The battle, the *Life of King Alfred* tells us, raged around 'a rather small and solitary thorn tree'.

Asser's account emphasizes that Alfred engaged the enemy 'like a wild boar', while his over-pious brother delayed in his tent hearing Mass. Alfred is given credit for the great victory. The Anglo-Saxon Chronicle takes a different tack, Alfred plays no such dominant role and Aethelred is credited with leading the attack against the heathen kings Bagsecg and Healfdene. Bagsecg was killed, along with many thousands of his men. It was said to be the greatest slaughter ever seen on British soil. The Danes withdrew back along the Ridgeway to Reading, but emerged to win a victory over the English only two weeks later. Ashdown was not the decisive battle later English patriots assumed.

Although the Reverend Wise's knowledge of the period was more limited, it was enough to stimulate him to leave his onerous Oxford duties for a few days of gentle fieldwork on the North Wessex Downs in 1738. He was attracted principally by the White Horse, which he believed was a memorial to Alfred's victory. In the manner of the times he published his observation as *A Letter to Dr Mead, Concerning Some Antiquities in Berkshire*.[25] Dr Richard Mead was a noted physician with an interest in the past.

Wise begins his pamphlet with a complaint about the state of antiquarian studies: 'The study of our natural antiquities has till of late wanted the encouragement, which it deserved.' He goes on to praise Camden's *Britannia* and the potential of the Society of Antiquaries (founded in 1717). He regrets the obscurity of ancient British history, 'the times preceding Julius Caesar's invasion being dark and impenetrable, wild, without letters and almost without monuments'.

Finally arriving on White Horse Hill, Wise says he 'was persuaded to look for the field of battle and was greatly surprised to find my expectations answered in every respect'. In other words, he was a great jumper to conclusions. He assumes that Uffington Castle was 'a large Roman

A View of White Horse Hill from the north, from Francis Wise's *A Letter to Dr Mead*, 1738. The Horse is depicted in a naturalistic form on the side of the hill.

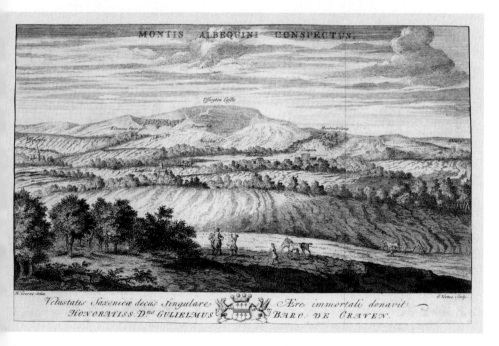

entrenchment' that was occupied by the Danes. Another nearby hillfort on lower ground, known as Hardwell Camp, was according to Wise 'fortified seemingly after the Saxon manner' (whatever that was supposed to mean), and this defended King Aethelred's English army. A third hillfort, to the south, Wise assumed was Danish (it is now known as Alfred's Castle).

Wise was aware that the White Horse was mentioned in twelfth-century documents and declared it to be a splendid work of art 'enough to raise the admiration of every curious spectator, being designed in so master-like a manner, that it may defy the painter's skill, to give a more exact description of that animal'. He makes it sound like a work by the contemporary artist, George Stubbs, famous for his paintings of horses, rather than the abstract shape that it is.

Accompanying Wise's *Letter* was a reproduction of a copper engraving by W. Greene belonging to the landowner Lord Craven, which shows a realistic representation of a horse galloping towards the east. This became the accepted view of the Horse and was frequently reproduced. However, elsewhere in his *Letter,* Wise writes: 'His Head, Neck, Body and Tail consist of one White line, as does each of his Four legs.' This sounds exactly like the image we see today. Wise continues: 'This is done by cutting a trench into the chalk about two or three feet deep.' Had he read Daniel Defoe's account? Or did he have access, a decade or so later, to the same sources?

The likelihood that the shape was sinuous and abstract is confirmed by a series of views of White Horse Hill produced in 1738 by Thomas Hammond from Lord Barrington's Park in the Vale. These sketches were made to illustrate Wise's *Letter* and to show the Horse as it was at the time, not someone's impression of how it ought to look. One of the sketches provides the foreshortened image as seen by the observer approaching from below. Unfortunately, the Hammond images were not published and remained relatively unknown.

Wise's *Letter* provides further information and speculation. The Danish king who died in the Battle of Ashdown was buried, he assumes, in the megalithic tomb known as Wayland's Smithy, along the Ridgeway to the east; the dead nobles were interred at Lambourn Seven Barrows. Wise had clearly walked the downland landscape, fitting the field monuments he saw into a preconceived model – everything had to relate to an event in AD 871: the Battle of Ashdown. Wise assumed that the battle occurred close to White Horse Hill, associating it with the local names Ashbury and Ashdown. However, the name Ashdown (Æscesdun) seems to have originally been applied to the whole of the North Wessex Downs. Margaret Gelling suggests that the name of the village Ashbury means 'the fort of

Four sketches of White Horse Hill and the hill figure drawn by Sir Thomas Hammond from Lord Barrington's Park in the Vale in 1738. These show the White Horse as a segmented, abstract figure.

the Ash tree' and refers to the hillfort that Wise calls Alfred's Camp. More recent studies place the Battle of Ashdown further east, near the Ridgeway south of Lowbury Hill, where the field name 'Ashdown' also occurs. This location would provide easier access to the Thames at Streatley, and on to Reading, where the defeated Danes are said to have quickly retreated to.

Wise's speculations about the White Horse were pretty much standard practice and innocuous for the time. The counter-attack must therefore have been unexpected. It came with a long title, but one that began with a superb squirt of vitriol: *The Impertinence and Imposture of Modern Antiquaries Display'd*. The author gave himself the pen-name 'Philalethes Rusticus'. In real life he was almost certainly another cleric, a jealous rival, the Reverend William Asplin (1687–1758), vicar of Banbury in north Oxfordshire. Although the eighteenth-century spat remains entertaining, the principal reason it is remembered today is that Asplin derided Wise's attribution of the Horse to the Saxons and, instead, suggested that its origins lay with the ancient British. He probably emphasized this because Wise was supposed to be knowledgeable about British coins, yet had failed to draw the parallel. Asplin, on the other hand, emphasizes: 'And this Conjecture would be strengthened also by the Figure and Posture of the *Horse* in every Circumstance, which are exactly the same with what we may observe upon some British Coins in Speed.'[26]

As mentioned above, John Aubrey had floated this idea of an ancient British horse on the basis of the image on a coin from Colchester. In 1758, William Stukeley's daughter Anna, after a visit to the Horse, had written to her father, telling him it was 'very much in the scheme of the British horses on the reverse of their coins'. William Stukeley refers to this in his *Family Memoirs* of 1758.[27]

The idea that the Horse originated in a dim and distant past, even before Caesar let alone King Alfred, was catching on in antiquarian circles. In spite of this, the new edition of Camden's *Britannia* that appeared in 1789 declared with 'great probability' that the Horse was a memorial to Alfred's victory over the Danes at Æscesdun (Ashdown) in AD 871.

This interpretation of the Horse – an emblem of the Christian English trouncing the heathen foreigner – inevitably continued to play well in Victorian England, and particularly to patriotic, upright, sporting gents such as Thomas Hughes, the Uffington-born author of *Tom Brown's School Days*, as will be seen in the next chapter. The argument would, however, resurface in the twentieth century.

CHAPTER FOUR

THE LAST PASTIME

There is no danger from hence of the whole
figure being obliterated ... the inhabitants have a custom of
'Scouring the Horse' as they call it, at which time a solemn
festival is celebrated, and manlike games with prizes exhibited,
which no doubt had their original in the Saxon times
in memory of the victory.

Francis Wise, 1738

20 AUGUST 1857: THE COMMITTEE

A small gathering of local worthies meet at the Craven Arms in Uffington.[1] They are the self-appointed Committee of Management gathering to organize the Pastime at White Horse Hill. Proper Victorian gentlemen – landowners and lawyers – they pride themselves on being business-like and modern. Mr Edwin Martin-Atkins chairs the meeting and will also be appointed treasurer. Clearly he is the man in charge. The group keep minutes and will announce their decisions to the community at large.

The past two decades have been troubled times, with increasing poverty and hunger in the countryside, riots, rick burnings and machine smashing. These men at the Craven Arms are looking forwards by turning backwards. They love the land and are proud of their local traditions – especially the Scouring of the White Horse and the 'Pastime' that went with it, a mixture of village fete, traditional sporting activities, horse racing and fairground entertainment, lubricated with drink. The Pastime and Scouring were theoretically held every seven years but the last had been in 1843, which was remembered because of the considerable difficulty encountered in hauling the elephant from Wombwell's Menagerie in its cart up the steep slope of the Downs. The self-appointed committee hoped to bring the community together by reviving this popular and patriotic event.

Edwin Martin-Atkins was a local landowner. Born in 1808 he was educated at Rugby School and Magdalen College, Oxford. On the death of his father in 1825, he inherited the Kingston Lisle estate to the southeast of Uffington village, just below the White Horse. Kingston Lisle Park

had been bought by Abraham Atkins in 1745. He was a lucky man who had emerged from the South Sea Bubble in 1727 without losing his entire fortune. Edwin enlarged the house and may have displayed his own architectural and Classical ambitions in the Staircase Hall, where 'the overall effect' is 'tenebrous and romantic', recalling the *Carceri* of Piranesi.[2] He was also a keen amateur archaeologist, and not a bad one for his day. In 1857 he was excavating on White Horse Hill. Believing the old tale that the Horse commemorated Alfred's battle against the Danes, perhaps he could find evidence in the barrows that dotted the Downs – the bodies of the glorious English dead, or even those of the heathen Danes.[3]

As an energetic Victorian polymath, he took on the organization of the 1857 Pastime, announcing that it would 'be held on the occasion of the Scouring of the White Horse, 17 and 18 September 1857'. To encourage participants there would be, for the first time, cash prizes for the most popular events: £8 for experienced backswordsmen, £5 for experienced wrestlers, £4 for the junior competitors. Pole climbers would compete for a leg of mutton; and the prize for the donkey race would be a flitch of bacon. The traditional headlong race down the Manger would be in pursuit of a wagon wheel and the winner awarded a cheese. In previous Pastimes the reckless and the foolhardy had pursued the cheese itself, which, rolling like a cannonball, didn't always survive the journey intact. Neither did all the pursuers.

Another member of the committee was lawyer Thomas Hughes – Uffington born and bred but now living in Wimbledon. His way of life had led him into the perilous paths of literature. Like Martin-Atkins, he had attended Rugby School and immortalized it in his novel *Tom Brown's School Days*, published that year. As Uffington's only well-known writer,

Thomas Hughes, author of *Tom Brown's School Days* and *The Scouring of the White Horse*, and Uffington's most famous author.

The title-page of *The Scouring of the White Horse* by Thomas Hughes
with illustration and lettering by Richard 'Dickie' Doyle.
Men are busy at work on an ancient scouring of the Horse.

Hughes was the obvious choice to chronicle the events on White Horse
Hill. This he subsequently did in the form of another novel, *The Scouring
of the White Horse*. Encouraged by the success of Hughes's previous work,
his publisher Macmillan & Co. produced a handsome book, bound in blue
buckram with gold lettering and images on the cover of the Horse (facing
the wrong way) and pastime sports (Pl. xiv).

The publisher must have had high expectations for the book because
it employed the well-known illustrator Richard 'Dickie' Doyle to decorate
it. Doyle came from a talented family of artists. His nephew Arthur Conan
Doyle would create the character Sherlock Holmes. Dickie himself was
best known for his rustic style and lively images, particularly of fairies, and
also his work on some of Dickens's Christmas books and the cover of *Punch*
magazine. In spite of his talent Doyle was a risk: he could be oblivious to
deadlines, once making the excuse that he 'had no pencils'. Nevertheless in
the case of the *Scouring*, he delivered. Arguably, the illustrations are more
memorable than the text.

17 SEPTEMBER 1857: THE SCOURING

It was 8.30 a.m. The morning was fine and Hughes had finished his break-fast of eggs, toast and coffee. 'A soft-boiled egg is not unwholesome', where had he read those words? He felt almost at peace with the world: he had a dutiful wife and a growing family, and his legal career was progressing. Perhaps one day he would be appointed a judge, or take up politics, and he could always tell his grandchildren how he had played cricket for the Varsity at Lords. Now his book *Tom Brown's School Days* was published and the arrangements for the Scouring all seemed to be in hand. He tapped the empty eggshells with his spoon. He had a niggling concern. He was a great believer in the value of manly sports and had strongly advocated reviving the backsword and wrestling events. Not everyone agreed. It could be disastrous if things got out of hand. The whole Pastime would be spoilt by violence and drunkenness. Much as he supported the reform movements and improving the lot of the poor, he hated and feared anarchy.

Hughes went to dress himself for the ride up the hill in his breeches, white shirt, waistcoat and black broadcloth jacket. He tied a plain green stock around his neck. This was an occasion for festivity, but Hughes did not wish to appear as some Westminster popinjay like Disraeli or Dickens. He might be an author, but he was also a lawyer and the sober Christian product of Dr Arnold's Rugby School. He pulled on his boots and jammed his beaver firmly on his head. It sat there like a well-mortared chimney pot. He was rather proud of his new mutton-chop whiskers. They made him look like a veteran of the Crimean War – and distracted from his balding pate. He picked up his whip.

Outside in the yard, the stable lad emerged with Hughes's chestnut cob. The summer had been exceptionally hot, but, as he mounted, Hughes was glad to see that, so far, there were no signs of gathering thunderclouds. He rode past the farmyard, where the pigs lay torpidly in the straw and the hens pecked the dust. The rick-yard was full of long stacks of hay and round stacks of corn. He passed a walnut tree whose branches drooped to the ground. Three turkeys perched in the tree watched him pass. 'They look like three old judges,' Hughes thought to himself. In the orchard the branches were heavy with apples and pears. He saw a young lad walking determinedly along the track. 'Young Piggott! Are you heading to the Horse? Jump up.' The ten-year-old boy climbed up in front of Hughes.

Ahead, Hughes could see the crest of White Horse Hill, crowned by the ramparts of Uffington Castle. The White Horse was dotted with figures already gathered for the Scouring. The ground grew steeper and he urged on his horse. At the crossroads with the Iggleton (Icknield) Way he took the steep road directly ahead. The great green hill seemed to be hanging right over him. On his right was the curious mound known as Dragon Hill. Here, they say, St George slew the dragon in olden times. Hughes was sceptical about these old tales, but they were harmless enough and promoted English patriotic spirit. Three children appeared on top of the mound. Hughes slowed his cob and young Piggott slid down. The boys were attacking the dragon with wooden swords. One, a pale, red-haired lad, dashed forwards and plunged his sword into the monster's throat. 'I am King George. Die you devil!' he cried. He turned to the second boy, skinny, with long blonde hair, 'Watch out for the blood, Caleb. It will burn your feet off.' Caleb leapt across the smoking stream. With his sword he slashed the bonds that tied his sister. 'Be not afraid,' he cried. She looked at him rather sceptically.

The slope of the Manger, known as the Giant's Staircase, was creased, folded like a curtain; these hollows were chutes rather than stairs. 'Perhaps', Hughes thought to himself, 'the megalosaurs had slithered down these slopes after the waters had retired from the Earth. Or were they connected to Monsieur Agassiz's new theories about glaciers? Perhaps not.' The Downs were hardly the Alps.

Undoubtedly it was a beautiful place and from horseback he was able to survey the view over the deep Manger and across the Vale. 'Pity about the state of the road,' he muttered to himself. The bare track coiled like a snake around the Manger. Its chalk surface was corrugated with deep grooves where heavy rains had poured down. These needed to be packed with hard flint instead of just pointlessly shovelling more chalk onto the surface. Really, these roads were not fit for the nineteenth century.

Hughes felt anxious to get on. He put the cob into a trot and rode past the steep footpath, opposite Dragon Hill, that led up to the Horse's tail. He continued until he reached a holloway in the chalk that ran, more gently, around the contour of the slope. He passed the thorn tree and the long mound that his friend Martin-Atkins planned to investigate. What treasures might lie therein?

Beyond, a marvellous sight appeared. Scores of local men were hard at work on the White Horse. Squire Martin-Atkins was there himself, a tall stalwart figure in yellow leather gaiters, supervising the workmen. Already the flanks of the Horse were gleaming white, as the weeds and the sheep muck, accumulated over several years, had been cleared away. Groups of men with shovels and besoms scraped and swept the surface, filling wheelbarrows with debris. Further along the slope children practised the ancient local art – cutting their initials into the turf.

The scouring of 1857, as depicted by Richard Doyle for *The Scouring of the White Horse*.
Thomas Hughes, the author of the book, was one of the committee who organized
the event, including the Pastime that accompanied it.

Hughes was already putting his mind to how he should compose a
description of these events. Perhaps, rather than straightforward report-
age, he might concoct a tale around the experiences of a visiting outsider,
some young radical from London, his head buzzing with Chartist ideas.
The lad, essentially good-natured, would soon come to see the wisdom
of the old ways: that not all squires were bloated aristocrats who, by the
time they were thirty, had addled with drink what little brain they had
ever possessed.

The energetic Martin-Atkins, observing Hughes's arrival, called for his
coat – a grey tweed shooting jacket. His wife said that of all manly dress
a shooting jacket was the most becoming. Some nonsense she had read
in a novel, no doubt. Still, it was a sturdy garment – capable of stopping
musket balls. The Squire picked up his riding whip. In a confident voice,
accustomed to giving orders, he urged the men to 'look alive' and 'get the
job done'. 'Then', he said, 'there's bread and cheese waiting at the marquee
in the Castle.' 'At least if they eat plenty it might mop up the beer,' Hughes
thought to himself.

Martin-Atkins and Hughes sat on a little grassy knoll just above the Horse's ears and watched the men working. The Squire lit a Trichinopoly cheroot and blew the smoke out over the Vale. Teams were digging clean chalk out of the shallow quarries behind them and barrowing it across to the hill figure. Once the surface was clean, the new chalk could be tamped in to ensure that the Horse kept its distinctive form. Hughes lit his pipe and listened to the skylarks, which hovered above. What a marvellous day! 'The work on the Horse should be completed by the end of the afternoon, provided there is no downpour,' said Martin-Atkins. 'Everything seems to be progressing satisfactorily for tomorrow's Pastime.'

Hughes plunged his hand into the pocket of his coat and pulled out a small book: 'Here is the Scott.'

'Ah, his *Letters on Demonology and Witchcraft*,' replied the Squire (see p. 249). 'Let me take a look.' He opened the cover and saw the red scrawl inside: 'Demon de Uffing' written over the sign of a pentacle. 'So this is the copy that the admirable Sir Walter gave to your family?'

'Indeed, indeed, Edwin. He would have been much pleased to learn that you have explored this ancient burial mound.' Hughes tapped the ground on which they were sitting.

The Squire signalled to one of his labourers: 'Ben, be a good fellow and dig a small hole, right here by Mr Hughes.' The man put his spade to the turf and brought down his boot. Four such blows and he was able to lift out a thick sod. With a little more effort he dug out the clean chalk below.

'That's champion, you are a worthy pioneer,' said Martin-Atkins. He took the book, placed it carefully into the hole and laid the loose chalk and turf back on top. 'Now, Ben, apply your boot to that.' The man stamped on the turf a few times. 'There we are,' said the Squire. 'Invested in Mother Earth! An offering to the ancient ones.'

'Alas, Poor Yorick,' Hughes announced theatrically. 'You have certainly found a sufficiency of skulls here on the Hill. A great contribution to the science of comparative cranioscopy I am sure.'[4]

The pair walked over to the gap in the ramparts of the Castle. Within the earthworks was (more or less) organized pandemonium. Scores of people were at work erecting booths, tents and wooden platforms and setting up banners. Men unloaded barrels of beer from carts that had been hauled to the hilltop by sturdy horses now flecked with sweat. Victuals were carried into the booths, along with wood and charcoal for the temporary kitchens.

Several fellow committee men attempted to keep order and ensure that the ground was parcelled out appropriately to those who had paid to rent a plot for the two days of the Pastime. It was a struggle to stop the booths encroaching on the 'streets', which were supposed to be kept clear to give passage to tomorrow's crowds. In the confusion old women had lost their donkeys and vice versa. Gypsies, with faces tanned and riven like the trunks of old oak trees, were trying to claim pitches they had not paid for; children pinched apples from untended baskets that sat outside the booths. In the centre of the hillfort a team of labourers were sawing and hammering, creating a wooden platform six feet high for the highlight of the Pastime – the backsword competition.

Martin-Atkins and Hughes walked along the emerging 'streets' checking that all was coming along, keeping an eye open for potential trouble-makers. Finally, they walked back to check progress on the Horse.

'I think we'll do very well,' said Martin-Atkins.

'It looks as bright and clean as a new sixpence,' Hughes replied.

The White Horse had not looked this good since Queen Victoria's coronation.

The lads who had worked hard all day on the Horse now sat in a group, consuming a large can of beer that Martin-Atkins had sent over to them. They were bawling out a song in their broad Berkshire dialect:

> The owld White Harse wants zettin to rights
> And the Squire hev promised good cheer,
> Zo we'll gee un a scrape to kip un in zhape,
> And a'll last for many a year.

18 SEPTEMBER 1857: THE PASTIME

The day of the Pastime dawned fine. Groups of people from local villages thronged the lanes leading towards the hill. The gentry, with their wives and children, came in carriages. There were barouches and berlins, old sporting curricles, landaus, phaetons, broughams and even a new Victorian driven by an adventurous young lady. Many of the coaches were accompanied by young men on horseback.

From the east and west came a flow of humanity along the Ridgeway. Some carried their coats and the women took off their bonnets as the day warmed. Often they jumped aside to avoid the motley collection of wagons. Some wit said, 'Them wagons look as if they were left over from King Alfred's wars with the Danes.' People were making their way from local towns: from Wantage and Faringdon and Swindon. There were rowdy flocks of scholars from Oxford. Gypsies with their lurchers left their painted wagons by the side of the Ridgeway. From further afield, from

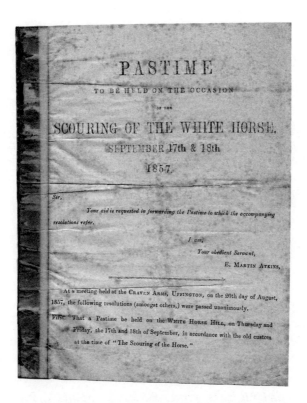

The original pamphlet setting out the Pastime of 1857, as agreed
by the Pastime Committee chaired by Edwin Martin-Atkins.

Wiltshire and Somerset, came the supporters of their sporting champions, already lubricating themselves with cider. The railway, which now crossed the Vale, had brought the curious and adventurous from as far afield as Reading and London, dropping them off near Uffington village.

At ten o'clock the committee men gathered to make the final arrangements. They were particularly concerned that the partisan crowd should not grow disorderly during the backsword events. Local clergy had preached against this traditional form of fighting. They regarded it as old-fashioned and barbaric, a blood sport unsuitable for modern times, for the new Victorian age. Many of the ladies agreed. They did not much approve of the drink either. Why couldn't Englishmen gather to watch sport without first filling their bellies with ale?

The carriages were parked neatly in rows on the lower ground west of the Castle. Youngsters dashed up the slope to the entrance while the older parties huffed and puffed, leaning on their canes. It was a welcome day out for nursery-maids, kitchen-maids and laundry-maids – all in their

A scramble taking place in the pig chasing, one of the less serious
events of the 1857 Pastime on White Horse Hill.

Sunday-best clothes and with rosy, freshly scrubbed faces, so clean they
looked skinned. During the Civil War the Vale had mostly sided with
Parliament, while King Charles sheltered behind the walls of Oxford,
playing real tennis. Many Vale people were still evangelical Christians, traditional in their attitudes. They looked to the Bible and the theological
virtues for their daughters' names: Faith, Hope, Charity, Prudence. There
were plenty of Ruths and Rachels. The boys also were given good, honest
biblical names like Joseph, Enoch, Jacob, Noah and Benjamin.

The countrymen had few clothes and these were made to last. The
traditional long white smocks were going out of fashion. Industrial
workers in the north had taken to jackets and trousers, tighter-fitting
garments that were less likely to be caught in machines. In spite of the
arrival of the canal and the railway, though, many Uffington farm labourers still wore the old smocks, albeit mostly shorter ones with trousers.
The better-off dressed for the occasion in velveteen and fustian coats
with coloured waistcoats – to cover their braces. Respectable local women
wore fetching scarlet cloaks, often passed down from their mothers.
The more fashionable had taken to wearing paisley shawls. Hughes preferred the red cloaks and thought the shawls 'did not become them half so
well'. All the women wore long skirts and bonnets. It was fortunate the
weather remained fine.

By noon over 20,000 people thronged the hill. Hughes hoped that
the crowd had come for the good of its education, to appreciate the significance of this place, so fundamental to the history of England and
Christendom. But he was a realist. There would be an opportunity to

enlighten his readers in his forthcoming book. In the meantime, the crowds thronged around the booths, watching the acrobats and rope walkers, playing skittles, listening to the musicians, the buskers and fortune-tellers, and the patter of the drummers, who stood outside their booths in front of painted sheets that advertised the wonders within. Was it worth a penny to see the pink-eyed lady or the strongest man in the world? A dilemma for a young housemaid with only a few coppers in her pocket.

The children were treated to gilded gingerbread and apples. Old farmers lit their pipes with lucifer matches and propped up the wooden bar that rested on a line of beer barrels; young farmers scouted the crowd for the prettiest girls. Here in the country, rarely was such a gathering seen. Uffington village held an annual 'feast', but that did not attract such a crowd from so far afield.

The men who were not chasing girls waited impatiently for the sporting events. There were daft ones like pig chasing, greasy pole climbing and sack races – a bit of fun. Serious horse racing on the hill was a thing of the past – the thoroughbreds now went to the courses at Newbury, Epsom and Ascot. Instead, there was a donkey race for the prize of a flitch of bacon and a carthorse race for a new set of harnesses.

Martin-Atkins, Hughes and the local parson had made a study of previous scourings and pastimes – tracing the events from old posters and records in the *Reading Mercury and Oxford Gazette,* which reported that a Scouring had been held on Whit Monday, 15 May 1780:

> The ceremony of scouring and cleansing that noble monument of
> Saxon antiquity, the White Horse, was celebrated on Whit-Monday,
> with great joyous festivity.... Upwards of thirty thousand persons were
> present, and amongst them most of the nobility and gentry of this
> and the neighbouring counties.... The origin of this remarkable piece
> of antiquity is variously related; but most authors describe it as a
> monument to perpetuate some signal victory, gained near the spot,
> by some of our most ancient Saxon princes.[5]

The earliest scouring of which the committee men could find a record was held in 1755. In the eighteenth century, events could be a little more scandalous. The backsword play was won by 'a fine dashing fellow, dressed like a gentleman'. As soon as he had his hands on the prize he jumped on his horse and rode off. Some of the locals claimed to recognize him: Tim Gibbons of Lambourn, who had not been seen in the area for several years, though racy stories circulated about him.

Martin-Atkins tracked down one of Gibbons's descendants, seventy-year-old Thomas, working in a field at Woolstone. This 'hale, sturdy old fellow' was Tim's great-grandson. 'Tim', according to his family, he said, had been a blacksmith at Lambourn 'till he took to highway robbin'. On one occasion he was surrounded by constables but, crying out, 'he'd shew 'em what a Englishman could do', he 'mounted his hos and drawed his cutlash' – and galloped off clean away. Some years later (after his success at the Pastime) Tim was taken by the authorities while drinking at a public house 'someweres up Hounslow way ... and I b'live 'a was hanged at Newgate'. The great-grandson, not surprisingly, claimed that Tim the Highwayman never killed anyone and gave some of his takings to the poor ('if he knowed they was in want'). Tim must have learnt his trade from the tales of Robin Hood and Dick Turpin. Or, more likely, the great-grandson was romanticizing his dubious ancestor.

The committee was determined that there would be no trouble at its Pastime – and the County Police and military were discreetly present, with their white tents and flagpoles under the western rampart of the hillfort, near to Lord Craven's tents. In fact, only two men were charged with pickpocketing in the course of the holiday and brought before Martin-Atkins, who, inevitably, was also the magistrate.

In the committee tent the sportsmen lined up to register for their events – a 'very tough race' of men, thought Hughes, averaging five foot eight and eleven stone – not very tall or stout. It was not unusual for such lads to enlist as soldiers. Hughes chatted to 'Old Mattingley', the Uffington blacksmith, who walked with a crutch and wore a new Crimean medal. Three of his sons had gone to the war in Russia, he said. One was shot in the hand at Inkerman on 5 November 1854, but carried on fighting until the Russians withdrew. He died of his wounds within a week. The second son was killed in the trenches at Sebastopol. The third survived the whole war only to be kicked by the horse of a wounded officer and lamed for life. The father hoped this lameness would not prevent him learning black-smithing, which, as he said, 'was mostly arm-work'. Hughes was 'rather ashamed' that England did so little for wounded veterans such as Young Mattingley and hoped that the powers-that-be and gentlemen who were knighted in the wartime might read this story in his book and do something about soldiers' pensions.

Once the participants had been sorted, the committee emerged from the tent and walked to the stage set for the wrestling and backsword contest. The chairman made an announcement, narrowing his eyes as he scanned the crowd, almost all men:

There has been a good deal of talk about these sports, as you all know; and many persons think they shouldn't be allowed at all now-a-days – that the time for them has gone by. They say, that men always lose their tempers and get brutal at these sports. We have settled, however, to give the old-fashioned games a fair trial; and it will rest with yourselves whether we shall ever be able to offer prizes for them again. For, depend upon it, if there is any savage work to-day, if you lose your tempers and strike or kick one another unfairly, you will never see any more wrestling or backsword on White Horse Hill.[6]

A packed crowd was keen to get on with the highlight of the day. John Bunn of Wedmore, in Somersetshire, threw his black hat in the ring and clambered up after it. George Gregory of Stratton, one of the best mowers in the Vale, jumped up to defend the honour of the locals. The two set about each other with heavy sticks, parrying, blocking and striking at each other in a flurry of blows. Suddenly the bout was over: blood could be seen running down the local man's forehead. Most of the crowd was silent.

While the bouts continued, to the east of the Castle the carthorses galumphed sturdily around a course marked with pink flags. The great horses wore their thill harness, which normally attached to a cart's shafts, that jangled and rattled as they moved. The carters perched on top, wearing white smocks and break-of-day hats with the brims turned up in front and ribbons on the side. Unlike regular jockeys they carried long cart-whips – except Joe Humphries, in full jockey fig and spurs, who was mounted on Dairymaid. The committee debated whether to disqualify Humphries for this blatant display of professionalism. Where did he think he was – Epsom? But none of the other riders objected. Perhaps they had no fears of a mare named Dairymaid, whatever her rider wore.

The race started and it seemed that Humphries did know a few jockey tricks. Dairymaid took the lead. But she found the course tough going and King of the Isle passed her as they crossed the Ridgeway, cheered on by the ploughboys, the shepherd and fogger who worked for Mr Whitfield, King of the Isle's owner. He had promised to divide three guineas – the value of the prize harness – between them all if his horse won. Which it did with ease thanks to the carter's skilful pacing.

Almost immediately the crowd shifted to the brow of the Manger to watch the races for 'the prime-coated Berkshire fives' (as they called the cheeses). The umpire, Mr William Whitfield of Uffington, looked, according to Hughes, 'like a model yeoman' in his broad-brimmed beaver, his brown coat, waistcoat with brass buttons, drab breeches and gaiters.

As he attempted to bring the competitors to order two wild-looking Gypsy women, their elf-locks streaming from under red handkerchiefs and black eyes flashing, dashed among the men screaming that their menfolk 'should not break their limbs down that break-neck place'. Then several giggling young couples wandered across the bottom of the course. The chairman, Mr Martin-Atkins, appeared on his white horse and rode down to the front of the line of men. Hughes looked on in admiration. There appeared to be footing for nothing but a goat on that steep slope. This brought some order to the events and the chairman gave the signal for Mr Whitfield to release the cartwheel on the cry of 'Off!'

The wheel careered down the precipitous slope, cleared the road in a monster bound of 40 yards and continued down in the Manger. Fourteen young men hurtled in hot pursuit, some slipping and losing their footing, some taking the course more carefully and trying to maintain their balance. Some fell flat on their faces and gave up the chase. The fastest of the Gypsies darted along a sheep walk, an easier track but one that took him away from the wheel. Two or three headed directly downwards. The swiftest was Jonathan Legg of Childrey. The Gypsy, realizing his mistake, changed tack. He gained rapidly, but Jonathan Legg reached the wheel first by 10 yards. The partisan crowd on the hill let out a huge roar.

Another wave of noise greeted the victory of Harry Seeley of Shrivenham in the backsword play. In spite of the chairman's warning, a Somersetshire man had fought dirty. Hughes was worried as the faces of the crowd around the ring turned 'savage and wicked-looking' (even the Oxford scholars). They howled for Seeley who, keeping his cool, had fought skilfully, but only after several hits drew blood, and so claimed victory. Seeley later said that the Somersetshire fighters drank vinegar for a week before a competition and this dried up the blood in their heads 'so it takes a "masin" sight of cloutin' to break their yeads as should be'.

Things calmed down when the jingling match started – a kind of blind man's buff in which blindfolded men chased a bellman. There was lots of good-humoured cheating, with young men peeking under their blind-folds and deliberately colliding with the girls who stood watching. Hughes did not think much of this so-called sport, nor the pig racing, though the crowd seemed to enjoy both and, at least, there were no frayed tempers.

The games were pretty much at an end. The victors lined up in the committee tent to claim their prizes and families began to drift away. The sun was low in the west and illuminated the newly scoured Horse. Hughes watched from the ramparts of the hillfort. He heard a cheer go up and was glad to see that the crowd was acknowledging the departure of

The most popular event at the 1857 Pastime was the backsword contest,
in which contestants fought with wooden swords or staffs. It was watched
mainly by partisan men, favouring their county champion.

Lord Craven's party. His was the only carriage allowed inside Uffington
Castle ramparts, hardly surprising since he owned the land, as well as
the White Horse and Dragon Hill. None of the day's events would have
happened without his say so. Nevertheless, it cheered Hughes to see that
the crowd was good-humoured. No sign of French revolutionaries; just
English bonhomie.

As the light faded, scores of oil lamps were lit in the booths where food
and drink were being served. Hughes, now armed with a fierce appetite,
sat at one of the supper tables and attacked a plate of beef, watercress
and walnut pickle. A grisly-headed old man, wearing a velveteen coat and
a blue bird's-eye-neckerchief, cleared his throat and began to sing 'The
Death of Lord Nelson'. Hughes, a collector of folk songs, frantically tried
to note down the words.

The local doctor sang 'The Vicar of Bray', an amusing and cynical ditty
about the ability of clergymen to change their beliefs and principles with
every wind that blows. The singing and drinking continued until nearly
nine o'clock, when the committee men, the doctor and the parson, seeing
the lateness of the hour, rose and headed towards their homes. Hughes
was mightily satisfied at the day's events: a great display from the rural
community and a successful revival of the Scouring and the Pastime. He
could not know that it would be the last.

CHAPTER FIVE

THE WHITE HORSE: THEORIES AND SPECULATION

Objects ... are there to be talked about and invested with
the memories and striking events associated with their use.
Objects of a durable kind assert their own memories ...

Mike Rowlands, 1993

THE BIRTH OF ARCHAEOLOGY

At the time of the 1857 scouring of the White Horse, archaeology was in a
state of flux, emerging from its origins as a mere antiquarian field sport and
beginning to develop into a more serious investigation of the human past.
In previous decades digging into or 'opening' barrows had become first
a fashionable activity and then an antiquarian passion. Across England,
from Cornwall to Yorkshire, local clergymen, doctors and country gents
like Sir Richard Colt-Hoare (see p. 35) set out to bag their prize of local
barrows. They did not, of course, dirty their hands by digging themselves. Gentlemen picked up shotguns not spades. Even in my own early
days in 1967 in the Middle East, our American excavation director simply
observed, wearing an immaculate explorer's costume, a red cravat and
dark glasses. He occasionally passed on a laconic order, via a supervisor, or
peered intensely at a particularly fascinating artefact. The only thing that
impressed me was how clean he was.

Some Victorian archaeologists appreciated the need for more careful
fieldwork and recording, realizing the importance of context and stratigraphy. The developing science of geology was influential, notably
Principles of Geology, by Sir Charles Lyell (1797–1875), published between
1830 and 1833. Lyell promoted the idea of 'uniformitarianism': that
the same natural processes that occur today – weather, floods, erosion,
vulcanism – also occurred in the past, gradually altering the Earth over

vast timescales. The history of the Earth could be read in its strata (layers of rock), like the pages in a book. Such ideas promoted careful observation in the field. The more mindful archaeologists, eschewing treasure hunting, developed concepts of biological and social evolution.

As Britain's middle classes grew in wealth and power thanks to the expansion of industry and trade, they became more willing to embrace such radical ideas. They themselves were a force capable of improving the world. Writers such as the philosopher Herbert Spencer flattered the ego of these individuals, would-be capitalists and empire builders. The horrors of the French Revolution were increasingly in the past. The new confidence was manifest in the Great Exhibition of 1851, a massive celebration of industry, manufacturing, wealth creation and new technologies. Lyell opposed the idea of biological evolution, but nevertheless influenced Charles Darwin, whose *On the Origin of Species by Means of Natural Selection* was eventually published, after about thirty years of work and hesitation, in November 1859.

The year 1859 was also remarkable for the visit by a group of British scientists, including Lyell, to the gravel pits of the Somme valley. Here they confirmed that ancient stone tools (now known as Acheulean biface axes), found by Frenchman Jacques Boucher de Perthes, lay stratified close to the remains of extinct animals. The antiquity of man became an issue of fundamental interest to Victorian scientists. When the polymath John Lubbock (1834–1913) published *Prehistoric Times* in 1865, in which he divided the Stone Age into Palaeolithic (Old Stone Age) and Neolithic (New Stone Age), he found he had a bestseller (see also page 238).

While Boucher de Perthes' stone tools were being given the imprimatur of English scholarly gentlemen (Boucher de Perthes was rather too lower class, an outsider, to be immediately accepted in Paris), other wonders emerged in the Dordogne in southwest France. Here, in 1863, Édouard Lartet, backed by an English banker, Henry Christy, began to reveal the Ice Age art hidden within the limestone caves. Lartet realized that these finds represented a long period of time, and he classified the periods on the basis of the animals he observed represented in the caves. Le Moustier, for example, belonged to the period of the Cave Bear and Mammoth. Being France, the archaeologists had to adopt a political stance. The second great researcher of the Dordogne caves, Gabriel de Mortillet, was a radical socialist who believed the study of human evolution and development would promote his views and undermine conservative monarchism. France takes enormous pride in its Palaeolithic archaeology, seeing the country as the birthplace of art 30,000 or 40,000 years ago. De Mortillet would be delighted that his discoveries can now, in many cases, be dated with remarkable accuracy, but shocked that his esoteric studies have spawned an international tourist industry.[1]

In the mid-nineteenth century, archaeology in Europe was making important discoveries and had established that the works of humans could be of considerable, but then unknown, antiquity. The traditional biblically inspired belief that humans had been on Earth for a mere six thousand years was increasingly being undermined, yet the depths of prehistory remained an incalculable void. Much archaeology in Britain and France was still dependent on written texts. Charles Warne, author of *The Celtic Tumuli of Dorset*, reflected the general pessimism when confronted by the problem of dating prehistoric monuments: 'By what distinct ethnic race or races were the tumuli of Dorsetshire ... raised ... are even now far from being satisfactorily determined .... the obscurity which now on every side surrounds all things connected with the era in which they lived is almost, if not wholly, impenetrable.'[2] In 1877 Canon William Greenwell, Yorkshire's great barrow digger, hazarded a guess: 'we need not fear that we are attributing too high an antiquity to them, if we say that they belong to a period which centres more or less on 500 BC.'[3] If Canon Greenwell had added another millennium to his estimate he would have been nearer the mark.

This is the context in which Squire Edwin Martin-Atkins conducted his excavations on White Horse Hill and the Lambourn barrows: a period of both excitement and frustration. His excavations were careful and reasonably well recorded by the standard of the day. Roman finds were accurately dated by coins portraying historically identifiable emperors (see Chapter 6). The age of the barrows remained elusive, however, and the White Horse an object of speculation.

MORE THEORIES

The Reverend W. C. Plenderleath (1831–1906) was rector of Cherhill, northeast of Devizes, in Wiltshire. Here, on the slope beneath the ramparts of the hillfort known as Oldbury Castle, there is a rather prosaic chalk figure of a horse. It faces to the left, with its right foreleg raised, and has a short, cropped tail. The year of its birth was 1780. Plenderleath recorded this, having spoken to an old man who heard it from those who had taken part in the construction. The Reverend's enquiries inspired him to research the local hill figures, publishing his discoveries in a useful series of articles between 1870 and 1883, and eventually in 'a most valuable little book', *The White Horses of the West of England,* in which he established the relatively recent pedigree of most of the hill figures.[4] However, he contradicted

The Reverend Plenderleath's relatively accurate portrayal of the
Uffington White Horse in his book *The White Horses of the West
of England*, in which he argued that the Horse was Iron Age in date.

Thomas Hughes by proposing that the Uffington Horse had its origins in
the Iron Age, the prehistoric period before the Roman Conquest.

This was still surmise, based on the older ideas of John Aubrey and
William Stukeley's daughter Anna (see p. 68); there had been no systematic fieldwork or investigations as yet. Then, in 1926, one of the great
founding fathers of modern archaeology, Sir William Flinders Petrie
(1853–1942), took an interest. He had revolutionized Egyptian archaeology from the 1880s with relatively meticulous excavations that carefully
recorded the location of pottery found. Ceramic sherds may not have the
glamour of gold masks or mummies, but pottery typologies would prove
fundamental to dating archaeological sites. His so-called sequence dating
of over two thousand graves in the cemetery at Naqada, in Upper Egypt,
was a world away from the smash-and-grab barrow diggers and treasure
hunters of a previous generation.

In relative old age Petrie took a brief look at the White Horse of
Uffington – and did what came naturally to him: he had it surveyed and
drawn accurately. He published the plan in his 1926 booklet, *The Hill
Figures of England*. Unfortunately, Petrie did not apply the energy or the
imagination that characterized his earlier Egyptian work. He presumably
thought that excavation of hill figures would be a waste of time.

STUART PIGGOTT AND THE IRON AGE HORSE: A MATTER OF STYLE

Five years later a much younger man tackled the problem, a young Turk
who probably took some pleasure in challenging one of the giants of
the previous generation. This was Stuart Piggott (1910–1996), the English
archaeologist of the mid-twentieth century whom I most admire. Piggott

was born in Petersfield, Hampshire, in the chalk landscape dominated by Butser Hill. His father was a local schoolmaster who was born in Uffington in 1874 and his mother was a Welsh woman from Breconshire. The Piggott family were rooted in the Vale of the White Horse. In 1983, in his 'Archaeological Retrospect', he wrote: 'Piggotts have been around in Marcham, Hatford and West Challow since the early seventeenth century, and the families died out or slipped quietly downhill to the status of farm labourers or at best small peasant farmers. My great-grandfather was one of these at Uffington ... and my grandfather at the age of 10 was taken up to the last of traditional festive "scourings" in 1857 by Thomas Hughes.'[5]

Piggott repeated this story to me in the early 1990s during one of my visits to see him in West Childrey, where he lived after his retirement from the Chair of Archaeology at Edinburgh University. His grandfather, he said, had ridden on Hughes's horse up to the hill. Piggott was obviously proud of his connection with the Vale and the Downs and their past and, although unwell in his later years, still spoke with remarkable fluency and lucidity of memory.

Sixty years earlier, when he was a mere twenty years of age, Piggott had produced his article, 'The Uffington White Horse'.[6] In those days most archaeologists still came from privileged backgrounds – the clergy or landed gentry. Piggott was a relative outsider; because of his modest origins he did not attend university – let alone Oxbridge. Instead, from the age of sixteen, he managed to put himself through a series of what one might call unofficial apprenticeships – working for the Ordnance Survey and then a poorly paid job at Reading Museum. As a result he learnt how to look both at the landscape of the Wessex Downs and at artefacts. He also developed a remarkable talent for draughtsmanship through a family friend, the artist Heywood Sumner.

Stuart Piggott (left) excavating at Dorchester-on-Thames (Oxfordshire).
On the right is the archaeologist Vere Gordon Childe,
inappropriately dressed for site visiting.

A number of perceptive people recognized this precocious talent, including the charismatic O. G. S. Crawford, pioneer aerial photographer, archaeological officer at the Ordnance Survey (from 1920 to 1946) and founder and editor of the quarterly journal *Antiquity* in 1927. *Antiquity*, still going strong today, was exciting and modern, and provided a platform for bright young archaeologists. 'Crawford's prime interest,' wrote Glyn Daniel, a distinguished later editor of the journal, 'was the face of the countryside in its archaeological aspects.' For him the landscape was a palimpsest of more value than any book, for those who would look and learn. The clues to the past also lay in ethnography and folklore. Piggott must have seemed the ideal disciple, and Piggott himself described Crawford as 'my archaeological godfather'.[7]

So Piggott, at an age when most archaeologists would be in their second year at university, produced this fluent and considered article about the White Horse, the sire of them all. Having described its documentary history, he strikes his colours by declaring that certain aspects of Flinders Petrie's description 'cannot go unchallenged'. Precocious stuff from a mere whippersnapper with no degree. Yet the article is a remarkably mature and balanced piece of work, in which Piggott approaches his subject in a logical and structured manner, and is very different from previous antiquarian efforts.

Piggott sets out his aims with a precision unusual for the time: he intends to examine the style of workmanship of the Horse, its associations and parallels with a view to determining its date, the culture to which it belongs, and the reasons for its making. No modern research design could be clearer. In fact, few modern research designs achieve such clarity, brevity and lack of pretension. He declares:

> When considering the date of any artefact, although many criteria may
> be employed, the two most important are associations and style of
> workmanship. The former can only be used in exceptional conditions
> – for instance, in an undisturbed grave-group a pot of novel form may
> be dated by an axe of known type, or a ditch cutting through a barrow
> would be later than the barrow. The White Horse has, however, no such
> inter-relation with objects of known date.

He emphasizes that adjacent sites of a certain period cannot be used as an argument for the date of the Horse, as Francis Wise did. So we are left with stylistic grounds alone for this piece of work of distinctive and conventionalized form – a work known from historical documents to be in existence a thousand years ago, but beyond which time 'there is no direct evidence'.

Piggott then describes the distinctive, attenuated, elongated and disjointed shape and its general lack of resemblance to what most people consider a horse should look like. So is it meant to be a horse? Or a dragon; or perhaps an ichthyosaur? He argues for the horse on the basis of the consistent story from folklore and early place names. The most striking feature of the head, he suggests, is the jaws, which are not unlike the beak of a bird. Significantly, Piggott continues, a horse with just such an attenuated body, disjointed limbs and peculiar head appears on a series of gold and silver coins, which were minted in England (sic) towards the end of the Early Iron Age (archaeological terminology has changed since 1931 – Piggott is referring to what, today, we would call the Late Iron Age). The British coins imitated the gold staters issued by Alexander the Great's father, Philip of Macedon (d. 336 BC), who distributed them to, among others, Celtic mercenaries serving in the Macedonian army.

The original Macedonian coins portray, on the reverse, a chariot drawn by two horses, urged on by a charioteer. Increasingly loose copies of such coins were minted in the west, in Gaul and eventually in Britain. This copying leads, Piggott states, to a gradual 'degeneration' of the design – a kind of visual Chinese whispers. Today we might question the assumption of degeneration: Celtic cultures seemed to love patterns and abstraction, unlike the more literal Classical world. In Gaul and Britain the chariot becomes simply a wheel, often used as a sacred symbol representing the sun or an attribute of the deity Taranis, god of thunder. The charioteer and the horse may fragment into a series of dots and 'a jumble of dumb bells and crescents'. Piggott reminds us, 'we have animals in all essentials like the White Horse', and he takes Sir Flinders Petrie to task for mistakenly claiming that the horse on coins 'is always a short, tubby beast'. He then goes on to note the presence of beak-like jaws and detached limbs on the coin horses 'quite comparable with the Uffington Horse'.

To strengthen his case Piggott draws attention to other British horses of this period. Iron Age art in England, he says, was essentially decorative and non-representational: 'In its sense of the balance of abstract designs and its triumphant use of curves of faultless certainty and matchless beauty it is probably unequalled.' He is thinking of such masterpieces as the Battersea shield, the Birdlip mirror and the curvilinear designs on the pots found in the Glastonbury lakeside settlement. He notes that the artists of this period saw the horse as an element to be incorporated into their designs, citing the beautiful curvilinear bronze handle in the form of

A pair of horses with beaked heads and each with a single eye,
depicted on a bronze bucket found in the Late Iron Age
cemetery at Aylesford, Kent.

the horse probably from a Romano-British tankard or bowl. Piggott would
have known this object well as it resides in Reading Museum. Could this
even be a representation of the White Horse itself? Other horses appear
on the bronze bucket found in an Iron Age cemetery at Aylesford, Kent.
These backward-turning, abstract animals also have beaked heads and
an isolated eye. Piggott draws attention to other cultures that incorporate
animals into more or less abstract patterns, such as the lions in medieval
heraldry, 'like no animal that lived'. He might have mentioned the heraldic
lions over the gateway of Bronze Age Mycenae in Greece, but his distant
travels were yet to come.

So on stylistic grounds 'we may date the White Horse as not earlier
than La Tène III'. Here he resorts to a rare example of archaeological jargon,
referring to a continental art style – but more clearly, he reckons the Horse
belongs to the first century BC. In spite of his earlier comment that sites in
near proximity are not necessarily associated with the people who made
the hill figure, he writes: 'One feels that there ought to be some relationship between the White Horse and the hill-fort.' We are suddenly reminded
of his youth, and his respect for his mentors, when he states: 'Mr Crawford
has suggested that it was the tribal emblem of the inhabitants of the
camp.' And then, 'Mr Crawford has suggested it was a token, and such a
conspicuous figure must have been a cult-object for a large area.'

The young Piggott also writes: 'Mr C. F. C. Hawkes tells me that there
is evidence to show that Uffington Camp was constructed in Hallstatt-La
Tène I times, but surface finds include two small enamels of typical late
La Tène style.' In other words, it appears that the hillfort was in use through

the Iron Age. The information came from Christopher Hawkes, only five years senior to Piggott (although this is an age to a twenty-year-old), who was public-school educated at Winchester College, with a first-class degree from Oxford and employed by the British Museum. He was also one of O. G. S. Crawford's 'ferrets' – the young men (and they were all men at this stage) whom he encouraged to get out into the landscape and explore.

Piggott concludes his article with a brief discussion of Celtic religion and the symbolism of animals. Perhaps influenced by Crawford, he also emphasizes the potential importance of folklore, proposing that the adoption of St George into the story of Dragon Hill might be an attempt to Christianize an earlier demi-god associated with horses. 'This substitution of a Christian saint for a pagan god is by no means uncommon,' he claims. And finally he states: 'We can only safely draw one conclusion, that the Horse is a monument constructed at the end of the Early Iron Age, probably in the first century BC. Beyond this we can be sure of nothing, and in many respects the White Horse still remains a mystery.'

In spite of the author's youth, this article was written with authority and published in the most influential journal of its day, with the imprimatur of O. G. S. Crawford. Piggott went on to become one of the 'three wise men' of British prehistory in the years between the 1930s and the 1960s. A professor at Edinburgh University, he was the leading Neolithic specialist in the country, while the other two – Christopher Hawkes (1905–1992) at Oxford and Grahame Clark (1907–1995) at Cambridge – dominated Iron Age and Mesolithic studies respectively. All three were invited to lecture at Harvard University on European prehistory. So Piggott's subsequent status gave weight to his opinion that the White Horse was created in the Iron Age. And this remained the general belief in archaeological circles in Britain.

DIANA WOOLNER AND THE ANGLO-SAXON HORSE

The challenge to this interpretation came not from an archaeologist but from a folklore specialist, Diana Woolner.[8] Woolner's discussion of the folklore and historical records relevant to the Horse, published first in 1965, was the fullest and most sophisticated to date. Her doubts about the Iron Age origins stemmed from the examination of photographs of the Horse taken by her husband, Alexander, from Dragon Hill, and from RAF aerial photographs. In these she detected various lines and gullies around the Horse that led her to conclude that the sinuous, abstract shape we see today was not original. Instead a larger, more naturalistic-shaped horse had, through time, become progressively thinner and more attenuated, gradually retreating uphill as the belly and neck became filled in with soil and turf.

Diana Woolner was not the first to question whether the sinuous shape was original. She pointed out that Wise, in his *Letter to Dr Mead* in 1738, had noted this process of soil crumbling and filling the white trench, 'which', he writes, 'is the reason likewise why the country people erroneously imagine, that the Horse, since its first fabrication ... is got higher up the hill than formerly'. She notes that the process of erosion and build up is particularly evident on the 'beak', 'which is now precariously maintained on a small embankment composed entirely of silt washed down from the head'.

As a result, she claimed, we have the survival of the fragments of an outline – an anorexic version of the original sturdy beast. If Diana Woolner was right, then it would drive a coach and horses through Stuart Piggott's argument, which relied on the stylistic similarity to horses on Iron Age coins. From her thorough examination of the folklore evidence and relevant features recorded in the Anglo-Saxon charters she concluded that the first theories to be published about the Horse, by Thomas Baskerville in his *Journal of Travels* of 1681 (see p. 225) and John Aubrey in the seventeenth century, were correct: 'that Hengist made the Horse, that is to say in the modern idiom, that the White Horse is a Pagan-Saxon survival'. So Woolner put the origins of the Horse in the fifth or sixth century AD, with the arrival of the pagan English and the collapse of the Roman imperial province.

And that was where the matter stood in the later twentieth century: various theories based on shifting evidence and contested meanings.

AN OPPORTUNITY ARISES

In the 1970s I had been mapping aerial photographs of the Thames Valley and identifying prehistoric, Roman and Anglo-Saxon sites that lay in the path of burgeoning development. Roads, housing, industrial estates and gravel extraction were gobbling up the open landscape. By ensuring that archaeology was built into the planning system it was possible to record ancient settlements, fields, trackways and cemeteries before they disappeared for ever.

Faced with this ongoing tide of destruction along the Thames Valley, well-known but ill-understood monuments like White Horse Hill had a low priority for investigation. Such sites were protected by Ancient Monuments legislation and not under immediate threat. However, it was also clear that not every important element within a supposedly protected area was necessarily identified and appreciated. I had recently been involved in discussions with the National Trust, owners and managers of the White Horse site, about this problem,[9] which responded by creating its own Sites and Monuments Records and a team of archaeologists to curate Trust property. At the time, there were also moves to improve the setting of the White Horse. The poor beast was corralled within a small enclosure surrounded with barbed wire, and much of the adjacent land was ploughed. Two prominent car parks completed the eyesore. Fortunately, the owner of the adjacent land, the Rt Hon. David Astor, proposed to donate it to the National Trust. So the questions arose: what archaeological features did the area contain and how should the site by managed?

To remind people of the White Horse's significance I wrote a brief article about it for the Trust's magazine. Rather stupidly I emphasized the Iron Age interpretation without mentioning Woolner's theory. The next thing I knew I received a note from Professor Christopher Hawkes, now retired from his Oxford chair, but living in the centre of Oxford – saying that his friend Diana Woolner had been in touch asking, 'Who is this idiot?' (or words to that effect). So round I go to the Hawkes's house to present my credentials. Hawkes was a complicated character who could be rather prickly. I had attended a few lectures by him on the Iron Age that were incredibly long and verging on the incomprehensible (at least to me). Fortunately, I found him in a good mood and he was very helpful.[10] I suspect he liked the Woolner article because it challenged his old colleague and rival, the upstart Stuart Piggott.

Professor Hawkes suggested a diplomatic mission to Devon, where Diana Woolner lived, and off I went into the deep Southwest, in the belief that it is better to make friends than enemies. Nevertheless, I did feel like Bertie Wooster being summoned to visit his Aunt Agatha, a *grande dame* of the old regime. The journey was worthwhile. Not only was Diana Woolner a bright and informative hostess, but she also lived in a fascinating house. Bradley Manor, with its own chapel, consecrated in 1428, lies in a wooded valley near Newton Abbot. Inside the house was a huge ship's wheel, a relic of the *Herzogin Cecilie*, a four-masted barque carrying grain from Australia on which Diana Woolner had been a passenger when it ran aground off the South Devon coast in April 1936. This seemed to be a family habit: her father-in-law survived the *Titanic*. She took me to the scriptorium (the kind of room you have if you live in a medieval manor) and began to open drawers. They were full of Egyptian artefacts: beads, scarabs, ushabti figures. Her father, Cecil Mallaby Firth, had been a serious archaeologist who had excavated at Saqqara and set up the museum at Aswan.

We eventually got round to talking about the White Horse and agreed that the date of the hill figure remained problematic. I did, however, point out that her theory had one advantage: it could be tested by excavation.

CHAPTER SIX

LIGHT FROM THE DARK

To describe a Country by other Men's Accounts of it would
soon expose the writer to a discovery of fraud; and to describe
it by Survey, requires a Preparation too great for any Thing but
a publick Purse, and Persons appointed by Authority.

Daniel Defoe, 1725

A PROJECT EMERGES: SEPTEMBER 1980

It had not been the most comfortable night, crammed into a small tent with my pregnant wife Gwyn and two-year-old daughter Jess. The two women in my life have a fondness for expensive hotels with large bathrooms. The tent was my idea. And for once I was right. As I crawled out from beneath the canvas at seven in the morning, the sun was emerging from behind White Horse Hill, bathing it in gold light, gilding the tops of the green turf and the Horse itself.

Our tent was perched on the slope below the ramparts of Uffington hill-fort. As I turned around to the north the view was surreal. A thick layer of mist, the edge of which was only a few metres below the tent, blanketed the Vale. I felt I was standing on a shoreline, above a still, opaque, white sea. White Horse Hill was an isolated green island. There was nothing else in sight, just the brightening blue sky and the impenetrable mist below.

A group of us were here because we had persuaded the National Trust and English Heritage to allow us to spend the weekend carrying out a field survey of the Horse and a detailed examination of the hill. We could have driven from Oxford, but it was more fun to camp – and you get the feel of a place by being there through the day and night, and in changing light and weather. Anyway, it was worth it for that early morning view.

The others in the group were: Simon Palmer, my colleague (the efficient, well-organized one) from the Oxford Archaeological Unit (OAU), of which I was then deputy director; a couple of members of our excavation team, away from their day job digging a huge Iron Age and Romano-British settlement across the valley near Lechlade in Gloucestershire; Nick Griffiths, a draughtsman from the Ashmolean Museum; and assorted local volunteers.

Simon and I had certainly not figured out how to tackle the problem of dating the White Horse. However, I have often found that it pays to work your way slowly into a project. Ideas and opportunities emerge, sometimes unexpectedly, and people you need to cooperate with, whether they be landowners, curators or authorities such as the National Trust or English Heritage, gradually get used to your presence (rather like the way Dian Fossey patiently introduced herself to the Mountain Gorillas). Perhaps we would appear to be part of the scenery and our proposals for research not too far-fetched.

We started with the survey. It could do no harm to the site and it would give us the opportunity for a long, detailed examination. Drawing something is a great help to observation. We spent the first hour erecting poles around the Horse, with lines of tape – like a police crime scene – to keep the general public out, and putting up notices to explain what we were doing and why we were standing on the Horse, as people are usually requested to keep off it. With so many visitors coming up the hill we knew we would be a form of public entertainment and be asked lots of questions, so members of the team took turns to be on guide duty.

Over the next two days we crawled over the Horse, examining it minutely and surveying the figure and its topography. One thing that struck us was the amount of fine detail that was present. The Horse is sited on a long narrow terrace and, as Diana Woolner and others had noted, there were signs of both erosion and deposition. It did appear as if the body had originally been wider, and the so-called 'beak' was certainly cut into an unnatural-looking mound of earth. I had looked at other hill figures such as the Cerne Abbas Giant in Dorset, which lay on steep slopes and where gravity and erosion could only carry material away downwards. Here at Uffington many parts of the figure lie horizontally across the slope, building up localized lynchet, or terraced, effects. It suggested that there might be layers of superimposed material. Could there be stratigraphy within the Horse – one of the key factors that enables archaeologists to unravel any site?

We knew from nineteenth-century records that there were other archaeological features on the hill that were now not clearly visible. We thought we could detect the Bronze Age barrow where Edwin Martin-Atkins had excavated Anglo-Saxon burials. The pillow mound, known as 'Long Mound', alongside the track that led up to the Horse clearly had a depression in the top, as Piggott observed, which probably was where Martin-Atkins had also uncovered a prehistoric pot in a stone chamber, and also many Romano-British burials.

i (*previous page*) Aerial view of the Uffington White Horse above the
dramatic folds of the Manger. Centre left is the circular mound of Dragon Hill,
while Uffington Castle dominates the summit of the Downs and behind it
the Ridgeway runs from left to right.

ii (*above*) Wayland's Smithy: the Neolithic tomb, with its façade
of megalithic sarsen stones, was a prominent feature of the Anglo-Saxon
landscape – hence its name.

iii, iv (*opposite*) A coin of the local Atrebates tribe *c.* 50 BC (*above*). The horse
has a distinctive triple tail and is associated with wheel/sun and moon symbols.
The abstract figure, with its beaked head, is superficially similar to the
design of the Uffington hill figure seen from the air (*below*).

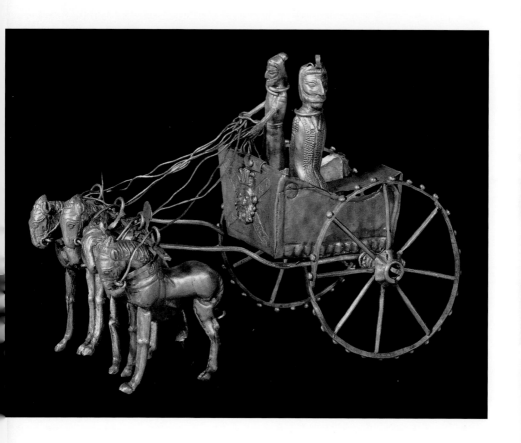

v (*opposite*) In the prehistoric frozen tombs of Pazyryk preservation is excellent. This felt hanging shows an aristocratic rider approaching a seated deity who carries a tree of life.

vi (*above*) A fine gold model of a chariot with light, spoked wheels from the Oxus Treasure, fifth–fourth century BC. Such technology spread from the steppes to transform warfare and symbols of power from China to Britain.

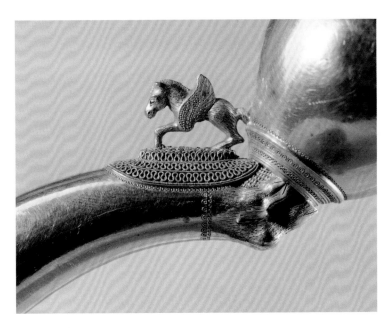

vii (*top*) Bronze cult chariot from a tomb at Strettweg, Germany, seventh century BC, depicting a goddess surrounded by mounted warriors; Hallstatt culture.

viii (*above*) The rich Vix tomb in France of about 480 BC included a fine gold torc. At each terminal a winged horse appears about to fly from waves represented by gold wire. These are rare Celtic representations of horses, clearly influenced by Greek and Scythian art and the Classical myth of Pegasus.

ix Among the extraordinary contents of the sixth-century BC Pazyryk frozen tombs
of the steppes are the 'fantasy' horses, with their elaborate regalia of gilded
leather, felt and carved wood.

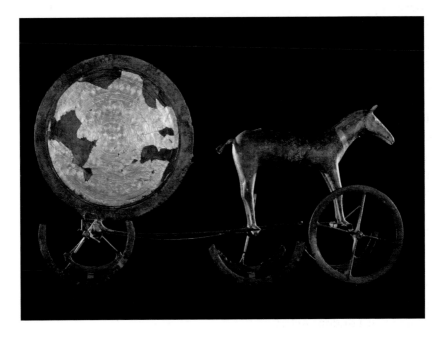

x (*top*) The Nebra sky disc (mid-second millennium BC), with astronomical features added in gold, as well as a possible stylized ship to transport the sun through the sky.

xi (*above*) The Trundholm sun chariot (*c.* 1460 BC): a cult object with one side gilded to represent the sun drawn by a horse across the daytime sky from left to right. On the dark reverse, the sun is drawn at night-time from right to left.

There were other features – holloways, traces of quarrying and field boundaries. The hillfort, of course, dominated the hilltop and was, clearly, a complicated monument. It had a major entrance in the west, with complex out-turned ramparts. Immediately opposite, in the east, the rampart and its ditch were swollen and enlarged, suggesting that an eastern entrance might have been blocked in prehistoric times. More problematic were the two small entrances roughly on the northeast and southeast sides of the hillfort. At one point a National Trust person said they thought these were made for a modern farm track and should perhaps be filled in. We pointed out that it must be an extremely old farm track because these entrances, though clearly secondary, existed a thousand years ago and are mentioned in the Anglo-Saxon charter bounds.

As well as archaeological detail in the landscape, there were also lots of visitor management issues – places where the natural slopes, ancient earthworks and ramparts were being eroded by people or by sheep. The donation of the surrounding land by David Astor in 1979 meant there was now an opportunity to remove barbed wire fences, put arable land under pasture and agree appropriate stocking levels with the tenant farmer to reduce the pressure on the grassland. But what to do about traffic, car parks, signs, litter bins (they accumulate litter!) and the many eroding pathways?

After our weekend jaunt it was back to the drawing board. The National Trust and English Heritage were beginning to see that it would make sense to undertake a field project to understand this landscape and the historic elements within it. This could inform the future management of White Horse Hill. However, they were not convinced about digging into the Horse itself. In spite of what both Daniel Defoe and Francis Wise had reported, the common belief was that the Horse was a sgraffito, simply etched into the chalk – so no layers, no dating opportunities.

AT THE ELEPHANT AND CASTLE

It was the Ancient Monuments inspector, Brian Davison, who told me about possible treasures hidden in the bowels of the Ministry of Works archives in London. Actually, this is a bit of poetic licence: Brian was a somewhat austere Ulsterman. He probably said, 'It might be worth looking in the ministry files.' So I took the train to Paddington, then the Underground south of the river to the Elephant and Castle. This may sound like a romantic spot, named after a pub – originally the Enfant de Castille – but it isn't. I emerged into the daylight and a crescendo of traffic tearing around a large roundabout. The Great Wen at its worst.

Being reasonably spry in those days I struck out across the maelstrom and made it to the far side. I found myself outside a grey, concrete and glass block. Grim was not the word. Actually, it was precisely the word. Here was where ministry files went to die, the Elephant's graveyard.

Inside, a jovial chap with spiky hair and a pallid complexion sat behind a desk. He seemed glad to have a visitor. I suspected he was Ben Gunn, deposited here after years of solitude on Treasure Island. I expected him to ask me if I had any cheese. Instead, he said, 'The files, the files. Follow me.' He scuttled off down a dark corridor. I wondered if he would drop breadcrumbs or unravel a skein of wool, or whatever you are supposed to do to find your way out of the labyrinth. Eventually we arrived in a room full of grey metal filing cabinets.

'Berkshire S to Z, this is what you are after.'

I sat at a small government-issue desk of about 1930 vintage and started to shuffle through layers of paper. After a short while of scanning routine ministry letters my eye was attracted to a drawing. 'Bloody hell!', I was looking at a very fine illustration of the beak of the White Horse with the outline of an excavation trench across it. There was also a cross section of the excavation itself. It clearly showed that the beak was made up of successive thin layers of chalk that were in total about 1 m (3 ft) thick. This really was a treasure. It showed that the White Horse was made up of stratified layers, something an archaeologist could get her or his teeth into.

There were notes attached that indicated that this small trench had been excavated after the Second World War when the Horse was uncovered and exposed to daylight again, after being hidden from the Luftwaffe. Whoever had drawn the illustration and written the notes had left no name. Fortunately, the style of drawing and the handwriting looked familiar. My guess was that they were the handiwork of the late William Grimes, until recently the director of the Institute of Archaeology in London and successor there to Sir Mortimer Wheeler and Vere Gordon Childe.

During the Second World War, Grimes had been employed by the Ministry of Works to record the archaeology that appeared during the construction of aerodromes and other defence sites. He had worked at the Neolithic henge at Stanton Harcourt, Oxfordshire – just across the valley from White Horse Hill. This was the site of one of the OAU's major projects in the 1970s as gravel pits consumed the old aerodrome, along with an enormous prehistoric landscape. We had examined Grimes's records, so I recognized his writing and style of drawing. Surprisingly, perhaps, Stuart Piggott knew nothing of this and, in spite of its implications, Grimes had never published the important findings of his small trench.[1]

This was a significant breakthrough. Now we could put forward a proposal that involved investigating both the wider landscape and the Horse itself. We could assist in the management and care of a much-loved and visited landscape, and tackle the old question: how old is the Horse? At the very least we might answer the Woolner question: how has the horse shape shifted over time?

Frankly, I would not have put money on us dating the Horse. Even if Daniel Defoe was right and we had stratified layers within a cut trench, would the people who made it, and continuously made repairs, have left anything that would provide dating evidence – in situ pottery sherds or fragments of bone that could provide radiocarbon samples? The odds were against it. After all, the Horse was not a settlement site or a rubbish dump. It was a figure that was constantly cleaned. For this reason, in our research design we emphasized that the project primarily aimed to assist with the management of the Trust's newly enlarged estate; it would have an important training element, and the impact of the investigation on the surviving archaeology would be minimal.

In the Thames Valley our excavations were on a huge scale, some of the largest ever undertaken in Britain up to that time. They were financed from the government rescue archaeology budget and, increasingly, by the developers themselves. They were also carried out relatively quickly, coordinated with the developers' timetables. White Horse Hill was not threatened by development. In fact, it was one of the most protected landscapes in England – a Scheduled Monument, a Guardianship Site and a Site of Special Scientific Interest (SSI). If we were going to investigate it then our work should target specific questions as efficiently as possible. At the time, I always said in presentations, 'This is brain surgery, rather than an autopsy.'

There was another factor. On the development-led excavations we had adequate budgets to employ big teams of archaeologists to complete the work to an agreed schedule. In contrast, there was very little money for research excavations on an unthreatened site.

We started with a contribution from the National Trust and the Inspectorate of Ancient Monuments, plus volunteers and students on Oxford University training programmes. Then W. H. Smith, the firm that ran the Ancient History Book Club and was based in nearby Swindon, made a vital contribution. This allowed us to proceed slowly, in limited seasons of work – not how we normally operated. I found it frustrating, but it turned out to be a godsend. In a dark Oxford laboratory, work was going on that would throw a whole new light on our project.

APPOINTED BY AUTHORITY

So in 1989, having negotiated our way through the tangled web of heritage bureaucracy, we had the permits to begin the serious investigation of White Horse Hill. One Monday morning a wagon train of Transit vans, site caravans and low-loaders with Portaloos balanced on the back crept carefully along the bumpy Ridgeway. We pulled into the flat ground alongside Uffington Castle and set up our site camp. There were none of the noisy mechanical diggers that usually tackle the preliminary donkey work for archaeologists. On this protected ground we would remove all the turf and topsoil by hand – and carefully replace it afterwards. The idea was that within weeks no one would be able to tell that a bunch of archaeologists had ever been here. We intended to tread lightly on White Horse Hill.

In fact, we did not begin by digging at all. In the first phase we threw a battery of non-destructive techniques at the site: geophysical surveys that provided images of what lay below the turf, and aerial surveys that recorded the subtle variations in topography – and allowed us, on a computer screen, to exaggerate the slight features, or change the direction of sunlight to highlight the shallow earthworks with 'unnatural shadows'. Simon Palmer and I went off to the offices of the survey specialists, W. S. Atkins, to see their technical bag of tricks. We were especially impressed when the technicians 'flew' us through the Hill, on screen, so that we could observe the surface of the ground from the inside, looking outwards. This was cutting-edge stuff at the time. Nowadays we could do it for ourselves with drones and easily available software.

The purpose was to understand as much as possible about the faint network of archaeological and geological features on the hill, to help us target our excavation trenches. We wanted to work as precisely and non-intrusively as possible to answer very specific questions. I will not try your patience by inflicting a blow-by-blow account of all our work, which has been published in a lengthy excavation report, complete with a CD-ROM.[2] I am afraid no excavation report will ever make the bestseller lists. They tend to be dry and technical, fascinating only to the geeky few, so here I will fillet out the interesting stuff.

DOWN IN THE MANGER

We decided to dig the first holes down in the Manger – the 'ring-pit' of the Anglo-Saxon charters, and a spectacular dry valley and natural amphitheatre that lies below the White Horse. The younger, fitter members of the crew were designated that job. It was a real slog to climb back up the steep slope for the lunch break. The base of the Manger was also, at times,

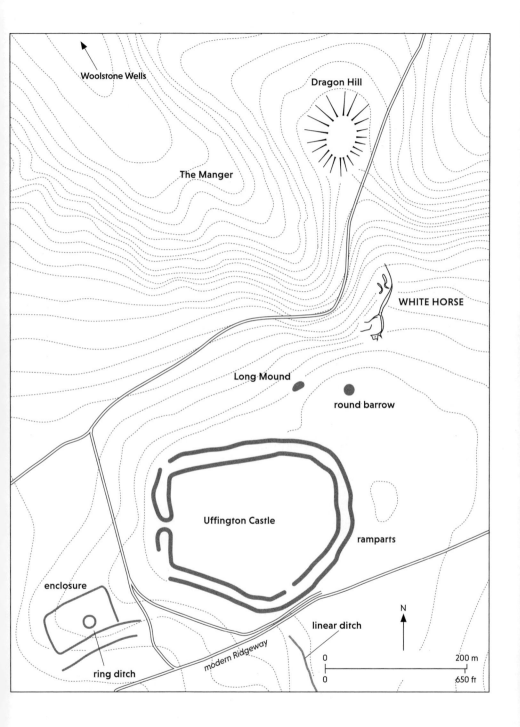

A plan of White Horse Hill and the location of the principal archaeological features mentioned in the text: Dragon Hill, the Manger, the White Horse, the Long Mound and round barrow, Uffington Castle hillfort and the ditched features to the south and west.

freakishly hot. The bowl trapped the heat and we found ourselves shovelling away in 90-degree temperatures, sweat dripping into our eyes. The following year at exactly the same time, as freezing air seeped down into the Manger, it was so cold that we needed to wear gloves while drawing the sections. Another day the fog was impenetrable; we had to use radios to locate a lost TV crew and their Land Rover. They were invisible only about a hundred metres from us. It is part of the charm of working on White Horse Hill that you get to experience English weather in all its variety, often on the same day.

The purpose of digging into the Manger was to find evidence for the evolution of the landscape and how it had formed. In the lower depth of the trenches there was a tumble of shattered chalk blocks, which had lain there for about 14,000 years since the last great freeze-thaw events at the end of the last Ice Age. We also found traces of huge mudslides that had carved out the distinctive waves in the side of the Manger. In the glacial winters cold had gripped the ground, which was solidified by permafrost. In springtime, the snow melted. The meltwater could not penetrate the still-frozen subsoil, so the snowmelt, mixed with soil and vegetation, skidded over the hard ground and plunged down the scarp. Over the years these chutes carved out giant furrows, which are such a characteristic feature of the Manger today.

Above the Ice Age deposits were layers of soil that told us about the later human presence. Fragments of flint tools, pottery and animal bones, washed downwards, indicated that there had been sporadic activity on the hills above in the period between 3000 BC and 2000 BC, but probably not intensive settlement.

Agriculture increased on the hill during the Roman period (first to fourth centuries AD). Ploughing on this higher ground created loose, bare soil. Gravity and rainfall caused the bare soil to wash downhill and accumulate in the Manger. Pottery sherds can get into the soil when farmers spread manure. In our trench one of the most distinctive sherds was glossy and red, a ceramic known as Gaulish Samian ware. The pots were made in southwest France and were traded across Europe. These vessels were the standard tableware of the Western Empire. The conscientious Roman matron could have any tableware she liked – as long as it was red.

The soil layers containing fragments of Roman pottery had accumulated rapidly. This happened in a period when the climate had deteriorated slightly. As conditions became wetter, some people abandoned their homes in the valley lowlands. In contrast, wetter soils could be good for the farmers of the chalk uplands, which, more often, suffered from dryness, so ploughing probably became more extensive on the chalk, as it did on the Cotswold Hills to the north. We know this partly because the upland soils were washed downhill and ended up accumulating in the Thames Valley, where we did much of our work. Soil erosion, caused by forest clearance and ploughing, has been a problem for millennia, and it still is. It is in our interests to take more care of the soil. Soil might just be muck, but life depends upon it.

THE HILL OF THE DEAD

Our first excavations on the hilltop itself aimed to tackle the question: was White Horse Hill a place where people buried their dead? We started with the so-called 'Long Mound', which some people had believed was a medieval rabbit warren. This mound lay alongside the footpath leading up to the White Horse, cut into the slope. Its siting was quite clever, for the builders had placed it on a false crest. This means that from below, in the valley, the mound stands out, silhouetted against the skyline. When it was new, made of freshly quarried chalk, the barrow must have been a prominent landmark to people who lived in the valley.

As mentioned, a distinctive hollow in the top of the mound seemed likely to be the trace left by Squire Martin-Atkins when he dug into it in 1857. He had discovered several human skeletons there, which were preserved beautifully in the chalk soil (in contrast, acidic soils consume bones). In addition, there were the bone fragments from several cremations. 'These', he wrote, 'were clearly of Roman date' because of the coins and pots placed with the burials. He also found a stone chamber in the centre of the mound, with traces of a cremation in a large pot. This sounds more like a Bronze Age burial, possibly placed in an even earlier Neolithic tomb. Martin-Atkins claimed that he sent this material to the British Museum. I tried to track it down. In the British Museum's leather-bound ledgers of 1862 there are beautifully written entries listing material from Martin-Atkins's excavations. But no cremation urn. The curators were insistent that it had never arrived. Martin-Atkins died prematurely and his unpublished excavation records were moved to the family home in Bath. The Luftwaffe may not have found the concealed White Horse during the Second World War, but they did manage to destroy the Martin-Atkins's Bath house and with it his archaeological records. Perhaps the cremation urn was blown to dust or lay shattered in the rubble. We will never know.

We do now know, however, that the Long Mound is the earliest monument on White Horse Hill, possibly contemporary with the Neolithic

Wayland's Smithy tomb on the scarp to the west. Later, in the Roman period, the mound was regarded as a place of significance, the work of ancestors. It was worthy to hold the remains of at least forty-nine individuals, men and women, aged from infancy to over seventy years, and at least nine cremations. Some of the burials had been deliberately decapitated after death. This seems weird to us, but it was a fairly common practice in the third to fourth centuries in this region. Perhaps these people had died in unusual or difficult circumstances, and decapitation was a way of persuading them to remain quietly in their graves and not disturb the living. Other burials received gentler treatment. Five had Roman coins in their mouths – the fare for the ferryman across the River Styx into the underworld.

In our excavations we found several burials that Martin-Atkins had missed because they had been infilled with clean chalk and were difficult to detect. We also uncovered the skeletons that he had found and left in their graves, removing only the skulls. Like the people who originally buried the dead, Martin-Atkins had a skull fixation. In this he was a man of his time: in the mid-nineteenth century there was a great interest in skulls and the study of phrenology – the lumps and bumps and shapes of skulls. Martin-Atkins sent his White Horse Hill samples to Dublin, where they were recorded and included in an impressive Victorian tome entitled *Crania Britannica: delineations and description of the skulls of the aboriginal and early inhabitants of the British Islands*, by J. B. Davis and J. Thurnham, printed in London in 1865. At the time such skull studies were taken seriously and regarded as valuable scientific work. Now they seem more of a curiosity. The Romano-British skulls were measured and declared, in the nineteenth-century jargon, to be 'platycephalic' – of flattened form – distinctive of the Romans, and, conveniently, the ancient Britons, too. The skull shape was supposedly an indicator of successful imperialists, according to the Victorian scientists.

In a letter of September 1857, Martin-Atkins said that he was digging the 'oblong mound' (our Long Mound), but that he would not be satisfied until he had also investigated the barrow further up the hill. Today a careful observer can just make out the remains of this low mound between the Horse's head and Uffington Castle. Our geophysical survey delineated its size and circular shape, and our excavation confirmed that this was, originally, an Early Bronze Age barrow of around 2000 BC, its dating confirmed by the fragment of a so-called Bucket Urn into which the prehistoric potter had pressed her fingertips. One of Martin-Atkins's labourers had tossed his broken clay pipe into the backfill. So two unknown people had worked with clay, almost four thousand years apart, their handiwork left in the same place.

Just as the prehistoric Long Mound had been reused for Romano-British burials, so the Bronze Age barrow had also been selected as a suitable place to bury the dead by later generations, in this case by Anglo-Saxons between about AD 500 and 600. They left distinctive grave goods, including enamelled metalwork and a characteristic shield of which we found the fragments of silver studs and iron boss and handle. In the sixth century, Anglo-Saxon men frequently carried, and went to their graves with, round shields, usually made of limewood covered in leather and with a large central boss. This meant that the shield could be used for defence and also quickly turned into an offensive weapon. A smash in the face with the iron boss would make anyone's eyes water.

A third barrow was also found to the west of Uffington Castle – invisible on the ground but detectable on aerial photographs. Our colleague Chris Gosden excavated this with Oxford University students. Only a shallow circular ditch remained, possibly early Bronze Age in date (though not proven). Again, a Romano-British burial had been inserted into the earlier monument – this was the body of a man aged about thirty.

It was clear from these three barrows that people had buried their dead on the hill for generations – possibly from the fourth millennium BC, in the Early and Middle Bronze Age around 2000 BC, and in the Romano-British and Anglo-Saxon periods. In fact, although it is not officially sanctioned, people still bring the ashes of their dead relatives and friends to be scattered on the hill. (It is better if they are scattered. 'When they are occasionally dumped in a pile they tend to kill the grass,' said the National Trust ranger.) Do modern people want to make contact with their ancestors, or to be close to nature, the earth and the sky? Is it simply the beauty of this liminal place that appeals – as if the dead will appreciate a fine view for eternity? Or is it for the benefit of the living: an opportunity to return to a landscape that will evoke their loved ones?

The local nature writer Richard Jefferies caught the spirit of the place when in *Wood Magic* he put these words into the mouth of the wind:

> this [prehistoric] man, and all his people ... were all buried on the tops of the hills.... There I come to them still, and sing through the long dry grass.... The sun comes too, and the rain. But I am here most ... I am always here.[3]

UFFINGTON CASTLE: 'A MAGNIFICENT CAMP'

The most prominent structure on White Horse Hill is, of course, Uffington Castle, the great hillfort. Thomas Hughes wrote: 'Yes, it's a magnificent Roman camp, and no mistake, with gates, and a ditch and mounds, all as complete as it was twenty years after the strong old rogues left it.'[4] We wanted to know who were these 'old rogues'; when did they build the great enclosure? What was the hillfort used for? Had it changed through time? And was its presence relevant to the White Horse?

Walking around the crest of the hillfort ramparts is an impressive experience. The huge bank and deep ditches enclose a space about 300 m (330 yd) across. The interior could hold about six standard football pitches (is it only the English who measure areas in football pitches?). From the top of the earthwork the view is panoramic: this is a place that dominates the landscape; a place to see out from and to be seen. We are on the highest point of the Downs at about 250 m (820 ft) above sea level. Not an imposing height on paper, but it feels high. There is a string of these hillforts along or near the chalk scarp. Liddington Castle, Rams Hill and Castle Hill and Little Wittenham, are a similar size to Uffington Castle; Hardwell Camp and Alfred's Castle are smaller, but Segsbury Camp is by far the biggest in the area. They beg the question: why did these Iron Age communities go to so much effort? Hundreds of people must have come together to hack out the chalk, pile it into ramparts and create elaborate gateways out of timber. We will consider the possible reasons why in a later chapter, but, for the moment, I just intend to outline the details of what we found.

Today the earthwork seems to consist of a simple bank and ditch with a slight, outer, counterscarp. There is a substantial entrance on the western side, which appears to be part of the original design. Our excavation revealed that the hillfort was built in two major phases. In the first, the builders erected a massive box rampart of timber. The largest timbers, forming the inner line, were the size of telegraph posts set a couple of metres apart, probably around the 747 m (2,450 ft) of the rampart. Here, whole trunks of trees may have been used, but at nearby Segsbury the excavations by our colleagues from Oxford University, Gary Lock and Chris Gosden, indicated that the timbers were split down the middle. Clearly, hundreds of trees had to be felled and transported to construct this major feat of carpentry. The chalk from the quarry ditch was piled over this construction to protect it, with a breastwork of timbers, and probably hurdles, projecting above to screen the guards who patrolled or defended the rampart while standing on the elevated walkway.

This first phase of construction took place about the eighth century BC, at the beginning of the Iron Age, when a distinctive coppery red pottery was in use, known to archaeologists as All Cannings Cross ware (from a site in Wiltshire).

Around this time the surrounding area was intensively farmed. The soils and snail shells that survived beneath the rampart showed that the hillfort was built on open downland, but clearly there were forested areas nearby, probably in the vale below, capable of producing serious quantities of timber. These were probably oaks deliberately cultivated for the purpose, in a carefully managed woodland of oak standards and hazel coppice.

The timber ramparts showed signs of deterioration and the hillfort may have fallen out of use, until in the fourth century BC people restored it, but with even deeper ditches and a larger, dump rampart, revetted with sarsen blocks to retain the earth.

We attempted to estimate the labour needed to dig the phase 1 earth-work using the tools available to prehistoric workers. Like archaeologists, they probably worked in teams of a picker, shoveller and two or three bucket carriers (perhaps more if they had to carry the stuff a long way). A single team would have required several years to build the phase 1 bank and ditch. More likely there were many teams, perhaps up to a hundred, which could have dug the ditch in about two weeks. This enormous commitment of labour would need to be organized to fit with the demands of the agricultural year. We do not know what motivated them: some driving political force, fear of an external threat or ceremonial activities that served to bind the community together?

In the 1970s two Oxford archaeologists, Brendon O'Connor and Bill Startin, had been working on the major excavations at the Danebury hill-fort in Hampshire with Professor Barry Cunliffe. The Danebury project is still the most complete investigation of a hillfort in Britain. At that site they had observed a thickening of the rampart, which subsequent excavation proved to be the location of a blocked entrance. O'Connor and Startin suggested that a similar thickening in the eastern rampart, and deepening of the ditch, at Uffington Castle might indicate the same phenomenon – keeping one entrance open, but blocking the opposite one. We tested this by excavation and the pair proved to be right. There had originally been a substantial timber gateway guarding the entrance in the east that was blocked in the Middle Iron Age by the builders of the phase 2 rampart. The surface of a rammed chalk roadway passed through the original eastern entrance.

THE SHIFTING RIDGEWAY AND ENTRANCES TO THE HILLFORT

This brings us back to the tricky question of the line of the Ridgeway. In the early days of the project I gave lots of talks about our work. I usually showed an aerial photograph of Uffington Castle with the modern Ridgeway, clearly defined, running on the southern side of it. I used to point out the phase I entrances and suggest that in the Early Iron Age the Ridgeway probably passed between them. The hillfort owners could then control the traffic along it. Once the eastern entrance was blocked, they had to build a bypass – hence the Ridgeway now passes to the south, outside the ramparts.

It was a nice theory and we decided to check it out. A linear field boundary ditch approached Uffington Castle from the south, still visible as a slight earthwork. We believed this feature belonged to the Late Bronze Age/Early Iron Age transition, contemporary with the construction of the early hillfort. Perhaps we could establish the relationship by excavating where the boundary met the Ridgeway. Gary Lock and Chris Gosden opened a trench and thereby complicated my neat, simple theory about shifting Ridgeways. It appeared that the boundary did run up to the south side of the hillfort and that they had probably been constructed at about the same time. The problem was that this boundary ditch had remained open until the Roman period, so the Ridgeway that crossed over it had to post-date the Romans. It was there by the time of the Anglo-Saxon charters, however, so this section of the Ridgeway was established between about AD 400 and 1000. This fits with the observations of Peter Fowler on Overton and Fyfield Downs, where he noted that the Ridgeway ran over earlier field systems (see p. 38).

One possible explanation for the two entrances to the early hillfort is that it straddled an important estate boundary and the enclosure could be entered by groups on either side. The unification of the estates might have removed the need for an eastern entrance, or was defence a priority in the fourth century BC? Entrances are a potential weakness.

So where was the Ridgeway? Gary Lock decided to take a different approach. He had begun his professional career as an IT specialist. Having used his skills to manipulate the vast quantity of data dug up at Danebury, he was enticed to Oxford, to specialize in archaeological computing, when Barry Cunliffe made him an offer he couldn't refuse. Gary specialized in the branch of IT known as Geographical Information Systems (GIS). He and a colleague used Digital Terrain Modelling to establish the route of least effort.[5] The 'grain' of the Downs runs, in fact, north–south along a series of dry valleys, and that is the way we approached White Horse Hill at the start of this book. Movement east–west is more difficult because it is necessary to cross valleys and streams. So a route along the crest of the scarp provides the easiest access in that direction.

For the most part the Ridgeway between Barbury Castle and Segsbury Camp follows the 'least cost' path predicted by the computer model. However, at Liddington Castle, Hardwell Camp and Rams Hill the 'ideal' route diverts from the present Ridgeway route and actually passes through these hillforts. At both Liddington and Rams Hill there were opposing entrances, one of which was blocked, and the Ridgeway shifted north to where it runs today. The computer-generated route is one determined by natural topography. In a real human landscape there can be lots of cultural reasons why routes have to bend, divert and shift around. If the 'migrating herds' theory for the origins of the Ridgeway is correct, then the deterministic explanation for the route would make sense, and perhaps its location influenced the position of some of our hillforts and the earlier burial mounds.

At Uffington Castle the 'ideal' simulated route did not pass through the hillfort, but on slightly lower ground to the north, close by the prehistoric Long Mound and the White Horse itself. The linear boundary ditch on the south side would have acted as an obstacle to a Ridgeway route until it fell out of use in the late Romano-British period. Sometime later the Ridgeway line shifted and the present line was established.

There are two other minor entrances into the hillfort, breaches in the northeast and southeast sections of the rampart, which gave rise to some questions about how this area was used after the Iron Age hillfort had gone out of use. As mentioned earlier, when discussing the management of the site someone at the National Trust suggested that these breaches were relatively modern, created to give access for farmers who ploughed the interior of the hillfort. Should they be infilled?

We could put paid to that suggestion straight away. These gaps are mentioned in the Anglo-Saxon charters – the bounds of Uffington and Woolstone ran through them – and on the aerial photographs there was a clear furrow visible on the ground running across the hillfort interior that marked this boundary. The land inside the hillfort to the west is covered in medieval ridge and furrow; to the east there is none. So the hillfort was probably divided between two medieval owners. The breaches were secondary, not part of the original design, but, nevertheless, of respectable antiquity, possibly late Romano-British in date. The southern breach gave access to the new line of the Ridgeway and the northern one to the White Horse.

INVESTIGATION OF THE HORSE: SCIENCE ILLUMINATES

Eventually, we tackled the most tricky problem – the White Horse itself. We started with the 'beak' as our geophysical survey confirmed the position of Grimes's post-war trench, whose plan had turned up in the Elephant and Castle archives. We re-excavated the hole he had dug thirty-eight years earlier and knew we had got it right when, on the bedrock in the bottom of the trench, we found a halfpenny of 1952. Grimes had left a calling card. Later we deposited a coin of our own when we backfilled the trench. More importantly, we could clearly see the stratigraphy of successive chalk 'beaks' down to a depth of just over 1 m (3 ft). The lower ones were longer than the present-day 'beak', but not significantly different. The creators of the Horse had not simply cut away turf and exposed white bedrock. The subsoil was a blotchy mix of eroded chalk and darker soils. To make a white horse it was necessary to dig out a trench and ram in pure chalk, dug from nearby quarries still visible on the hilltop. Significantly, it seemed that the 'beak' was an original design feature, as Piggott had suggested. However, to confirm Piggott's theory that the Horse was prehistoric in origin we needed something we could date.

In the 1970s my wife and I lived in the village of Wheatley, west of Oxford. One of our neighbours, Rob Hedges, was a modest but brilliant

A television crew films the team excavating a trench
into the body of the White Horse in 1989. The author is standing
on the left, with his lurcher Meg.

and remarkably productive scientist who worked at Oxford University's Research Laboratory for Archaeology and the History of Art. He kept me abreast of what was going on in their warren on Keble Road – a place devoted, among other things, to cracking the problems of archaeological chronology using scientific techniques.

I sometimes used to call in at coffee time to gather intelligence from Rob and his colleagues. On one occasion the director of the lab, Professor Teddy Hall, appeared, straight off a flight from Italy. He held aloft a sample bag, rather idiosyncratically closed by what looked like a great medieval wax seal. 'It's the Turin Shroud,' he said. Well, it was a very small strand of material from the Turin Shroud, along with a second, control sample. The lab, led by Rob Hedges, had developed high-precision radiocarbon dating using very small samples, so it was one of the few places where the Archbishop of Milan could entrust these precious fibres. Unwise in my opinion. Many Christians still do not accept the scientific results: that Christ's image on the Shroud is medieval in date and a marvellous piece of work, but not miraculous.

On another visit to the lab I heard about interesting new developments. It was well known that they were world leaders in the development of thermoluminescence dating, which the deputy director, Martin Aitken, had worked on since the 1950s. This was a method capable of dating fired clay, whereas radiocarbon dating requires samples of organic material such as bone. One of the reasons I admired the scientists at the lab was that with thermoluminescence dating they had proved that a group of six prehistoric pots, bought by curators in some very grand museums, were in fact forgeries. These Turkish pots had been purchased without a secure provenance; if they were genuine, then they had probably been robbed from Turkish archaeological sites – and the curators should not have touched them. But they had been fooled.

Thermoluminescence was a well-established technique – not very precise but relatively reliable. Now, it seemed, there was a new development, with a tongue-twisting title: Optically Stimulated Luminescence (OSL dating). Martin Aitken began to explain it; within two minutes I was baffled. This was normal when talking to Martin about his subject. He assumed everyone had PhDs in physics and chemistry. Fortunately, Rob Hedges was on hand to interpret. In a nutshell this was a new technique that presented the possibility of dating buried sands and silts, or more specifically, when the grains of quartz and feldspar had been buried and last seen the light. Wow! Did this mean we might date the buried layers within the White Horse? 'Well,' Martin replied, 'It's on chalk and that's not the ideal material. Pity it's not in Cornwall. There's more radiation in the ground there. Still it's worth a shot.'

Scientific interest in luminescence goes back a long way. In the mid-seventeenth century Robert Boyle (1627–1691), arguably the father of modern chemistry, set up a private laboratory in Oxford's High Street, ten minutes' walk from the modern research lab. Boyle's researches into luminosity involved such things as rotting fish and imported American insects. Later, in London, he had the piss pots of Pall Mall collected and their contents boiled in the hope of reproducing a phosphorescent glow, which he eventually did by increasing the heat. He had more success in 1663 by holding a large carbuncle, a type of diamond, against his body. As the electrons in the gem warmed, they escaped their traps and emitted a feeble glow. It was the discovery that electrons can be trapped and then counted when the addition of heat or light allows them to escape that laid the foundation for modern thermoluminescence dating.[6]

OSL dating is a method of dating ancient material such as geological sediments. In simple terms, electrons are trapped in the crystalline structures of carbon minerals, notably quartz and feldspar. When the minerals are transported by water or wind and exposed to sunlight, the electrons escape and the luminosity clock is set to zero. If the minerals are then buried, what is called the dosimetric clock is reset and the minerals are exposed only to a low level of natural radiation from the surrounding sediments or rock. The electron trap will fill again at a rate determined by the background intensity.

Two scientists, Mike Tite and Julie Rees-Jones, arrived at our White Horse Hill excavation to take their samples. They drove 50-mm (2-in.) diameter steel cylinders into the layers exposed by our work in the Horse's belly, deep enough to collect buried samples that had been hidden from sunlight since the Horse was created. The samples were then wrapped in black plastic. Back at the Oxford lab, in darkroom conditions, the samples had to remain caressed by darkness until they were exposed to an external stimulus – in this case the green light from an argon ion laser. On exposure, electrons are released; the emitted light is measured and the age since burial calculated. We waited anxiously for Mike and Julie to provide the results. Would they answer the question: how old is the Horse?

Eventually the report arrived, and we felt like we were receiving our exam results. Simon Palmer opened the envelope. Slowly he turned through several pages until he arrived at the last one, with the conclusion. 'It's old!' he said.

Much of the scientific report is technical in nature, describing the laboratory procedures. The later published report covers OSL samples from other features on White Horse Hill, some of which did not produce satisfactory results for various technical reasons. Importantly, though, Mike and Julie concluded:

> The accuracy of the Horse data is further reinforced by the agreement in the dose rates as determined by two independent methods.... In addition there is no risk of the age over-estimate that can arise.... Similarly there is little likelihood of a lower age as a result of a lower water content.... In summary, taking the earliest date as that given by sample 962b from below all the preserved chalk figures and the latest date as that given by sample 962a from above one chalk figure, the luminescence data from the White Horse suggest an appropriate age range of 1380–550 BC for the construction of the first Horse.[7]

So the White Horse was prehistoric. Morris Marples in his 1949 *White Horses* book had come closest to the scientific date, although few people had taken much notice.

It is most likely that the Horse was first constructed between the Late Bronze Age and Middle Iron Age. This range overlaps with the suggested date of 750–650 BC for the construction of the hillfort, so the White Horse and the hillfort could be contemporaneous. It was almost a thousand years old by the time the Anglo-Saxons buried their dead on the hill, and it had probably been made several centuries before Stuart Piggott's proposed date of about the time Julius Caesar inflicted his megalomaniac presence on southern Britain.

One thing is clear: in the transition period between the Late Bronze Age and Early Iron Age, the communities who lived around White Horse Hill were experiencing a period of enormous change: in the way they controlled and exploited land, in their technology and trade, and in the way they proclaimed their identity. The ramparts that girdled the hilltop were visible across the Vale, a powerful symbol of a community who laid claim to the land. Was the White Horse a banner for those people, a sign announcing their presence and their power? Or was it more: a message carved into the earth announcing how they viewed their universe? And why a horse?

CHAPTER SEVEN

THE
WONDER HORSE

The paintings on rocks, they are the earliest dialog
of the human being with eternity.

Herbert Kühn, 1972

WONDERS TO BEHOLD

The philosopher Martyn Evans has described 'the attitude of wonder' as 'one of altered, compellingly intensified attention towards something that we immediately acknowledge as somehow important – something that might be unexpected, that in its fullest sense we certainly do not yet understand, and towards which we will likely want to turn our faculty of understanding'.[1]

This just about sums up my approach to the White Horse. Not everyone agrees. The journalist and romantic cynic Richard Ingrams takes a sharp poke with his pen at archaeologists – spoilsport 'experts' who dig for facts. In *The Ridgeway: Europe's Oldest Road* he writes:

> Like all prehistoric survivals – Avebury, Silbury Hill, the Ridgeway itself
> – it [the White Horse] cocks a snook at the historian, the expert and
> other professional seekers of information…. Nobody knows for certain
> what its purpose is, what it commemorates (if anything) or even who
> put it there. In the modern world when every secret is out and instant
> factual data are available for all fields of inquiry, such lack of information
> is reassuring. No one who walks along the Ridgeway need feel ignorant.
> He [sic] is just as knowledgeable as the professional archaeologist.[2]

Ingrams would probably agree with the author of Ecclesiastes 1:18: 'he that increaseth knowledge increaseth sorrow'.

In a world of fake news, propaganda, false myths and lies, I do not support this 'ignorance is bliss' approach. It seems an odd view from the former editor of the satirical current affairs magazine *Private Eye*. Neither do I accept that knowledge must dissipate wonder, or that a search for facts turn us into grey gradgrinds. I prefer Albert Einstein's optimism: 'the eternal mystery of the world is its comprehensibility'.[3]

At the same time, Stuart Firestein, Professor of Biology at Columbia University, makes an interesting point: 'Questions are more relevant than answers.'[4] Good questions can start the process of revealing layers of answers and deeper research. It is not a good idea to get bogged down in facts. New facts, though, can be a key that opens a door on the fascinating depth of our ignorance. The search for origins has been out of fashion with some academics, and dating the White Horse does not solve any significant problem. But it does signpost appropriate avenues of exploration and explanation.

Richard Jefferies, that great naturalist and mystic of the downlands, described lying on the ground and gazing at the stars: 'they were not above, nor all round, but I was in the midst of them'. 'Full to the brim of the wondrous past,' he said, 'I felt the wondrous present.' He was stating a literal truth and engaging with humanity's greatest wonder: the heavens.[5] But would Edwin Hubble's calculation in 1925 – that the Andromeda nebula was 900 million light years away – have reduced Jefferies's wonder? Or the discovery a few years later that the galaxies were hurtling away from us? Would Jefferies's wonder at the cosmos have been undermined if, like us, he could have been privileged to witness the revelations of the *Voyager* missions: the volcanoes of Io, the oceans of Ganymede and Callisto? To reveal the wonder of the universe is not to diminish it.

I find it remarkable that scientists have been able to develop techniques that allow us to estimate the age of the White Horse. Medieval chroniclers believed it to be a wonder because the hill figure, miraculously, remained white. They were wrong. The Horse is a wonder, and white, because for almost three millennia local communities continuously cared for it. Can we say this about any other such delicate, ephemeral figure?

During the excavation of the White Horse, I was also captivated by a very small discovery: a scatter of snail shells in the earliest layer of sediment on its body. Some of these belonged to a species known as *Abida secale*, a tiny survivor of the dry, open limestone screes of the last Ice Age.[6] The bare chalk of the Horse's body provided a rare habitat, a home where this scarcely noticeable creature could cling to life. For this snail, the chalk of the Horse was a white tundra and an island refuge. Eventually, it became an unnoticed victim of the Second World War – its habitat destroyed when the Horse was camouflaged.

The snail may be an unconsidered trifle – an anonymous creature, disregarded except by members of the rare tribe of conchologists. Yet it provides a glimpse of tenacious life that, I think, would have played on Edward Thomas's imagination, as an image of continuity and vulnerability. He wrote:

> The shell of a little snail bleached
> In the grass; chip of flint, and mite
> Of chalk[7]

HUNTING THE HORSE

Establishing the age of the White Horse does not, I believe, take away from the sense of wonder that we feel when standing on White Horse Hill. Now we have some idea of the age of the White Horse, however, can we get any closer to those who made it and why? Why was the image of a horse so important at this time? This is a story that begins long ago and quite far away.

The English artist (of French descent) Elisabeth Frink (1930–1999) said that she sculpted dogs and horses because they have been man's best friend for thousands of years. In fact, horses are relatively recent human companions. For millennia we slaughtered wild horses for food. It was only several thousand years after sheep, goats, cattle and pigs were domesticated that the horse joined the select band of animals entangled, for better or worse, with the big-brained, bifurcated ape known as a human being.

Anatomically modern humans, with large brains capable of symbolic thinking and language, developed in Africa from about 300,000 years ago. Our ancestors had great potential, but it took time to develop, acquire knowledge and create complex cultures. For ninety-nine per cent of our existence we saw animals as sources of food, and of skins, bone and sinews, to be used for clothing, shelter and tools. Some also seem to have played powerful symbolic roles – as clan totems, spirit animals or objects of taboo. For millennia, across the Ice Age tundra of North America and Eurasia, the relationship between horses and humans remained, essentially, that of prey and hunters. Some have argued that it is because of humans, the deadliest of hunters, that horses disappeared from the Americas.[8]

Nowhere is the Stone Age hunters' impact more clearly demonstrated than at Solutré in France's south Burgundy region. Here, a great white limestone buttress breaches from the land – what geologists term a 'cuesta'. Today, regiments of vines, the source of buttery Pouilly-Fuissé wines, climb to the foot of the great rock. The plants are tended by strange machines that look like giant insects. In the 1860s archaeologists dug into the ground here and found deep beds of animal bones. For generations, Stone Age hunters had trapped migrating herds of bison, aurochs, reindeer and horses against the cliff faces, killing them with flint-tipped spears powered by atlatls (spear-throwers) that extended the human arm and human power. Which animals predominated in the kill depended upon the changing climate of glacials and interglacials.[9] Each of them, however, was capable of surviving the Ice Age tundra in its varying degrees of severity.

In 1872, archaeologist Adrien Arcelin wrote a popular novel entitled *Solutré, or the Reindeer Hunters of Central France* (*Solutré, ou les chasseurs de rennes de la France centrale*). He created a myth, which still persists, that Stone Age hunters stampeded herds of animals over the top of the cliffs to crash to their deaths below. It is much more likely that the Solutrean people coordinated in teams to drive the herds against the cliffs and corralled them with brushwood and hurdles made for the purpose. From the great kill, the Solutrean people would – like Plains Indians – have supplied themselves with meat and fat, and also hides, bone, antlers, sinews and glue. To survive in northern Europe, human lives depended upon these herds, and humans were the top predator thanks to their big brains, language, organization and developing technology.

CREATING IMAGES: THINKING WITH THINGS

Until relatively recently archaeologists regarded early *Homo sapiens* as biologically or anatomically modern but culturally 'primitive'. It was argued that it took many millennia before modern humans learnt to think symbolically, and complex technologies emerged slowly. Not far from Solutré, Ice Age hunters left evidence of the supposed intellectual breakthrough in the caves of the Dordogne, the Pyrenees and the Ardèche: magnificent works of art, principally representations of animals, first decorated the cave walls from 30,000 years or more ago. Of course, it fitted the imperialist Europeans' image of themselves that fully developed humans should emerge in France and neighbouring countries.

More recent discoveries have undermined this Eurocentric human cognitive revolution. Pinnacle Point lies on South Africa's south coast, halfway between Cape Town and Port Elizabeth. Appropriately, today it houses that pinnacle of modern civilization – a golf course. As anthropologist James Suzman writes: 'some seventy-one thousand years ago Pinnacle Point was home to another group of people also preoccupied with trying to get small projectiles to fly accurately over large distances'.[10] In caves that penetrate the sea cliffs below the golf course, archaeologists have found traces of human occupation dating as far back as 150,000 years ago. In levels dating to 71,000 years ago, skilled human beings left complex tools for fishing, hunting and digging. At Border Cave, in KwaZulu-Natal, preservation was exceptional in dry conditions. About 50,000 to 45,000 years ago people here made bone arrowheads, resin-based glues and beads made of ostrich eggs. By 24,000 years ago, at the latest, local hunters were tipping their arrowheads with ricin-based poison.

At Pinnacle Point the humans gathered lumps of ochre to grind into powder that, mixed with heated fat, could make a paint for body decoration and as an insect repellent. At the now famous site of Blombos Cave, 65 km (40 miles) west of Pinnacle Point, the world's first artist's studio was found, or at least a place where ochre-based paints were ground and mixed in saucers made of abalone shell.[11] How the pigments were used – for some of the world's first artistic efforts, or for bodily decoration or protection – is uncertain, but clearly the artistic impulse was a fundamental aspect of being human. Humans think through visual representation, images and decoration. Pictures and symbols convey messages and reveal our obsessions.

THE DEPICTION OF ANIMALS IN THE ICE AGE

In September 1940 a group of French boys rescued their dog from a cavity in the ground into which it had disappeared. A few days later they returned to explore the hole for themselves. Cavities in these limestone hills, overlooking the River Vézère in the Dordogne region of France, had a habit of revealing wonderful things. The boys were not disappointed; they tumbled into a parallel universe, a spectacular gallery of rock painted with images of aurochs, prehistoric Europe's huge and now extinct wild cattle. They had discovered the cave of Lascaux, where, over 20,000 years ago, people felt the need to create marvellous images of animals.

Bulls dominated this particular gallery; however, in the words of Paul Bahn, an expert on prehistoric art, 'the horse ... is the most important animal in Palaeolithic iconography'.[12] Many of the animals portrayed were possible food sources for Palaeolithic hunters, notably bison, reindeer, mammoths and horses. Others, particularly those depicted in the more recently discovered Grotte Chauvet-Pont d'Arc, Ardèche, are powerful competitors to humans, even a potential threat: beasts such as lions, rhinoceros and cave bears. Were they seen as a source of strength, as the lion was to the medieval knight or the bear to the Plains Indian?

Palaeolithic humans created images over a vast period of time – roughly 40,000 to 12,000 years ago. Some images are undoubted masterpieces, others are simpler: quick sketches, sometimes crude, perhaps the work of beginners or children. These image-makers painted with natural earth pigments or charcoal – applied with brushes, then spray-painted using the mouth, or stencilled or etched into the rock surface – and drew with pencils or simply with fingers in the soft, clay-like surface, such as the owl at Chauvet. Some images are charming. One carved fawn is remarkably similar to the lovable Disney figure Bambi. The Chauvet lions look sinister to our eyes; the horses are beautifully shaded, mostly quiet and gentle.

The Chauvet and Lascaux images have a surprising cinematic quality; the artists utilized the shape of the cave and the rocks to enhance the sense of movement and provide a three-dimensional effect, which would have been exaggerated by the light of flickering torches and lamps. Some of the earliest artists understood how to use the Earth itself to enhance their work. Did Stone Age storytellers also bring these places to life with words and music? Images, stories and music go together to provide a powerful human experience, dissolving time and removing us from everyday concerns. Science constantly moves forwards but, as Picasso said, there were great artists from the beginning; art doesn't get better. A steam engine cannot be ten thousand years old, but a great image can.

A horse – 'the most important animal in Palaeolithic iconography' – painted on the wall of the cave of Lascaux in France over 20,000 years ago. The person who painted it had clearly observed horses closely.

A tiny figurine of a horse carved from ivory, from Vogelherd
in Germany, around 40,000 years old. Even in miniature, the carving
captures the essential qualities of the animal.

In the caves, artists often worked on a large scale, but other Upper
Palaeolithic images may have been more for private use, mementoes for
the individual. Models of horses appear in virtually every medium – modelled or carved in clay, ivory, antler and stone. Some of the finest come
from the rock shelter of Duruthy in Landes, France: a beautiful little horse's
head carved in limestone (71 mm/2¾ in. long) and a kneeling horse carved
in stone (*c*. 260 mm/10¼ in. long). Arguably the finest, most sensitively
carved sculpture of a horse is the tiny (less than 50 mm/2 in. long) ivory
figure from Vogelherd in the German Jura. Its beautifully modelled, curving
back and neck form a continuous line, and it has the same vigour, in miniature, as the Uffington White Horse.

Like the Uffington Horse, the Vogelherd sculpture illustrates the difficulty of relying on style as a dating mechanism. Few would have assumed
that such fine work belonged to the Aurignacian period (*c*. 40,000 years
ago) if it had not been found in a stratified layer.[13] Similarly, the remarkable sophistication of the black charcoal images (horses, rhino, lions etc.)
in the Chauvet Cave led to considerable scepticism about the surprisingly
early radiocarbon dates. These indicated that the artists also worked in
the Aurignacian period, 35,000 years or more ago. On stylistic grounds the
Chauvet animals seemed to belong with those of Lascaux, which were
made about 21,000 years ago. More recently, however, a new chronology for
activity in the Chauvet Cave has been proposed based on 88 radiocarbon
dates. Humans first used the cave 37,000–33,500 years ago (when the black
paintings were made using pine charcoal) and again 31,000–28,000 years
ago.[14] I mention these early dates because they make us appreciate that the

human obsession with the horse is very ancient, and they also warn us not to be over-reliant on artistic style as a dating mechanism.

Modern science helps us to date some of the earliest images, but not necessarily to answer other questions. Since the significance of cave art was first recognized in the late nineteenth century, scholars have speculated endlessly about why people went to so much trouble, often in difficult, inaccessible places, to create these impressive images. What was the purpose? The motivation? Was there a message? Or were there many motives, many messages?[15] This is not a problem unique to the deep past. We will face it again with the Uffington hill figure.

What we can say with certainty is that this was the art of hunting societies. Horses were chased and killed for their meat and other useful resources, but these animals were also sentient beings, perhaps with symbolic meaning for humans. For example, horse teeth and skulls were placed around hearths at Pincevent, near Paris, yet here reindeer, not horse, were the main source of food. At Duruthy in southwest France there was a possible horse sanctuary, with the kneeling horse sculpture resting on two horse skulls and a fragment of jaw. Nearby there were three horse-head

Horses, rhino and aurochs (extinct wild cattle) depicted with great sensitivity on the walls of the Chauvet Cave in France. These animals were painted in the depths of the cave around 30,000 years ago.

pendants. The horse was more than a source of calories. It must have loomed large in human myth-making, storytelling and rituals.

The horses are often depicted with great clarity. The people who drew or modelled them had obviously spent a great deal of time observing the animals in life – they have barrel-shaped bodies, short legs and stiff, upright dark manes. Some have shaggy winter coats; occasionally they are spotted. Some have elongated bodies suggesting speed, but most are stocky horses, typical of breeds living in cold environments.

In fact these wild horses most resemble, physically, the small, tough horses first brought to the attention of the West by the Russian explorer Nikolay Mikhaylovich Przhevalsky (Przewalski in Polish), who first encountered them in Central Asia in 1879. Przewalski's horses, as they are now known, live in groups consisting of a stallion with several mares and their foals. In the early twentieth century, five mares were captured and taken to the Ukraine. A successful breeding programme has resulted in the reintroduction of the endangered Przewalski's horse to Mongolia. Another group has successfully bred on the Causse Méjean in France, a high limestone plateau where vultures soar. Approaching these nervous animals slowly, across the grassland, is perhaps the closest we can come to reliving the Aurignacian. Yet not quite. Although the resemblance is close, genetic studies suggest that Przewalski's horse is not the same animal as those depicted so beautifully in the Chauvet Cave some 70 km (45 miles) to the east. Nevertheless, for those familiar with the Palaeolithic masterpieces, contact with these animals in the wild sends a tingle down the spine.

FINDING MESSAGES AND MEANINGS

At one time, Ice Age hunters pursued wild horses across the tundra of North America, western Europe, Russia and Central Asia. At the dramatic kill site at Solutré, as mentioned earlier, migrating horses were corralled and slaughtered. One theory about Lascaux is that the cave itself and its images represent an animal drive – the barriers of rocks and scrub and corrals indicated by painted spots and lines and barbed signs. At Lascaux small horses arguably gallop towards an enclosure and at the far end a frantic horse tumbles upside down, its body wrapped around a rock – it is an incredible composition, as gut-wrenching as the stricken horse in Picasso's *Guernica*.

However, few depictions of animals in cave art are convincing as hunting scenes. In fact, all we can really say about these marvellous images, in terms of explanation, is that animals played an essential part in the thought and culture of Upper Palaeolithic humans in Eurasia. It is also apparent that from very early in our human history some people felt a powerful urge to express themselves through the creation of images, by leaving their mark: a handprint on a rock wall or an animal frozen in time. This was part of becoming human.

The creators of these images were physically, genetically and even mentally very similar to us, but their culture and world were vastly different. We can identify the animals they depicted, but not the ideas, the myths or meaning they conveyed to those who penetrated the caves of Lascaux and Chauvet many thousands of years ago. Alfred Gell wrote one of the most interesting books about art by an anthropologist. In *Art and Agency*[16] he explained that artists make works for some reason: they usually have an intended public, an audience. In the case of artists in the ancient world, however, that audience was certainly not us. These images were not meant for our eyes; nevertheless, we assume they had a purpose. Gell emphasizes the importance of context – such as with the spectacularly carved Trobriand Island canoes whose purpose was to impress would-be trade partners and put them at a psychological disadvantage. King Charles I was attempting this trick with his equestrian portrait (see p. 126) and I have met businessmen who used their Porsches or Ferraris to the same effect.

Upper Palaeolithic people were as intelligent as us. They were experts in a world in which the presence of wild animals loomed large. They knew their smell, their sound, their habits. But they did not have the accumulated knowledge, history or technical and cultural complexity of our society. Picasso's elegant little drawing of a dove is certainly not an encouragement to hunt birds (though some people on the Mediterranean coast today might see it as that). Rather, in our culture, the dove carries ideas of hope, peace and love, which are conveyed in stories as old as the Flood myth, and endlessly repeated and transformed.

If my office caught fire I think the first thing I would save is the lithograph above my desk by Elisabeth Frink. Two powerful horses are depicted by a few simple lines. Frink said she didn't draw from life; she closely observed her subjects and then later attempted to catch their characters – much like the best Palaeolithic artists. A naked man is tied by his ankles to the nearest horse. His body is flayed by the horse's hooves and the rough ground. Behind them is a chariot, again indicated by just a few simple lines, and the chariot seems to have become disconnected from the horses. So what is going on? The subject of the drawing is obvious to anyone who has read Homer's *Iliad*. It is the disfigured body of Hector, being dragged around the walls of Troy, in full view of his wife and his parents, all to satisfy the rage and fury of Achilles.

Hector is one of the more sane and balanced characters in the *Iliad*. Homer calls him 'the breaker of horses'. In the Late Bronze Age world of Greek warriors, horses were used principally to pull war chariots. The *Iliad* is the first, and arguably the greatest, European literary masterpiece, which gazes frankly into the hollow eyes of death. War, for the Greeks, was cruel, brutal, painful and inevitable. For some the joy of battle is intoxicating. War is driven by the lust for glory and honour, or the blindness of revenge. 'Friend, you too must die,' said Achilles, but the suffering and the glory, even the physical traces of wars in the landscape will be erased by the passage of time. The *Iliad* denies us the comforts of paradise, or even the boozy, raucous nights-out in Valhalla. Darkness will engulf the dead. Ultimately we have to face our own mortality and our own insignificance.

Elisabeth Frink was born into a military family, between two of the most disastrous wars in human history. In this drawing of Hector she, like Homer, confronts the impact of war. A naked, vulnerable figure, once a glorious hero, is dragged through the dust. Yet the horses dominate the composition. Frink said that she depicted animals because they are an important part of our lives and totally dependent on us. Of course, this is the view of someone who has experienced the horse as a domestic animal and, itself, often a victim of man's senseless wars. The Palaeolithic artists would have had a different view of the world: their thoughts and motivation are less accessible to us than Elisabeth Frink's.

CHAPTER EIGHT

DOMESTICATING THE HORSE

Out of the earth
I sing for them
A Horse nation
I sing for them

A song of the Teton Lakota, recorded c. 1900

TRANSFORMING THE WILD

About 12,000 years ago the last cold spell of the Ice Age came to an end and we then entered the geological period known as the Holocene (meaning the 'recent' period) when the climate around the world gradually became generally milder and wetter. The great glaciers retreated and sea levels rose. In many parts of the world humans adapted to the changes by shifting away from a dependence on wild animals and plants for food. Instead, we began to cultivate grasses – the ancestors of wheat, barley and rice in Asia – and maize and potatoes in the Americas. Domestication caused plants to become dependent on humans as we became dependent on them. Around 10,000 years ago humans also domesticated a few species of animal, particularly ones that were cooperative or capable of flocking and following a leader.

In the early Holocene in the Near East, human beings thus began what is arguably the most important transformation in our way of life. This domestication of plants and animals is often known as the Neolithic Revolution. The cultivation and management of selective plants and animals led to genetic changes. Hunter-gatherers became farmers, with a different attitude to nature and the wild. The earliest farmers in the Near East manipulated a flexible suite of domesticates – einkorn and emmer wheat; barley, peas and lentils; sheep, goats, cattle and pigs. Ultimately, communities settled down and grew in size; men and women adopted different roles. Trade, urbanization and forms of communication – notably writing – developed. Rivalries and warfare resulted in the growth of kingdoms and empires. Great art and architecture was fuelled by growing social inequality, and the pursuit and demonstration of power.

Although horses were late to join the animal farm and not present in the initial package, they came to play an essential part in the rise of tribes, kingdoms and empires. The farm, in fact, was not the horse's natural habitat or the setting for its most important role. What the horse had to offer humans was speed, power and stamina, and a means of reducing distance. It also offered status, another form of power. King Charles I (1600–1649) of England may have eventually lost his head, but when he wished to look impressive he commissioned an equestrian portrait of himself on a magnificent grey horse (by Sir Anthony van Dyck in 1633). It took a worthy and capable person to control such a powerful beast. Unfortunately, in the painting, the King's Master of Horse stands alongside looking rather

Map of Eurasia showing the east–west corridor formed by the steppes from Mongolia to Hungary, with major sites and cultures in the region mentioned in the text.

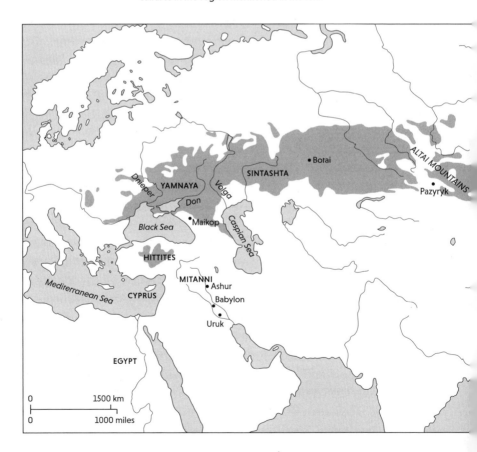

anxious. The King was said to be a good horseman, yet he does not look quite in control. Charles was just one of many rulers, aristocrats and generals who used the horse to emphasize their status, to lift them above the common herd of humanity. Sometimes it was wishful thinking.

THE ORIGINS OF THE HORSE

Horses as a family (Equidae) are essentially American, and that is where most of them evolved. In the late Miocene, about ten million years ago, twelve species grazed or browsed across the continent. In the Lone Bone Bed, northern Florida, about 60 per cent of the ungulate (hoofed) fossils belonged to nine different species of horses.[1] From America horses dispersed across Beringia, the ancient northern land bridge that existed when sea levels were lower, into Eurasia and Africa. The true, single-toed horse made the passage eastwards about three million years ago. Like us, the horse has a single stomach, but is a hind-gut fermenter with long intestines, so its digestive system allows it to survive on a diet of poor-quality forage.

In the early post-glacial, about 13,000 years ago, horses became extinct across the Americas and most of northern and western Europe. They may have survived in a few favourable pockets such as Iberia. However, they certainly continued to thrive in parts of the dry grasslands – the steppes – that stretched for thousands of miles from present-day south east Hungary and the Ukraine eastwards through Turkmenistan and Kazakhstan to Mongolia. The landscape of this vast area contains many local and regional variations, but the steppe is essentially a belt of open, dry grassland as vast as an ocean, bounded by cold forests to the north, deserts to the south and high mountain ranges. The steppe climate is harsh, with bone-shattering winters and hot summers. However, the rainfall is sufficient for grass to grow, and this open landscape, with few natural obstructions, provides a convenient corridor between eastern Europe and China. Eventually it would become a routeway for traders, for the exchange of animals and plants, and for religious ideas and invaders such as the Huns, Mongols and Turkic peoples seeking the wealth of the rich farming lands and civilizations that developed both to the east and west. These raiders sliced into the settled farming communities of Europe and China and were deadly because they rode horses and were armed with short, powerful bows.

TAMING THE HORSE

So where and when did the innovations develop that allowed humans to appear as centaurs, to strike terror into central Europe, China and eventually into the Americas? It is a question that has been thrashed over for decades. Only recently has archaeology begun to provide some answers.

Around 7000 BC, the occupants of the large farming settlement at Çatalhöyük in Anatolia (modern Turkey) and neighbouring sites occasionally hunted wild horses, which were probably relatively rare in the surrounding region. As agriculture first spread westwards into Greece and the Danube countries, about 6000 BC, there is no evidence that early European farmers exploited horses at all. In northwest Europe, small isolated bands of horses were sometimes preyed upon by Mesolithic hunter-gatherers, but their bones amount to only a small proportion of the total discarded in their camps. In the Near East and Europe, horses were not very significant to either the early farming communities or the traditional hunter-foragers.

Things were very different on the great grasslands.[2] At hunters' camps on the Dniester steppes and early farming communities in the Azov steppes (north of the Black Sea and the Caucasus Mountains), into the Caspian Depression and beyond, archaeologists have found that over half the identified animal bones belonged to the wild horse (*Equus caballus*). Here humans and wild horses still existed in close contact. This seems, then, to be the most likely place to find evidence that humans first figured out that a live horse might be of more use than a dead one.[3]

Hunters and early farmers, closely observing wild horses, would have been aware of their habits: that small herds of females and colts were serviced and protected by a dominant stallion, but, like cattle and sheep, were led by an experienced female. Less dominant and younger stallions were ejected from the main herd and lived in male groups, some of them frustrated and ambitious, keen to take on the role of super-stud. As with sheep, the tendency of horses to gather in herds and follow a leader proved advantageous to humans. Once humans had developed the idea of domestication, horses became candidates for recruitment.

Wild horses are strong but nervous, fast runners and quick to bolt. They are also adapted to cold, snowy winters. Like the mammoth, which once thrived on the Ice Age steppes, or the bison of the North American prairie, they were capable of pushing the snow aside (with their hooves) to reach the grass below. Domesticated sheep, which arrived in the steppes with farmers, had evolved in more temperate conditions and were incapable of feeding themselves in harsh winters. In this new environment they had to be cared for by humans. On the endless steppes the mounted shepherd or cattle herder was far more effective than the pedestrian.

Horse remains are not difficult to identify if you are familiar with their bones, and particularly their teeth. It is far harder to assess whether the horse they belonged to was wild or domesticated. Specialists have attempted to answer this question in different ways: studying the varying size of the animals and their ages at death; searching for pathologies in vertebrae caused by riding; and by examining the lower second premolars (P2s) for evidence of bit chewing.[4] It is now generally accepted that horses were first domesticated in the steppe region north of the Black Sea, into which flows the River Dnieper, and the Caspian Sea watered by the River Volga. Horses once again became a frequent subject of art, their images carved in bone and stone.

Botai is a key site in northern Kazakhstan, which has produced some of the finest evidence yet for the changing human interaction with the horse. At this large settlement, dating to about 3700 BC to 3000 BC, less than fastidious inhabitants discarded hundreds of thousands of animal bones. A few were those of wild animals, including bear, elk and red and roe deer, but the vast majority belonged to horses. It now seems most probable that the Botai people had learnt to ride the horse and used it to round up and hunt its wild fellows. There was clear evidence that horses were kept in the settlement: pits filled with horse manure, pots impregnated with the lipids (fats) from their milk, and the carcasses of dead animals. Hunters on foot, like those at Solutré in France, always butcher the horse at the kill site, so intact bodies found in the settlement probably came from domesticated animals that lived there. Further confirmation that some horses at Botai were domesticated came with the significant number of P2s with the wear marks created by bits inserted into their mouths to control them. The majority of horses, however, did not show the bit-wear pattern and these were probably victims of the mounted hunt. Horses now assisted humans to catch their own kind.

In the northern Kazakh steppes about 3700–3500 BC, human communities changed with the adaptation of horse domestication. Settlements grew in size and wild horses became the principal hunted animals. The horse-riding hunters used polished stone weights with a central perforation attached to multi-stranded rawhide ropes – ideal for lassoes or bolas and hobbles. Increasingly, horse riding can be identified by the presence of specialist equestrian tackle.

THE SPREAD OF HORSE RIDING

Horse domestication and riding appeared first in the western steppes, promoted by the knowledge of the earlier domestication of sheep and cattle that spread from the Near East. The new skills rapidly dispersed, even beyond the steppes. Just north of the Caucasus and inland from the Black Sea is the famous site of Maikop (Maykop, in southwest Russia). This is an enormous burial mound (kurgan), excavated in 1897, which contained the spectacular burial of a rich chieftain with his female companions lying in a wooden chamber. In the early fourth millennium BC the people of Maikop were predominantly sheep herders. About 3700 BC their way of life was transformed – at least for the elite – because of their location.

About 1,500 km (930 miles) to the south, the farming communities along the southern Euphrates and Tigris had developed a sophisticated civilization with the world's first cities. Between 3700 BC and 3100 BC, the city of Uruk grew to about 100 hectares (240 acres) in size. Agriculture and the population were booming. The cities were controlled by elite groups, including literate priests and administrators, whose roles demanded impressive monumental buildings. They adorned themselves with prestige artefacts made by local craftsmen from exotic materials. The Maikop sheep herders were ideally placed to control the gateway between the steppes, the supplies of valued lapis lazuli, turquoise, carnelian, copper and cotton from the lands to the north and east, and the new, demanding markets of Mesopotamia and its status-conscious rulers. Certainly by 3300 BC horses were traded in considerable numbers along this route. These animals of the steppes were now in demand in the 'civilized' south.

In the early to mid-fourth millennium BC conditions in the steppes changed as the climate became warmer and drier. People began to exploit larger territories in search of grazing. Instead of settling in one place they moved around. Covered wagons rolled across the grasslands from the Dnieper, the Don and the Volga. By living in wagons drawn by oxen, and riding horses, these groups, often known as the Yamnaya culture (from the Russian for 'pit-grave'), could push their herds and flocks onto the open steppes and claim previously wild and scarcely exploited lands. The new way of life was adaptable. Wagons provided shelter as well as slow, steady

La llegada de Cortes al puerto de Cempuala de la nueva España) con su
armada y gente, y quando hiso barrenar los navios y hechar los a fondo /

A horse is lowered into the waves from a Spanish ship moored off the
coast of the Gulf of Mexico, an illustration from Diego Munoz Camargo's
'Descripcion de la ciudad y provincia de Tlaxcala', 1581–84.

transport for families and bulky materials, such as food supplies. Horseback riding allowed the herders to control much larger groups of animals and travel rapidly over large distances to trade or attack their enemies. Horse riding promoted raiding, rustling and warfare. Warriors and horses were natural partners and an irresistible unit.

A similar transformation of societies would appear over 4,500 years later in North America when groups such as the Apache, Comanche and Lakota exploited the feral horses that had escaped from Spanish herds and spread north. In 1493, Columbus brought the first European horses to the New World, to Hispaniola. In 1519, Hernán Cortés imported them to the mainland and his mounted conquistadors caused consternation among the Maya and Aztecs. The Aztec capital Tenochtitlan fell to the Spanish on 13 August 1521, the feast of St Hippolytus, patron saint of horses. In just over two centuries the horse spread across North America.[5] Both foraging and horticulturalist tribes took to horseback and became mobile hunter-pastoralists, traders and raiders. The horse was back in its original homeland, but its relationship with humans had changed. The Wild West was born.

Increasing the number of one's horses became vital to Plains Indians. However, not everyone voted to adopt the new 'elk dog',[6] the name given to the horse by Algonquin speakers, such as the Blackfoot. Some communities mainly subsisted by growing vegetables in environmentally sensitive areas. The horse simply did not fit into their way of life. Unfortunately, this could cause problems for them as their horse-riding neighbours became increasingly aggressive. And among the most enthusiastic equestrians, such as the Comanche and Lakota, there were consequences: more horses meant that men could have more wives (horses commonly became the currency in establishing the bride price, as cattle did in much of sub-Saharan Africa). Horses increased mobility and more stuff could be carried, so families acquired more possessions. More wives meant greater household production, particularly on the Plains, where women processed bison robes for trading with the non-indigenous population. So the acquisition of horses and material wealth increased social distinctions in, previously, fairly egalitarian societies.

The influx of material also promoted inflation in bride prices, which, in turn, required more raiding to capture more horses and, in some areas, human beings to sell as slaves. Dominant figures also arose, as a result of bison hunting on horseback. This activity encouraged small groups to amalgamate, thus creating more powerful forces. From these, leaders emerged capable of organizing the hunt, raids and mutual defence. Such leaders made a habit of developing spiritual sanctions to justify their authority.

We cannot draw simple analogies from the relatively well-documented introduction of the horse into early-modern America. It is a different continent with different societies from prehistoric Europe. We can, however, perhaps learn a few lessons. It is remarkable how rapidly horse riding spread into communities in America that had previously never seen the animal. Within three centuries, horses had made an impact – northwards into Canada and south as far as remote Patagonia: about 14,500 km (9,000 miles) in total. In prehistoric Eurasia the horse moved east and west, into China and Britain, in the third millennium BC. Horse riding in the Americas impacted the social, economic and religious lives of indigenous communities. It totally changed the way many people lived – and where they lived. With horses some people prospered; others were enslaved, abandoned their traditional homes because of warfare, or took to building fortifications. Increased mobility spread ideas, technologies and disease.

New rulers emerged with new mythologies. Sometimes the myths were inscribed into the land.

Back in the Eurasian steppes of the fourth and third millennia BC, the domestic horse continued to spread rapidly. It was not an easy animal to tame, but the advantages, once it was domesticated, were enormous. A shepherd alone can handle 60–80 sheep, with a good dog perhaps 200, but on horseback the flock can be far larger and the rider can cover over 50 km (30 miles) a day. The horse can also provide milk, blood and meat, and large quantities of fertilizer.[7]

Unlike most other ungulates, the wild horse developed both speed and stamina to outrun its oldest predator (before humans came along), the wolf. It is hardly surprising that the horse, perhaps more than any other animal, has helped to revolutionize human society. We still use 'horse-power' as a unit of measurement, the term developed by James Watt in the late eighteenth century to compare the output of early steam engines. It is commonly thought that one horse has the strength of seven men, although that, of course, depends upon the horse – and the men.[8]

WAGONS ROLL

The mobile pastoralism of the Yamnaya culture proved to be a new, remarkably adaptable and popular way of life. Their barrow burials mark the trails of seasonal movements in search of pasture. In these graves, dug across the Pontic steppes between 3000 BC and 2200 BC, archaeologists have found over 2,500 wagons – timber constructions with a box seat on which the driver could perch. The four wheels were crudely made of thick planks dowelled together. One or two poles were attached to the wagon and took the yoke that harnessed the oxen, the steady but reliable means of traction. Light hoops provided support for a colourful cover of felt and reeds, which sheltered families and their possessions.[9]

These wagon trains trundled across the steppes, carrying supplies and accompanied by huge flocks and herds and outriders on horseback. Mounted riders, rather like skilled sailors, could navigate the vast terrestrial seas of grass, covering large distances to trade, and also raid. Flocks and herds were wealth on the hoof – easily transported but also easily rustled. The mounted warrior became a heroic figure in this society as inter-community aggression increased, promoted by horse theft. Successful horse rustlers probably enhanced their prestige by distributing the stolen animals among their communities. At the end of the fourth millennium BC, Yamnaya groups began to move westwards, following the natural steppe corridor that led into the Great Hungarian Plain and into Europe.

Recent research projects, combining archaeology with genetics, isotope studies and linguistics, have thrown up fascinating theories about the Yamnaya people. They seem to be the most likely carriers of the inflow of genetic changes that are observable in the population of temperate Europe after 3000 BC.[10] We are in the early stages of much of this scientific analysis of the past and no doubt ideas and details will change as more data accumulate. But to reduce complex uncertainties to a simple narrative: it is consistent with the present evidence that Yamnaya bands, consisting often of young men, spread from the Caspian-Pontic steppes in search of the usual things – wealth and wives. Exactly what pushed them at this time is uncertain. They brought their horse riding and pastoral way of life, and over several centuries their culture hybridized with that of the local European Neolithic farmers.

The genetic evidence points to exogamy – the incoming men finding wives from among nearby communities. The anthropological jargon 'exogamy' sounds rather neutral. In reality the strategy may have been similar to that practised by the early Romans and reflected in the story of the Rape of the Sabine Women. Horse-riding nomads tend to be more aggressive than settled farmers (another popular story – filmed as *Seven Samurai* and *The Magnificent Seven* – dramatizes mobile horsemen preying on sedentary farmers). The new scientific evidence shows that as a result of their innovative pastoral lifestyle, the Yamnaya were well fed, relatively long-lived (commonly up to sixty years), increasingly lactose-tolerant, so able to digest milk (they probably helped to spread the gene into northern Europe), and becoming taller. By abducting and marrying local Neolithic women they mixed cultures as well as genes and, arguably, introduced their Indo-European tongue, which hybridized into proto-Germanic languages in western Europe.

As in *Seven Samurai*, however, farmers can fight back. Archaeologists found the evidence of a vivid incident at the cemetery of Eulau in central Germany. Here they found four multiple burials containing the remains of single families. In each case the mother was not local. The women originated in the Harz Mountains about 50 km (30 miles) to the north. The arrows that killed them came from the same area, made by Neolithic farming groups who also produced distinctive pottery that appeared in the new mixed Corded Ware communities. If this was a revenge massacre initiated by frustrated farmers then the women paid the price. Similar incidents occurred in America when European women were taken captive, as in the 'captive stories' mythologized by James Fenimore Cooper in his novel *The Last of the Mohicans* and by John Ford in his film *The Searchers*.[11]

Eulau is just one incident, but it provides a vivid reminder that archaeology is about people. And when new peoples come into contact with each other life gets exciting, complicated and sometimes dangerous. Like Europeans arriving in the Americas, there is also a possibility that the Yamnaya brought new diseases, probably the plague, which was to strike Europe again from a similar source in the Middle Ages.[12]

This, necessarily, is a simple glimpse of what may have been a much longer, gradual process of interaction between the people of the steppes and the farmers of Europe. The Yamnaya interlude happened, approximately, between about 2800 BC and 2400 BC. Horses, however, appear in eastern Germany, Hungary and the Czech Republic up to a thousand years earlier, an indication of even older contacts with the steppes. In some areas there was an exchange of ideas and material culture. But increasingly, steppe peoples themselves moved west under the pressure of climate change – drought in the east and expanding grasslands in the west. Their descendants, in the Netherlands, marked archaeologically by their use of Bell Beakers, migrated on a large scale into Britain and Ireland after 4,500 years ago.[13] Like their horses, it seems that the descendants of the steppe people also colonized the northwestern isles of Europe.

FAST AND FURIOUS CHARIOTS

The Yamnaya ox-drawn wagons with their solid plank wheels have a 'Flintstones' look about them. The technology was about to improve. In the southeast Urals there were groups of pastoralists known to archaeologists as the Sintashta culture. These people were unusual because they worked copper mines in the Urals and constructed strongly fortified villages. It is arguable that the stress of increasing aridity and warfare drove technological change in this area. Within the safety of the village the early metallurgists smelted arsenical copper, casting shaft-hole axes (like most modern axes, these were cast with a central hole through the metal head to take a wooden shaft) and spearheads in moulds and ingots for trade. They were leaders in an early industrial revolution.[14]

The Sintashta people kept small, milk-producing cattle and some sheep. They also rode horses, whose significance is obvious from the burial mounds and grave pits located outside the settlement. Their burials included horse sacrifices – as many as eight in a single grave. In one, the remains of six horses, four cows and two rams would have provided 2,720 kg (6,000 lb) of meat for a funerary feast capable of satisfying three thousand mourners. Other burials had animal sacrifices for smaller but still substantial funeral gatherings. For these people status was not reflected in their houses, which were remarkably uniform, but in their control of animals, social alliances and the scale of feasting. Feasting became a means by which surplus production could be converted into social capital, the fuel that drove the self-aggrandizers of society.

Among the Sintashta some geniuses came up with a most remarkable technological innovation: the world's first chariots with spoked wheels. These appeared in graves about 2100 BC and were drawn by a pair of horses, probably yoked to a pole. The horse gear in the graves includes circular cheek pieces of antler or bone with short spikes on the inside to allow charioteers to control the horses (like spurs operated through the reins). The Sintashta community must have developed new skills in carpentry, horse training and the manipulation of these new vehicles. They needed expert drivers. It remains uncertain whether the first chariots were used primarily in warfare, for racing or as status symbols (a means of transport that literally elevated the passenger).

These sleek, swift and impressive machines were soon in demand throughout the ancient world, along with horses and the copper mined in the Urals. Carved seals from the Assyrian colony at Karum Kanesh, in central Anatolia, show the earliest image of spoke-wheeled chariots outside of the steppes – much more sophisticated vehicles than the solid-wheeled war-wagons depicted on the so-called Royal Standard of Ur (c. 2400 BC), which were drawn by some form of ass–onager cross-breed. Asses were originally royal mounts. To a modern audience the image of Jesus' entry into Jerusalem mounted on an ass may suggest humility, but this was not the perception of a contemporary audience steeped in Middle Eastern tradition.[15]

By 2000 BC horses were well known in the cities of Mesopotamia and beginning to replace the asses that drew the traditional war-wagon. In this period there was a huge demand for metal ores. The search for tin encouraged merchants to travel between the steppes and the Middle East – and beyond, even to the remote misty islands off the northwest peninsula of Europe. As these routes opened, so horses, horse technology and even horse-riding mercenaries moved between the different worlds.

The spread of pastoralism, wagon technology and metallurgy across the steppes also made an impact in the Far East, reaching China by the mid-second millennium BC. For the next thousand years chariots played a vital part in elite culture, and were a symbol of aristocratic power (Pl. vi). Generations of Jin rulers at Beizhao in Shanxi province (tenth–eighth centuries BC), were buried alongside pits containing horses and chariots – the largest with 107 horses and 48 chariots. The Jin lands lay close to the steppes, from which flowed the abundance of selectively bred, swift and strong animals. From about 1000 BC horse riding and the use of iron became increasingly important in China.

To the west of the steppes the horse played an equally dominant role. Although donkeys did most of the hard work in Egypt, by the 18th Dynasty (1550–1307 BC) elegant, fine-limbed horses are portrayed pulling light chariots in ceremonial processions and royal hunts. In Tutankhamun's tomb, his Asiatic and African enemies fall beneath the hooves of his magnificent horse, while the young pharaoh stands proudly in his chariot, drawing a powerful bow. In reality, Tutankhamun was disabled: he had fused vertebrae, a deformed foot and suffered from malaria. He died aged about nineteen in 1323 BC, so this portrayal of power is idealized – image-making on a scale that might embarrass even a modern advertising agency. But, of course, in the ancient world most people saw the myth; few witnessed the reality. Egyptians certainly campaigned against Nubians and Asiatic peoples, but the weak, young pharaoh probably played no active part in the fighting. His tomb contained his walking sticks, as well as the dismantled chariot that was so vital to maintaining his royal image.

An archaeologist working at the No. 3 Horse and Chariot Pit, one of a cluster of tombs belonging to noble families of the Zheng State, dating to around the mid-first millennium BC, found near the city of Xinzheng, Henan Province, China.

The Assyrian king Ashurnasirpal II hunting lions from his chariot drawn by three
fine horses, in an alabaster relief from his palace at Nimrud. The king, armed with a bow,
shoots arrows at a lion attacking the back of his chariot.

Egypt's most powerful enemies, the Hittites, commissioned a horse-training manual, perhaps the first of its kind in the world, by Kikkuli the Mitannian.[16] He describes the ideal feed for warhorses and the training regime for both them and their human passengers. The time and expense involved in creating such a force promoted the development of powerful warrior clans among the Hittites, similar in some ways to the mounted knights of medieval feudal Europe.

As Egyptian influence declined, the Kushite state emerged a few hundred kilometres to the south in Nubia, in what is now present-day Sudan. The remains of two dozen horses were found at el-Kurru, the site of the Kushite royal cemetery. An important horse burial dating to about 900 BC, discovered at Tombos, emphasizes the animal's growing significance, especially as this horse, a mare aged between twelve and fifteen years, had a cheek piece made of iron, one of the earliest uses of the metal in Nubia. Wear and tear on the bones indicates that the mare had been used to pull a chariot. By 729 BC the Assyrians admired the superiority of Kushite horses. For the Nubians, the horse, through innovations in breeding and training, became a means of exerting and demonstrating their newly found strength and influence, while at the same time harking back to the memories and images of the glorious Egyptian past, irradiating themselves in its fading power.[17] In France and England the barbarian successors of Rome would do the same.

As empires rose and fell, the images of power, symbols of authority and deeper religious ideas persisted for generations. The idea of the horse was firmly embedded in the minds of people and in the mosaic of cultures across Eurasia and into Africa. The horse was the symbol of speed, power and authority.

The great French historian Fernand Braudel noted that 'the dazzling civilizations we have glimpsed may have been no deeper than a layer of goldleaf'.[18] Certainly, empires and civilizations came and went in the east Mediterranean, spreading like puddles in the rain and then evaporating in the heat. After the Hittites, the next great power to emerge in the Near East was Assyria, from their capital at Ashur. The Assyrians had their ups and downs in a turbulent period of history, but by the end of the tenth century BC they were once again in an expansionist mood. One of the highlights of the British Museum is the gallery lined with the alabaster reliefs of Ashurnasirpal II (883–859 BC) from his palace at Nimrud. Armed with a deadly bow – and the world's most threatening beard – the mighty monarch stands arrogantly in his chariot, which is controlled by his expert charioteer. The three horses are large and muscular – different beasts from the ancestral, shaggy, short-legged steppe dwellers. Over the previous millennium some serious breeding programmes had resulted in the emergence of specialized animals: warhorses, hunters and speed merchants. Ashurnasirpal II boasts that he has killed 450 lions from his chariot. He was a man in control of all he surveyed, or so he wanted us to think, and, as in nineteenth-century England, riding for sport also kept imperial warriors in battle-trim.

Another panel in the British Museum shows human beings, the enemies of Ashurnasirpal II, pierced by arrows, falling beneath his chariot wheels. The Assyrians have adopted the iconography of Egypt. Their chariots are decorated with standards that represent the gods Adad and Nergal, respectively the deity of storms, lightning and rain, and of war and the underworld. Like crusaders, Assyrians were licensed to kill by their gods and assisted by their mastery of the horse.

While such powerful dynasties may have rapidly evaporated, their ideas – for example, how to project power and status – spread widely and persisted. This is clearly demonstrated in Cyprus, which became entangled in the Assyrians' political and economic web. By the seventh century BC the island, closely linked with Phoenician traders from the mainland, was tied into an international trading network that had bases in Naucratis (in the Nile Delta of Egypt) and Greek islands such as Rhodes and Samos. Through these conduits, ideas – as well as art, animals and foodstuffs – spread around the Mediterranean and beyond. From the ninth to the seventh centuries BC, burials in the monumental Royal Tombs of Salamis, Cyprus, reveal an elite who probably paid tribute to the dominant Assyrian kings, from Sargon and Esarhaddon to Ashurbanipal. At the same time, the elite aped the ways of their superiors even in death, going into their tombs with chariots and horses, fine furniture inlaid with ivory and the trappings of feasting, especially magnificent bronze cauldrons adorned with the figures of griffins or lions. Painted terracotta statues found at Cypriot shrines in the seventh century BC show male worshippers wearing Assyrian fashions, and even sporting those fearful beards.[19]

The significance of rituals involving horses and chariots or parade vehicles appears vividly on large ceramic vessels from eighth-century BC Greece.[20] In the Dipylon cemetery, outside the city of Athens, large pots – kraters for men and amphorae for women – marked the position of graves. The most elaborately decorated, in the Geometric style around 750–730 BC, illustrate funerary scenes. First the body is laid out on a bier observed by lines of mourning women. This is the *prothesis*, or what we called the Wake in my Irish Catholic childhood. The stylized female figures wail and tear at their hair. Then comes the *ekphora*, or transportation of the body for burial or cremation. An honour guard of warriors, equipped with distinctive hour-glass shaped shields, accompany the body, along with columns of horse-drawn two-wheeled chariots and a four-wheeled vehicle as a hearse. These scenes look like funerals out of the *Iliad* or the Greek Bronze Age, and perhaps they do represent the heroic ancestors or the funeral games to honour the dead. However, such displays of lordship – horse riding, chariots, feasting and fine craftsmanship – spread across the Mediterranean, and would soon appear in the graves of the barbarian north.

In the centuries before and after 1000 BC, societies from China to the Near East, in Greece and deep into Africa depended upon the horse as their engine of power and their symbol of authority. It is hardly surprising that these animals were also making an impact in northern Europe and into Britain.

A PEOPLE OF CHARIOTS AND HORSEMEN

They were a people of chariots and horsemen.

Winston S. Churchill, 1956

VENI, VIDI, VANESCI: CAESAR MEETS THE BRITISH

Our scientific dates from the body of the White Horse suggest that people carved this great image some time between the Late Bronze Age and Middle Iron Age, focusing on the years around 800–600 BC. The obvious question now is: do these dates make sense? Is it likely that the image of a horse would loom large, at that time, in the imagination of the community that dominated the high chalk Downs and controlled the valley below?

Winston Churchill may not have been Britain's finest historian, but he had a journalist's instinct for a good story and an eye for a visual image. His British 'horsemen', from the quote that heads this chapter,[1] belonged to the tribe known as the Belgae, 'the proud or puffed up people', which, he assumed – and it was a common belief at the time – had invaded and settled in southern Britain in the Late Iron Age. Churchill's primary source was no less an authority than Julius Caesar, who launched a brief expedition into Britain in 55 BC and another in the following year.

Caesar was the first person to leave a detailed, written record of Britain: its geography, tribes and chieftains, and the events of his campaign. He describes these in his famous work *Gallic War* (*Commentarii de Bello Gallico*). Caesar landed in Kent, where, he said, the people were 'the most civilized' (*humanissimi* in Latin). They were little different from the Gauls, in Caesar's opinion; not surprising, as they were said to be recent arrivals from across the Channel. In contrast, the indigenous tribes, living further inland, supposedly dressed in animal skins, painted themselves with woad and lived on a diet of meat and milk. Furthermore, they did not grow cereals. Caesar was wrong about this primitive dark interior: it was, in fact, mostly well populated and extensively cultivated. He was probably more reliable, however, when it came to military matters, and the evidence of his own eyes. He describes how his forces were attacked by British cavalry and chariots. For 'chariots' he uses the Latin word *esseda*. The modern English word comes, in fact, from the Celtic root *karros*. Caesar describes the British tactics:

> First they drive in all directions, hurling missiles. This inspires terror and compounded by the racket of the wheels throws our ranks into confusion. In this way they break up our cavalry and then leap down from the chariots to fight on foot. The charioteers withdraw a little way off so that the warriors, if pressed, can leap back on board and be carried to safety.[2]

According to Caesar, the chariot crews and their horses were incredibly skilful, able to drive down steep slopes, manoeuvre and turn rapidly. The warriors darted back and forth along the chariot pole and stood on the yoke. Caesar admits that, at first, his troops were confused by this strange way of fighting. But, of course, his presence soon calmed them down (remember, Caesar was writing, or dictating, this account himself, for his audience in Rome). Near Eastern chariot skills had clearly spread to Britain by this time.

In the centuries before Caesar, the armies in the Mediterranean world had evolved, becoming professional, disciplined and integrating their infantry with cavalry. By Caesar's time, Romans raced chariots for sport in the circus not around the battlefield,[3] and during his campaign against the Gauls, he seems not to have encountered them at all. The British were behind the times. Nevertheless, clearly their horses were vital to them by the first century BC.

EARLY HORSES IN BRITAIN

So when did the horse begin to play an important role in the British way of life? With Julius Caesar, Britain enters the light of history for the first time. Before 55 BC we are in prehistory, reliant on archaeology – on physical remains not written texts. To establish when domesticated horses first appeared in prehistoric Britain we must look for the relevant evidence: the traces of their bones, the gear associated with riding, such as bridles and terrets (rings the reins pass through), and the paraphernalia from chariots or carts. The first clue appears in East Anglia. Today, Norfolk is a flat land with big skies and isolated churches. Once, it had the largest flint mines in Britain, an industry that supplied the stone axes of Neolithic farmers and, almost six thousand years later, the flints for the muskets of British Redcoats. Grime's Graves today is pitted with the hollows that mark the position of ancient shafts and galleries where prehistoric people penetrated deep into the chalk to reach the valuable seams of glossy black flint.

It was at Grime's Graves that archaeologists unearthed the skull of a horse dating to the end of the Neolithic or the Early Bronze Age (2900–1600 BC). This is probably the earliest domesticated horse yet found in Britain. The skull belonged to an aged mare, who was more than thirty-five years old when she finally died. This venerable animal had lost most of her teeth, and her owners must have taken some trouble to feed her. So was this horse exotic and highly valued, a rare import from the Continent?

One horse skull does not, of course, make an equestrian revolution.[4] For that, we have to move forward several centuries into the Middle to Late Bronze Age. The use of horses becomes increasingly apparent across Europe from about 2000 BC. By the Late Bronze Age they were widespread in Britain and horse bones are found in most settlements with sizeable, well-preserved assemblages.[5]

Their numbers are, however, still limited compared with cattle and sheep. The site at Potterne in Wiltshire is an exception to the rule.[6] To a modern observer, prehistoric Potterne seems an odd place – a huge accumulation of cattle dung and rubbish. Such Late Bronze Age/Early Iron Age dumps or middens have been found elsewhere, in Wessex, South Wales and East Anglia. The reason archaeologists are attracted to these super-dung heaps is that they also contain a remarkable quantity of rich objects. At Potterne there was bronze metalwork, iron slag in the upper levels, fine pottery and evidence of spinning, weaving and bone and antler working. The sheer quantity of animal bones indicates that people were organizing feasts at these places. What was the attraction of giant heaps of dung? Were they symbols of fertility, perhaps a visual display of cattle wealth? Literally, the bigger the pile the richer the clan? Whatever the message, people gathered here to make and exchange valued materials, to feast and presumably to cement alliances. Some were on obvious routeways, and varied styles of pottery suggest that people were coming together from wide areas to exchange gifts, animals and even bridal partners.

READING THE BONES

At Wallingford in Oxfordshire and Runnymede Bridge in Surrey, such midden sites occupied islands in the River Thames. Horse bones were unusually frequent, and at Runnymede, in particular, it is clear that horses were butchered and consumed.[7] This is not uncommon at that time. Gravelly Guy is a site that we spotted from aerial photography (near Stanton Harcourt, Oxfordshire) alongside the River Windrush. The crop-marks revealed a rash of Iron Age pits. Fortunately, we found this site shortly before an active gravel quarry consumed it. We excavated, believing the pits would contain the debris of cereal processing – good evidence of prehistoric arable farming in the area where Caesar had believed it had not taken place. In fact, the pits were also rich in animal bones, and the horse bones found there were scarred with even more marks of butchery than the pig bones. At this Iron Age settlement, about 20 km (12 miles) northeast of the White Horse, people were routinely consuming their most recently domesticated animal. Yet these horses were not, primarily, kept for meat, as they lived to a ripe old age compared with other animals and were eaten at the end of their working lives. Clearly, Iron Age farmers were not sentimental about their animals; some of their dogs also ended up in the pot. They did not have our food taboos.

At another Iron Age settlement, known as Mingies Ditch, just upstream from Gravelly Guy, the occupation layers were unusually well preserved and not scoured by modern ploughing. So our archaeozoologist (the bone guy), Bob Wilson, was able to analyse how animal remains had been distributed around the site. Bob observed that prehistoric dogs complicated the picture by carrying prized bones to the edge of the settlement, where they could settle down and gnaw them in peace. The settlement consisted of conical round houses in a central space surrounded by two ditched and hedged boundaries. To modern eyes this homestead would probably look more African than British. Hoof prints showed that the area between the two ditches was used as a corral for the community's herds.

At Mingies Ditch, sheep and cattle outnumbered horses, but horses lived four times as long as sheep, on average. A horse also consumes four times as much food as a sheep, so the horse made a much greater impact on the community's grazing. The long-lived horses were used for riding or pulling vehicles, not killed young like most animals reared for meat. It is suspected, however, that the Windrush valley in the Middle Iron Age was a horse-breeding area, and animals were exchanged with other communities, so there may have been more horses around than the bones alone indicate.[8]

Back at Gravelly Guy, all those pits containing bones and plant remains allowed us to model the economy of the mixed farming settlement. It is suggested that about 50 head of cattle, 65 sheep, 15 pigs and 11 horses were kept at any one time.[9] Of course, if Gravelly Guy was part of the Windrush valley network of horse breeders, then many of the animals must have trotted off the site for a life elsewhere. Some may have been traded, but others could have been given as gifts. In Iron Age society men achieved status by acquiring horses, and giving them away;[10] although, of course, only those animals that remained until their deaths left their bones for us to find on the site. Some, at that stage, received special treatment. It is a common phenomenon on late prehistoric settlements to find deposits that seem to have been specially selected and placed in the ground as a kind of religious offering. This is where most of the adult horse bones ended up: in these 'special deposits'. Even if horses were eaten in old age they retained some symbolic importance to their owners. Perhaps that is why they were eaten, not just for the sake of calories, but to pass on power, status or fertility.

RITES AND PASSAGES

Indo-European literature and mythology is full of references to horses and to rites in which they were involved. One of the most famous stories, because it is so startling, was told by Gerald of Wales in the late twelfth century, in his *Itinerary of Ireland*. Gerald says that at a royal coronation in Donegal the king-to-be declared to his assembled people that he was a horse, and then, in front of them, copulated with a white mare. The sacrificial mare was slaughtered, butchered and its flesh boiled. The royal candidate then climbed into a broth-filled barrel and proceeded to sup the liquid. At the same time, the cooked meat was consumed by the onlookers. Now, Gerald of Wales is not the most reliable guide, nor is he, exactly, a flatterer of the Irish. However, he may be recounting a story of a past ritual, as this strange coronation has echoes of ancient Indian rites, such as the Asvamedha – when a white stallion was sacrificed in order that the queen could lay with its body during the night, while priests chanted verses calling upon the animal, dead but still potent, to impregnate her – a supernatural coupling that also occurs in Greek mythology and is known as 'hieros gamos', a sacred marriage.

Throughout Indo-European cultures horses were admired. In literature such as the ancient Indian Vedas they attract common epithets including 'swift' and 'flying'. In the *Iliad* the father of Achilles' horses was the West Wind and they 'flew with the winds' – a description that occurs in the Indian Rigveda and the great Irish epic *Táin Bó Cúailnge* ('The Cattle Raid of Cooley'), where steeds 'seemed to fly in the air'. Horses partner heroes, who sometimes talk to their mounts as if they were human. In the Welsh poem 'Song of the Horses' (*Canu y Meirch*) in the fourteenth-century manuscript known as the Book of Taliesin, the horses are themselves heroic.

Bones found on archaeological sites are a relatively dry, forensic form of evidence. They whisper to us about the past, but the literature of Indo-European communities speaks of the strangeness of ancient societies – rites that to us seem weird, even objectionable. But in the past our ancestors did do things differently, and their relationship to animals and to their gods was not necessarily the same as ours.

The most impressive local collection of horse bones in the White Horse region came from Blewburton Hill, the large hillfort on the edge of the Downs, about 24 km (15 miles) east of the White Horse.[11] The hillfort was prominent in the landscape not only because of its massive defences on an isolated hill, but also because of the coloured bands of its geology exposed on the hill slope. Like White Horse Hill, Blewburton Hill demanded attention. The hillfort builders emphasized the importance of the place by interring the remains of ten horses in the entrance. Horse skulls were also buried in the middle of the street that led through the fort's entrance passage, and there were two complete horse skeletons under the collapsed northern revetment wall.[12] It is not unusual in prehistoric contexts to find animal or human bones placed either as foundation deposits or to mark the closure of a structure: an offering to recognize the beginning or the end of life and a time of change – a ritual that probably involved music, chanting and rites of purification presided over by priests, priestesses and chieftains. The buried horses may have been out of sight but they were certainly not out of mind.

TOP GEAR

Aside from their bones, another form of evidence for the use and status of horses is equipment for riding them and for chariots or carts. From the Middle Bronze Age into the Iron Age, antler cheek pieces (part of the harness used to control horses), are the commonest element to be found. Several turned up at Late Bronze Age Runnymede and there was an Early Iron Age example at Yarnton, upriver from Oxford. At this site, a well-made prehistoric road crossed the valley floor. Bronze objects had been ritually placed in the make-up of the road, providing a form of ancestral protection to travellers.[13] The Yarnton prehistoric road was a rare survival, made of stone brought to the site from at least 4 km (2½ miles) away. By this time the landscape was being systematically managed and controlled.

This was even more obvious when we excavated a relict channel of the River Thames (before the construction of the Eton Rowing Course at Dorney, in advance of the London 2012 Olympic Games). Most of the Thames channel has been dredged many times, scooping out any archaeological remains and leaving it historically sterile. Here, though, an abandoned channel had silted up and, consequently, been left intact. In one short stretch we found the remains of six late prehistoric timber bridges. The earliest, belonging to the Middle Bronze Age, had two parallel rows of oak uprights. Here again, at these river crossings, important places in the landscape, there were ritual deposits, ranging from pots and carbonized cereals to human skulls and long bones which, judging from the cut marks on them, had been deliberately severed from the body and defleshed.[14] Ancient British roads may not have been up to Roman standards, but we have probably underestimated the extent to which the landscape was crossed by tracks and droveways, with bridges and metalling where needed. The Ridgeway along the chalk uplands was not the only prehistoric route in the region.

In the vicinity of the White Horse itself, there is some evidence of horse riding or horse-drawn vehicles. Bronze fittings were deposited close to the megalithic tomb of Wayland's Smithy, and, in 1803, a strange collection of metalwork was unearthed at Hagbourne Hill, on the North Wessex Downs near the Icknield Way. This contained objects of several periods, including a pair of three-link bits made of finely decorated cast bronze, but with an iron core. This kind of bit was an Iron Age invention, and so effective it remained in use for the next 2,500 years.[15] There were also three terret rings and a pair of horse bits, which suggests we are dealing here with the gear from a chariot. Unfortunately, the early nineteenth-century antiquarians might have been digging up potatoes for all the care they took with their precious finds.

It is clear, albeit from fragmentary evidence, that horses and horse-drawn chariots and carts were present in Britain from the Middle Bronze Age. For a more vivid picture of the importance of horses as high-status animals, often drawing vehicles, we need to look further afield, first into Europe, then once more to the steppes, before we return to northern Britain.

ELITE BURIALS: VIX, HOCHDORF AND HOHMICHELE

On the Continent, horses and wheeled vehicles were clearly important features in the display of power and status for the Early Iron Age elite. The practice of burying the dead with four-wheeled wagons, and sometimes the horses that pulled them, seems to have originated in the northern Pontic steppes in the ninth century BC.

As we have already seen, centuries earlier in the mid-second millennium BC, warriors, kings and at least some pharaohs tore across the dry steppes and deserts of Asia and Egypt in light-weight, two-wheeled chariots. Several centuries later there were important technological changes in horse equipment: improved harnesses with metal bits, cheek pieces and sophisticated rein-fastenings. These allowed drivers to control four-wheeled wagons, and riders to more easily handle their mounts. Although the wagons look practical, capable of carrying useful loads, their high-quality workmanship and appearance in high-status graves in southern Germany in the eighth century BC, and later further north and west, indicates that these vehicles were more than everyday forms of transport. The Queen's fairy-tale carriages are based on the same structure as farm carts, but clearly play a very different role – and in royal pageants, horses still trump Rolls-Royces.

A number of factors generated enormous changes in Late Bronze Age and Early Iron Age central Europe. In the eastern Alps copper mining developed on a massive scale from about 1200 BC. The mines at Mittelberg in Austria are estimated to have produced in total some 20,000 tonnes of raw copper. These communities developed into what archaeologists term the Hallstatt culture (Pl. vii).[16] There was increasing use of both bronze and horses: Professor Barry Cunliffe of Oxford University put it in a nutshell when he said Europe was 'swamped with bronze horse-gear'. This includes not only horse harnesses and chariot fittings but also long slashing swords. Mounted warriors had scabbards with wing-like extensions (chapes) on the tip so that they could be held in place with the foot while drawing out the sword.

Around 600 BC these people, north of the Alps, began to show increasing signs of contact with the civilizations of the Mediterranean. The establishment of Greek colonies, such as that at Massalia (modern-day Marseilles), played an important part in opening up trade routes, but the growing influence of rivals to the Greeks, the Etruscans, who spread into Italy's Po Valley, also promoted contacts across the Alpine passes and into southern Germany. The Mediterranean traders brought luxuries: wine, olive oil, fine metalwork, glass, coral and ceramics – in particular, the equipment involved in feasting and drinking. Such stuff brought lustre to the lifestyles of the northern elite, who may have maintained a monopoly of control over it, and so enhanced their own status. In return for southern luxuries they traded metals, furs, amber, timber, foodstuffs and slaves. As tribal leaders increased their wealth, power and prestige, their status was reflected in their burials.

In my frequent journeys across France I occasionally stay at Châtillon-sur-Seine (north of Dijon). Here, in the local museum, is one of the great treasures of Iron Age archaeology: the Vix burial, dating to about 480 BC.

This tomb, excavated in 1953, was sited on the slope below the hillfort (or oppidum) of Mont Lassois. It is characteristic of these rich burials in France and Germany that they were placed within sight of dominant, defended strongholds, which were occupied by the tribal elite. Mont Lassois is an obvious strategic location on the Upper Seine in Burgundy, close to the watershed where French rivers flow both north and south: a vital place on the route from the Mediterranean to the English Channel and the North Sea. The Vix burial is one of the most westerly of a group of elite (they are sometimes known as 'princely') burials that date to the Early Iron Age.

In the Vix tomb, the most remarkable object is a vast bronze krater. I can vividly remember my first encounter with it many years ago, in the previous Châtillon museum. I walked into a small gallery and was over-whelmed by this massive, dark green, gleaming object that dominated the room. A krater is an urn-shaped vessel used to contain wine for serving at feasts or symposia. I had seen lots of them in the National Archaeological Museum in Athens as well as the museum in Thessaloniki, which holds the treasures of Macedonia. But this was on a different scale: over 1.6 m (5 ft) high and with a capacity of 1,100 litres (242 gallons). It is the largest metal vessel to have come down to us from antiquity.

The krater had been made in a Greek workshop (possibly in Sparta or southern Italy) and then packed, in segments, to be transported and reassembled in Gaul: a gift for a very important person, someone who could open the routes to trade. The grimacing faces of gorgons glare from the vessel, their tongues protruding from gaping mouths. Around the neck of the krater marches a frieze of Greek warriors, hoplites wearing crested helmets and greaves, carrying large round shields, and with them chariot-eers in small mobile vehicles drawn by four horses.

The objects in the Vix burial are exceptional. They include one of the finest pieces of goldwork from ancient Europe: a torc with swollen termi-nals and on each side a beautiful figure of a small winged horse (Pl. viii). The little winged horses are masterpieces in their own right: they perch on gold discs filled with gold wire shaped to look like waves. The Pegasus figures are taut and crouched, ears forward, appearing to spring from the waves and about to fly into the air. The influences may come from Greece and the steppes, but the liveliness and craftsmanship are Celtic.[17]

The tomb contained another surprise, at least to anyone expecting to find the body of a powerful 'prince'. The occupant was a woman: elderly, diminutive, with a deformed face, who probably walked with a limp. Her status in the community was clearly high, but was she a 'queen-mother' figure or perhaps a priestess or a shaman capable of guiding her people?

She is not the only important Celtic woman that we know of. Boudica, of the Iceni, and Cartimandua, of the Brigantes, played important roles in first-century AD Britain. But we should not overestimate Celtic feminism. Boudica and Cartimandua were members of high-status families that, at the time, had a shortage of appropriate male leaders.

The famous nineteenth-century statue of Boudica (or Boadicea as she was then known) on London's Embankment, opposite the Houses of Parliament, shows her in a chariot drawn by fiery horses. The real Boudica may well have ridden in a chariot, but certainly not one with scythes on the wheels like this Victorian fantasy vehicle. Our lady of Vix lay on the bed of a beautifully made cart, its four-spoked wheels with iron tyres removed and propped against the walls of the burial chamber, rather like Tutankhamun's. Unfortunately, no records survive from pre-literate Gallic society, so we have no record of her name or achievements.

The wealth in this grave reflects the strategic importance of the nearby Mont Lassois hillfort. It dominated the navigable headwaters of the Seine, the major routeway into the Paris Basin, the agriculturally rich Champagne region and the Channel coast. Greek and, later, Roman traders could use the Rhône and Saône corridor to transport their goods from the Mediterranean northwards. The massive krater and the gold torc were probably brought as diplomatic gifts to help forge alliances with and guarantee the cooperation of the ruling elite of Mont Lassois. As a result, the elite could cement their own power in the community by supplying wine and other luxuries to their retinue of followers, and with this power they could protect the peasants who cultivated the land. This kind of protection racket operated for centuries in societies with mounted warriors.

There are many more similar elite or 'princely' burials further east, particularly in Germany and Bohemia, close to major river routes. The most opulent, like Vix, contain horse-drawn vehicles, probably specially built for the funeral parade. As East End London gangsters are aware, there is nothing better than a team of glossy horses, preferably bedecked with black plumes, pulling a carriage containing your coffin, if you want to make an impression in death. The community will turn out to watch, pay their respects and be reminded who was the boss (and is now).

Something similar happened about 530 BC at the Hallstatt site of Hochdorf, north of Stuttgart. A large tumulus, one of several, was excavated in 1978–79. Inside was an exceptionally well-preserved timber burial chamber. The body proved to be that of a man in his forties and 1.87 m (6 ft) tall – larger than average and well built. Archaeologists become accustomed to seeing material that is familiar, even predictable, but not here. Hochdorf

A four-wheeled chariot or cart depicted on the bronze couch found
in the rich Hochdorf burial in Germany. The chariot is drawn by two stylized horses
and carries a man armed with a shield and a javelin.

was a revelation, a new window on the Iron Age, especially its remarkably modern-looking couch, made of bronze. The dead man lay along it, as if he were taking a post-prandial nap, made comfortable by fine textiles and a badger pelt. He was a glitzy fellow, dressed to kill, wearing a gold torc and bracelets and shoes decorated with gold leaf. He also had a gold belt plate and a dagger in a fine, gilded scabbard. The Hallstatt elite clearly intended to make an impression in death, and presumably he also did so in life.

Decorated panels on the back of the couch showed a four-wheeled cart pulled by a pair of horses, obviously stallions. A stylized human figure stood in each cart, holding a shield and brandishing a javelin. The central panel depicted pairs of men fighting with swords and small shields or bucklers. Was all this a battle scene or perhaps funerary games, of the kind described in the *Iliad,* which provides our earliest documentary account of chariot racing?

The funerary cart itself stood on the opposite side of the chamber. This was an elaborate vehicle, almost certainly made for the funeral, its wheels and yoke still attached, and with decorative harnesses for the horses. The animals themselves had not been sacrificed and left in the grave. However, there were two small horse figurines, cast in bronze, attached to the yoke. Hochdorf provides us with some of the best evidence of the varied ways that horses could be depicted in the mid-sixth century BC.

The grave also contained many vessels for feasting. Nine drinking horns, a local touch, hung from the chamber wall, and cups and bowls were stacked in the cart. The most impressive vessel was a spherical bronze cauldron that originally contained mead. Around the rim stretched three rather docile-looking lions cast in bronze. My friend, the late Professor Noel Gale, analysed the metal used in this vessel in Oxford and identified it as a product of the Laurion mines – the source of the lead and silver that generated much of the wealth of Classical Athens (and a hell-hole for the enslaved miners). Craftsmen may have manufactured the vessel itself in one of Greece's Italian colonies, not far from the Bay of Naples, which was the source of coral, also supplied to the Hochdorf elite.

Another major centre of 'princely' power in the late sixth century BC was the hillfort of Heuneburg, which stands prominently above the Danube in southwestern Germany. Its architecture and use of mud brick feels distinctly Greek in style and is unique in the north. Nearby, to the west, is the cemetery of Hohmichele, where massive barrows were highly visible monuments to the aristocratic families who controlled this section of the Danube. One woman was buried with a dress embroidered with Chinese silk. This exotic rarity was probably more valuable than gold.[18]

In 2010 German archaeologists discovered a further burial ground (the Bettelbühl necropolis) outside the Heuneburg, this time on the floodplain of the Danube, but on the opposite bank of the river.[19] The most important burial here contained a wooden chamber beneath a mound that once stood 4 m (13 ft) high before modern ploughing denuded it. Remarkably, the archaeologists lifted the entire chamber *en bloc* – all 80 tonnes of it – and removed it to a laboratory, where it could be carefully dissected in ideal conditions.

The richer of the two burials inside was that of a woman aged between thirty and forty years, accompanied by a spectacular array of gold or gilded jewelry, some decorated with amber, jet arm-rings and bronze ankle-rings. No horses or funerary carts were included in the burials, but the importance of horses in elite society was reflected in circular (or penannular) mounts formed of opposing boar tusks held by a bronze clasp and with suspended chains and tulip-shaped bells. These jangly objects are thought to have been breast ornaments for horses and are remarkably similar to horse decorations used in Turkmenistan today.

A second burial was poorly preserved. The remains probably of an adult woman lay in the southeast corner of the chamber. Her jewelry was rather basic, but by her feet were very significant objects including a bronze sheet decorated with sun symbols, a design closely paralleled in Slovenia. Along with this were the remains of an iron horse bit and cheek pieces. Detailed forensic examination showed these came from a piece of bronze armour, padded with fur, which was designed to fit over a horse's head. This is the first 'chamfrein' to be found in a Hallstatt culture context. It brings to mind the 'Torrs chamfrein' found in Scotland: a contentious piece of horse decoration, with attached horns with bird's head terminals.[20]

This chamber burial is of paramount importance because, in the wet conditions of the floodplain, the oak and silver fir timbers of the structure were well preserved, so it proved possible, using tree-ring dating, to pinpoint the exact year when the latest timbers were cut and the chamber constructed: 583 BC. So this elite woman pre-dates la Dame de Vix by a century. Objects in the grave also show that the Heuneburg elite had contacts beyond the Alps into Italy, supporting the theory that their mud-brick fortifications were the result of Mediterranean influence.

These south German burials demonstrate the importance of contacts with the Mediterranean for the changing societies of central and northern Europe. Here was a source of new ideas, foodstuffs and prestige goods to enhance the status of the elite. Their contacts, however, ultimately went further east.

LUXURY FROM THE EAST AND FANTASY HORSES

If silk could travel across Eurasia, so could horses. At about the same time as the Hohmichele tombs, the elite horse riders of the eastern steppes and the Altai mountain foothills were also burying their dead in timber chambers, notably at Pazyryk, in southern Siberia. In the cold conditions these chambers froze and became icehouses in which preservation was remarkable: the earliest pile carpets in the world and Chinese silk and felt hangings cosseted the dead, and fine examples of horseflesh accompanied them into the afterlife.

In 1975 I travelled to the USSR in the depths of the winter and the height of the Cold War. In Leningrad I informed my Intourist guide, or minder, that I would not be staying with her group because I wished to spend a couple of days looking at the archaeological collection in the Hermitage. She put a brave face on it and, the next day, off I went, followed, I eventually realized, by a nice young man from the KGB.

At the Hermitage a long queue of visitors – mostly Russians or visitors from the far-flung reaches of the Soviet Empire – were directed towards the Western art galleries. Rembrandt was clearly top of the agenda. I wandered the corridors until I reached a gloomy inner sanctum that held the prehistoric material from Siberia: doors locked, lights out. I approached a squat old lady dressed in black. Her expression was sour. I went into a pantomime, indicating the locked rooms and the absolute necessity of opening them. With my long hair and beard, I suspect she took me for a holy fool. The chatelaine pulled out her keys, opened the doors and switched on the lights.

Wonders were revealed. Here were the treasures of the frozen tombs of the Altai mountains: human bodies, sliced open and stuffed with herbs, their skin covered with swirling, dragon-like tattoos. Their tight-fitting leather suits were studded with gold medallions in the form of mythical beasts. The animal art of the steppes captures the sheer power of panthers, deer and horses. Huge felt hangings and silk carpets covered the walls of the timber burial chamber and life-sized swans of stuffed felt flew above. Most remarkable were the horses buried with their riders. Fantastic beasts, some masked, swathed in technicolour textiles and decked out with antlers carved in wood and covered with gold leaf, these horses resembled fantastical hybrid creatures (Pl. ix). The horses and their sparkling, gilded riders must have made an impressive and terrifying spectacle as they galloped across the steppes.

I saw some of this so-called Scythian art again in 2017, at an exhibition at the British Museum, beautifully displayed but not with the same impact of sheer barbaric splendour as that day in the Hermitage when suddenly the lights were switched on and I was alone with the golden horses of the steppes.

Scythian riders perhaps resting under a tree with their horses, depicted in a fine gold belt buckle, southern Siberia, fourth to third century BC. The tree, from which hangs a quiver, may be an allusion to the tree of life.

In one Pazyryk kurgan, a man had been placed in his grave with ten horses. The exceptional state of preservation allows us to see how incredibly caparisoned these horses were, each with a differently decorated saddle, blanket, bridle and in some cases face mask and headgear. It has been suggested that the reason for the different decorations is that each horse was brought by a different group or clan as a sacrifice for the funeral of the great man. The American academic Gala Argent, after examining the ages and equipment of the horses, had another suggestion: that the horses had different careers as hunters, travelling horses, warhorses or animals used in ceremonials. The older animals, who had received greater schooling, were dressed accordingly, rather like soldiers, clergy or academics who literally wear and display their achievements. As Mark Twain is supposed to have said: 'Clothes make the man. Naked people have little or no influence in society.' The ten horses of Pazyryk had made their mark.

Gala Argent makes the interesting point that only calm, experienced horses could wear the most elaborate paraphernalia we see in the Altai burials, such as mock-antlers and face masks. However, her suggestion that specific images, such as panthers or eagles, literally indicate events in the horse's life, is more contentious. Perhaps these other animals represent the virtues that the horse possessed – or should possess. The decoration and painting of horses on the North American Plains told of spirit qualities or 'medicine'. They increased the animal's power.[21]

Horse skulls from the Arzhan 2 tomb in the Altai mountains. The excellent preservation allows us to appreciate in detail both the variety of horses and their elaborate gear and decoration.

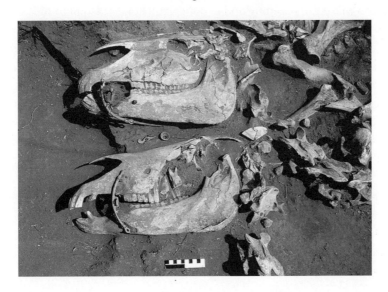

Across the steppes, from the Scythians near the Black Sea to the great Pazyryk burial ground in the Altai mountains, horses appear as hybrid animals, seemingly acquiring the qualities of others – speed, strength, ferocity. These attributes were transferred to the horse riders themselves through tattoos, which even show the influence of Egyptian imagery, such as the deity Bes, who won much favour in the Achaemenid Empire of Persia from the sixth century BC. The image of the griffin, a winged lion with the head of a bird of prey, combined the attributes of the most powerful animals of earth and sky, and was also associated with gold and the sun. A particularly well-preserved carpet (from Pazyryk, Kurgan 5) was made of densely knotted wool and embroidered in silk. Griffins and horse riders process around its border.

Also in the Kurgan 5 burial, a wall-hanging of felt (dated to about 240 BC) shows the seated Scythian goddess Tabiti, deity of the hearth and home, holding a tree of life. An elegant, cloaked rider, with a dashing curled moustache, approaches her mounted on his fine, tall horse (Pl. v). This image of the goddess passing the tree of life to the ruler appears across Eurasia for centuries. The ruler's horse is impressive. Centuries of breeding had produced fast, powerful animals, more specialized for war and raiding than the traditional strong, shaggy ponies. The many sacrificed horses in the frozen Pazyryk graves include ponies, but also animals that reach 15 hands (152 cm/60 in.) and more – magnificent and probably with great endurance. Most are chestnut brown with a golden mane.[22]

The Russian archaeologists noted that the richest chieftain's tomb contained the highest-quality horses. To achieve such fine mounts was not simply a matter of breeding and genetics, the horses also required consistently good grazing and fodder. Much Mediterranean land is grass-poor. The Medes, who lived in modern Iran, found a solution: the leguminous fodder crop lucerne, or alfalfa (*Medicago sativa*; the botanical name derives from the Medes), which has a high protein content, almost double that of grass hay, and can be cut up to six times a year if well irrigated. Almost a tenth of a hectare (about a quarter of an acre) of lucerne can feed three horses and at the same time enrich the soil with nitrogen. Lucerne travelled west. It also went to China, along with what the Chinese called 'Heavenly Horses'.

The Heavenly Horses are coming
Coming from the Far West
They crossed the Flowing Sands
For the barbarians are conquered
The Heavenly Horses are coming[23]

HORSES IN GAUL

We have travelled a long way from Uffington and the English downland. However, the point of this diversion is to emphasize that horses, their equipment, vehicles and the ideas associated with them spread over vast distances, across an entire interconnected continent.

The elite burials of Hallstatt Europe demonstrate the prestige goods, contacts and practices by which Celtic rulers displayed their power. Some of these things trickled down to lower members of society. The idea of cart or chariot burials was also picked up by other groups further north in Europe – for example, in the Marne and Champagne in France.

Archaeological evidence for the spread of elite ideas and prestige goods can be seen in northern France in the burials of the Marne/Aisne valleys in the fifth century BC. We now know from the discoveries of rescue archaeology and aerial survey that this area was densely occupied. The elite were interred in chambers under barrows, along with two-wheeled vehicles, drinking paraphernalia, swords, daggers and jewelry. They also went to their graves suitably provided with foodstuffs, including joints of boar, poultry and frogs' legs. These people were not of such elevated status as the earlier Hallstatt 'princes' further south (there was much less gold), but they had adopted and adapted some of their status symbols – the emblems of power.

Wealthy chariot burials and swords found in the southern Netherlands and north Belgium bring the prestige package even closer to the English Channel, in the Late Bronze Age/Early Iron Age (800–625 BC). There was a dramatic increase in the wealth of material interred in graves, notably beneath the massive barrow (built on top of an earlier one) at Oss, near the mouth of the Meuse/Rhine in the southern Netherlands. Here a chieftain was accompanied by a four-wheeled cart, horse gear, a large bronze vessel and a fine sword with gold inlay that had been deliberately bent into a circle.

The southern Netherlands underwent an interesting process of change at the Late Bronze Age/Early Iron Age transition. A landscape of well-defined fields appeared, suggesting increased concern about territoriality. Houses are numerous but smaller in size than before. A minority of graves of men and women reflected the shared ideas of what the elite should look like: their dress, a warrior ideology with weapons, and most notably the artefacts of drinking and driving. The evidence from shipwrecks – for example, off Dover – suggests that large quantities of bronze artefacts and scrap were moving around Europe in the Bronze Age. It was a continental exchange network along which ideas and cultural information flowed, much of it coming from central Europe and southern Germany. It is not surprising that – via the Low Countries and France – these same ideas and artefacts reached Britain.[24]

BACK IN BRITAIN: CHARIOTS IN YORKSHIRE

The fluid nature of late prehistoric society and the pressures to acquire new land and treasure were, perhaps, similar to those that launched the Vikings and Normans into the desirable south. The acquisition of the horse in the later Bronze Age promoted the warrior ethos and the ability to launch raiding parties, particularly to rustle cattle. The Irish epic *Táin Bó Cúailnge* ('The Cattle Raid of Cooley') emphasizes the role of cattle as wealth on the hoof, and cattle raiding as a path to glory and power.

The bones of domesticated horses, riding equipment, new weapons and transformations of the landscape into controlled territories of fields, tracks, boundaries and enclosure all indicate a context in which the creation of the White Horse makes sense. However, the people who actually made the figure remain elusive. Unlike in earlier periods – the Neolithic and Bronze Age, for example – burials with intact human remains, let alone grave goods, are relatively rare in much of later prehistoric Britain, so it is difficult for archaeologists to study the population physically, and understand its social organization, such as the differences in gender, age and hierarchy, which can be explored in large cemeteries.[25]

Fortunately, there is one area to which we can turn: the chalk wolds of the East Riding of Yorkshire. Here, in the early nineteenth century, excavators dug into a group of unusual barrows that had square-shaped ditches around them. In the richest graves they found men and women buried with dismantled two-wheeled chariots. Some men had weapons, including swords. In the richest woman's grave there was a mirror. Many of the dead were buried with distinctive brooches, rather like safety pins, which held their clothes together. These East Yorkshire sites became known to archaeologists as the Arras culture, after a local farm near Market Weighton. One of the cemeteries, with the notable name of Wetwang Slack (in the local dialect a 'slack' is a dry chalk valley), has currently produced 446 graves, making it the largest Iron Age inhumation cemetery in Britain. At present some 21 chariot or cart burials are known from Britain, all but two were found in Yorkshire.

The chariot burials, not surprisingly, led to the idea that later Iron Age people in northern France had migrated to the Yorkshire Wolds, bringing their funerary practices with them. The invasion hypothesis was encouraged by the name of the East Yorkshire tribe, the Parisi. Modern Paris is named after the local Gallic tribe, the Parisii, so the two tribes on either side of the Channel had the same name.[26]

There were, however, problems with the theory that a band of Gauls deserted the Paris region for the delights of Yorkshire. The British chronology was uncertain; the Yorkshire chariots were dismantled in the grave and had different iron tyres; and most of the brooches found in the graves were distinctly British in design and manufacture. Furthermore, the nearby settlements contained typically British round houses. If the Gauls had come to Yorkshire they did not bring their rectangular houses or their fondness for frogs' legs.

More recently, science has thrown new light on the Arras people and, predictably, given rise to more questions. It now seems that the rite of chariot burial in East Yorkshire took place over a shorter period than previously assumed: probably about 250–200 BC, spread across two or three generations.[27] There have also been new discoveries in France: less spectacular vehicle burials have turned up in rescue excavations during road and railway construction that have criss-crossed northern France. These are comparable in date with the Yorkshire chariots and the tyre technology is also similar. Other insights into the Arras people have come from isotope analysis of their bones and those of animal remains in their graves: horse skulls under the chariot wheels and joints of pork and lamb to accompany the dead. The big question, of course, is did these people come to Yorkshire from somewhere else? The answer seems to be no – they were mostly born close to where they died.

One of the most interesting burials was found on the edge of the village of Wetwang Slack in 2001. A woman lay crouched on her left-hand side, possibly within or under the wooden box of a chariot. By her feet were the remains of two wheels and an elaborate collection of horse gear – but no horses. Food offerings of pig accompanied the woman, and the remains of suckling pig had probably been consumed at a funeral feast. This woman was clearly an important member of her local community. *The Yorkshire Post* (19 February 2002) labelled her a 'Yorkshire Boadicea' – a slight exaggeration. A relatively tall woman (1.71 m/5 feet 7½ in. tall), her life was not without incident – she had suffered a severe injury to her right shoulder, possibly in a heavy fall that also damaged her teeth. She also had some malformation of her face, or distinguishing mark, which set her apart in the eyes of her community. The style of burial and the elaborate mirror which accompanied her reflected her importance, and reminds us of another distinguished woman, the Lady of Vix, who also had physical deformities.[28]

The Arras burials are important because they provide a uniquely large sample of burials, of varying degrees of status and of mixed ages and gender. Those buried with chariots would seem to be the most important people in their cemetery and they include both men and women, probably members of high-status families.

At Wetwang Slack the isotope evidence tells us about their diet – people consumed considerable quantities of animal protein: meat and dairy products. Marine food was notable for its absence, as it is elsewhere at this time. There was, however, no observable difference between the diet of the 'rich' chariot burials and the rest of the population, or between men, women and children. It is possible that the 'rich' ate better cuts of meat, while the poorer survived on stews and cheese. But in the graves, the richer occupants were often provided with the pig forequarters, while the meatier hindquarters may have been shared out at the funeral feasts to all-comers. There was also a fondness for roasted suckling pig in Iron Age Yorkshire. So these prehistoric Britons on the northern chalk wolds ate well and lived in round houses of similar shape and size. Status was important in society, but it was most clearly reflected in the use of horses and chariots, in weapons and dress, and the ability to provide feasts for the community.

As well as the fragmentary remains of chariot equipment at Hagbourne Hill already mentioned (p. 147), evidence of chariot gear has been found in Wales and, in 2001, a uniquely intact chariot burial was discovered in Scotland, at Newbridge, just west of Edinburgh airport. This chariot burial is earlier than the Yorkshire examples (fifth century BC). So the Auld Alliance with the Continent may already have been in operation. Chariot burials continue to emerge, most recently in 2017 in a large cemetery at Pocklington, East Yorkshire. Here the chariot was accompanied by two horses.[29] A burial, unusually within an intact two-wheeled chariot placed in a grave pit, was also found during road construction at Ferry Fryston in West Yorkshire.[30]

To return to the question that launched this chapter. Would the White Horse be an appropriate symbol to carve into the landscape in the Late Bronze Age or Iron Age? Clearly the answer is 'Yes'. Not only was the horse an animal of great practical value – for transport and herding cattle and sheep, and as the companion of warrior raiders – it also played an important role in displaying the status of the elite across Asia, Europe and Britain in life and in death. But could the horse have played an even more complex role in prehistoric society, as an animal with spiritual and mythical meaning, an important actor in the cosmological drama?

CHAPTER TEN

THE SUN HORSE

Dawn leads the sun over the dark sea
She leaps over the hill-top. Behold the sun.

Peter Vansittart, 1981

HERE COMES THE SUN

Prehistoric peoples respected the sun and felt it as a powerful force to which they should appeal with carefully choreographed ritual. The Egyptians, the Inca, the Maya and the Europeans made offerings to the sun and observed its movement. Until recently humans lived in the 'homely Holocene', the geological period since the last glacial. In the Holocene, temperate environments spread across much of the world and were essentially kind to people and the domesticated plants and animals that lived with us. Not all the time, of course. Biblical plagues, droughts, floods and famines occurred with frightening arbitrariness, reminders that humanity needed to placate the gods, to ask 'What have we done wrong?' The question is still relevant. We are now living in the uncertainties of the Anthropocene, the new geological epoch in which humanity has started seriously to impact the Earth, and to throw the climate out of kilter. The old gods have abandoned us. We had better take responsibility ourselves.

In the later Bronze Age in northern Europe, humans were exerting increasing control over their environments – clearing forests, laying out fields, hedges, ditches and routeways, intensifying their agriculture. People were then, like us, subject to the powerful forces of nature, and the unintended consequences of their own actions. For example, in Britain early farmers stripped the trees from the slopes of the Cotswolds, the Downs and the Thames Valley and laid bare the soil for the cultivation of winter wheat. As a result, water ran off the hills, increasing flooding downriver. Near the confluence of the Thames and the Kennet, the low-lying Late Bronze Age landscape of pastoral fields was dotted with hamlets, each with a cluster of thatched round houses. These communities were hit by the floods, their land buried under waterborne silt. No wonder this section of the Thames has produced a harvest of bronze daggers, swords, spears

The Ezelsdorf gold cone, with a detail showing wheels and sun discs. This is
one of a number of spectacular gold hats, decorated with astronomical symbols,
which have survived from the European Bronze Age.

and axes, offerings to the powerful river god. But it was the people themselves who had unleashed the problem. They moved to higher ground. The
problem got worse. Today, the low land is drained; no longer farmed, it is
covered with the giant sheds of a science park powered by windmills.

BRONZE AGE GEOMETERS: GOLD HATS AND SKY DISCS

In a secular world we look to science and ourselves for explanations and
solutions. Prehistoric communities had a different approach. As Klaus
Randsborg of the University of Copenhagen wrote: 'Bronze Age cosmology
is based on the worship and study of the sun.'[1] Colin Renfrew reminds us:
'We have no direct access to the mythic narratives formulated during the
prehistoric past. We do, however, have access to traces of the activities by
which early societies sought to grapple with these realities through their
actions in the world, which have left some material trace.'[2]

Some ancient artefacts speak louder than others. As his first witness, Randsborg calls the model of a sun chariot found in the Trundholm Bog on the island of Zealand (Sjælland) in Denmark (Pl. xi). Black bogs can be sinister places, yet they tenderly caress the sacrifices people placed in them. They preserve human bodies, like that of the man in the Tollund Marsh on Denmark's Jutland peninsula – even his fingernails, the mild pods of his eyelids, and the two-day stubble on his chin. Around his neck is the harsh rope that was used to throttle him. Beauty and atrocity survive in this fragment of humanity. The Trundholm sun chariot is almost as delicate; one of the most famous artefacts to come down to us from north European prehistory, it may represent a Bronze Age ritual from about 1400 BC, in which an image of the sun, on a wheeled vehicle, was drawn by horses through the expectant crowds.

The model gives us a fascinating insight into the elusive beliefs of Bronze Age people. One side of the disc is golden: the glowing sun in daytime, moving from left to right, from east to west. The surface is decorated with concentric circles – sun motifs. The other side of the disc is dark, and, when facing the observer, moves from right to left: the sun's night-time journey. The eyes of the horse also resemble suns. The spoked wheels of the cart suggest the sun in movement. Out of context, symbols such as wheels, discs and spirals can be ambiguous. The Trundholm vehicle leaves little doubt about its intrinsic meaning: the importance of the daily journey of the sun, carried by a horse-drawn chariot, which disappears at night, beneath the earth or the sea, hopefully to reappear the next day.

There are other rare and remarkable objects that support the idea of a Bronze Age sun cult. For example, there are four spectacular conical hats of finely beaten gold that encased an organic lining. These look like the hats of wizards or witches, to be perched on Gandalf or the magi of Hogwarts. The most magnificent specimen, almost 90 cm (35 in.) high, was found at Ezelsdorf in Bavaria, Germany. It resembles a gleaming rocket or a ballistic missile. The hat is decorated with bands of circles and sun wheels. Another from Schifferstadt, Bavaria, is only slightly more modest and has similar decoration.

These fragile survivors give us a glimpse of the rich ritual world of prehistoric Europe, when people invoked the sun at critical times of year. The sun brought light and warmth, and caused life to resurrect, seeds to sprout, corn to turn gold. The Provençal poet René Char (1907–1988) wrote in his poem *Le Paysan* ('The Peasant'):

nul ne croit qu'il meurt pour de bon ...

No man believes that his death is a final end
If after a day's harvesting he sees the sheaves shine
And the grass smile as it pours into his hand.

The sun can also be both harsh and elusive, and it disappears at the end of each day into the netherworld, into the land of the dead and eternal winter.

It is hardly surprising if elite groups, priests or 'time-lords' attempted to predict the passage of the sun and moon, and choreograph the rituals that controlled life and fertility. Such practices may have given power to a priesthood, but they also helped people, who had real concerns and anxieties, who needed reassurance in a tough world. This is not especially contentious; however, arguments arise among researchers about the degree of sophistication of prehistoric cosmology or astronomy in northern Europe. German scholars have argued, for example, that the sun and moon symbols on another golden hat in Berlin correspond to the 'Metonic cycles' discovered by the fifth-century BC Athenian astronomer or geometer Meton, which explain the variation in sun and moon years.[3]

There is general agreement that the sun played a major role in European Bronze Age religion (as it did in contemporary and well-documented Egyptian beliefs). Stonehenge, in its developed form, is the obvious example of a monument created as the setting for the enactment of ritual theatre at the sun's midwinter and midsummer solstices. However, the suggestion that northern barbarians might have been ahead of the Greeks in the observation of the skies is disputed. Societies that have sophisticated astronomical systems, such as the Babylonians, the Maya and the Greeks, also have systems of writing. In the second millennium BC, northern Europeans remained doggedly illiterate.

Such arguments have persisted about another unique survival, a discovery made in 1999, unfortunately dug up by illegal metal detectorists, in Saxony-Anhalt, Germany. After the Berlin Wall came down, black-marketeers in the West equipped people in East Germany with metal detectors and set them loose across promising archaeological areas in search of loot. They could not have predicted the discovery of the Nebra sky disc, a unique circular tin-bronze object inlaid with gold images of the sun, moon, stars and a curving arc, possibly representing a ship (Pl. x). The sky disc could have disappeared into the dark underworld of illegal antiquities had it not been for the efforts of the director of the regional museum, Dr Harald Meller. In an operation that resembled the sting in a Hollywood movie, he tracked down the looters and arranged to meet them at a Swiss hotel. The police, meanwhile, staked out the hotel, so when the bad guy pulled the disc out from under his shirt, wrapped in a towel, they pounced and seized him, the disc and his glamorous blonde companion.

It is a good story, yet Dr Meller wanted to do more than catch the villains and save the sky disc. Importantly, he also discovered where the disc had originally been buried, along with a cache of swords, axes and bracelets. For such cult objects, their location, in a specific landscape, can be the key to understanding. At Nebra the prehistoric worshippers had placed the disc and other offerings in a pit, inside an enclosure that encircled a hilltop in Germany: the Mittelberg. This high place overlooked land that contained up to a thousand burial mounds. In the distance, 80 km (50 miles) to the northwest, the Brocken, the highest peak in the Harz Mountains, is visible. From the Mittelberg enclosure the sun can be observed setting behind the mountain at the solstices. It seems that prehistoric geometers were using the same techniques as Meton – locating a fixed point on the horizon to establish the positioning of the sun – almost a thousand years earlier than the Classical Greeks, about 1600 BC. The midwinter and summer solstices loomed large in the minds of prehistoric people and were probably vital to the calendar and rituals of the farming year.

Other remarkable claims have been made for the Nebra sky disc: that it was a portable device recording the precise angle between the solstices at this particular place, and that the seven gold stars represent the Pleiades, a star group recorded in ancient Mesopotamia, Egypt and Greece, and in the mythology of many cultures around the world. Furthermore, could the golden curved strip on the disc represent a solar boat or barge? The solar boat in Egyptian mythology carried the sun god Ra on his nightly voyage and may have preceded the horse-drawn chariot as the means of mythological transport.[4] The Nebra people also had wide-ranging contacts: some of the metal they used came from Cornwall.

NORTHERN IMAGES

It may seem speculative to build a Bronze Age cosmology and sun cults on the basis of a few, rare objects. However, there is more widespread evidence in carvings found widely in Europe where there are suitably hard rocks: in the Alps, northwest Spain, Norway, Sweden and Britain – for example, on Ilkley Moor in Yorkshire.

I first became aware of Scandinavian rock art, with its images of ships and suns, when digging in Orkney in 1967 and 1968 with Peter Gelling of Birmingham University. Dr Gelling was not a great excavator (I learnt what *not* to do), but he was a brilliant linguist, speaking at least a dozen languages fluently or competently, including a language of ancient Mesopotamia (Akkadian), ancient Greek, Latin, Russian and the Scandinavian languages, so he was very familiar with the religion and mythology of the ancient and medieval world. During the long summer daylight of Orkney, when the sun disappears so briefly, Gelling told me that he was trying to get a book published on Scandinavian rock engravings. His approach to comparative religion and mythology was out of fashion at the time and his prospective publishers would only go ahead if Professor Christopher Hawkes, one of the triumvirate of powerful British prehistorians (see p. 92), agreed to write a foreword to the book. Hawkes did this and the book was eventually published, entitled *The Chariot of the Sun and Other Rites and Symbols of the Northern Bronze Age*. Hawkes's imprimatur bestowed a degree of academic respectability.

While anthropologists took to the field to study the realities and complexities of religion, many British and American prehistorians either lost interest in the subject or became drily descriptive. Gelling's *Chariot of the Sun*, in spite of introducing the fascinating Scandinavian rock art to an English-speaking audience, was largely ignored. One distinguished prehistorian, Richard Bradley, who went on to analyse rock art rigorously, in various landscape contexts, did at least notice the book but accused Gelling's study of being 'anachronistic' – in other words he and his co-author, Hilda Ellis Davidson, had used the evidence of later Norse mythology to interpret the prehistoric symbols. Non-prehistorians remained more attached to the study and continuity of religious ideas, such as solar symbolism, notably the historian Ronald Hutton[5] and archaeologist Miranda Aldhouse-Green, who has written prodigiously about the sun cult in the Romano-Celtic world.[6] In the wider world the subject continued to inspire writers and artists.

The title of this chapter comes from one of my favourite childhood authors. At the age of nine, for two or three years, I was obsessed by historical novels, and there were some excellent authors at that time: Geoffrey Trease, Henry Treece, Ronald Syme, Ian Serraillier and, not least, Rosemary Sutcliff. Sutcliff spent her life in a wheelchair, translating her love of history and mythology into books for children (though many adults enjoy her clear, poetic prose, and her books are certainly not childish). She gained inspiration from Sir James Frazer's *The Golden Bough*, particularly the idea of the king sacrificing himself for his people.[7] This trope reoccurs in one of her later novels, *Sun Horse, Moon Horse*, which tells the story, with a mythical simplicity, of the carving of the Uffington White Horse.[8]

The premise of the story is highly unlikely, based on theories found in T. C. Lethbridge's book *Witches*.[9] Lethbridge was a 'conventional' Cambridge archaeologist who, in the 1960s, became more and more eccentric in his views. (His followers will condemn me as a typically close-minded archaeologist.) Notably, Lethbridge was an avid promoter of dowsing. He also believed that Boudica's East Anglian tribe, the Iceni, once lived on the North Wessex Downs, giving their name to the Icknield Way, and built the hillfort of Uffington Castle. He claimed that the tribal name *Iceni*, meant 'Horse People' (unlikely) and that they were pushed out by the incoming Atrebates. The Iceni then headed north into southeast Scotland and became the Epidii (which does mean 'People of the Horse', from the British *epo-s* – 'horse').[10]

Rosemary Sutcliff concocted a compelling story out of all this. Lubrin Dhu, the son of an Iceni chieftain killed in the battle with the Atrebates, is an artist who sketches the horses galloping on the Downs. The victorious Atrebatic chieftain agrees to allow the Iceni to leave with their horses (once they have refurbished the hillfort) providing Lubrin Dhu creates a giant figure of a white horse on the downland scarp – a symbol of the sun and moon gods. Lubrin Dhu is sacrificed on completion of his work, to invest the image with great power.

As I said, the story is historically dubious. Nevertheless, Sutcliff describes beautifully the motivation of the artist and the practical way he creates the large White Horse image by scaling up a small drawing (exactly how I painted a large mural myself many years ago, by placing a grid over a small drawing and then scaling up about twenty times on the wall). She evokes the flight of swallows and how they convey the image of speed and elegance to the artist. She sees the White Horse image as an abstract masterpiece, capturing the essence of the Sky Horse, galloping at speed across the heavens.

This is a different approach from that of some archaeologists. For example, Grahame Clark said that similar horse images on British coins 'took the form of devolution or degeneration' from the prototype stater of Philip II of Macedon (Alexander's father), as did Stuart Piggott (see p. 90).[11] In other words, the Britons and Gauls produced horse images that were a primitive form of the naturalistic Greek originals. An alternative view is that the best of these depictions of horses created by northern 'barbarians' show an imaginative design capability far more interesting than the literal, prosaic imagery of the Macedonian Greek coins. Rosemary Sutcliff got it right when she saw the White Horse as a deliberate, considered design, not a result of sloppiness, accidental erosion or a process of degeneration.

We can see the brilliance of prehistoric artists in other animal designs. The two, beaked flagons from Basse-Yutz in northeastern France, made between the mid-fifth and early fourth centuries BC, convey the skill, elegance and humour of Celtic artists. The style of the bronze flagons is Etruscan and the vessels are inlaid with Italian coral, which the northerners believed warded off evil. On the end of the spout, where liquid would emerge, sits a perky little duck. The handle is made in the form of a stylized wolf (itself not unlike the White Horse), whose elongated body and spirals on the shoulder convey speed and power. The wolf bears a distinct resemblance to the animals in the art of the steppes. We cannot be sure how this style travelled west, but Greek traders in the Black Sea may have helped to distribute and popularize it.[12]

THINKING ALOUD: DISCOVERING THE PREHISTORIC MIND

In the 1960s and 1970s 'New Archaeology' largely ignored the study of religion, ritual, symbolism and myth. It was not until later in the twentieth century that academic fashion moved again. What is known as 'cognitive archaeology' encompasses the study of the human mind, and how people think and express themselves through the symbolism of physical objects, natural places and artefacts.[13]

This approach can be seen to advantage in the recent research project at Stonehenge, where Mike Parker Pearson and his colleagues have investigated how the land of the living is connected to the place of the dead along the meandering River Avon. Remarkably, their discoveries seem to fit their original concept – an anachronistic one, perhaps – derived from the study of contemporary megalithic monuments in Madagascar, where the permanence of stone is connected with the ancestors.[14]

Joshua Pollard of the University of Southampton is a member of the Stonehenge team. He recently turned his attention to the Uffington White Horse, arguing that its creators located it specifically to be seen as the

An Iron Age silver coin from Drayton (Hampshire), depicting a horse beneath a crescent or partially eclipsed moon, with a solar disc beneath. Though not naturalistic, such designs show an imaginative design capability.

horse that drew the sun across the sky.[15] He emphasizes the uniqueness of the White Horse geoglyph – a very different beast in scale and character from the abstract, non-figurative images found in considerable numbers in the Bronze Age rock art of upland Britain. This lack of comparanda has made it difficult to 'accommodate' the White Horse within accounts of later prehistory and so it has tended to be marginalized – a slight embarrassment, often ignored in narratives of prehistoric Britain and Europe.

Recently, European rock art has attracted a plethora of researchers.[16] Peter Gelling would be delighted. From Scotland and northern England to Sweden, Galicia and the Alps there are abstract symbols carved or pecked into hard rock. The dates of the carving vary, but much of it belongs to the Early Bronze Age. The meaning of one of the commonest signs, the so-called cup and ring mark, is not transparent unless you remain a believer in the Mother Goddess, as had been strongly advocated by the archaeologist Marija Gimbutas. The human imagination is almost infinite and the meaning of the cup and ring marks, a relatively simple circle with a central hollow, can vary depending upon the context: where they occur in the landscape, who is looking at them and their association with other images.

Similar circular marks occur on rocks in Amazonia where they carry messages about incest taboos, a complex set of ideas that no prehistorian could unravel from the marks alone.[17] A study of indigenous groups in northwest Amazonia (Colombia and Brazil) provided a fascinating insight into their complex religion, cosmology and ethics. These people see the sun as the primary creator of life, and one of their most important myths tells how the Sun violated his young daughter. Marks on the rocks signify this mythical act. A witness to this shocking event blew his trumpet as a warning. Spirals carved into rock indicate where he put the trumpet. Other abstract signs, some painted, others carved into rock, indicate the dwelling places of the Master of Animals (who can also be a sexual predator). Such signs are also clustered to create specific meanings, and the meanings can change over time as myths, stories and ideas adapt.[18] Amazonian rock art is a warning against over-simple explanations. We might, for that matter, consider the multiple meanings of the cross in our own society, which has decorated both the shield of the holy warriors in ruthless pursuit of infidels and the ambulance bringing relief to the injured.

In different parts of Europe the rock carvings emphasize other images: stags in Galicia (northwest Spain); cattle with huge horns pulling ploughs, and also daggers and halberds, on Monte Bégo, at over 2,000 m (6,560 ft) high in the Maritime Alps in France. There are possible sun-worshippers with exaggerated, outstretched hands and fingers in Val Camonica, Italy.

In Sweden, as well as abstract images there are 'whole fleets' of ships (in Richard Bradley's words), horses, phallic humans and life-sized 'footprints'. Bradley has approached the question of Bronze Age iconography by comparing Scandinavian rock art with the images engraved on bronze razors found mainly in Denmark.[19] These images, he suggests, depict the path of the sun, across the sky in daytime and beneath the sea at night. Horses draw the sun from left to right, representing daytime; ships complete the night-time voyage from right to left. This imagery occurs both in the rock art and on the metal razors, suggesting that there were links to the north from central Europe, and even Egypt and Mesopotamia, which influenced the northern ideas of cosmology throughout the Bronze Age.

Razors and rocks are very different, and they occur in very different places. The razors were placed in cremation burials, but not actually burnt in the pyre. Were they objects perhaps given to young men to remind them of important truths at an initiation rite?[20] What the razors and rocks do reveal is the ubiquity of the sun imagery, both on small personal items and out in the landscape. We also know that there was a widespread trade in Bronze Age textiles. Unfortunately, only fragments now survive in Europe. Was this also a means of conveying imagery and ideas, as certainly was the case in the prehistoric steppes and, later, in medieval Christendom?

Clearly, there was no single, straightforward iconography across Europe, though there were common elements. The rock art was often positioned near routeways – tracks taken by herders or wild animals – in high places, overlooking the land or sea, in locations relating both to the land of the living and the land of the dead. Some rock art is found in situations that may have been relatively open and public; other images are difficult to access, perhaps meant to be seen only by initiates where arcane knowledge is the privilege of the few. Such locations are also characteristic of the sites where Neolithic stone axes were quarried – for example, the precipitous ledges of Pike O'Stickle in Langdale, Cumbria.

At least, for archaeologists, there is plenty of prehistoric rock art to analyse and discuss. Even the great images of Nazca in Peru occur in numbers. Rock art is also practised, or was until recently, by many traditional communities – for example, in Australia, South Africa and the Americas. Ethnologists have been able to gather information about the images and locations from local witnesses. Writing-on-Stone, Alberta, Canada, is a place of weirdly shaped landforms, cliffs and canyons, and, as its name implies, has extensive rock art, much of it of a 'biographical' nature, recording specific events. In particular, it demonstrates the

Scandinavian rock art from Brastad, in Sweden, depicting abstract
human and animal figures and wheel/sun symbols, ships and footprints.

changing methods of warfare.[21] First, there are pedestrian warriors armed
with clubs and lances and carrying shields in hand-to-hand combat.
Then horses appear, protected by armour at a time when guns were rarely
available. Subsequently (in the early 1800s), armour and shields were
abandoned, and more varied weapons appear, including rifles and steel
hatchets.[22] One complex scene shows eighty horses, represented by the
head and neck only, which may indicate the tally of horses captured by
one man.

As societies developed writing, they inscribed their myths for posterity.
The spread of the horse from the steppes into Europe and also eastwards
into the Indian subcontinent is often associated with expansions of Indo-
European languages and mythology. Their pursuit can lead into quagmires.
I particularly like Hellenist scholar M. L. West's description: 'the unreada-
ble in pursuit of the unpronounceable'. However, in spite of the mists that
blur the vistas of the past, he agrees that 'There is extensive evidence for
the recognition of the Sun as a deity among Indo-European peoples.'[23]

Across Eurasia, Indo-European languages use related words for the sun (English): *Sonne* (German), *Sol* (Latin), *súil* (Irish). The Irish word also means 'eye', and a common trope is that the sun is all-seeing, the watcher who supervises justice. As late as the nineteenth century, old men in the Western Isles sang a Scots Gaelic song that addressed the sun as *sùil Dhe mhoir* ('eye of great God'), an epithet that occurs in ancient Rome, Armenia and India.

The ancient Greek playwright Aristophanes recalled a myth which told how sight was given to living creatures in imitation of 'the wheel of the sun'. The concept of the solar wheel again occurs in the Indian Rigveda, and the wheel is drawn by a horse whose name means 'swift'. In the Rigveda (7.63.2) we are told:

> Up goes the arouser of peoples, the great waving banner of Sūrya
> To set rolling the common wheel that Etaśa conveys, yoked in harness[24]

In the Avesta (the sacred book of Iran) a formulaic epithet is used for the sun: 'possessing swift horses'. Herodotus tells us that the Massagetae (a nomadic tribe of the steppes, east of the Caspian Sea) worshipped only the sun and sacrificed the swiftest horses to him, and the Roman historian Tacitus recounts a story that he heard from the Baltic region (in *Germania*, 45): when the sun rose the sound was audible and the outlines of horses and the rays from the god's head were visible.

ON WHITE HORSE HILL: AN UNFOLDING DRAMA

White Horse Hill is a very specific place; however, we can see similarities to sacred sites elsewhere. It is a dramatic landform within a gentle rolling landscape that otherwise lacks many distinctive features. It also provides a high point that overlooks the valley below and the hills beyond. The chalk scarp falls steeply to the northwest and enfolds the deep combe, the natural amphitheatre of the Manger. Dragon Hill alongside is a distinctive, artificial-looking platform that resembles Silbury Hill, the great prehistoric mound near Avebury. At the open mouth of the Manger water pours out, now hidden among the scrub and neglected fallen timber in Woolstone Wells.

It is easy to see this landscape in terms of the human body: smooth, curved, sensuous. The artist Eric Ravilious perceived the sweep of the land around the Manger as a person lying on their side. In 1994, artist Chris Hoggett painted this landscape. He said: 'I became subliminally aware of some underlying form just beneath the surface of the land, and was suddenly jolted into a realm which could not have been anticipated – where only Gods and Goddesses reigned. I empathized so closely I now glimpsed parts of something so monstrous it caused a sharp intake of breath.'[25]

White Horse Hill is a liminal place: you feel that you are at the boundary of the sky and earth. Woolstone Wells, which may have been more prominent in the past, is a portal where water emerges from the underworld, cold and dark beneath the chalk. On the hilltop above, you feel and hear the wind, and the song of skylarks. The light continuously changes as clouds skim across the sky. It is a landscape of 'terrific animation', a 'fusion of nature and artificial design'.[26]

This is the kind of high place that attracts people to create shrines and bury their dead. From the hilltop, you can survey the earth below. And from below, the scarp provides a stage, a setting for monuments silhouetted against the sky. In this way, the landscape memorializes the living and the dead, and lends itself to stories and myths. It is not only a memory of the past but also a place where people continue to engage with the land, to reimagine both the past and the future.

So why did people around three thousand years ago create the White Horse image in this place? In purely visual terms the position is not ideal. Here, the curve of the scarp both foreshortens the image for the viewer below and hides it from the northeast. Our excavations into the horse's body showed that the image was originally slightly more substantial and that it was tilted into a more upright position in relation to the scarp slope, so the image would have been clearer to an observer down in the Vale to the northeast, in the Manger or on Dragon Hill. But its position was still not ideal if the aim was merely to display some tribal banner, some sign to visitors announcing the presence of the People of the Horse. Recent viewshed analysis suggests that there are a number of alternative positions on the nearby chalk scarp that would provide better visibility for the distant viewer, if the aim of the makers was simply to announce their presence.[27]

The excavation also showed that the unusual design that we see today has not changed substantially over time. The fragmented limbs, the 'violent foreshortenings' noted by Paul Nash (see p. 256), the running posture and head tilted downwards convey a sense of movement, of speed. But the design does not maximize visibility. More recently created horse figures are static, even hieratic. The Westbury Horse is a much less exciting design, like a child's hobby horse, but it is certainly unavoidably visible. Ravilious found it easier to incorporate it as an icon into his paintings.

Joshua Pollard has made the valid point that visibility, for a group symbol or banner, was not the primary concern of the Uffington White Horse designers. Nevertheless, they paid great attention to the details of the local topography. We have seen how the earliest human 'artists', for example, at the Chauvet Cave and Lascaux, were remarkably sensitive to the medium of the rock, integrating natural swellings and cracks to enliven their images, using curving, smooth surfaces as panels or screens for impressive panoramas of herds of horses and prides of lions. At Stonehenge, pilgrims approaching along the Avenue (as unfortunately few visitors do today) would have seen the great sarsen stones literally rise before them above the horizon, to provide a dramatic theatre for the solstice sun. Across Britain and Europe, sites were carefully chosen for their potential involvement in cosmological dramas.

At White Horse Hill, some prehistoric dramaturges were sensitive to the possibilities of the landscape. Imagine that the sun horse – like the Trundholm model – loomed large in their sense of the universe. The location of their carving, on the brow of the hill, was such that for a viewer standing in the mouth of the Manger, near where the spring emerges, the sun rose above the top of Dragon Hill, out of which the Horse appears to leap. At midwinter the sun rolls low across the brow of the hill, and just above the body of the running Horse. The hill figure seems to be carefully placed to exploit this solar choreography, and designed to convey movement to the west, as if Horse and sun are moving together in partnership. So the Horse is more than a static symbol. Neither is the land itself a mere backdrop or blank canvas. As the dawn light scans across the downland it enhances the Bronze Age round barrow, then the Neolithic long barrow, just southwest of the Horse's head. It reminds us that this is an ancient land of ancestors. The dead are always with us. It also illuminates the ramparts of Uffington Castle and a further barrow near the Ridgeway, which itself appears to track the sunlight. Beyond is the megalithic tomb of Wayland's Smithy. Bronze Age horse gear was found buried by this Neolithic tomb, perhaps an indicator of its link to the White Horse in the minds of those who inhabited this land.

At the right time, in the right conditions, the White Horse, the sun and the landscape together create an animated cosmological drama. Remarkably, we can still witness it today.

CHAPTER ELEVEN

CHANGING HORSES: SURVIVAL IN DIFFICULT TIMES

But the past was another country. In the British case indeed,
the past was a great many countries.

Linda Colley, 2010

THE VULNERABLE PAST

The scientific dating of the White Horse of Uffington confirms that, give or take a few centuries, the hill figure has existed for three thousand years. Bill Bryson, England's favourite American commentator, made the valid point:

Consider the famous White Horse of Uffington, one of the many ancient chalk figures commanding hillsides in the extraordinary country of yours ... it seems to me what is truly remarkable about the White Horse is not that people some time in an immensely ancient past took the trouble to cut it into the hillside – though that is extraordinary enough, goodness knows – but that continuously for around twenty centuries others have made the effort to maintain it.... The White Horse has been preserved simply because people like it. I think that's splendid.[1]

There are, of course, older images in the world, although the Uffington White Horse is England's only surviving ancient chalk figure. The delicate horses in the Chauvet Cave in France are 30,000 years old, but they remained lost for millennia, forgotten in the dark, securely cocooned in a stable temperature until French speleologists crawled into their hidden world. At Pazyryk, in the Altai mountains, the glowing textiles survived because their grave-chambers were transformed into icehouses. The geoglyphs of Nazca inscribe the surface of a desert in Peru, where conditions are the closest Earth comes to replicating those on the Moon or on Mars.

The footprints of Neil Armstrong, impressed into the dust of the Moon, should remain there indefinitely unless some thoughtless human drives a moon-buggy over them or builds a lunar golf course.

The Uffington Horse is unique because it requires continual, conscious care. It is high maintenance. Every generation, for a hundred generations, has had to weed and clean and repair the image to keep it pristine and intact. During its lifetime the Horse has occupied a steep slope, mostly surrounded by grassland. It is subject to constant erosion and deposition: through rain, frost, wind and gravity. Sheep wander across it depositing their dung, adding to the silt that accumulates naturally, creating a mulch for seeds. Without human care the Horse image would disappear in a few decades. If this happened, a later generation, who still remembered the Horse's presence, could resurrect the image because the Horse was created by digging and filling a trench, not by simply removing the turf to expose chalk; the image is recoverable, like any buried archaeological feature. But out of sight and out of mind: how long would the memory last?

Although the steep location promotes erosion it has one definite advantage: the ground does not lend itself to ploughing. The great circle at Stonehenge survives because it stands in a relatively remote area between settlements such as Amesbury and Salisbury. The stones were too big for a few local farmers to shift. Unfortunately, many of the more fragile surrounding monuments, such as the great avenue known as the Cursus, have succumbed to the plough. The best-preserved area for archaeology on Salisbury Plain is the land restricted to the use of the British Army. Here it is still possible to walk along the lanes of Romano-British villages, between the platforms where houses stood over sixteen hundred years ago. These remain unscoured by the plough, like the White Horse itself.

In contrast, across the Thames Valley at Stanton Harcourt, the henge known as Devil's Quoits was ploughed almost flat, its stones pushed over and buried. In spite of the site's name, its destruction was probably carried out in the cause of agriculture rather than because of Christian disapproval. The henge stood on valuable flat, fertile land. A few miles downriver, below Oxford, the name Barrow Hills records an impressive Neolithic and Bronze Age barrow cemetery. The place name is Old English, so the burial mounds must have been prominent in the landscape until the seventh or eighth centuries AD. In the Middle Ages, the land at Barrow Hills belonged to Abingdon Abbey (which also held Uffington), a wealthy monastery not shy of expanding its coffers. The barrows were gradually ploughed flat, to reappear as dark circles in the barley crop on aerial photographs taken in the 1950s. Now this land, and the Iron Age farm, Romano-British villa and

Anglo-Saxon hamlet that once stood in the neighbouring field, have disappeared beneath the expanding suburbs of Abingdon.

People do not often let the past get in the way of the present. So why did the White Horse buck the trend?

A STORY OF SURVIVAL

The White Horse has certainly not survived because the people of Uffington or Woolstone retained the pagan beliefs of their ancestors. On the contrary, the past two thousand to three thousand years have seen massive changes. Settlements have moved like pawns on a chessboard. The tongues of their occupants and their masters have switched between Celtic, Latin, Old English, Norman French, the dialects of Berkshire and estuarine English, and beliefs have shifted from Paganism to Puritanism, from Anglicanism to atheism. We might well ask: why did local people not regard the Horse as an image of heathendom and, at best, neglect it, or even indulge in one of the occasional bouts of iconoclasm that inflict the righteous? Many local churches were scoured by the pure of heart. The English destroyed the works of medieval Christendom with all the enthusiasm of the Taliban.[2]

So the Horse's survival is remarkable, and I cannot pretend to fully explain it. Certainly there were once other geoglyphs along the English scarplands – we know of about sixty that have disappeared. The Red Horse of Tysoe existed on the ironstone slopes of Warwickshire in the seventeenth century, but its age remains uncertain. Only the White Horse of Uffington is of proven antiquity.

Part of the explanation for its survival must be the malleability of its meaning: a flexible icon for constantly changing times. The weeding and scouring of the Horse is a communal activity; it requires cooperation, and cooperation that requires people subscribe to a particular story – a myth, a belief, a feeling of loyalty, a sense of identity – something that brings them together. Its survival must represent the Horse's adaptability to contemporary values. It may communicate a message, but the message changes. As Graham Greene said: 'The imagination has its own geography which alters with the centuries.'[3]

'Public Works' like the White Horse, the nearby hillforts and the linear boundaries need a community willing to come together first to create and then to maintain them. During much of the past, on the Downs and in the Vale, these communities remain frustratingly elusive to archaeologists. The first farmers, five thousand to six thousand years ago, created monuments such as causewayed enclosures like Windmill Hill above Avebury, or megalithic tombs such as West Kennet and Wayland's Smithy, places where relatively mobile and scattered groups came together. But where they lived remains difficult to pinpoint. In recent years archaeologists have begun to see the Middle Bronze Age as the time of a new farming revolution, with fields, trackways and more permanent settlements. This may be an oversimplification, as the more we find out, the more complicated the picture becomes. There is enormous variation in different regions: sometimes settlements are invisible to archaeologists and at others they shift with frustrating frequency.

In terms of conventional or even old-fashioned history, the Horse witnessed the presence of prehistoric Britons (Celts if you like), Romans, Anglo-Saxons, Danes and Normans. Some of these people are visible to archaeologists when they lived in substantial buildings like Roman villas, or buried their dead in rich cemeteries like the Anglo-Saxons. They can also fade into the mist. Nevertheless, the land continued to be farmed, ditches were cleared and woodland coppiced. The grass grew and sheep grazed. Inevitably, there was a calendar of agricultural activities, seasonal feasts, social and religious obligations. People needed to come together: to maintain alliances and friendships, to help each other in difficult times, to exchange animals and seeds, to match-make and bring together sons and daughters. On the Downs, and even in the Vale, settlements were often not permanent, moving around relatively often. But community obligation remained, regardless of where people lay their heads. This must partly explain the survival of the White Horse. In a constantly changing world, people still needed to understand or forge links with their past, to remind themselves that this land was their land. They needed to maintain the habits of mutual support with their neighbours.

Rudyard Kipling (1865–1936) tried to convey this sense of continuity, the age of the occupied landscape and the presence of the past in his book *Puck of Pook's Hill*[4] set on the southern downland. T. S. Eliot wrote that Kipling aimed 'to give at once a sense of the antiquity of England, of the number of generations who have laboured the soil and in turn been buried beneath it, and of the contemporaneity of the past'.[5]

> 'Let's see,' he said at last. 'It must have been some few years later – a year or two before the Conquest, I think – that I came back to Pook's Hill here, and one evening I heard old Hobden talking about Weland's Ford.'
> 'If you mean old Hobden the hedger, he's only seventy two....'
> 'You're quite right!' Puck replied. 'I meant old Hobden's ninth great-grandfather. He was a free man and burned charcoal hereabouts.'

Kipling tells us that – regardless of who was in charge – a Roman governor, a Saxon thegn or a Norman lord – generations of anonymous country dwellers cared for the land. Their feet trod the dirt; their hands turned the soil and filled the pails with milk. Like contemporary government ministers, all rulers are here today and gone tomorrow. Not so the ordinary folk – according to Kipling.

Unfortunately, the question of continuity is not quite as straightforward as this. The more we reveal the shifting kaleidoscope of settlement and the complexities of genetics, the more difficult, and intriguing, the questions become, which does not make it any easier to explain the survival of the White Horse.

Nevertheless, the figure meant something. It was important to the community's sense of identity. The work of scouring may have been done willingly; alternatively, was it a task required by the masters, encouraged by religious leaders, made palatable by supplies of drink and the kind of communal gathering and sense of fellowship that archaeologists believe took place during the past six thousand years at causewayed enclosures, henges, midden sites and hillforts?

AGES IN TRANSITION

The White Horse was made at a time of great change on the Downs and the surrounding area. In the conventional terms of the Three Age system used by prehistorians, the Bronze Age was giving way to the Iron Age. This was not an overnight event. The Three Ages are an archaeological construct or model, originally invented to provide some logic for frustrated museum curators sorting artefacts whose date was not known. When we tackle the realities of the landscape, this three-act play of stone, bronze and iron begins to blur. The scenes overlap and reality is more confusing than the simple model of prehistory. For example, a recent excavation at Hartshill Copse, Upper Bucklebury in Berkshire, on the north side of the Kennet Valley, revealed two 'Bronze Age' round houses dating to about the tenth century BC. Yet the archaeologists found clear evidence for ironworking, smelting and blacksmithing, with one of the houses used as a workshop.[6] This is the earliest-known ironworking site in Britain, a century or more before the conventional end of the Bronze Age. Unfortunately, none of the actual iron products survived.

The earliest dated iron object we have is an iron socketed axe dredged out of the Thames at Buscot, just across the Vale from the White Horse. As the axe had been left in the river mud, part of its wooden handle had survived and provided a radiocarbon date of 790–410 BC. Once iron technology caught on in Britain the pathways of metallurgy shifted, no longer reliant on long-distance contacts for raw materials. Hartshill Copse had iron ores on its doorstep. Sources were common in Britain, so, once they had the knack, British communities, or at least their specialists, could make tools and weapons without needing traders and middlemen.

It seems likely that the Thames Valley was in the forefront of innovations in metallurgy because of contacts with northern France and the Low Countries. Below Hartshill Copse is one of the greatest concentrations of Late Bronze Age settlements and fields in the region, on the flat lands where the River Kennet meets the Thames near Reading. Their flourishing agricultural economy and, arguably, textile production could account for the thriving cross-Channel contact, which stimulated new ideas, technological development and even practices like chariot burial.

THE AXES OF TOWER HILL

During the White Horse project I received a phone call from the owner of the neighbouring estate, Erik Penser. He told me that some interesting objects had recently been found on his land and asked whether I would like to take a look at them. I arrived at the hamlet of Compton Beauchamp one snowy Sunday morning. The picturesque church of St Swithun – a simple chalk building with a thirteenth-century tower – stands alongside a medieval spring-fed moat that surrounds the rather grand Compton House. I crossed the bridge over the moat. Erik Penser emerged and we went into a large, warm kitchen. The table was set with a gleaming array of Bronze Age axes. They looked brand new – which in a sense they were.

Erik introduced me to Liz Philips, a local schoolteacher, who, he explained, had found the axes while walking her dog over Tower Hill, a high point of the nearby downland. It seemed that the ploughman, in order to incorporate straw stubble into the shallow soil, had ploughed deeper than normal. She had followed the prominent tractor tracks up the hill believing (wrongly) that they indicated the footpath, and, fortuitously, had found herself in the middle of a huge arable field where she spotted the coppery-green axes gleaming in the chalky soil.

As context is everything in archaeology (well, almost everything), I suggested we brave the wintry weather and head towards the find-spot. The top of Tower Hill was certainly bleak – completely open and exposed, the wind sliced across the ploughed field, driving the scattered snowflakes into the furrows. This was as wuthering as it gets in southern England. Fortunately, Liz quickly located the slight disturbance in the ground where she had pulled out the axes. We ran a metal detector over the spot; it went berserk. Clearly there was more to be found. A few minutes of careful trow-elling revealed more axes and other, stranger objects, probably parts of horse harnesses, stacked within a shallow pit.

Museums in Britain are full of Bronze Age metalwork. What made Tower Hill particularly exciting was that here the objects were in situ: they lay where they had been buried about 2,800 years ago. Over the next few weeks we investigated the site more carefully. Excavation uncovered the rest of the hoard, which consisted of ninety-two pieces of metalwork, including twenty-two complete socketed axes, ornaments, scrap and casting debris that had been freshly made. Some of the axes were unfin-ished. They had been taken out of their moulds but not sharpened, so the blades were still rough. The axes, in this unfinished condition, had been placed in a pit by the doorway of a round house. Our trenches revealed that Tower Hill was home to a Late Bronze Age farming settlement, covering about 4 hectares (10 acres), set in open country. The settlement was short-lived and was occupied during the eighth century BC.

Tower Hill illustrates some of the problems of understanding this period. Decades of aerial photography and field survey had failed to locate the settlement because the house remains were slight: just postholes with no enclosure ditches. The pottery was also friable and broke up in

The Tower Hill hoard of bronze (copper alloy) axes, some fresh from the mould and unsharpened, as well as rings and casting debris.

the topsoil. Fortunately, Liz Philips happened to come across the hoard shortly after it had been exposed by the plough. The land was also overlain by Romano-British fields, which served to mask the traces of the earlier settlement. We recruited a local metal-detecting club to search extensively across Tower Hill in case there were further bronze hoards, but none turned up. A scatter of worn Roman coins and abraded pottery showed that the fields had been manured and rubbish spread over them in the early centuries AD by Romano-British farmers.

Tower Hill provided us with the houses of a relatively short-lived settlement during the Bronze Age/Iron Age transition, about the time that the Horse was carved into the hillside. These people, as we experienced ourselves, lived in an extremely exposed position, with panoramic views over the Downs and to the Wayland's Smithy tomb, beneath which they may also have deposited bronze horse gear. Were they members of the scattered farming communities – herders, shepherds and cereal growers – who came together to create and maintain the White Horse?

HILLFORTS AND OTHER PUZZLES

So why suggest that scattered local farming communities built the Horse? The more obvious answer might seem to be that the people who occupied Uffington Castle created it. Unfortunately, things are not so straightforward – it seems that few people if any actually lived there.

Hillforts – Iron Age enclosures surrounded by substantial earthworks – are found across the Wessex chalkland. They are conspicuously frequent in the White Horse section of the Ridgeway: Liddington Castle in the west, overlooking modern Swindon; Alfred's Castle, less prominently sited south of the Ridgeway near Ashdown House; Hardwell Camp, hidden in the scrub and almost in the shadow of Uffington Castle and never investigated. Only 2.5 km (1½ miles) east of Uffington Castle is Rams Hill, originally a Bronze Age enclosure built about 1400 BC that was encircled by a larger Iron Age earthwork. The monument is scarcely visible today thanks to the tender mercies of the plough, but it occupies a prominent position, controlling a routeway northwards down into the Vale and south into the Lambourn valley and the ritual landscape of Seven Barrows. In contrast, the largest hillfort – about 9 km (5½ miles) along the Ridgeway from Uffington Castle – is Segsbury Camp, which was constructed in the sixth century BC on land where there seems to have been little earlier activity.

Originally, archaeologists assumed that hillforts were defended strongholds, either well populated or places of refuge where herds and flocks, and probably women and children, could be protected from raiders. During his campaigns in Gaul, Caesar besieged great tribal centres like Gergovia, on a hilltop near Clermont-Ferrand, taking Bibracte in the Morvan, where he overwintered and wrote his memoirs, and Alesia in modern-day Burgundy, where he defeated the forces of Vercingetorix. In Britain, hillforts in the southwest, such as Maiden Castle and Hod Hill, were assaulted by the Second Legion under the future emperor Vespasian in the first century AD.

The panoply of weapons found across the country – swords, daggers, spears and shields – supports the idea that British Iron Age society was familiar with conflict and had a warrior class eager to display its mettle. At the hillfort of Fin Cop in the Derbyshire Peak District, archaeologists found the evidence of the warriors' ruthlessness. About 400 BC, the bodies of women and children had been thrown into the hillfort ditch and the massive stone walls were partly toppled onto them.[7] On the other hand, studies of ramparts also suggest that display occasionally came before defensive practicalities. Exhibitions of power are sometimes a substitute for the real thing.[8]

On the Downs, investigations of hillforts have revealed a complicated picture. Some, like Liddington and Uffington castles, appeared as early as the eighth century BC. Most were much modified and maintained over the next four hundred years, but abandoned long before the Claudian conquest of the first century AD. Segsbury came later, enclosing 11 hectares (27 acres). Alfred's Castle was constructed in the early fourth century BC and was about a mere 1.2 hectares (2.7 acres), yet made use of earlier Bronze Age enclosure ditches as an annexe, perhaps to hold its flocks.

Elsewhere on the Downs, so-called 'developed' hillforts like Danebury had substantial populations living in densely packed round houses, with streets, facilities for storage of crops and areas for craft activities. None of the Ridgeway hillforts demonstrates activity on this scale. Segsbury, for example, has scattered round houses – rather odd constructions difficult to interpret, but which may have been seasonally occupied by people involved principally in sheep farming. In fact, although farmers kept pigs and cattle and grew cereals such as spelt and emmer wheat, sheep rearing seems to have been the dominant activity. One witty osteologist noted that if it was left to bone specialists, the Iron Age would be known as the 'Sheep Age'. Of the local hillforts that have been investigated only Alfred's Castle was found to have been permanently occupied, and then only by a small group of people, an extended family, who lived there for about a century. Spinning wool was an important activity there, judging from the number of clay loom weights they left behind.

So the impression is that the bigger hillforts like Segsbury and Uffington Castle were probably communal gathering places, built by people who lived scattered across the Downs and in the Vale below. Segsbury seems to be a place where shepherds could come together with their flocks, perhaps exchanging animals to improve the gene pool. But we cannot discount the need for security – they did build substantial earthworks and timber ramparts. Wolves may not have been the only threat in a society where mounted warriors valued glory and other people's herds and flocks. Hillforts could provide protection when it was needed.

Of course, ramparts were also designed to impress, like the medieval moated manor at Compton Beauchamp or the walls of many medieval towns. The boundaries restrict access and tell visitors they have arrived somewhere important. Uffington Castle's initial rampart – gleaming white, topped with a palisaded walkway and approached through two substantial gateways – would certainly have been impressive, yet inside the hillfort we found relatively slight traces of occupation. So was its function also to provide a ceremonial enclosure, a space for those who gathered to curate the Horse, who took part in the seasonal rituals, perhaps even the prehistoric 'Pastimes'? Neither the Horse nor Uffington Castle itself were created by a population who lived permanently inside the hillfort.

Their actual homesteads remain elusive, as we saw at Tower Hill. Across the Downs there are a substantial number of smaller enclosures (known as 'banjo' enclosures because of their shape). These have not been investigated, but elsewhere in Wessex they have proved to be small, Mid-Iron Age farmsteads in which animals could be corralled. Other open sites, like Tower Hill, may simply be invisible to conventional archaeological survey.

Perhaps many of the White Horse's people lived in the Vale. It was often assumed that the Vale was boggy, forested and sparsely inhabited in late prehistory. This seems unlikely. In the 1980s I taught an evening class in archaeology in Faringdon, the market town that lies just across the Vale. I stuck my neck out and said that if we went out into the Vale and started field walking we would be bound to find previously undiscovered sites. We chose an area of land about 4 km (2½ miles) long and 1 km (about ½ mile) across to the southeast of Faringdon, along Frogmore Brook to Stanford-in-the-Vale, one of the largest Vale villages.

The topography of the Vale is complex. Southeast of Faringdon, a sandy ridge leads towards Stanford. The straight road that runs along it is known as the Ridgeway (not the famous one). It looked suspiciously like the line of a Roman road and alongside it, near Bowling Green Farm, we found the traces of a substantial Romano-British settlement. Nearby, on the lower land near Frogmore Brook, we located the clearly defined earthwork of a Roman villa, and running across the valley bottom the foundations of a wall with glossy red Samian pottery embedded in it – the distinctive shiny red tableware made in Roman Gaul. Across the brook, not far away, the foundations of another small Roman building appeared. On the slope above at Hatford there were traces of an Iron Age settlement. So this supposed forested marsh was densely inhabited almost two thousand years ago and possibly earlier. A section of the valley where no one lives today was littered with Roman settlements.

In Stanford-in-the-Vale local people also began to tell us that they were finding Roman pottery in their gardens. Was this evidence of substantial settlement at the 'stone-ford' crossing of the River Ock? The picture has also changed recently thanks to a vast archaeological programme around Didcot at the eastern end of the Vale, in advance of the expansion of the town. An area with few identified ancient settlements is now known to have been covered with Iron Age and Roman farmsteads, fields and trackways.

The Vale is an area of rich farmland and good grazing, criss-crossed by streams. It is very different from the open downland where water can be in short supply. In the Anglo-Saxon charters we hear of settlements at Pusey, Goosey, Charney and Hanney. These '-ey' endings represent the Old English word *ieg*, meaning 'island' – dry spots between the many streams and rivulets. Other villages have names like Shillingford, Hatford and, as we have already encountered, Stanford – places where the streams can be crossed. These places could mask much earlier settlement.

Several years after our White Horse excavation, English Heritage's aerial photographers captured a new site lying just northwest of Uffington. The cropmarks seemingly indicated a typical Thames Valley Iron Age settlement of round houses, animal enclosures and trackways. When I visited the place shortly after seeing the photographs I realized the people who had lived there had a good view of the White Horse, only 3 km (1¾ miles) due south. From where I stood, on slightly elevated dry ground, the Horse seemed to leap out of the top of Dragon Hill.

Of course, on the surface, there was no obvious trace of the settlement itself, which had been thoroughly ploughed. However, it stood on a dry platform of Greensand. I had seen lots of Iron Age settlements like this in the Thames Valley, where people lived, sometimes seasonally, on slightly elevated islands surrounded by rich pasture enriched by seasonal flooding. The aerial photograph begged the question – were these people living in the Vale when the Horse and the hillfort were constructed? Could they be part of the community of builders?

Oxford Archaeology came together with the Tom Brown's School Museum in Uffington to organize a community project, with support from the Heritage Lottery Fund. Geophysical survey and limited trenching confirmed that this was a long-lived settlement, with two concentrations of round houses. Surrounding ditches may have protected these from flooding. The pottery included the familiar All Cannings Cross style that we found at both the Uffington Castle hillfort and Tower Hill, the hoard site, indicating that all these places existed in the eighth century BC. However, there was also some Late Bronze Age pottery, and sherds belonging to the second century BC. This settlement in the Vale may have been there when the White Horse first appeared on the hillside above, and these Vale people may have helped to make the Horse and the hillfort. The small excavation produced some evidence for how the occupants made a living: they grew cereals and raised cattle and sheep, and they also kept horses. At least, the excavators found three horse teeth.

THE LATE IRON AGE – RIPPLES OF CHANGE

Stuart Piggott argued that the White Horse was originally made in the Late Iron Age, about the first century BC, because of the similarity of its shape to some of the images on the first British coins. In fact, there is remarkably little evidence of activity at this period around the White Horse. It was certainly a period of major change in southern Britain, partly caused by the shock waves from the Roman Empire expanding from the Gallic shores of the Channel. The downland hillforts were abandoned at this time, or even before.

New centres emerged, known to archaeologists as 'oppida'. Some, like Dyke Hills, just outside Dorchester-on-Thames in Oxfordshire, are at nodal points where overland routes meet the River Thames. Others are very extensive tribal centres, and for the first time the tribal names are known. The Dobunni were on the Cotswolds at Bagendon, north of the White Horse. To the south, and probably including the White Horse itself, was the territory of the Atrebates, centred on a new oppidum at Silchester in Hampshire (Calleva Atrebatum to the Romans). Beyond the Thames to the east lay the territory of the Catuvellauni and the oppida of Verulamium (St Albans in Hertfordshire) and Camulodunum (Colchester in Essex). London was not yet a significant population centre; it was probably a landscape of scattered farms, possibly with an important religious focus by the Thames. This is suggested by the deposits of rich metalwork, such as the Battersea Shield, and large numbers of human skulls found in the river.

The White Horse Hill area may have been a backwater at this time, but its position was significant. It lay on the boundary of three of the most important tribes in southern Britain. Did the Atrebates maintain the Horse as a badge of tribal identity? Or was the White Horse on more neutral territory, on the borderlands, where people gathered to express their insular solidarity and identity? Caesar said that there were pan-Gallic gatherings of Druids in Britain. This was where the old lore was taught. We know very little about the liturgies of Iron Age religion, in spite of the vivid imagination of modern neo-pagans, but places seem to have been more important than buildings. The survival of the White Horse suggests that the hill was one such powerful place.

Rich graves of this period show that exchange with the Roman world was increasingly important. The elite enjoyed amphorae of wine, and the paraphernalia of wine drinking. For the first time they had fine, wheel-thrown, locally made pottery, which copied imported drinking vessels. And coinage, made first of potin (a base metal alloy), then gold, silver and bronze circulated among the tribes of southeast and central Britain.

PENNIES FROM HEAVEN: BRITAIN'S FIRST COINAGE

Britons first began to use coinage early in the second century BC, when the coins were mostly imported from the Continent. These derived ultimately from two sources: the fourth-century gold staters of Philip and Alexander of Macedon, often acquired by Celtic mercenaries, and the potin coins that imitated the lower-value bronze coinage of Massilia (Marseilles) and which, by the early second century BC, was being manufactured in Kent. Gold coins, known as Gallo-Belgic A and B, first appeared in the Thames Basin and Kent, manufactured in Gaul and then copied. By 100 BC new coins (Gallo-Belgic C) appeared and then were also extensively copied in Britain. At the time of Caesar's campaign in Gaul in the 50s BC, Gallic coins flooded into Britain, possibly reflecting attempts to buy British support in the struggle against the Romans. These spread northwards as far as Derbyshire and South Yorkshire.

At this time the British, especially in Wiltshire, Berkshire and on the south coast, produced their own fine coins: gold staters, quarter staters and, more numerous, silver coinage in great variety. By 20 BC there seems to have been more standardization and control over coin production. Coins appear inscribed with the name of Commius, followed by those of his supposed sons Tincomarus, Verica and Eppilus, who calls himself 'King of Calleva'. For the first time we have the name of a British king in the region, and he modelled his coins on Roman prototypes. Verica probably succeeded Eppilus and, according to Roman sources, he was forced to flee to Rome when attacked by enemies from north of the Thames – or possibly by internal rivals. It is at this point in the story of the White Horse region that we can shed some light, however faint, on political and personal histories.

Gold was also back in demand at this time: for coinage and for ornaments, particularly spiritually powerful, high-status torcs such as those found at Clench Common, near Marlborough, and the magnificent flexible necklaces with Roman-style clasps and gold brooches in a north European style found near Winchester.[9] In the mid-first century BC there were clearly some very wealthy individuals in the Wessex area, possibly they were refugees from Gaul carrying pure gold from the Mediterranean world.

The coins are relevant to our story of the White Horse because of their imagery. The Macedonian coins showed the head of Apollo on the obverse side and a chariot drawn by two horses on the reverse. By the time Gallic copies reached Britain the imagery was more abstract. In many, including British coins, the symbol of the horse and solar wheel was emphasized. Some have segmented limbs and beaked heads (Pl. iii).

The Dobunni, the tribe to the north of the White Horse, often portrayed an animal with a triple tail. The Iron Age coin specialist John Creighton suggested that fragmented designs were the psychedelic images of drug-fuelled druids or shamans.[10] This idea came directly from the interpretations of Palaeolithic art by David Lewis-Williams – a South African archaeologist whose view of rock art is influenced by his observations of the trance states of the San people, hunter-gatherers now principally living in the Kalahari Desert. Lewis-Williams points out that while the Egyptians, Maya and Greeks, among others, invented supernatural beliefs about natural phenomena, the San manage without mythological beliefs about the changing seasons: 'For the San, the seasons just happen.' In their cosmological concerns the late prehistoric people of northern Europe were closer to the Egyptians. Elements of the so-called 'entropic states' (spots, zigzags, horses with human heads), rather than being universal as one would expect if generated in the human brain during drug use or trance, have distinctly regional distribution on the coinage designs. Archaeologists, like everyone else, can be infected by fashion – in this case, a tendency to see shamans everywhere.

However, the coins might well tell us something relevant to the White Horse. There seems to be a relatively brief period in the middle of the first century BC when abstract horses and sun symbols were dominant. This was also a time when new religious structures were being built – for example, the timber temple on Hayling Island in Chichester Harbour, Sussex. Could this represent the authority of traditional British (Druidic) religion exerting itself in the face of the threat from Rome? The White Horse was not influenced by the coinage, contrary to Stuart Piggott's theory, so much as vice versa. The segmented sun horse represented the independence of the British and their attachment to their ancestral lands.

If there is any truth in this interpretation, I am afraid the British independence movement did not last. The royal house that ruled at Calleva (Silchester), the local tribal centre, became pro-Roman. This shows in their coins. There are gold quarter staters using Roman lettering, marked VERIC and COME, with a naturalistic horse and a sun on the obverse and the Latin title REX (King). The British quislings still claimed the horse, but theirs was prosaically Classical. Other gold staters even combined Verica's name with a vine leaf (how Roman can you get?) and a mounted horseman, an image used by Octavian/Augustus when he came to power after the civil war that followed Caesar's assassination.

We tend to think of coinage as cash – loose change used to buy commodities. At this stage, however, gold staters were very valuable, and probably their function was as high-status objects used in the highest levels of gift exchange. This is why archaeologists often find gold coins in buried hoards near sacred places such as springs and marshes, or in shrines like Hayling Island, where they are gifts to the gods. As bronze coins became more common, they were used as money. In contrast, gold coins helped to forge alliances: they were a medium to send messages. At Calleva, the coins declare 'we love Rome'. Calleva seems to have become a focal point for the pro-Roman party. The house of Verica provided the Romans with the age-old excuse: 'We moved in our troops because they asked us to. We are helping our allies against aggressive usurpers.'

THE ROMAN GODS

If the Claudian invasion of AD 43 was assisted by some Britons, it was fiercely opposed by others. These traditionalists lost in the long run. So if the White Horse was their emblem, this is a time we might expect it to suffer neglect or worse. In fact, this does not seem to be the case. The Romans were a pragmatic power, particularly where religion was concerned. They were polytheistic and generally willing to give regional gods a place in the Pantheon. Those who stood out determinedly against the cult of the emperor, attempting to assert a non-Roman identity, however – such as the Jews in Jerusalem and Masada, or the Druids on the Isle of Anglesey – were severely repressed. Pliny the Elder justified this in his *Natural History*, as, he said: 'Today Britain is obsessed by magic.' Rome, he argued, was extending *humanitas* by clearing out the cruel Druids who practised human sacrifice. For the most part, however, local gods were respected and often identified with the principal Classical deities.

Rome had a strong sense of its own civilizing mission: a brutal manipulator of military power that, nevertheless, saw its own Classical culture as opposed to barbarism. The Empire supported and promoted civilization. The two were synonymous.

While we were excavating alongside the River Thames in its upper reaches at Somerford Keynes in Gloucestershire, we found what seemed to be a Roman depot. Around a large, aisled, barn-like building there were lots of red-fired building tiles of varying sizes. This was something new to Britain: a place where building material was gathered to supply the construction sites of the newly founded city of Corinium Dobunnorum (Cirencester). On the edge of marshy ground lay several finely carved pieces of stone sculpture, including the figure of an eagle. These were fragments from a cult statue of the Capitoline Triad of Juno, Jupiter and Minerva: an emblem of official Rome. While the eagle was the formal Roman representation of Jupiter, the god was also associated with other familiar symbols, such as the sun wheel. In Gaul and, to a lesser extent, in Britain, Jupiter was linked with scores of local gods.

On the Cotswolds, at Uley in Gloucestershire, an important regional temple was built on the site of an earlier native shrine and dedicated to Mercury. Worshippers sacrificed cockerels to him and left curses, written on lead tablets, which requested retribution for supposed offences. Mercury was popular in Roman Britain and appeared in many different aspects.

Nearer to the White Horse, another religious complex existed at Frilford, Oxfordshire, where a Roman road meets the River Ock. The dedication of the temple is uncertain owing to the lack of inscriptions, but the place must have attracted crowds of pilgrims. When examining aerial photographs, my colleague Richard Hingley (now a professor at Durham University) and I noticed a large, dark, oval mark near the temple site. We eventually showed it to the local farmer. 'Any idea what it is?' I asked. 'That's where I had my slurry pit,' he replied. I had my doubts; it would have been the biggest slurry pit in the country. 'What do you call that field?' Richard asked. 'Trendles,' he said. My eyebrows shot up: *trendel* is an Old English word meaning 'the circle'. We knew of no record of the name in any of the Vale's Anglo-Saxon or medieval documents, and neither did the place-name expert Margaret Gelling when we told her about the new discovery.

Subsequently, Richard dug a trench into the edge of the oval mark and found that it was the remains of a Roman amphitheatre built into a natural hollow, a place for ceremonies and games held in association with the temple. The survival of the name 'Trendles' is remarkable. It must have been passed down by word of mouth for about fifteen hundred years, long after the amphitheatre itself had been lost in the ground – another miracle of continuity, like the Horse itself. Further excavations have revealed that the amphitheatre (or possibly theatre) had been constructed around a spring that emerged in a natural hollow. The deposits of artefacts indicate that this was a sacred spring where offerings were made.[11]

White Horse Hill has produced no trace of a temple, but that is not to say the hill lost its ritual significance. A number of British hillforts were marked with Romano-British shrines, as was the hilltop of Lowbury, east of the White Horse. This high point was capped with a Bronze Age barrow (the *hlaew* or 'low' of Lowbury) two thousand years before the temple arrived. There are magnificent 360-degree views across the Vale of the White Horse, the Thames Valley and the Downs from the hilltop. It seems an obvious place to talk to the gods and to leave offerings: archaeologists found the shrine was littered with them, indicating that pilgrims had come to this high place from at least the first to fifth centuries AD.[12]

Hilltops and hillforts often continued as sacred spaces during the Romano-British period. While no sacred structures have been located inside Uffington Castle, there were a considerable number of Romano-British finds – including coins. Twenty of these were found close to the flue of a fourth-century AD oven or corn-drier. Other material included bronze jewelry, glass and fragments from coarse-ware cooking pots and food vessels. Clearly, people were coming to the hillfort that, by then, was an ancient monument over a millennium old.[13] At the same time they were burying their dead, often decapitated, in and around the Neolithic long barrow on the flank of the hill. Was this all in connection with people gathering to scour the Horse? One thing is clear: the Roman period saw a dramatic increase in population, agricultural activity and the number of settlements in the region.

The earliest known local stone-based farmhouse – a small villa – was, unusually, built inside Alfred's Castle about AD 100. There are many other Roman villas in the area: on the Downs, for example, at Maddle Farm; close to the urban settlement at Wanborough; and along the spring line in the Vale and in the valley itself. When I analysed aerial photographs and actively excavated in the White Horse region, it was clear that the gravel terraces of the Thames Valley were covered with small farmsteads, whose origin often went back into the Iron Age. These were mixed farms, growing a variety of cereals, beans and flax, but exploiting the rich pasture for cattle – and horses. The Downs were also extensively cultivated – covered in small fields, with sheep the predominant farm animal, and where villas exploited estates of about 150 hectares (360 acres).

We knew less about the lowlands below the Downs to the north – geologically the landscape of Greensand and Gault Clay. However, in the past few years there have been massive archaeological evaluation exercises in advance of development, particularly around Didcot, as mentioned above. These have revealed an intensively farmed Late Iron Age and Romano-British landscape, with a hierarchy of settlements from villa estates to small farms and villages. The animal bones tell us that cattle-raising was an important activity in the area. The sheer density of Romano-British farms and fields on both the Downs and the lowlands indicates an active agricultural population linked by a road network to the Thames Valley and the minor and major urban centres at Wanborough, Abingdon, Dorchester-on-Thames, Silchester and Cirencester. These towns were small by modern standards, but the countryside was busy. More people worked the land in the first to fourth centuries AD than do today.

While Britain saw an inflow of foreign soldiers, administrators, traders, slaves and craftspeople, the majority of people were descendants of the Iron Age population, and probably 90 per cent of them were farmers and peasants, attached to the land. We can only guess who took responsibility for the care of the White Horse, but there was no shortage of possible candidates with motivation.

Aside from landowners and peasants with an attachment to their ancestral roots, there was another group that might respect the Horse. Many of the cavalry in the Roman army were recruited in Gaul and they looked to the horse goddess, Epona, for protection and good luck. Epona was said to have been the offspring of one Fulvius Stellus who was not attracted to women but copulated with a mare. The name 'Epona' derives from Indo-European words meaning 'mistress of horses', which can be traced back to the Linear B tablets of Bronze Age Greece. There is more evidence for her cult in Gaul, where she is sometimes shown riding a horse, or seated, a fertility goddess associated with a sun cult. It is a little far-fetched to associate her directly with the White Horse, as some have done. On the other hand, Romano-Celtic religion and beliefs were notoriously complicated. There was no simple catechism or Guide to the Approved Gods.

The Gallo-Roman horse goddess Epona, sitting side-saddle on her mount.
This limestone carving was found at Alesia, Alise-Sainte-Reine, where a Christian
shrine still survives by a spring below the hillfort.

From the Cotswolds there are carved images of the Three Mothers –
a triad of fertility figures marked with spoked wheel/sun images. Further
afield, at Backworth in Durham, there is a fascinating hoard that includes
a silver dish dedicated to the Deae Matres (the mother goddesses) and gold
jewelry, all with solar amulets. Clay models of a 'Venus' figure are frequently incised with wheels and sun symbols. Many were made in the

tribal capital of the Redones (near Rennes in Brittany), but widely distributed, turning up in health shrines and in burials. There was a widespread obsession with the sun in the Romano-Celtic world, associated with fertility, child-bearing and mortality. The mother figure was not the sun god, but rather his divine consort.

The ultimate sky god in the Roman world was Jupiter. Interestingly, he is shown as the solar victor over death, particularly in a series of monuments found near Stuttgart in Germany. These Jupiter Giant Columns show a bearded horseman, a solar sky-warrior, sometimes carrying a solar wheel, riding down a monster or dragon figure, atop a large stone column representing a tree. The tree grows out of the underworld and supports the sky, like the ash tree Yggdrasil in Norse mythology. Here, the sun repels evil and the forces of death in an image that combines Classical and northern European ideas. Stuttgart may seem a long way from the White Horse, but fragments of a Jupiter Tree have been found at Corinium (Cirencester), not far from it, and similar iconography – with a charioteer – was used on widely distributed Roman coins in the second century AD.

If the White Horse had become a symbol of such powerful religious ideas, then this could explain its survival during the time that Britain was part of the Roman Empire. The presence of burials on the hilltop and material left inside the hillfort is consistent with White Horse Hill continuing to play a significant role in the spiritual and social life of the local community. This is a place that united the heavens and the underworld 'in mutual dependence', both life and death ruled over by the sky god.[14]

CHAPTER TWELVE

STRANGE MEETINGS: OLD GODS AND NEW GODS

Old gods can easily become new gods in an identity shift.
Timothy Ingold, 2000

SUN GODS AND THE SON OF GOD

In the centre of Istanbul there is a blackened stone column held together with metal bands. A maelstrom of yellow taxis swirls past it. No one takes much notice of this stump, yet it is all that remains of one of the great monuments of early Christianity. Time has ravaged the Çemberlitaş (the 'hooped stone' in Turkish). Historian Edward Gibbon (1737–1794) knew it as the 'burnt column'. It was once a gleaming giant made of blocks of porphyry (the purple-red 'imperial' stone from Egypt), the biggest of its kind in the world, erected on the orders of the Roman emperor Constantine in AD 330 to mark the centre of the Forum in his New Rome: Constantinople.

The emperor was not a modest man. In fact, he rather suspected that he was not a mere man at all. Constantine the Great (AD 306–337), as he became known to a grateful Church, was the emperor who championed Christianity and set it on the path to becoming the new state religion of Rome, and of medieval Europe. The ravaged column represents the launch of Christianity. So, whose image did Constantine set atop the great pillar? Not Christ's but his own, in the form of Sol Invictus, the Unconquered Sun. The emperor was not so much a subject of God as a partner. His figure carried an orb that contained a fragment of the True Cross:[1] the crucified God and the imperial sun god combined.

The cross was important to Constantine. Before the Battle of the Milvian Bridge (by the River Tiber just north of Rome), where he confronted the forces of his rival Maxentius in AD 312, Constantine communicated with the Supreme Being. To describe this as 'praying' might give a wrong idea of their relationship. As the sun declined, Constantine saw a pillar of light inscribed: 'In this conquer'. Constantine got the message, especially when Christ then appeared to him with a design proposal for a new standard that would guarantee victory. Hence the Chi-Rho – Christ's initials and the cross in the form of the sun symbol: the banner of imperial victory.

I have wandered off to Istanbul because the Column of Constantine represents the ambiguity of early Christian thinking nearly seventeen hundred years ago. Ideas and practice were changing, but they still emerged from and were amalgamated with the past. The past was not simply shed like a snake's skin. It is an anachronism to see early Christianity as a reflection of the later, highly organized medieval or modern institutions. The old gods and myths did not just disappear – they helped to provide the roots and foundations of the new religion. Constantine, for example, built his main church, dedicated to Hagia Eirene (Holy Peace), on top of the temple of Aphrodite. Like the White Horse, the Column of Constantine is a lesson in survival. It demonstrates the hazards of time, the unpredictability of events and the flexibility of human myth-making.

RELIGION IN LATE ROMAN BRITAIN

The arrival of Christianity in Britain represents the start of one of those key transformations in society that might have resulted in the loss of the White Horse through neglect or iconoclasm. The new Eastern religion certainly took hold in late Roman Britain, but perhaps not so firmly as in other provinces. There is also some evidence for a resurgence of paganism in later fourth-century AD Roman Britain. This may explain the damage done to a lead tank, marked with a Chi-Rho, which we found thrown into a late Roman well near Caversham, Berkshire. Such tanks are unique to Roman Britain and are believed to be part of the equipment of the Christian baptismal ceremony, specifically used for ritual foot-washing.

The word 'pagan' came into use in a Christian context in the fourth century. It is often claimed that the term first referred to a country dweller, and that most early Christians were to be found in towns. There is some evidence for this, with possible churches in Roman Silchester, Canterbury, Lincoln and Colchester, and historical evidence for the presence of bishops in London, Lincoln and York. However, it is also clear that some wealthier rural landowners adopted Christianity – for example, at Hinton St Mary, Dorset, the image of Christ is portrayed on a mosaic in close proximity to Bellerophon, the famed monster-slayer who rode the white, winged horse Pegasus. The Oxford classicist Robin Lane Fox has convincingly argued that the word *Pagani* referred to civilians who had not registered by baptism as soldiers of Christ, in the struggle against Satan.[2] They were not specifically country dwellers.[3]

However, at White Horse Hill it appears that those who came to bury their dead in the fourth century were still practising pagan rites, especially the removal of skulls after death, and placing coins on the body to pay the ferryman to cross the River Styx to the underworld. In AD 391, Emperor Theodosius banned all pagan cults, but out in the Vale of the White Horse, on the edge of a crumbling empire, was anyone listening?

In fact, within five decades after AD 400 Britannia was drastically transformed as England emerged. The Western Roman Empire shuddered and retreated; after almost four hundred years, Britain was no longer a Roman province. In the previous century, southern Britain had been relatively prosperous. Large, comfortable, even luxurious villas – like Chedworth or North Leigh in the Cotswolds – seem to reflect an Arcadian idyll. Tile roofs and stone foundations kept the buildings secure, and underfloor heating systems kept them warm. Elaborate mosaics, made by specialists based in towns such as Corinium (Cirencester), reflected the sophistication and good taste of the owners: men and women who plunged regularly in their own heated pools, and pampered themselves with unguents and perfumes. Other benefits of the empire appeared in kitchens and dining rooms: quality tableware, ceramic and silver, glass, herbs and spices such as coriander and cumin, olive oil and wine. The level of comfort enjoyed by the Romano-British elite was perhaps unequalled in England until the eighteenth century with its great country houses.

This privileged existence was for the few: slaves stoked the boilers and milled the flour. Ninety per cent of people toiled on the land. Nevertheless, there was an agricultural surplus that fuelled trade and a degree of prosperity. The countryside was intensively exploited, as we can see from the quilted surface of the Downs, stitched together with fields. And nearby there were large-scale pottery industries – for example, around modern Oxford, potters shipped their distinctive wares along the Thames to customers across the province, and even beyond. Britannia was at the edge of the empire, but in the later fourth century it was not peripheral. Emperor Julian (AD 361–363), who tried to reverse the Christian tide, even supplied his armies on the Rhine with British corn.

From archaeological evidence (and lacking the evidence of censuses, birth and death records or even taxation and rent assessments) it is difficult to estimate population. However, we can confidently say that around AD 370 Britain's population was at a peak, perhaps reaching four million people, comparable with fourteenth-century Britain before the great plague struck. Of course, precision in numbers is impossible. Nevertheless, relatively, there were a lot of people in late Roman Britain and many enjoyed a lifestyle that was more comfortable than that of their ancestors. In numerous places there are signs that ancestral rites were respected. Shrines and temples marked hillforts, hilltops and ancient ritual centres – places where people continued to gather. White Horse Hill clearly retained its significance, at least to the local population.

THE ANGLO-SAXONS ARRIVE

Then things started to go wrong. Fast! The Roman Empire in the West came under what we would now call an existential threat. Social, political, financial and military problems created a perfect storm. In AD 410 the imperial authorities pulled the troops out of Britain. There was already evidence of decline: no supplies of imperial coinage entered the country and major towns had defensive walls yet there was little evidence of new building. On the contrary, public works deteriorated. In the countryside, owners and farmers abandoned their villas as the infrastructure that supported them, and trade with the outside world, collapsed. The fires were finally extinguished in the industrial kilns of the Oxford area. By AD 450 southern Britain was a very different place – less populated and no longer fully integrated into the political world of the Roman Empire.

Until recently the story of the Anglo-Saxon arrival – whether seen as an invasion, a seizure of power or a longer process of settlement and integration – depended upon the interpretation of historians who were reliant on limited sources. The source that was closest to the events is by Gildas (c. 500–c. 570), a Christian monk writing about the early sixth century. He was probably educated in the Vale of Glamorgan, the most Romanized region of Wales, and in Corinium. *De Excidio Britanniae* ('On the Ruin of Britain') is an angry diatribe, both polemic and sermon, a rhetorical dagger plunged into the breasts of the British rulers whose moral backsliding had left the country open to the ravaging heathens.

Not noted for temperate language, Gildas proclaims that from the north came 'the foul hordes of Scots and Picts like dark throngs of worms who wriggle out of narrow fissures in the rocks ... they were readier to cover their villainous faces with hair than their private parts ... with clothes'. And then there were 'those wild Saxons, of accursed name, hated by God and men ... admitted into the island like wolves into fields ... first fixed their dreadful tribes in the eastern part of the island'.

Gildas paints a picture of destruction, of towns sacked and pillaged and Britons in retreat until, at the Battle of Mount Badon, they halted the

Anglo-Saxon advance for a generation. Later stories associated this temporary victory with Arthur, and one of the possible sites for the clash of the Britons and Anglo-Saxons is the hillfort known as Badbury Camp (or Liddington Castle), in a dominant position by the Ridgeway overlooking the Roman road (Ermin Way) and the Roman town of Durocornovium near present-day Wanborough, Wiltshire. However, there are many claimants for the honour of being Arthur's battlefield and, to be frank, we do not know which was the battle site, if any.[4]

As Gildas saw it, God wreaks havoc, punishing the Britons and their rulers for their moral weakness. He is not the stuff of objective history, nor is he strong on dates. In fact, he does not provide us with any. The Venerable Bede (673–735), the first English historian, composed his great work *The Ecclesiastical History of the English People* (*Historia ecclesiastica gentis Anglorum*) two centuries after Gildas. Nevertheless, Bede relied on his predecessor as a major source. The lack of dates presented Bede with a problem. He saw the arrival of the Saxons in Britain as a specific event – the *Adventus Saxonum* – which he calculated to have happened in the year AD 446. Bede also had access to the records of the Kentish dynasty and, with the help of these, estimated that the newcomers controlled Kent by about AD 450.[5] Bede tells us that the first ships carrying the invaders arrived at Ebbsfleet on the Isle of Thanet (now near Ramsgate on the Kent coast) led by Hengist and Horsa, whose names mean 'stallion' and 'horse'.

Charles Dickens told his young readers in *A Child's History of England* (1852): 'the Saxons, like many other nations in a rough state were fond of giving men the names of animals, as horse, wolf, bear, hound'. He did not point out that the supposed British leader, Arthur – the victor at Mount Badon – had a name that meant 'Bear'.

According to Gildas, British rulers invited in the first Saxons as mercenaries to help with defence. Relations soured, and the Saxons turned against their British employers. The consequences were disastrous: 'All the major towns were laid low by the repeated battering of enemy rams; laid low, too, all the inhabitants – church leaders, priests and people alike, as the swords glinted all around and the flames crackled. There was no burial to be had except in the ruins of houses or the bellies of beasts and birds.'

Archaeology indicates that the events of the fifth century were more complicated and drawn out than either Gildas or Bede suggest. On the continental North Sea coast we can see why the Germanic peoples may have headed for Britain. They occupied settlements, raised on artificial mounds and known as *terpen* in Dutch, which increasingly suffered from flooding. The rising waters drove them out, and these refugees needed a new home.[6]

Some came to the Thames Valley. The village of Sutton Courtenay is not far from White Horse Hill, about 20 km (12 miles) to the northwest where the Vale meets the Thames. E. T. Leeds (1877–1955), a curator at Oxford's Ashmolean Museum, first recognized an early Anglo-Saxon settlement in a gravel pit just outside the village in the 1920s.[7] There he noticed dark marks, shaped rather like playing cards. He dug into them and realized that they were sunken chambers originally set beneath small timber huts with thatched roofs. These holes contained material such as loom weights, bone tools, animal bones and most importantly, for Leeds, the distinctive handmade pottery known from Anglo-Saxon cemeteries. To Leeds, the settlement he had discovered seemed a primitive place: the newcomers lived in sunken-floored houses, rather like large dog kennels, amid their own rubbish. In fact, he was wrong. Anglo-Saxons did not wallow in the filth, they simply used the abandoned huts as rubbish dumps. Such buildings have since turned up in large numbers and are known to archaeologists as *grübenhauser* ('dug-out houses', after the German name for similar structures common in the continental homelands) or, in cumbersome English, sunken-featured buildings (SFBs). These huts were probably used for craft activities and storage, or as sleeping places for the community's slaves.

What Leeds did not appreciate when he first made his important discovery was that on the rough surface of the gravel, bashed about by the quarry machines, there were small postholes of more substantial rectangular timber buildings – or halls – which were the Anglo-Saxons' principal dwelling houses. In 1973, my colleague Don Benson and I were mapping the archaeological features visible on aerial photographs when we observed the shapes of several large timber halls immediately next to where Leeds had excavated his sunken huts.[8] The Anglo-Saxons were not quite as primitive as he first imagined. They were expert at building in wood, and archaeologists had to learn how to recognize and excavate their buildings if they were to understand the newcomers.

Over the last few decades this area of the Thames Valley, between Dorchester-on-Thames and Abingdon, has produced prolific evidence of the first Germanic settlers. At Dorchester, the Roman or later British authorities employed Germanic troops. North of the town, from about AD 430 to 450, an Anglo-Saxon community of about thirty to forty people buried their dead in family groups for several generations. Many of the men went to their graves covered by iron-bound, limewood shields and with spears hafted with ash. Only a small minority had swords. The women wore distinctive jewelry that identified them as belonging to the West Saxon people, or *Gewisse* – a name John Blair of Oxford University translated as 'The Trusties'.[9] At this stage the grave goods suggest that these were communities with a relatively flat hierarchy. Some families were more important than others, but not yet elevated onto aristocratic or royal pedestals.

The Gewissan women's jewelry often showed their continuing belief in the power of the sun. Some women were buried wearing a pair of gilded saucer brooches, whose shape and decoration included sun symbolism. These brooches were pinned on the women's dresses at the shoulders, and between them hung strings of beads. The most impressive were large swags of amber (fossilized tree-resin), probably gathered on the shores of the Baltic Sea. Amber's electro-static properties and glowing, golden quality had made this exotic material valuable across Europe for millennia. In the ancient Greek world amber was known as *electron*, also meaning 'beaming sun'. In the Greek myth, Phaethon ('the shining one') was the son of Helios, the sun god. Phaethon demanded that his father, to prove his paternity, should allow him to drive the sun chariot. The reckless boy could not control the fiery horses and, to prevent a catastrophe on Earth, Zeus hurled a thunderbolt at the chariot and killed Phaethon.[10]

A short distance further up the Thames from Dorchester, near Abingdon, another group of settlers occupied the land of an abandoned Romano-British farmstead.[11] There were no signs of conflict; the local occupants had left their house sometime after AD 400. When Anglo-Saxons arrived about 450 they could see a chequerboard of open ditches surrounding the relics of the farm buildings. They built timber halls and SFBs within the old enclosures and threw their rubbish into the ditches. Their pottery was relatively crude and handmade, and their material culture simpler than that of the earlier Romano-British occupants. Nevertheless, they continued to farm the land of the Romano-Britons, keeping similar animals and growing cereals and flax, although less intensively. The land did not revert to a dark forest or dank swamp. The new settlers used the ruins of the old buildings as burial places. One man, placed within the Roman rubble, wore a beautiful small gold mount in the form of a dragon. Anglo-Saxon settlement sprawled across the adjacent flat gravel terrace onto land crossed by an avenue of large Bronze Age barrows. The field still, today, has the English name 'Barrow Hills', although the mounds disappeared centuries ago, worn down by medieval ploughs.

In recent years interpretations of this period of English history have swung like a pendulum between opposing views. From around 1970 some younger archaeologists became rather obsessively opposed to the idea that change came about because of invasions. Invasions were the standard go-to explanation for a dreary older generation, they argued. It became fashionable instead to see the fifth-century population as British survivors, with a minimal German presence – in spite of the drastic transformation of material culture, settlements, burials and language. Now the pendulum has swung back and some genetic studies indicate a substantial presence of Germanic immigrants into eastern Britain. Arguably, though, the issue of the proportion of incomers versus natives will only be settled with further scientific studies.

It is difficult to believe that the countryside, in which several million Britons lived until about AD 400, had become totally deserted. Certainly, the population decreased – hit by disease, warfare, migration or collapsing morale – but some remained to live alongside incoming Anglo-Saxons. This was sometimes as slaves, but others intermarried with the newcomers and some Britons achieved positions of high status. If the first Germani to arrive were warrior bands, they were soon followed by migrants seeking a new life in the hollowed-out lands of eastern Britain, where forests had been long cleared and fertile fields were there to be cultivated. It was precisely these easily ploughed, well-drained areas of land where earlier generations had invested their efforts that attracted the new settlers. Their first settlements were scattered and unplanned. It was two hundred to three hundred years before the typical English village began to appear.

UNDER NEW OWNERSHIP

If the fifth century AD was a period of catastrophe or, at best, drastic change, then we should ask: how could the White Horse survive? Yet it did. Diana Woolner, in her well-argued article 'New Light on the White Horse', wrote: 'the most reliable period for the creation of the White Horse would seem to be between the Saxon settlement of the Middle Thames region and the mission of St Birinus, that is to say during the fifth century or the sixth century of our era'.[12]

Our excavations into the White Horse have undermined this theory, yet Woolner makes a good case for why the Horse would retain its significance for Anglo-Saxons. It is debatable whether Hengist and Horsa were real people or mythical ancestors. However, they were relevant to Anglo-Saxons, who traced the origins of their royal houses through them to the god Woden.[13] Horses loomed large in their mythology. It is also worth remembering that these people originated in northern Germany and southern Scandinavia, where the horse-drawn sun myth had an ancient pedigree. They were also a people who had not been invaded or

A Scandinavian rock art carving depicting a horse drawing the sun-disc, from Balken, Tanum, Sweden.

conquered in previous centuries; their myths were persistent and had much in common with those of prehistoric Eurasia.

The most important deity was Woden (still commemorated in 'Wednesday', or *mercredi* in French – after Mercury). Not far from the White Horse, Woden is remembered in several places in the Vale of Pewsey, Wiltshire, where Woden's Dyke (Wansdyke) can still be seen crossing the landscape. Thunor was the sky god and 'thunderer' (Thursday); Tiw was a war god, like Mars (Tuesday, or *mardi* in French). Bede tells us that the fertility goddess Eostre, counterintuitively, gave her name to Christianity's most important festival, Easter. There is limited evidence for Anglo-Saxon temple structures (Bede mentions a few), but the words *hearh* (hilltop sanctuary) and *weoh* (sacred space) occur across much of southern and eastern England.

We should also remember that the Angles, Saxons and Jutes were closely related in language and culture to the Norse inhabitants of Scandinavia. We know more about their myths and beliefs from later writers. The Norse earth was linked to the underworld and the heavens by the great ash tree Yggdrasil, which means 'the horse of the terrible one', a reference to Odin. Horses feature extensively: Odin took Night and her son Day and placed them in a horse-drawn chariot that carried them through the sky and around the world. The horse of the night was Hrimfaxi, while Skinfaxi was the horse of the day, whose gleaming mane lit up the sky.

An important god, like Loki, the cunning shape-shifter, was associated with a white horse, Sleipnir – a symbol of fertility and death – who could run through the air. Sleipnir had eight legs – a symbol of speed or, as some have suggested, the eight legs of coffin-bearers. If stories such as these circulated among the Saxons, it is not hard to see how the Uffington White Horse could have been adopted.

There is an important question for all immigrants, strangers in a strange land: 'How do you build a homeland on alien soil, full of someone else's dead?'[14] In fact, the land of the White Horse, close to some of the earliest Anglo-Saxon settlements and cemeteries, was soon incorporated into Germanic mythology. The sight of a giant White Horse must have impressed the newcomers. This was not an alien Roman temple of collapsing stone pillars and pediments, like those described in the melancholy Anglo-Saxon poem 'The Ruin':

Wrætlic is þes wealstan, wyrde gebræcon ...
This masonry is wondrous; fates broke it, courtyard pavements
were smashed; the work of giants is decaying.[15]

These tumbled, Classical buildings, probably in Aquae Sulis (Bath), impressed the author of 'The Ruin', but belonged to a very different culture. The work of fate and time was not to be restored. All things must pass. The Horse, in contrast, was more relevant to the Anglo-Saxons. It fitted into their view of the world. As one specialist has written: 'In the early Anglo-Saxon mind the horse stands out as a motif with socio-political, heroic and spiritual significance. Horses played a major part in pre-Christian Anglo-Saxon belief and cult.'[16]

The Anglo-Saxon origin myth was based on the twins Hengist and Horsa, both named for the horse. War leaders rode horses and gave them as gifts to their followers. Horses were placed in the graves of clan leaders and frequently appear in Anglo-Saxon art, on brooches and ceramics. The horse carried a warrior not only into battle, but also into the afterlife.[17] Such ideas were widespread and enduring in the pan-Germanic cosmological belief system and beyond. They can be traced back to the prehistoric steppes and the earliest horse riders.

Around the Vale of the White Horse and the Thames Valley most West Saxon cemeteries were relatively small, and inhumation was the prevalent rite for disposing of the human body (though some were cremated). In contrast, in the Anglian heartland, Spong Hill in Norfolk was the site of a massive cremation cemetery with over two thousand burials. It was

A cremation urn from Spong Hill (Norfolk), with decoration
stamped into the clay including both a procession of horses
and swastikas, the ancient Indo-European sun symbol.

customary for the ashes and bone fragments collected from cremation to
be placed in a pottery urn. One of these is remarkable for the decoration
stamped into the clay showing a procession of horses and swastikas, the
ancient Indo-European sun symbol that, unfortunately, has been tainted
by its twentieth-century associations. Some of these Anglian men were
accompanied by cremated horses.

Elsewhere, burial rites included horse harnesses and bones of sacrificed horses, some of which were from large males of around 14 hands
(142 cm/56 in.). These were the bones of 'companion' animals, not joints of
meat for the afterlife, like the remains of sheep and cattle. Horse sacrifice
seems to increase in frequency among second- or third-generation Anglo-
Saxons, suggesting that a horse cult developed in England in the sixth
century AD. By the later sixth/early seventh centuries only high-status
burials included horses, such as the 'royal' cemetery at Sutton Hoo, with
its spectacular ship burial. Interestingly, Anglo-Saxons referred to ships as
sund-hengesta (sea-stallion) or *yd-meares* (wave-steed).[18]

On continental and English metalwork the iconography of paired or
fighting stallions occurs frequently, as well as the horse rider trampling a
fallen victim. This is a common Classical image – for example, on Roman
military tombstones – which was then translated into Germanic art,
notably on the magnificent Sutton Hoo helmet now in the British Museum.
The rampant horseman is similar to that on the Jupiter Columns in Germany

and Cirencester, and which, to a medieval Christian audience, became St Michael or St George conquering the dragon and overcoming evil. To a heathen Anglo-Saxon, this image could represent Odin or Thor. New communities transformed the meaning of the horse-rider iconography.

A SACRED LANDSCAPE

The Anglo-Saxons created a homeland by making the land itself sacred. They named the ruinous megalithic tomb that was near to the White Horse, Wayland's Smithy, after the legendary master-smith of Germanic mythology (known as Weland). Like the Classical smith-god Hephaestus, Weland was also lame. His story was depicted on the whalebone casket known as the Franks Casket.[19]

Eighth-century Northumbrian craftsmen made this fine, carved box, possibly in the abbey at Ripon, Yorkshire, one of the first Romanized stone churches in England and said by Bede to be 'clothed in gold and purple'. The casket depicts Jewish, Roman and Christian scenes such as the adoration of the Magi, but, surprisingly perhaps to a modern viewer, it also illustrates the legend of Weland: how he was captured and held by King Nidhad and hamstrung so that he was, in effect, tied to the forge and made to exercise his craft for the king (Weland was said to have made the mail shirt for Beowulf, the great Germanic hero). On the casket, Weland decapitates the king's son and makes a goblet of his skull. He offers the goblet, containing spiked beer, to Nidhad's daughter Bodvildr, whom he rapes once she falls unconscious. This may not seem ideal Christian behaviour, but the Germanic world saw things differently: Weland disposes of the wicked and triumphs over evil. He is a heroic figure like Beowulf or, later, St George. He is justified. Pragmatic Christian missionaries adapted their message and their voice to their audience. To Anglo-Saxon rulers, Christ offered both success and revenge, as he did to the would-be Roman emperor Constantine. Meanwhile, their old gods could be transformed into heroes, humans to be admired rather than deities to be worshipped. So Weland persisted in Christian England.

Born near Wantage, King Alfred (c. 847–899) would have known the downland landscape well. He had confronted the Danish army on the Ridgeway at the Battle of Ashdown in AD 871. As ruler he promoted literacy, and his scholars translated the philosopher Boethius' (c. 480–524) *Consolation of Philosophy* into English. Where the Latin text refers to a distinguished Roman, Fabricius, Alfred replaces it with a more familiar reference: 'Where now are the bones of the famous and wise goldsmith, Weland?'[20] Alfred probably knew the answer. He must have ridden past

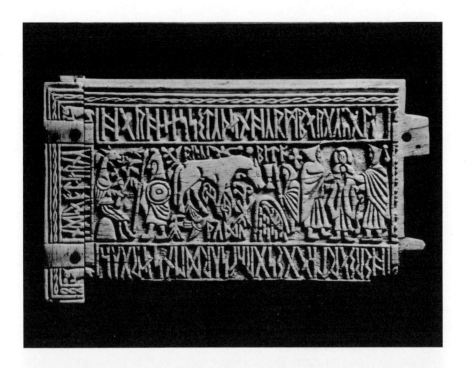

Two sides of the Franks Casket: above, the horse and mound, and below, Weland (left) presents the poisoned skull goblet to the king's daughter; Weland's brother, Aegil or Til, captures birds for their feathers; and the Three Magi (right) present their gifts to Jesus.

the megalithic tomb on the Ridgeway. For Alfred, brought up on a diet of Germanic heroic poetry, 'Boethius offered a radical and alternative view of the cosmos.'[21] Fame was doomed to oblivion. Ironically, in Alfred's circles, Fabricius was forgotten, but not, apparently, Weland.

Chris Fern, an Anglo-Saxon specialist, has pointed out that on the Franks Casket the traditional Anglo-Saxon image of rearing horses appears in the scene of the Fall of Jerusalem. The horses support the Ark of the Covenant, so uniting 'the Christian Holy of Holies with the Germanic double-horse icon'. The horse theme continues on the right-hand end panel of the casket. What is going on here is obscure, to say the least, and may represent a 'lost' Germanic legend (or the Beowulf story). However, in two scenes a horse is shown with a burial mound. Fern argues that these scenes indicate the practice of shamanism among the Anglo-Saxons: the frequently claimed elements of shape-shifting, the mixing of human and animal, transformation and communication with the spirit world, and of journeying to the afterlife.[22]

The relevance of these fascinating and enigmatic images on the Franks Casket is that horses and burial mounds are adapted for a new eclectic world view. The Uffington White Horse may have enshrined much more complex beliefs, myths and stories than we can imagine today, including ideas that enabled the Horse to have meaning to pagans and Christians.

There are other links between the White Horse landscape and the Franks Casket. On the scarp between Wayland's Smithy and Uffington Castle there is another hillfort, now known as Hardwell Camp. Today it is scrub-covered and used as a pheasant shoot, and has never been investigated by archaeologists. In the tenth-century bounds of Compton this place was referred to as *telles byrg* (Tell's Fort). This personal name is well known through the story of William Tell, the Swiss bowman who, supposedly in the fourteenth century, was forced to shoot at the apple placed on his son's head. In fact, this tale has an ancient pedigree. 'Tell' is another name for Aegil, Weland's brother and an expert archer. He also appears on the Franks Casket helping Weland to escape by making a pair of wings from bird's feathers, and slaughtering his brother's enemies. So the Anglo-Saxons laid claim to the land by integrating it into their mythology. Early charters also refer to Tell's Fort as *horduyllae* or *hordwelle* – 'the spring of the hoard or treasure'.[23] Is this a reference to the ancient practice of depositing hoards of metal or other treasures into water, a habit familiar in prehistory but almost certainly continued by the Anglo-Saxons?

The mention of a hoard is also a reminder that just below the White Horse is the natural though rather artificial-looking mound of Dragon Hill.

At last a short break in the rain
on the Ridgeway walking east towards
Barbury Castle. At easy fading light
The Ridgeway passes up through the
castle on sth. 835 29/11/09

xii (*top*) A downland landscape of the Ridgeway, looking towards
Barbury Castle, painted by Philip Hughes, 2009/10.

xiii (*above*) The White Horse as it appears on the Sheldon Tapestry map
(late sixteenth century). While not accurately depicted, the Horse is correctly
located north of Lambourn and east of Ashbury.

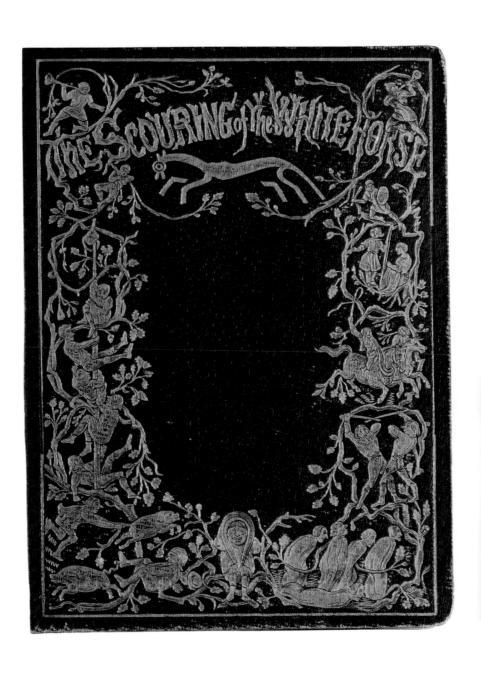

xiv The cover of Thomas Hughes's *The Scouring of the White Horse* (1859), elaborately decorated by Richard 'Dickie' Doyle. Unfortunately the White Horse faces the wrong way.

xv (*top*) *Remembrance*, the autobiography of H. J. Massingham, with a dust jacket created especially for the book by Paul Nash and featuring the White Horse and Uffington Castle on the back. Massingham was suggested as a possible author for Eric Ravilious's Puffin book on the White Horse.

xvi (*above*) Keith Grant, *Uffington Horse and White Horse Hill*, from the 1986 exhibition at the Francis Kyle Gallery.

xvii (*above*) Wittenham Clumps, the eastern extension of the Downs by
the Thames, painted by Paul Nash in 1913. A man-made, rook-racked downland
landscape, but without human figures. 'Grey, hallowed hills
crossed by old, old places', said Nash.

xviii, xix (*opposite*) Tania Kovats's homage to the White Horse and all
things equine: *The Museum of the White Horse* (2007), a horsebox filled with
horse memorabilia, which travelled the country.

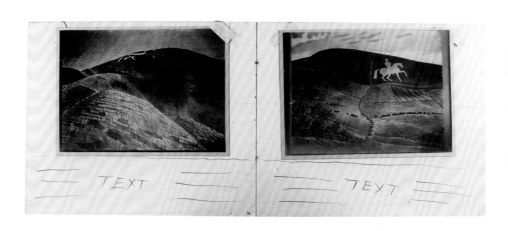

xx–xxii In Eric Ravilious's painting *The Vale of the White Horse* (1939; *opposite above*), the hill dominates the foreground and resembles the pelt of an animal, while the abstract Horse seems about to disappear over the horizon. It was featured in his mock-up for his proposed Puffin book *White Horse* (*above*), along with his paintings of George III on a horse at Osmington, near Weymouth, and the Westbury Horse seen through a railway carriage window, as well as the Cerne Abbas Giant. The project was abandoned on Ravilious's death in 1942.

xxiii (*above*) The Shell poster of the Cerne Abbas Giant (1931)
by Frank Dobson. In a bright landscape intended to be attractive to children,
the priapic Giant is emasculated by a passing cloud at the request of Shell's
marketing department.

xxiv Anna Dillon's painting of the White Horse
as viewed from the air, *Frost on Uffington* (1996).

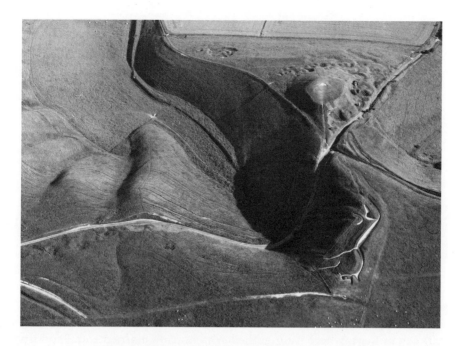

An aerial photograph which shows the relationship between the flat-topped
Dragon Hill (top right and surrounded by the marks of quarrying)
and the White Horse above the Manger.

In Anglo-Saxon mythology the job of the dragon was to guard treasure:
Draca sceal on hlaewe, frod, fraetwum wlanc ('A dragon must dwell in the
mound, ancient, glorifying in treasure').[24] When I flew low over Dragon Hill
in the evening sunlight, or stood in just the right place below it as I have
already mentioned, I was struck by how the White Horse appears to leap
out of Dragon Hill. To Anglo-Saxon eyes, perhaps the figure looked like a
dragon. There is, I am afraid, no direct evidence for this speculation.

The name 'Dragon Hill' was first recorded by Francis Wise in 1738, in relation to the local St George legend. In the charter bounds the hill is recorded
as *eceles beorh*, which, as discussed in Chapter 3, may refer to the presence
of a Christian church or to a personal name. However, as we saw in the previous chapter, the 'Trendles' (circle) name survived by word of mouth at the
Frilford temple complex, so it is possible that 'St George and the Dragon' is
a Christian transformation of an older myth that related to this distinctive
barrow-like hill – a place where a hero slew a monster. It is significant that
a horse and dragon appear on the medieval bell in Dorchester Abbey (see
p. 59) – the prehistoric horse and the pagan dragon both absorbed into the
iconography of Christianity, in the region's mother church.

ONWARD CHRISTIANS:
CREATING ANGLO-SAXON RELIGION IN ENGLAND

The Anglo-Saxons arrived in Britain carrying centuries-old baggage of mythology relating to the sun and to horses. The surviving Romano-Britons, whose ancestors made the White Horse, had much in common with this mythical tradition. The two groups soon mixed their ideas, their beliefs and their genes. This period, which is sometimes known as 'the Dark Ages', was, in fact, a time of fascinating change, creativity and cultural hybridization, from which new societies emerged.

The early generations of Anglo-Saxons were heathen. Gildas, a Briton, emphasized this, as did Bede, himself a descendant of the Anglian incomers. A Christian monk in the Italian papal tradition, Bede played down the importance of Celtic Christianity, which had survived and thrived in the west of Britain, Ireland and Scotland. He blamed British Christians for their laxity. God's punishment, Bede claimed, was to inflict his own heathen ancestors on them. Bede credited Augustine, Pope Gregory's missionary from Rome, with re-establishing Christianity after his arrival in AD 597 in Kent, where King Aethelberht, already married to a Frankish Christian, adopted the religion of his wife and the continental royal houses. The papal strategy was to insert Christianity from the top down, from where it would penetrate through the rest of society. The aim was to hitch a ride on power and politics. Cultivating the grass roots would come later.

A letter from Pope Gregory to his English mission in 601 suggests that diplomacy and tolerance of old ways was the best approach. He advised 'that the temples of the idols in that country should on no account be destroyed'. Dispose of the idols, but purify and Christianize the temples with relics and altars. The foreign missionaries should be careful not to upset the natives, it seems. However, shortly afterwards, Pope Gregory took a harder line. In a letter to Aethelberht, he urges the king to make the conversion of the English a top priority: 'Abolish the worship of idols and destroy their shrines.' Had Gregory changed his mind or did he believe the local ruler could be more heavy-handed than his own vulnerable mission?[25]

Christianity did not sweep in and wash away older beliefs and practices overnight. From the historical and archaeological records it is clear that some areas – for example, Sussex and the Isle of Wight – were more resistant to change than others. The Sutton Hoo ship burial reflects the complexities of seventh-century religion and alliances in East Anglia, with its hybrid mix of heathen and Christian influences.

In 2003 archaeologists made a remarkable discovery at Prittlewell in Essex.[26] Here they found a wooden chamber, the burial place of an elite man. The grave goods and two Merovingian coins date it to the late sixth century AD. The man was equipped with the gear of a warrior: a gold-mounted iron sword, spears and a gold-buckled belt. His chamber for the afterlife resembled a feasting hall, with drinking horns and vessels for cooking and serving food. A lyre and gaming pieces would provide him with entertainment in the long hours of eternity.

As at Sutton Hoo, we seem to have entered the world of heathen Anglo-Saxon warriors and kings, but at this time, they were developing contacts with the more Romanized Continent, with Francia (Merovingia) and even Italy and beyond. The Prittlewell 'prince' also had a Byzantine silver spoon incised with a cross, possibly a baptismal spoon, and two gold foil crosses (placed on his eyes) of a type usually found in Lombardy, or just over the Alps from there, about AD 600. So this could be the burial of Saeberht, or of his brother Saexa, interred as a heroic Germanic ruler, but with objects from the Christian south.

In AD 604, Augustine gave Mellitus the unenviable job of missionary to the East Saxons. Saeberht was their ruler, and nephew of Aethelberht of Kent, who was himself the over-king of southern England. Mellitus's initial success resulted in Aethelberht funding a new church in London – the first St Paul's – in the territory of the allied Middle Saxons (hence the county of Middlesex). Aethelberht died in AD 616 and was succeeded by his son Eadbald who was, initially, a follower of the old gods, as were the sons of Saeberht. Christianity's advance was clearly not without hiccups, and royal burials could reflect the dichotomies at a time of hybrid religious beliefs.

The papal missionaries penetrated the Upper Thames Valley in the 630s. Their leader, Birinus, intended to progress northwards, but arriving in the territory of the Gewisse (by then a powerful group occupying present-day Oxfordshire, north Berkshire and part of Wiltshire: the heartland of what became Wessex), he found them to be *paganissimi* – 'very pagan' – and in need of his ministrations. The Christian message, probably for political rather than theological reasons, found favour with the king, Cynegils. Birinus baptized him in the presence of King Oswald of Northumbria, who was the dominant partner in this new Anglo-Saxon–Christian alliance. The two kings agreed to establish the first bishopric at Dorchester-on-Thames, whose defences must still have surrounded the decayed Roman town. For Anglo-Saxons it was becoming increasingly important to attach themselves to sites with a historic pedigree. White Horse Hill became a place of elite burial, as did other hilltop sites with barrows, such as Lowbury. The Anglo-Saxon rulers respected the past and drew upon it to burnish their own authority.

At the same time, one impressive barrow by a Roman road and above the River Windrush (at Asthall, Oxfordshire) contained the cremation of an important man, who was buried with a Byzantine bowl, a Frankish bottle, a silver cup, a board game and the remains of his horse. Cremation was not approved of by Christian priests, who awaited the Resurrection.[27] So was this burial a statement of allegiance to the old ways?

The Thames was a significant channel of communication and trade from Kent to the Cotswolds. In its upper reaches near Lechlade in Gloucestershire, while investigating prehistoric fields we discovered a particularly important cemetery. The earliest burials of the later fifth and sixth centuries were distinctively Gewissan, although surprisingly wealthy for this period, especially those of some of the women. One had been buried with so much stuff we called her 'Mrs Getty'. As well as having the Gewissan saucer brooches and festoons of amber beads, she was influenced by Kentish fashions, with a great gilded square-headed brooch pinning her cloak, a purse of elephant ivory, a comb, a wooden bowl and so-called 'girdle-hangers', or symbolic keys. In Kentish law the woman who carried the keys (*lochore*) was of a high status. 'Mrs Getty' was relatively wealthy judging by her grave goods, but she was a member of a Gewissan society still without extremes of hierarchy.[28]

A century later, Anglo-Saxon society had developed a more pronounced social structure – with distinctly aristocratic burials. The Gewisse also lost their tribal signifiers and regional style. During the later seventh century the women adopted a pan-Anglo-Saxon style of dress, which would not have been out of fashion in Kent and was widespread across eastern England and westwards into Gloucestershire.

In the Lechlade burial ground in the later seventh century, the grave orientation turned west–east, possibly, but not necessarily, an indication of Christian affiliation. Christians customarily lie in the grave west–east, rising to face east to meet their maker on the Last Day – except priests, who face their congregation. Amber beads and saucer brooches disappeared. The richest women now had gold jewelry mounted with garnets, and almond-shaped amethyst beads, and some wore silver crosses or gold pendants with cross decorations. These were objects clearly reflecting the influences of the Continent, the Mediterranean and beyond. One woman was buried with a large cowrie shell, a beaver tooth pendant and a circular copper alloy casket, or 'workbox', most probably a religious reliquary.[29]

So were these people the first generation of West Saxons to adopt aspects of the Christian religion and its allegiances? Even if so, folk religion was still entangled with elements of Christianity – as it was for the emperor Constantine. In Ronald Hutton's words, this was a 'world of fluid religious identities' in which people 'pick and mix'; Christianity is not and never has been a single phenomenon.[30]

At Lechlade, in spite of Christian missionaries, the clan retained their ancestral burial ground for a generation and their tradition of burying their dead clothed, with grave goods that reflected their status, gender and beliefs. As a result of their changing religious allegiance and the direction of trade and political alliances, the Gewisse/West Saxons abandoned their use of more blatantly pagan or Germanic materials – such as amber. Their influences were shifting away from the North Sea province – their ancestral lands and sea lanes – to the more Romanized world of Francia across the English Channel. New materials appeared, indicating new values and symbols. They still believed in the power of amulets to protect – in childbirth, or against disease and witchcraft – but garnets glowed with the blood of Christ and amethysts symbolized heaven.[31] These people were creating new identities, which mined their Germanic past while adopting new influences from the Continent with memories of Roman power.

THE APPEARANCE OF CHURCHES

After about 680 the local community abandoned the Lechlade burial ground that had been in use for almost two centuries, and also their nearby settlement of scattered houses. Today by the market place in the small town of Lechlade is the fine late-fifteenth-century church of St Lawrence – funded, like many of the local Cotswold churches, by the wealth of the medieval wool trade. It was here in 1815 that the poet Shelley wrote 'In a Summer Evening Churchyard'. This church was built over the foundations of an earlier one – how much earlier we do not know. However, the construction of the first church on this site, prominent from the river, could explain the abandonment of the ancestral cemetery and the relocation of both the burial ground and the settlement. St Lawrence is also an interesting dedicatee. This third-century martyr had several early basilicas dedicated to him in Rome, and Pope Vitalian sent some of Lawrence's relics to King Oswald of Northumbria in the seventh century. The West Saxon alliance with the powerful northern kingdom could explain why Lawrence was honoured by this wealthy Thames-side community, controllers at the head of the river, the main artery to Kent and the Continent.

At this time Anglo-Saxon rulers began to sponsor new churches, notably minsters (from the Latin *Monasterium*), with monks, nuns or priests attached. In this way Christianity percolated through Anglo-Saxon society. Bampton in Oxfordshire, like Lechlade, is today a small town by the Thames, but in Domesday Book it was the second-most valuable manor in that county. For several years John Blair has investigated Bampton – attempting to unravel its complicated history: the site of a Bronze Age barrow cemetery, a Romano-British settlement and an early Anglo-Saxon settlement and burials. There was a Lady Well associated with cures, and evidence that heathen Anglo-Saxons made ritual deposits into the water. This was an ancient sacred landscape adopted by the new religion, one of those 'numinous places' that 'may have evolved by repeated use and visitations, by familiarity with the broad tapestry of the land and its resources'.[32]

Bampton's minster church is precisely aligned on a building 1 km (about ½ mile) to the east, a cottage known as 'the Beam'. This is the word from which Bampton gets its name, first recorded in 950, though originating earlier. In Old English, *beam* means a timber post or tree (as in hornbeam). In the early Anglo-Saxon world the name could also refer to a sacred place and a place of sacrifice.[33] In 1317, the Chapter of Exeter held 5.25 hectares (13 acres) *iuxta Beme* ('next to the Beam'). The cottage, it seems, was rebuilt from a twelfth-century chapel, itself built over a heathen ritual site. Blair suggests: 'Beam chapel is arguably our most convincing Anglo-Saxon case of that celebrated process, the conversion of pagan shrines to churches.'[34]

Secular rulers founded minsters with 'extraordinary enthusiasm' in the late seventh century. In the White Horse region a number of these were established within or close to prehistoric enclosures – at Eynsham, Oxford and Abingdon – all sites prominently sited by the River Thames. On the Downs, near White Horse Hill, a minster existed at Lambourn in 1032, and is now the fine parish church of St Michael, himself of course a heroic slayer of dragons and a guardian of high places.

By the early 700s most English people were at least nominally Christian, and Christianity had proved skilful at accommodating and adopting old ways – mostly, but not entirely, without force. The minsters acted as launch pads for further developments – the emergence of urban centres, markets and bureaucracies in what was a traditional, rural, kin-conscious society. Initially, aristocratic women played an important role in establishing new monastic centres – most famously Hild at Whitby, but closer to home a Mercian noblewoman, Frideswide, was the abbess of a double monastery in Oxford. St Ebbe's in Oxford may also be named for one of the 'aristocratic cousinhood', whose name (Aebbe) occurs in Abingdon – site of what would become the region's richest monastery. In early Anglo-Saxon communities women seem to have played an important role as 'wise women' healers, midwives and organizers of rituals – a role that apparently continued in the early phases of Christianity. However, as the Church became established, men exerted greater control.

The growing authority of the Church spread outwards from the minsters. New local parish churches were often built alongside the residences of thegns, initially as their private chapels, as we see today at Compton Beauchamp, below the White Horse. Local noblemen, along with the Church, dominated their communities.

In the later Anglo-Saxon period, landholdings tended to become smaller and large estates were dismembered, as at Bampton and Eynsham. In the Vale and downland area, 'strip-townships' appear in the tenth and eleventh centuries, as we have seen earlier from the charter evidence. Immediately under the White Horse, Woolstone (Wulfric's *tūn*) took its name from the thegn Wulfric, who was granted the land in 960 by King Eadgar. Woolstone was carved out of the larger estate of Æscesbyrig (the name of Uffington Castle). Uffington ('Uffa's Farm') appears as a name for the first time in the mid-tenth century and was also originally part of the larger estate. John Blair explains: 'We are witnessing here the creation of the English country gentry: a new class of small resident proprietors for whom manorial fragmentation provided an economic base.'[35] The tenth century saw urban development, more productive agriculture, population growth and the foundations of parishes, villages and churches that we can still see today. The common fields and nucleated villages began to emerge, which culminated in the manorial system of the high Middle Ages.

In spite of changes of land tenure, there is a strong current of continuity in land use. It would be fascinating to know who stimulated the curation of the White Horse – was it local tradition, the enthusiasm of the peasantry preserving the engrained habits of their ancestors, or were the scourers following the instruction of local lords, on whom the figure bestowed some kind of status? We cannot tell. And the person who composed the 'Wonders of Britain' (see p. 58) did not seem to know either. The Horse's cleanliness was associated with godliness, with wonder-working rather than with hard labour. But local people had to make the effort – time and time again – to keep the Horse alive.

CHANGE AT THE TOP

The Norman Conquest of 1066 was a disaster for the English – a papally approved land-grab, and a protection racket imposed by William's gang of bully boys. One of them, Miles Crispin, muscled his way into the lordship of thirty-one Oxfordshire manors. Yet there was also a remarkable degree of continuity in southern England – of population, villages, parishes, shires, law courts and towns. The Normans formed the new aristocracy, but beneath them the people remained English or Anglo-Scandinavian (in the north and east) and spoke English.[36] The bishopric of Dorchester-on-Thames was transferred to Lincoln, but Abingdon Abbey, under Norman abbots after 1071, remained a major local landowner.

After the setbacks of 1066, and the disruption that followed, the English economy and population continued to grow. The Domesday Book accounts indicate that north Berkshire was well populated. In the Vale and on White Horse Hill the familiar corrugated effect of ridge and furrow – the mark of medieval fields – expanded: for example, into the Manger and up into Uffington Castle (on the west side only, which belonged to Abingdon Abbey). This was the high-water mark of medieval arable agriculture.

Nearby, the magnificently austere barn at Great Coxwell still proclaims the productivity of the Vale. For William Morris (see also p. 248) it was 'unapproachable in its dignity, as beautiful as a cathedral'.[37] Recent tree-ring dating confirms that the building, with its impressive timber roof, went up about 1300. The barn was part of a grange (farm) belonging to the Cistercians of Beaulieu Abbey in Hampshire. The accounts of the abbey for 1269–70 detail Coxwell's output. Grain production was mostly wheat, oats and rye, amounting to 582 quarters. The monks sold the greater part and ground the rest in a windmill for flour. The stock consisted of 13 horses, 45 oxen, 1 bull, 11 cows, 18 calves and 20 pigs. There were 144 swine earlier in the year, but sales and disease reduced their numbers. The previous year's output included 4 tonnes of cheese, 6 tonnes of butter and about 20 litres (4½ gallons) of honey. The number of sheep is not specified, although the Beaulieu flocks totalled over five thousand animals. An unspecified number of lay brothers ran the Great Coxwell grange, with about fifteen hired servants. It was a productive place with a large labour force.[38]

New churches stitched together the parish system. About 1250, Abbot Faritius of Abingdon, himself an immigrant from Tuscany, founded the fine early Gothic 'Cathedral of the Vale' – St Mary's Uffington: 'To stand under the cross-tower and gaze up at the undulating lines of its arches and vaults is to see medieval architecture at its most pure.'[39] Two familiar figures now guard each side of the porch: Alfred the Great and St George, carved by local sculptor Heidi Lloyd in 1975 – heroes as much mythical as historical, both woven into the local landscape.

In 1341, Berkshire was the sixth-richest county in England. The exceptionally good records of Woolstone show that it was a two-field manor, which was routinely rotated, and that sheep were important, presumably grazed on the Downs and folded on the parish's corn lands in the Vale.

Animal dung was vital to fertility and the health of the soil. Conditions deteriorated, however: an inquest of 1342 shows that disease was decimating the flocks. At the same time Lambourn pleaded poverty, and cultivators were abandoning their land. Persistent bad weather was probably to blame. Nevertheless, at Woolstone there were signs of improvement by 1348, when the profits of the manor increased.

Then the plague hit – the catastrophe that originated on the Eurasian steppes and came to be known as the Black Death. About a third of the British population died. In 1352, Woolstone's corn sales fell from £33.13s.2d to £8.17s.1d – almost certainly because of the loss of labourers on the land. The Woolstone records tell us that stock sales also declined, but not drastically. The solution was to hire labour at increased rates. Two women taken on to milk ewes were paid 2 pence a week (almost twice the normal rate for labourers). This was 'in defect of the customary tenants who were dead and their lands in the Lord's hands'. Payment also had to be made for washing and shearing sheep, weeding and mowing. The rate for reaping pulses and barley was 3 pence per acre, 4 pence for wheat.[40] These were activities necessary to provide food, to keep the surviving population alive. What priority was Horse scouring in such times? Or could it wait?

Fortunately, it seems that at Woolstone recovery from the plague was relatively rapid – at least in economic terms. God knows what the emotional damage must have been after such human losses. By 1354 there were signs of improvement and by 1361 some things were back to normal – for example, customary tenants took on the work of the hired dairy-women and hired hands were no longer needed for weeding.

The plague and then the Peasants Revolt of 1381 made a long-term impact on traditional feudal arrangements, promoting emancipation and an increase in rent-paying tenants. In the mid-fifteenth century, one farmer at Woolstone leased land for seven years. In 1458, just before the lease came to an end, the farmer scarpered, taking with him 7 sheep, 5 cows, 4 oxen, 10 quarters of wheat and 13 of barley, 7 quarters of beans and various tools. We do not know what became of him. Undeterred, the lord let out the land again in 1463, on a lease of eight years, to one Richard Westhrop. By 1450, only Norfolk, Oxfordshire and Middlesex were wealthier counties than Berkshire. The Vale and downland prospered while the Horse looked on.

CHAPTER THIRTEEN

REINVENTING
THE NATION'S PAST

Civilization comes from what men call greed.

Plantagenet Palliser in *Can You Forgive Her?*,

Anthony Trollope, 1864

FROM MYTH TO HISTORY

The Black Death of the fourteenth century scythed through the population of England and fractured the feudal world of the Middle Ages. An increasingly powerful group of people in southern England began to see the land in a different way: a resource generating productivity, income, profit and status. The intellectual, artistic and economic movements on the Continent, now known as the Renaissance, were also lapping against English shores, ultimately bringing about the religious Reformation of the sixteenth century. The Italian Polydore Vergil (*c.* 1470–1555) arrived in England in 1502 as a papal tax gatherer, a collector of 'Peter's Pence'. He must have like the place – he stayed for over fifty years, eventually in the service of the Tudors, and wrote a history of Britain, the *Anglica Historia* (published in 1534). Polydore attempted to scrub away some of the fables of the past, and he had the temerity to point out an English characteristic: a dogged belief in their own myths.

In particular, he attacked the story of national origin compiled by Geoffrey of Monmouth in around 1133, the *Historia Regum Britanniae* (*History of the Kings of Britain*), perhaps the most influential, if not the most accurate, 'history' ever written in Oxford. The Britons, Geoffrey claimed, were of Trojan descent, like the Romans. They travelled to an island in the sea, beyond the setting of the sun: 'Now it is empty and ready for your people.... A race of kings will be born there from your stock and the round circle of the whole earth will be subject to them.' These heroes included King Arthur – who supposedly conquered swathes of Europe. Polydore did not think much of this national fairy tale, or King Arthur. He preferred to consign it, and him, to the dustbin of medieval storytelling.[1]

His dismissal of Arthur did not make Polydore Vergil popular with British nationalists, 'that most rascall, dogge knave in the worlde', who undermined the glory of ancient Britain at the bidding of the Pope. His opponents claimed that he smuggled important ancient documents (evidence of the British version of history) back to Rome. In fact, he did great service both to the Tudors and the Protestant Church.[2] The Tudor king, Henry VIII, continued to claim descent from Arthur, the 'Once and Future King', whose tomb had been 'discovered' by the medieval monks of Glastonbury Abbey in 1191.[3]

Polydore Vergil was a man of his times, on the cusp of a more rigorous approach to the study of history. But change does not happen overnight. While Polydore Vergil was critical of dubious sources, he still relied on 'Fortune' and 'divine intervention' to explain events. His greatest influence was unintended. He was the source for the sixteenth-century histories of Edward Hall and Raphael Holinshed, on which Shakespeare based his history plays, thus providing the English with a vivid, coherent narrative that still tugs at the national imagination today. Many people know, for instance that for Richard III the price of his kingdom was a horse; or that English and Welsh archers could see off any overwhelming continental armies with a bow and a V sign.

STRIPPING THE ALTARS

In the 1530s and 1540s, John Leland, a poet and scholar (who vehemently disagreed with Polydore about the glorious British past), travelled the country armed with a royal commission from Henry VIII (see also p. 61). In his *Itinerary* he reported on the state of the nation, its towns and activities. In particular, he documented the contents and condition of the ancient monastic libraries.

The Dissolution of the Monasteries was part of the process that shifted and diminished the role of the Church – no longer the main provider of medical welfare, education and administrators. Henry's attack on these institutions resulted in the greatest land-grab since the Norman Conquest, which permanently altered the English landscape and society. In about six years up to 1541, in 'an operation of remarkable efficiency', the King's agents extinguished all monasteries, friaries and nunneries in England and Wales. Over eight hundred religious houses were demolished, left to become romantic ruins, or converted to houses and workshops. Altars were stripped of their treasures, roofs of their lead. A few survived as cathedrals or became parish churches, such as St Peter and St Paul, Dorchester-on-Thames, which was bought by Richard Beauforest, 'a great rich man of

Dorchester', and presented to the parish. As much as a third of the land of England and Wales was confiscated. The process was arbitrary, sometimes brutal and of dubious legality. As frequently happens, people who gained financially held their noses and turned a blind eye.

Henry, however, was proud of his achievements, comparing himself to the Old Testament priest Phineas, who recognized God's hatred of idolatry and persuaded the Israelites of the error of their ways. For Henry it was a very convenient form of self-righteousness; hardly surprising, then, that he thought the church windows of Oxford's Rewley Abbey were better employed illuminating the exertions on his bowling alley at Hampton Court.[4]

In the Vale of the White Horse, and nearby counties, the estates that had belonged to such great religious houses as Abingdon, Reading and Beaulieu were carved up and privatized almost overnight. The manor of Uffington had belonged to Abingdon Abbey since the tenth century. After almost six hundred years it was seized by the Crown in 1537–38. Uffington went through a succession of owners until, in 1620, the Jones family sold it to Elizabeth Craven. Elizabeth's son became Viscount Craven of Uffington and the family retained the manor of Uffington until the 1950s. For a period, the Cravens choreographed or at least gave permission for the scouring of the White Horse.

Ironically, the developing study of monastic documents, especially for county histories, benefited those families that had themselves acquired land and profited from the suppression of the monasteries. Landowners found the surviving documents useful, as they helped support their title to new acquisitions from the religious houses.

PUTTING ENGLAND ON THE MAP

By the seventeenth century, the landed gentry were avid customers for the spate of publications devoted to antiquities, genealogy, and the natural history and history of English counties: Sir William Dugdale's *The Antiquities of Warwickshire* (1656), followed by many others, notably Robert Plot's *Natural History of Oxfordshire* (1677) and then *Staffordshire* (1686). The English gentry took a pride in their families, their land, their nation – and especially their county. Thanks to the printing press the number of books increased enormously and many landowners built up substantial private libraries.

There was also a rapid growth of interest in cartography and the acquisition of maps, which visually represented the nation with its counties and hundreds as essential elements, as well as detailed estate maps. The land

The arrival of Hengist in Kent, holding his shield with its device of a white horse, from John Speed's map, 'Britain as it was devided in the tyme of the Englishe-Saxons'.

surveyor Ralph Agar, in a 1596 treatise, advised the landowner to 'Know his own'. This increasing interest in landholding and boundaries influenced the approach to the past. Sir Robert Atkyns, author of *The Ancient and Present State of Gloucestershire* (1712), claimed that it was impossible to give an account of such matters before the arrival of the Romans, because Britain was a 'multitude of barbarous Kings' who kept shifting around. Hence, to Atkyns and other antiquarians obsessed by the descent of property, prehistory and the study of barbarians provided 'little edification'.[5]

Christopher Saxton's *Atlas of England and Wales* (1579), with its superb county maps, was the first of a series, which included John Norden's *Speculum Britannia* (only partially completed) and John Speed's *The Theatre of the Empire of Great Britain* of 1611.[6] A pocket version of the atlas followed in 1627. Speed (*c.* 1552–1629) based his maps on those of Saxton and others, but made them even prettier and more patriotic, depicting fine buildings, towns, battlefields and heraldry. The shield of Kent bears the insignia of a white horse, which also appears on the shield carried by Hengist. Delving into Speed's world, one can almost believe in Shakespeare's rural idyll – 'This other Eden, demi-paradise ... set in the silver sea' – even if the famous patriotic speech was put into the mouth of John of Gaunt (Ghent, now in Belgium), a man who did not speak English and spent much of his life on the wrong side of the Channel.

The Berkshire sheet of Speed is dominated by the towers and turrets of Windsor Castle. The map itself is divided by a range of hills – the Downs

– depicted like a line of molehills (cartographers had not yet solved the problem of indicating height). 'Whithorse hill' is labelled as such, with 'The Vale of Whitehorse' to the north, though the scale does not allow for an image of the hill figure. For this we have to turn to the huge Sheldon Tapestry map (Pl. xiii; see also p. 60). The gentry demonstrated their taste and influence not only with books and atlases, but also with large tapestry maps displayed on their walls. The Sheldon Tapestry map for Oxfordshire was big enough to include an image of the White Horse itself, albeit an inaccurate one.

Another type of map indicated the growing interest in travel and commerce. In 1675, John Ogilby (1600–1676) produced the first road atlas, entitled *Britannia*, although it covered only England and Wales. The next edition, in the same year, was retitled, less ambitiously, *Itinerarium Angliae*. The busy frontispiece shows surveyors pushing their 'way-wiser' – the handwheel used to measure distance – past a flock of sheep, while a coach and horses struggles up a meandering road to the top of the chalk downland, which is capped by a windmill. Travel was still slow and often difficult. After the Romans left, the British never do seem to have got the hang of road-building.

TRAVELLERS AND TRAVEL GUIDES

Leland had doggedly travelled the length, though not always the breadth, of England in the sixteenth century – he tended to stick to coasts and valleys. In Berkshire, he notes: 'the fertile Vale of the White Horse begins about Sinodun [the hillfort on Wittenham Clumps overlooking Dorchester-on-Thames] and stretches away southwest to the Faringdon area. The Vale has not much woodland.'[7] His travels, and his focus on towns and churches, took him to Abingdon, Wantage and Lambourn – which he calls 'Cheping Lanburne',[8] with its 'poor Friday market'. The White Horse lay off the beaten track and merited no mention, though on a good day Leland might have seen it from the road to Faringdon.

The arrival of road maps in the late seventeenth century encouraged other determined travellers. Between 1682 and 1712 Celia Fiennes (1662–1741) progressed around the country, largely on horseback, and recorded what she saw in her journals.[9] She encouraged travel to 'form such an idea of England, add much to its Glory and Esteem in our minds and cure the evil itch of over-valuing foreign parts'.

Fiennes should be the patron of the British tourist industry. Her aim, she said, was to save the English from 'ignorance and being strangers to themselves'. Born near Salisbury, she came of good Roundhead and

Nonconformist stock. Her father was a colonel in Cromwell's army and her grandfather, Viscount Saye and Sele of Broughton Castle, Oxfordshire, was a leading light in planning the Civil War against the king. In George Eliot's words (describing Dorothea Brooke in *Middlemarch*), 'the hereditary strain of Puritan energy ... glowed' in her. She preferred 'the convenience of the modern to the romance of the old' and did not conform to any clichéd image of a delicate gentlewoman: her interests included mining, manufactures and money-making. While willing to tackle rough roads, Fiennes was also partial to the comfortable houses of rich men. However, she was an accurate witness and, unlike some writers who followed in her tracks such as her contemporary Daniel Defoe, she did not describe what she had not seen for herself.

She began her series of journeys shortly after Ogilby's book of road maps appeared in 1675. Turnpike roads were legalized in 1663, which generated funds for much needed repairs. Yet, as she often tells us, roads were still frequently rutted, pot-holed and even, at times, impassable. No wonder she preferred horseback to carriage. Nevertheless, people were increasingly on the move – patronizing the growing number of spas such as Bath, Epsom, Tunbridge Wells and Buxton, for example – all of which Fiennes sampled, for better or worse. She seems to have become something of a specialist on which waters were 'diaretick' or 'good for scorbutick humours' and which malodorous 'stinking spaws' to avoid.

Celia Fiennes travelled with her mother 'into Oxfordshire by Berkshire' – so perhaps, this time, taking to a coach. The ladies stopped off at 'Farington' and Celia provides us with a lengthy description of Sir George Pratt's fine house at Coleshill (built in the 1650s in consultation with Inigo Jones). When it comes to gardens and furnishings she was no puritan, unlike Defoe who had no time for 'geegaws'. 'From thence', she writes, 'we enter over the Vale of the White Horse which takes its name from a Ridge of high hills on which is cut out the shape of a horse in perfect proportions, in broad ways, and is seen a great distance very plaine, the hills being a chalke look's white and the great valley in the bottom is term'd the manger.'

Daniel Defoe wrote a similar itinerary – his *Tour through the Whole Island of Great Britain* (1725) – though it was, at times, mischievous and, certainly by modern standards, politically incorrect (he supported slavery, disliked foreigners – especially the Irish – hated Papists and their architecture. One could go on...). Defoe liked to tease his readers – he makes crossing the Pennines in summer seem like an epic expedition in the Himalayas. On the other hand, his statement that the White Horse was dug out and filled with chalk (see p. 64) has the flavour of first-hand report-ing. Nevertheless, most subsequent commentators on the Horse, with the exception of Francis Wise, ignored Defoe's explanation.

The enormous increase in documentary sources means that we have a more nuanced picture of the place of the White Horse in English culture for the past three or four centuries: how politics, rural economy, social change and intellectual trends affected attitudes to the hill figure. In the eight-eenth and early nineteenth centuries, the White Horse leapt to a peak of popularity. It became an English icon, only to slither into neglect by the end of the century. So what brought about this turn of events?

SAXONS AND ENGLISH NATIONALISM: 'OUR HISTORY BEGINS'

The growth of English nationalism and the emergence of a national Church under Henry VIII and Elizabeth I did not make the past irrelevant. There was no year zero. In fact, throughout the history of early modern Britain, rulers justified change by claiming to resurrect the past. The past provided the English with the material they needed to construct a new national myth, and they increasingly found it in the Anglo-Saxons. This was a dramatic change of tack, as Philip Schwyzer, a specialist in early modern English literature at the University of Exeter, points out, refer-ring to the Tudors: 'The general silence on the subject of the Saxons in this period, and the low esteem in which they were held, stands in remarkable contrast to the Teutonomania of later centuries.'[10]

It seems that in the sixteenth century only Catholic dissidents had any interest in the Anglo-Saxons – a people converted to Christianity by the agents of the Pope. The shift of attitude begins to be apparent in Richard Verstegan's *A Restitution of Decayed Intelligence in Antiquities: Concerning the Most Noble and Renowned English Nation* (1605), a work that kick-started the rehabilitation of the Anglo-Saxons. Verstegan's *Restitution* included an illustration of Hengist and Horsa landing in Kent (as described by Bede). A follower bears their standard – a galloping white horse. Verstegan pro-moted the idea that the Anglo-Saxons were the ancestors of the English, and gave birth to distinctively English virtues and institutions: to liberty and common law. The later seventeenth century saw Anglo-Saxon schol-arship flourish in Oxford and Cambridge, with the publication of early English sources, although Bede – still tinged with Papism – was not made available for popular consumption.

The Anglo-Saxons received a further fillip with the accession of the Hanoverians to the throne of Great Britain (the Act of Union of 1707 had united Scotland with England and Wales). Britannia was once again united as in the days of the Romans. Edmund Gibson, bishop of London and a leading antiquary, was also, it seems, a skilled sycophant. In 1722 he dedicated his revised edition of Camden's *Britannia* to the new monarch, George I, welcoming a fellow Teuton:

> Not only our Histories, but our Language, our Laws, our Customs, Our Names of Persons and names of Places, do all abundantly testify, that the greatest part of your Majesty's Subjects here, are of SAXON Original. And if we enquire from whence our Saxon Ancestors came, we shall find, that it was from your Majesty's Dominions in *Germany*.[11]

William Stukeley, the great antiquary and bizarre promoter of the Druid myth, was also a Hanoverian supporter. He claimed that the royal family was descended from Hengist himself: the man who, according to John Aubrey, had given his name to England – 'Hengist's Land'. It is hardly surprising that an ambitious scholar like Francis Wise, at Oxford, should jump on the bandwagon. The White Horse, Hengist's emblem, was on his doorstep. It suited him, and the politics of the time, to promote this symbol of Englishness. The Romans departed, 'And here,' Wise pronounced in his *Letter to Dr Mead* of 1738, 'our history may be said to begin.'[12]

Wise drew attention not only to the White Horse, but also to other hill figures: the nearby Westbury Horse (an earlier version), the Whiteleaf Cross on the Chilterns, and the Cerne Abbas Giant in Dorset (which he had not seen). These hill figures, he hoped, would be his passport to membership of the Society of Antiquaries, which had been formally founded in 1717 and provided the gateway to the 'Republic of Letters' for any gentleman devoted to the past.[13]

The Society of Antiquaries was much concerned with 'construction of national honour'. European nations competed to promote their ancestral glories; 'Bryttish antiquitys' must be as good as anyone else's. Wise echoed Celia Fiennes: the English should stop wandering about 'seeking adventure in foreign lands' and pay attention to their own history. And nowhere deserved attention more than the White Horse and its landscape – where the Christian army of Alfred had triumphed over the heathen Danes. Alfred's celebratory monument – and Wise seems to be the first to link the White Horse to Alfred – may 'hereafter vye with the Pyramids for duration, and perhaps exist, when those shall be no more'.

Wise was aware of the practice of scouring the Horse; it was no longer a 'Wonder' that had simply appeared and remained bare. He reports that in the 1670s, Thomas Baskerville (of Bayworth, near Abingdon, 'a gentleman of learning and curiosity', according to Wise) visited the site and was the first to explain that the White Horse had to be cleaned:

> From this pleasant town of Faringdon in Barkshire Travellers may go two ways to Bristow, either by Leachlade in Glocestershire, or by Hyworth in Wiltshire. [By this latter route] ... you shall go by Coltfwell [Coxwell] ... Here I may take occasion to speake of that Ancient Land marke or remarkable work of Antiquity, which gives name to our Country the Vale of White Horse; for in the way betwixt Faringdon and Hyworth, some five or six miles distante, you have the best prospect of the White Horse, cut in the side of a white chalky hill, a mile above Uffington. The Manger, as they caleth it, or sides and bottome, where this Horse is cutt, is now in the possession of my loving friend and neighbor, Mr Wiseman of Sparswell's Court: and some that dwell hereabout have an obligation upon their Lands to repair and cleanse this Land marke, or else in time it may turne green, like the rest of the hill, and be forgotten. As touching the original of this eminent landmark, which gives its name to one of the best Vales of England, I heard my Father say, who was a man well read in Antiquityes, that he thought it was Hengist, the Saxon conqueror, who in remembrance of his exploits, this being his Armes or Crest to them, caused this figure to be cut there. This Hengist came into England in AD 450 being sent for by Vortigern to assist him in his warres.[14]

Aubrey's idea that the Horse had an earlier, British, pedigree did not go away. However, in the minds of most scholars, and certainly in the view of the people at large, the White Horse was associated with King Alfred. The Saxons were essential to the post-Reformation national origins' myth because the Church of England needed to establish its roots in the pure English Saxon church before it had been corrupted by medieval popery. The second, and perhaps more important, reason to cling to the Saxons was that they were the people supposedly who established the system of common land, the nation's constitutional principles and Parliament: 'The great seed plot of our national history', according to the often fanciful, but widely read antiquary John Whitaker.[15]

The English took pride in qualities that they claimed to have inherited from the Saxons. And the embodiment of these qualities was King Alfred, born in Wantage in AD 847 or 848: England's champion, warrior, father of the navy and scholar. Above all, he was victorious over the great heathen army of the Danes, who fought under Odin's black raven banner, in battles on the Downs, at Ashdown in 871 and in 878 at Ethandune.[16] Alfred is the staunch, plucky Englishman, his back to the wall, against the odds over-coming the barbarian hordes from over the sea. A complex history of compromise was simplified into a national myth.

So Alfred's reputation rose as the nation's model king and the great-est Englishman, and the Uffington and Westbury hill figures became celebrated as memorials of his success. Of course, it is false logic automat-ically to associate an ancient and distinctive monument with a known and celebrated ancient event, but that is what Wise did on White Horse Hill. National myth-makers are rarely fastidious about the facts of history. Alfred became the new Arthur. The prehistoric earthwork southwest of the White Horse was labelled Alfred's Castle; the many Bronze Age barrows on the Downs were the burial places of Danish leaders.

My favourite story on the Alfred tourist trail was concocted in Devizes, Wiltshire. In 1826, the travel writer known as the London Hermit went from an inn in Wantage – Alfred's Head, 'the very house' of Alfred's birth – to Alfred's Castle, a 'rude, rotund rampart of earth' and the site of the Battle of Ashdown, he was told. At Devizes, he saw some recently discov-ered cannon balls that, locals assured him, had been fired by the Dane Guthrum at the Battle of Edington (Ethandune). The London Hermit set out for Edington, only 11 km (7 miles) away as the cannon ball flies, to view the battlefield and the Westbury Horse, which was said to celebrate the English victory: a remarkable feat in the face of Danish cannon!

At this time, the English heritage prioritized Christian monuments: everything else was an oddity, a curiosity or, worst of all, foreign. The London Hermit, in his tour guide, set out sites in order of importance. The White Horse topped his list, above Avebury, Stonehenge and Silbury Hill, because it was blessed with an English and Christian origin.

ATTRACTING THE CROWDS

It is easy to question the veracity of White Horse myths, whether they relate to pagan sun chariots or Christian battles with the Danes. What matters is that they meant something to people at the time – the stories defined their identity. As a result, the English admired and cared for the White Horse, and began to replicate it.

Wise describes the festivities that accompanied the scouring of 'this noble antiquity' and speculated that the origins lay with the 'Saxon Olympicks'. He felt that these 'manlike games' had gone downhill, debased at the hands of local rustics. In order to restore the Games 'to their ancient splendour, of which, without question, they are fallen much short', Wise argued for 'the countenance and presence of Nobility and Gentry; which would have a good influence upon the assembly, add decency to the meeting, and restrain the excesses of the population'. The snooty Oxford don wanted to attract the patricians and sideline the plebs.

The history of changing attitudes to popular culture in England following the Reformation – to seasonal rituals, feasts, revels, pageants and processions – is fascinating and complicated, but, to a considerable extent, the pastimes of the gentry, with their grand houses, parks and gardens, were increasingly divorced from the rustic revels of the ordinary folk.[17]

Traditionally, seasonal tasks that required cooperation and hard work – such as harvesting and mowing – were followed by communal sports, feasting, drinking and dancing, sometimes at the expense of the Lord of the Manor, but often organized by the labourers themselves. Innkeepers also promoted revels, just as today they might organize a pig-roast or have a huge screen to display a sports event. Crowds are good for business. Home brewers capitalized by setting up unlicensed 'bush-houses' on the routes to the revels to attract thirsty visitors. Such places were notoriously unruly, and the authorities clamped down on them.

Eventually Wise got his way and the gentry took control – of the land through enclosure, the Courts and what they saw as archaic, uncouth and unruly activities.

WHO RULES BRITANNIA?

Wise's appeal in 1738 that the 'Nobility and Gentry' should take part in the scouring pastimes (Olympicks) did not meet with immediate success. Things changed, however, in the 1770s, not least because of the Enclosure Acts. Enclosure was the process of reorganizing land ownership, to bring parcels of land together into tidy and economical units that could be more efficiently farmed by one person. This had gone on, in a piecemeal fashion, for centuries – the earliest reference in Berkshire to enclosure was in the fourteenth century. However, in the eighteenth century the whole business became much more systematic. The growth of population and the improvements in agricultural techniques tempted landowners to pursue the potential increases in productivity and profitability of their assets. This involved doing away with the ancient rights of the peasantry, such as grazing on common pasture and 'wastes', collecting firewood 'by hook or by crook' or gleaning for leftover grain after the harvest. Each parish, or group of parishes, to be enclosed required a separate Act of Parliament – but as the large landowners controlled both Parliament and the Courts this did not usually present too much of a problem. Between 1760 and 1800 Parliament passed almost fifteen hundred Enclosure Acts, including in 1778 the 1,485 hectares (3,670 acres) of Uffington, Baulking and Woolstone.[18]

Powerless poets, like John Clare in 'The Mores', might bemoan the changes:

Inclosure came and trampled on the grave
Of labour's rights and left the poor a slave

But power lay with the landowners, who argued, as many still do, that big is best and productivity trumps and tramples on all other interests – animal, vegetable and mineral. Proselytizers for the new agriculture, such as the writer on agriculture and economics Arthur Young (1741–1820), condemned the traditional open-field cultivators as 'Goths and Vandals'.

Today, from White Horse Hill, we look down on a patchwork landscape of fields defined by hedges, most of them planted at enclosure. Ironically, lovers of wildlife and scenery now complain when efficiency-driven farmers, in their mega-machines, grub out these hedges to create a prairie landscape. Fortunately, the hedge loss in the Vale has not been drastic and most of those that existed two hundred years ago still remain. On the Downs, hedges were not a major part of the enclosure package. Instead, fields were often simply defined with marker stones until the appearance of that great American invention of the 1860s – barbed wire, the stuff that severed traditional footpaths on the Downs, tamed the Wild West and is now the symbol of Amnesty International.

The Uffington Enclosure Award provides us with the names of the largest landowners. These included Abraham Atkins of Kingston Lisle and Lovelace Bigg of Woolstone, who, one of his tenants said, 'had a face that could have been very fine if a horse had not sat on it'.[19] Heading the list of landowners was the 6th Baron Craven, William Craven (1738–1791). A 1788 map of the Craven estate shows that, as a result of the Enclosure Award, Craven land had been extended to include the White Horse and the whole of Uffington Castle, the hillfort that had previously been divided between two properties. When Elizabeth Craven had acquired Uffington Manor in 1620, the White Horse stood on Woolstone Down, land belonging to Lord Barrington.[20]

We are told in *The Scouring of the White Horse Country*:

That ancient piece of antiquity ... the White Horse was cleaned for many years by William, Lord Barrington, but the grounds on which the Horse is cut being allotted by the Commissioners for Uffington inclosure 1775

to William, Lord Craven His Lordship has since that time cleansed
it annually at His expense and has twice celebrated the Scouring
of the Horse with many country diversions viz horse racing, ass racing,
men running in sacks, men running down the steep part of the hill for
a cheese, boys dipping in a tub of meal for a bullet etc. At both which
sports there were computed to be upwards of 30,000 spectators. His
Lordship gave a most elegant cold collation in a large booth to all
gentlemen of the neighbourhood who were present and likewise strong
beer to the common people.[21]

This confirms an account in 1720 by Thomas Cox, author of *Magna Britannia et Hibernia, Antiqua & Nova*, that the Horse was weeded each year, and the scouring and revels took place on a less regular basis. Wise suggested this should be every four years for his 'Saxon Olympicks', instead of being left 'to the discretion of the inhabitants'. Thomas Hughes believed that the scouring took place on a seven-year cycle, but there is no evidence of such consistency.

As landowners tightened their grip 'the scouring revels were transformed from a communal recreation for the masses, into a spectacle to entertain the upper classes'.[22] The local newspaper, the *Reading Mercury and Oxford Gazette*, for 22 May 1780 records: 'The ceremony of scouring and cleansing that noble monument of Saxon antiquity, the White Horse, was celebrated on Whit-Monday with great joyous festivity.... Upwards of thirty thousand persons were present, and amongst them most of the nobility and gentry of this and the neighbouring counties.'

The White Horse had been successfully reinvented as a unifying symbol of Christian England, bringing together the monarchy and aristocracy, along with the population as a whole. Like the River Thames, it could be seen as a national symbol and a 'balm for political friction'.[23]

The Georgian elite was delighted to see such a display of unity at a time when the 'common people' were coming under increasing stress, and in France and America the authority of monarchy was being challenged. In June 1789, 'Farmer' George III (1738–1820) stopped off in the New Forest, on his way to the newly fashionable bathing resort of Weymouth. He was accompanied by his wife and three of his daughters. So, while Louis XVI barricaded himself into Versailles and Paris rioted, Great Britain's popular Hanoverian royal family dined *al fresco* and the watching public cheered every mouthful. But there were limits: 'the populace became rather riotous in their joy (and) there was a necessity to exclude them'.[24] One simply couldn't trust the plebs to behave!

HORSES MULTIPLY

That the Uffington scouring was popular among the elite can be seen from the way hill figures began to proliferate. Each scouring seems to have given birth to yet another 'horse', as can be seen in the list below:[25]

Uffington Scourings	New Horse Hill Figures
1776	Westbury (1778), Wiltshire
1780	Cherhill, Wiltshire
1785	Pewsey, Wiltshire
1803	Marlborough (1804), Wiltshire
1808	Osmington, near Weymouth, Dorset
1812	Alton Barnes, Wiltshire
1838	Hackpen, Wiltshire
1843	Devizes Snob (1845), Wiltshire
1857	Kilburn, North Yorkshire

These new horse images, reproduced on prominent slopes, occurred as landowners became fond of creating eye-catching features in the landscape. They could be conspicuous brands of ownership – or signs of patriotism and allegiance. Many were dedicated to the remarkably popular George III, who came to the throne in 1760 and, unlike the previous Georges, had been born in England. During his long reign Britain lost the American colonies but expanded its empire and scraped to victory over Napoleon in 1815. He had been labelled 'Farmer George' by satirists, but, as he proved himself to be a thrifty and moral 'man of the people', the name worked to his advantage. He was a John Bull character, standing for British 'values' against French tyranny – even if revolting Americans, always eager to avoid paying taxes, did not see him in the same way.

It seems likely that landowners were inspired to create this spate of new horse figures by the ubiquitous Hanoverian white horse that appeared on coinage, medals and the royal coats of arms displayed in most churches. The appearance of the new Westbury Horse in 1778 coincided with George III's fortieth birthday and, in total, six chalk horses sprang forth during his reign, but after that only sporadically. The white horse represented not only the Hanoverians, but specifically George III himself, who emphasized the connection by riding a white horse – Adonis, his 'favourite charger' – when he reviewed his troops in Hyde Park on his birthdays. He had others harnessed to his spectacular royal coach designed by Sir William Chambers, the eighteenth-century architect of the Kew Gardens pagoda and Somerset House.

The Osmington hill figure, near Weymouth, Dorset, carved in honour of the rider,
King George III, in 1808, who visited the fashionable bathing resort with his family.

A most distinctive white horse, dedicated to the king, appeared in 1808
at Osmington, Dorset, not far from Weymouth, the resort he put on the
map. This one showed George himself in the saddle. Perhaps the carvers
were promoting the healthy sea air of Weymouth – King George had
arrived ill and debilitated, and now look at him: back on his horse, riding
towards London. The Osmington Horse is a forerunner of those distinctive
seaside posters – Skegness is so bracing! – created by John Hassall in 1908.

Other horse figures appeared on the Downs, closer to Uffington. The
best known is the Westbury White Horse, on land that belonged to the 4th
Earl of Abingdon, Willoughby Bertie (1740–1799). Like Lord Craven he had
a survey of his land carried out in the run-up to enclosure. The hugely successful Uffington scouring of 1776 may have inspired him to create the
Westbury Horse, possibly replacing a smaller figure of uncertain date.

Willoughby Bertie was notoriously fond of horses and horse racing, an addiction that proved to be a financial roller coaster. His debts made him unpopular with some, his support of American revolutionaries with many others. He also made serious business errors – selling his best horse Pot8os,[26] a son of the great Eclipse, to his rival, the lascivious racing fanatic, the Earl of Grosvenor. In spite of his unflattering name, the horse went on to win at least twenty-eight races. Horace Walpole, antiquary, author and man-of-the-world, described Willoughby Bertie as 'rough, wrongheaded, extremely under-bred, but warmly honest ... eager in every pursuit without any knowledge of the world'.[27] His lack of business acumen led him to sell off the family estates in America after the Revolution – the piece of land now known as Greenwich Village in New York. Nearer home, the new Westbury hill figure is a monument to his fondness for horseflesh.

The Earl of Abingdon was not alone. This was the period (through the eighteenth century until the Repeal of the Corn Laws in 1846) when English racing was dominated by the great aristocratic landowners, after which rich, upstart industrialists and newspaper barons came to the fore. Successful horses were so popular that their proud owners commissioned their

The Westbury Horse, Wiltshire, was carved in 1778, possibly on the site of a previous figure of a smaller horse. It was created for the 4th Earl of Abingdon, Willoughby Bertie.

portraits. These fine animals, English thoroughbreds, had been created by crossing English mares with imported Arabians – the Godolphin Arabian from Yemen, the Byerley Turk, and the daddy of virtually all modern thoroughbreds, the Darley Arabian – bought from Bedouin near ancient Palmyra (in Syria), and shipped slowly and dangerously to Yorkshire in 1704. The greats of modern racing, such as Red Rum and Frankel, were all his descendants. The first winner produced by Mr Darley's Arabian was a colt named Whistlejacket, which won at York in 1712, confirming the potency of his sire's genes.[28] Unfortunately, the first Whistlejacket is not the magnificent animal made famous by George Stubbs's painting of the same name in 1762.

On 4 July 1776, 'erstwhile English Protestants' issued the Declaration of American Independence. The battle at Saratoga (October 1777) was a bloody disaster for the British, and the Americans (sometimes portrayed as an unruly, out-of-control horse) allied themselves with England's hated enemies, Catholic France and Spain. The British roused themselves to a pitch of patriotic fervour, bellowing the new stirring anthem 'Rule, Britannia!' (still the highlight of the flag-waving, post-imperialist Last Night of the Proms). The British could also rally under the new Union Jack, created for the union of Great Britain and Ireland proclaimed by George III on 1 January 1801.

The English thoroughbred thrives on the Downs: Best Mate, trained by a female trainer, won the Cheltenham Gold Cup a record three times in a row.

The historian Linda Colley notes that this period also witnessed a rise in the patriotic interest in antiquities, which saw the membership of the Society of Antiquaries more than double.[29] Pride of place among antiquities was the White Horse – a banner of the King and of Protestantism.[30] For the British, both beleaguered and aggressively expansionist, the White Horse figures were a public display of patriotism and private ownership.

DIVISION AND DISSENT

Thomas Hughes listed the scouring events for which he had dates back to 1776. One of them stands out as odd: 1825, 'the largest gathering that had ever been,' he said.[31] Apparently, this gathering was not on White Horse Hill, but a short distance away at the relatively remote Lambourn Seven Barrows, and there was, in fact, no scouring of the Horse itself. Historian Brian Edwards suggests that the 1825 gathering was organized without the 'co-operation or consent of Lord Craven', and rather was 'an underground event organized by ordinary locals.'[32] So what was going on?

The late eighteenth and early nineteenth centuries were a time of relentless change and civil rupture in Britain. Thanks to enclosure and new machinery the landed gentry became richer while the rural workers declined into poverty or left the land in droves for the new industrial towns and cities. By the middle of the nineteenth century almost half the British population were urban dwellers.[33] But landowners still ruled the roost and, politically, the industrial centres were grossly under-represented, as were the swelling numbers of industrial workers. The landless had no voting rights.[34]

In 1815, following the Battle of Waterloo and the end of the Napoleonic Wars, manpower and imported goods flooded the market. Prices and wages crashed. The landowners protected their pockets by imposing the Corn Laws (from 1815 to 1845), a tariff on imported foodstuffs that boosted the price of grain and their own profits. For the hard-pressed poor, food prices rocketed while wages stayed low. Before the Dissolution, the monasteries had provided a safety net for the poor but that role then passed to the parish, which distributed 'poor relief'. Landowners exploited this by paying minimal wages, knowing that their workers could turn to the parish to avoid starvation. At the same time, however, the relief contribution declined. In 1795 in Berkshire, a man's sustenance was calculated at three and a half 'one gallon' loaves of bread a week. By 1817 only two loaves were provided for each man.

These factors all contributed to widespread unrest in the early nineteenth century, and the reaction of the ruling elite exacerbated the deep sense of injustice. On 16 August 1819 thousands gathered in St Peter's Field

– Peterloo – Manchester, for a protest rally. The sabre-wielding, mounted Yeomanry charged into the crowd, killed fifteen people and wounded hundreds more. Suppression, not reform, was the tactic of choice for the powerful elite.

The rural uprising known as the Swing Riots occurred in 1830 – threatening letters sent to landowners, magistrates and others were signed by 'Captain Swing'. In reaction to rural hardship, rioters in Kent smashed horse-powered threshing-machines and burnt tithe barns and hay-ricks. The unrest spread through much of England. The authorities again cracked down hard. In 1830–31 nearly 2,000 people were tried: 252 were sentenced to death, although 'only' 19 were executed, and 481 were transported. In 1834 in Dorset, the six 'Tolpuddle Martyrs' were sentenced to transportation to Australia on a concocted charge: in reality for cooperating to demand an increase in wages – from 7 to 10 shillings a week.

It is hardly surprising that England saw a widening chasm between employers and labourers – a chasm witnessed by the White Horse. After 1776 the Earls of Craven controlled the scouring revels, rather than the local people. Thomas Hughes and the fine local folklore writer Alfred Williams documented the popularity of the scourings and the fondness for this traditional event. The local newspaper makes no reference to the 1825 event – so it may not have had 'official' approval. Lord Craven, William the 2nd Earl of Craven, was no admirer of rural dissidents – he led the reaction to the Swing Riots in 1830, organizing Special Constables, Yeoman Cavalry, house-to-house searches and arrests. He also sat as a magistrate and served on the Grand Jury 'that crushingly reasserted the ruling elite's position and power'. The 1825 gathering at the Seven Barrows may have been a popular collaboration. Lord Craven apparently kept his distance.

With the landowners firmly back in control and holding the reins of power, the Cravens must have felt more comfortable about reviving the scouring. The coronation on 28 June 1838 of the last of the Hanovers – the youthful Queen Victoria – provided the incentive for the celebrations. The Queen's popularity initially waned, but was then given a huge boost by contrasting events: her marriage in 1840, and, while she was pregnant, an assassination attempt, followed by another in 1842.

In reality, however, Britain was a seething mass of discontent. The 'Plug-plot' riots and strikes brought northern factories to a standstill. In my home town of Halifax, on 15 and 16 August 1842, the anniversary of Peterloo, hundreds of striking men and women, many malnourished and barefoot, faced down a platoon of Prince Albert's Own that left six people dead. Nevertheless, the northern strikes petered out and the massive 1842 Chartist Petition failed to gain the support of the House of Commons.[35] A combination of patriotism, support for the threatened Queen and self-satisfaction probably encouraged Lord Craven to initiate the scouring and revels of 1843.

MUSCULAR CHRISTIANS REVIVE THE SCOURING

It was against this background of unrest and division, when the scouring had lapsed again for fourteen years, that the Uffington Committee met in the Craven Arms on 20 August 1857 to organize 'a pastime to be held on White Horse Hill on Thursday and Friday 17 and 18 September'. Although Lord Craven must have cooperated, the committee, led by Edwin Martin-Atkins and Thomas Hughes, was now the motivating force.

Their motives were different from those of the previous organizers. Hughes was a conservative (with a small c) reformer, and a Christian Socialist of the 'muscular' variety. He sympathized with the exploited and under-represented labouring class, realizing that both the landowners and their allies, the Church of England, were seen as the enemy. The White Horse provided an opportunity to bring people together to celebrate a joint past, and to promote 'manly' and healthy activities. Hughes wanted to retain what was best from the good old days and promote a Utopian, Christian, English community. Workers, he believed, deserved and needed holidays, decent pay and education. In 1854 he joined the Reverend Charles Kingsley (1819–1875), author of *The Water Babies* and *Westward Ho!*,[36] and later Sir John Lubbock, among others, in founding and supporting the Working Men's College. The college not only provided conventional education, but also promoted sporting activities. Hughes coached boxing, which, he believed, taught young men restraint and endurance, and was character building. These ideas lay behind the new scouring pastime. There were others in the air.

Several of this Christian Socialist set were friends or admirers of Charles Darwin, whose *On the Origin of Species by Means of Natural Selection* was published in 1859, the year Hughes's *Scouring* novel appeared. Darwin's great work was one of the wedges hammered into the walls that the English had doggedly retained around their national mythology. The intellectual advances from across the Channel, especially those developed in Germany, had been ignored for as long as possible. But now they were flooding in – notably ideas about theology, critical biblical studies, history and natural history: ideas reflected in the novel *Middlemarch* (1871) by George Eliot (Mary Anne Evans), which was set in the 1830s.

As we have seen, Edwin Martin-Atkins, the chairman of the scouring committee, was a forward-thinking landowner and a competent archaeologist. He invited the Secretary of the Society of Antiquaries, John Yonge Akerman (1806–1873), who lived nearby in Abingdon, to join the committee. Akerman was not an automatic follower of the patriotic flock – he rejected the Alfred origin story and argued that the White Horse was 'Celtic' based on the coin evidence: 'The figure of the White Horse at Uffington appears to be one of the rudest of its kind, and so strongly resembles those on the more barbarous British coins, that I do not hesitate to class it with the same period.'[37]

In the mid-nineteenth century the concept of deep time entered popular consciousness. The traditional 'biblical' date of 4004 BC for the creation of the world crumbled in the face of accumulating geological and archaeological evidence. The word 'prehistory' entered the language. But the cutting-edge ideas of scientists, critical theologians and archaeologists were not always popular with those who found comfort in the traditional ideas of the past. Sir John Lubbock, one of the Darwin set and supporter of Hughes's Christian Socialism, wrote *Prehistoric Times*. When he announced his wish to stand for Parliament in 1865 his agent told him to delay publication, as such a radical book would make him unpopular with the traditional, God-fearing electorate. Lubbock published that same year and was damned: he lost the election. However, *Prehistoric Times* was a massive bestseller. In 1870 he stood again for Parliament and this time was successful. Like Hughes, he supported the idea of a national holiday for workers, not just an arbitrary 'pastime' dependent on the whim of the elite. Lubbock's 'Bank Holidays' were passed by Parliament in 1871.[38] In practice, it was a small recompense for the loss of the Holy Days that once brought respite in the rural calendar of drudgery.

In the same year, Thomas Hughes gave a lecture to the Newbury District Field Club on the 1,000th anniversary of the Battle of Ashdown: 'I am afraid I must now run the risk of shocking many of you,' he said. He went on to admit that no one knew precisely where the battle had taken place. 'Nor am I sure, and this is perhaps greater heresy, that our White Horse was cut out of the hill after the battle. Instead I incline to believe that it was there long before.' Akerman had won over the best-known supporter of the Alfred White Horse.

All this was not good for the immediate future of the White Horse. If it was carved by the barbaric Britons then it no longer served the purpose of the landed elite or of the Church of England. Ordinary people may have retained their affection for it, but would that be enough to maintain it?

In contrast, King Alfred remained enormously popular in Victorian England.
The successful, but dreadful, versifier
Martin F. Tupper wrote in his poem
'The Anglo-Saxon Race' of 1850:
'Break forth and spread over every
place / The world is a world for the
Saxon race!'[39] Increasing imperial
success reflected well on England's
greatest monarch, King Alfred.
A statue was erected in his honour
in Wantage in 1877 (see p. 245), and
another in Winchester in 1901, when
huge crowds gathered and the military
heroes of the Boer War marched past to celebrate
Alfred's supposed millennium. English popular history was still not noted
for its fastidiousness: the Winchester organizers got the date wrong and
'England's darling' was promoted as the champion of universal education
and the founder of Oxford University. In 1899, Arthur Conan Doyle hailed
Alfred as 'an educationalist on a scale to which we have hardly yet
attained'.[40] The 1902 Education Act introduced primary education throughout Britain and Alfred was celebrated as the champion of progress. English
mythology was alive and well.

However, the advances in science and history, and the expansion of
basic universal education did not immediately benefit the White Horse.
The scouring of 1857 was popular and well attended, but it was the last
of its kind. Hughes's *Scouring* novel did not sell well and interest waned
in the ancient hill figure. The English had become town dwellers. They
preferred music halls, theatre, public houses and organized sports: football, cricket and horse racing at Epsom, Ascot, Newbury and York. By the
late nineteenth century the United Kingdom was at its most prosperous
and populous, yet the White Horse was in danger of neglect to the point
of disappearance.

The fame of the White Horse spread widely: this dessert plate ornamented with a view of White
Horse Hill is part of the Frog Service made for Catherine the Great of Russia by the Wedgwood
Manufactory (Staffordshire) in 1773–74, now in The Hermitage Museum, St Petersburg.

CHAPTER FOURTEEN

INTO THE MODERN WORLD

The owld White Harse wants zettin to rights

'Ballad of the Scouring of the White Horse', in Thomas Hughes, 1859

THE FADING HORSE

The festivities of 1857 might have breathed fresh life into the traditional gathering and kick-started a new era of celebrations on the hill. Unfortunately, this was asking too much in the changing circumstances of the later nineteenth century. When origin myths emphasized early English Christianity, whose icon was the White Horse, wealthy landowners found support for their world view. The scouring was a demonstration of their rightful place at the peak of society. As Victorian intellectuals like Darwin and Lubbock shone a penetrating light into the prehistoric past, new ideas challenged the comfortable assumptions. The elite became uneasy. They only had to look about them to see the fissures in Victorian society. As Florence Nightingale declared in 1848: 'England is surely the country where luxury has reached its height and poverty its depths.'

Both the rural and burgeoning urban poor challenged the status quo, and the profiteering and power of agricultural and industrial capitalism. Providing opportunities for large crowds to gather was, perhaps, not a great idea. The White Horse itself remained popular, and there was certainly growing interest in prehistory. Nevertheless, when field clubs wrote to the 3rd Earl of Craven in support of a future scouring he showed no enthusiasm.[1] We have no direct evidence for Craven's motivation. He may have felt the pressures of changing times; he may have had his own, more personal reasons. However, the continuing neglect of the White Horse clearly worried Thomas Hughes.[2]

Around this time, other more recent hill figures were restored: the Westbury Horse was outlined, rather unsympathetically, with kerbstones; at Marlborough, a Captain Reed paid for restoration work, claiming that as a child he had assisted in the figure's creation. In 1876 it was the turn of the Cherhill Horse to be spruced up. However, these were all 'modern' figures that did not come with the historical baggage of the Uffington White Horse.

In 1877, Wantage saw the culmination of its plans to erect a statue to King Alfred in his birthplace (see p. 245). The booklet produced for the unveiling ceremony announced that Lord Craven 'intends to revive the old custom' at the White Horse.[3] However, this was still a divisive issue. It was fine to celebrate a work of heroic Christianity, an emblem of Englishness, but not a 'pagan and foreign' monument. The pro-Alfred author of the booklet even turned on local hero Thomas Hughes for changing his mind about the origins of the Horse and joining the 'prehistoric pagan' camp.

It was now twenty years since the last scouring. A decade earlier the Bath Field Club complained of a disappointing visit, finding the White Horse 'almost obliterated'. Three years after the unveiling of King Alfred, in 1880, Reverend Plenderleath confirmed that the hill figure was 'so over-grown with weeds as scarcely to be discernible from a distance, except by a person who knows precisely where to look for it'.[4]

When the 3rd Earl of Craven died in 1883, no one had cared for the Horse in twenty-six years. The following year and in 1892 Craven's succes-sors made belated and half-hearted attempts to clean the hill figure. Only two years later, in 1894, the British Association field trip reported that the White Horse was in a poor state.[5]

PROTECTING THE PAST: THE FIRST NATIONAL MONUMENTS ACT

Clearly the unfortunate Horse was in a bad way. After centuries of care, neglect had set in at a time when the country had never been more populous or wealthier. But values were shifting. Early antiquarian fieldworkers, like Aubrey and Stukeley, had long complained about the destruction of ancient sites: for example, the smashing and burning of Avebury's stones, and the ploughing of earthworks around Stonehenge. The survival of national treasures seemed to be at the whim of landowners. Landowners, in turn, pointed the finger at antiquarians who, in their obsessive hunt for the past, had casually quarried prehistoric burial mounds with no thought for care or conservation.

Then in the mid-nineteenth century the approach to the past became more scientific, measured and considered. Turnpike roads, canals, quarries and railways had turned up remains, such as Roman villas and Anglo-Saxon graves, in unprecedented quantities. The intellectual value of such things was increasingly appreciated, yet there was no mechanism to

(*Top*) A photograph by Henry Taunt of Oxford, taken in 1899, of
people enjoying themselves on a Bank Holiday on the rampart of Uffington Castle.

(*Above*) A modern scouring organized by the National Trust: a pleasant but sedate affair,
without the boisterous 'Olympicks', and 'Pastimes' of earlier such events.

prevent destruction or ensure that a record was made of such discoveries. The British Archaeological Association was launched in 1843 to promote a positive interest in the past and, increasingly, in prehistory.

Once again, Sir John Lubbock emerged in the forefront of the new movement. Lubbock visited Denmark in the 1860s (having learnt Danish, like any hard-working Victorian polymath would) to see what was happening among the pioneers of archaeological studies.[6] The Danes had already appointed a conservator of national antiquities and Lubbock seized on the innovation. He said, 'We cannot put Stonehenge or the Wansdyke into a Museum – all the more reason why we should watch over them where they are.'[7]

One place that was not being watched over initially was the great Iron Age oppidum of Dyke Hills, in the bend of the River Thames below Wittenham Clumps in Oxfordshire. Here, the well-meaning landowner had come up with a job-creation scheme for under-employed farm workers. Unfortunately, this consisted of quarrying away the prehistoric fortifications for gravel to resurface local farm tracks. Lubbock and his ally, archaeologist estate owner Colonel Augustus Lane-Fox (later General Pitt-Rivers), rode to the rescue and persuaded the owner of Dyke Hills to voluntarily put a stop to the destructive work.

Lubbock was convinced that Britain's ancient monuments needed legal protection. However, his proposed parliamentary bill faced an uphill battle: *The Times* reported in 1877 that the bill would be 'as roughly treated as the monuments that it seeks to preserve'. And so it was, by parsimonious politicians and others determined to defend the privileges of the landowning classes. For nearly a decade Lubbock batted his private member's bill against the stone wall of the Commons, only to see it bounce back at him.[8] Wits labelled it 'The Monumentally Ancient Act'. In 1880 a more skilled or influential parliamentarian, George Shaw-Lefevre (1831–1928), took a hand, boosted by the fact that he was First Commissioner of Works (in Gladstone's Liberal government), with practical experience of restoring the Royal Parks and the Tower of London. He drafted ancient monuments legislation that had government support and that allowed a landowner to place his (or occasionally her) monument in the care of the state. Lefevre's bill became law as the Ancient Monuments Protection Act on 18 August 1882: 'Thus the mountain of ten years of debate produced the molehill of an act.'[9] Its powers were limited, but it was a start.

The initiation of the first legal protection for national monuments in Britain is relevant to our story of White Horse Hill. Attached to the Act was a schedule of 68 sites (26 in England, 21 in Scotland, 18 in Ireland and 3 in

Wales), all noteworthy places recognized as deserving preservation. Most of these were prehistoric sites because Lubbock and Lefevre appreciated that these would be cheaper to deal with than the crumbling medieval ruins of monasteries and castles. Included among the select 26 in England were the megalithic tomb of Wayland's Smithy and the Uffington Castle hillfort, but not the White Horse itself. We do not know why it was excluded, but it was probably because of the uncertainty and continuing argument about the date of its origins. Legal protection was withheld until 13 December 1929, three years after Sir Flinders Petrie had bestowed a degree of academic respectability with his survey and his, albeit unconvincing, argument that the White Horse was Bronze Age in date (see p. 87).

Fortunately, the Horse had survived the vicissitudes of the later nineteenth century. In a letter of 18 August 1894, Thomas Hughes, now an elderly judge, bemoaned the fact that since the passing of the Ancient Monuments Act in 1882 the Craven family, as Lords of the Manor, had considered itself relieved of all responsibility for the hill figure. G. K. Chesterton (see below) wrote a barbed sonnet: 'On hearing a Landlord accused ... of neglecting one of the numerous White Horses that were or were not connected with Alfred the Great'. Nevertheless, in 1892 Lady Craven, at her own expense (of £10), had employed a dozen men, over three days, to clean the White Horse.

However, the Ministry now responsible was apparently not overconscientious. In an article on 26 August 1922 headlined 'Famous Landmark Which Requires Cleaning', the *Daily Mail* reported: 'The famous White Horse on the Berkshire downs near Uffington ... is but a shadow of its former glory. It can scarce be seen for want of scouring.' Travellers on the Great Western Railway were complaining that it was so dirty 'that something ought to be done about it'.[10] It seems something was, because according to reports the Horse was in a good state prior to being covered over in 1940 for the duration of the Second World War. Presumably the men from the Ministry had been taking care of it, although scouring festivals, attended by great crowds, were a thing of the past.

TWO CULTURES: NORSEMEN AND SAXONS

I grew up in Calderdale near Mytholmroyd in Yorkshire. Nearby were villages with names like Slaithwaite and Micklethwaite, we ate fish from Grimsby, went on holiday to Whitby and walked up Langstrothdale. Place names and the dialect we spoke (we 'laiked' football and splashed in the 'beck') reminded us northerners of our Scandinavian ancestry. The southerners had a different attitude: King Alfred was the hero of Wessex who had defeated the heathen Danish hordes, driven them out and preserved the country for Christianity – and, incidentally, kept the Wessex place names Anglo-Saxon. In the late nineteenth century Victorians erected statues to Alfred and even as late as 1911 that prolific popular writer G. K. Chesterton (1874–1936) produced what some consider his finest literary work, *The Ballad of the White Horse*, a romanticized account of Alfred's exploits in a traditional epic form (a poem 2,684 lines long).

It is difficult now to appreciate Chesterton's popularity – his generation of Edwardian writers (such as George Bernard Shaw, Hilaire Belloc and Rudyard Kipling) have been overtaken, first by the recorders of the horrors of the First World War and then by literary fashion. The usually po-faced and sternly anti-romantic T. S. Eliot made an amusing jibe in defending modernist verse: 'I have seen the forces of death with Mr Chesterton at the head upon a white horse.'[11] The biblical image, also referring to *The Ballad*, was funny because Chesterton was a huge man, the last person to imagine on a white horse. He also had a large and generous personality and probably saw the joke.

The unveiling of the statue of King Alfred in Wantage,
by Albert Edward, Prince of Wales, depicted in an illustration
from *The Graphic*, 21 July 1877.

As a jocular, unpretentious Edwardian, and an admirer of Dickens and 'Merrie England', it is not surprising that Chesterton went out of fashion in the dour later twentieth century, riven by wars, pessimism, pretentious literary academics and the diet conscious.[12] However, occasional champions emerged. The contrarian and serious 'popular' writer, Graham Greene, said that he was not sure that he did not prefer *The Ballad of the White Horse* to T. S. Eliot's *The Waste Land*.[13] I would not go quite that far – *The Waste Land* is arguably, thanks to the severe editing of Ezra Pound, a twentieth-century masterpiece. However, *The Ballad* is still worth reading as a traditional epic poem, in which Alfred, with the help of God and the Virgin Mary, defeats the Danes at Ethandune – placed incorrectly in the land of the White Horse.[14]

The White Horse is a witness to English history – Alfred scours and cleans it, in contrast to the Danes, but he did not create the figure, which was already ancient:

> For the White Horse knew England
> When there was none to know;
> He saw the first oar break or bend,
> He saw heaven fall and the world end,
> O God, how long ago.

Alfred, in the guise of a minstrel, visits the Danish camp of the 'dread King' Guthrum and sings them a warning:

> 'All things achieved and chosen pass,
> As the White Horse fades in the grass,
> No work of Christian men.

> 'Ere the sad gods that made your gods
> Saw their sad sunrise pass,
> The White Horse of the White Horse Vale,
> That you have left to darken and fail,
> Was cut out of the grass.

> 'Therefore your end is on you,
> Is on you and your kings ...
> But because it is only Christian men
> Guard even heathen things.'

According to *The Ballad*, the White Horse was made long ago in pagan times. As a symbol of English continuity it must be scoured, yet only Christians can be trusted with this task of conservation. The Danes meet their fate at the Battle of Ethandune:

Great shields groan like a gong –
Horses like horns of nightmare
Neigh horribly and long.

Horses ramp high and rock and boil
And break their golden reins,
And slide on carnage clamorously,
Down where the bitter blood doth lie ...

'The high tide!' King Alfred cried.
'The high tide and the turn!' ...

'The Mother of God goes over them,
Walking on wind and flame,
And the storm-cloud drifts from city and dale,
And the White Horse stamps in the White Horse Vale,
And we all shall yet drink Christian ale
In the village of our name.'

As a result of his victory, Alfred wisely rules a peaceful land, which lays 'Like a dog in a patch of sun', but he reminds his people to: '...keep the White Horse white / As the first plume of the snows.'

For Chesterton, the White Horse is the symbol of the health of the nation: ordinary people must work constantly to prevent the infestation of weeds – of cruelty, injustice, tyranny and barbarism. Like Kipling, who produced *Puck of Pook's Hill* in 1906 (see p. 178), Chesterton believed that it was the work of ordinary people, peasants and farmers that made the English landscape. Chesterton was a vitriolic opponent of imperialism in general, and the recently fought Boer War in particular. At home he believed that the land should be in the hands of smallholders who cared for it, not aristocratic, capitalist land barons. Neither did he think much of the forward-thinking admirers of science and Soviet Russia, nor supporters of eugenics and cleanliness, such as H. G. Wells, G. B. Shaw and the Bloomsbury set.

PRE-RAPHAELITES AND RADICALS

On behalf of the White Horse, one might ask: with friends like Chesterton who needs enemies? With the development of modernism in poetry and art, urbanism and industrial farming, and an increasingly secular society, an interest in the White Horse and its curation might seem hopelessly romantic and old-fashioned. However, English culture in the late nineteenth and earlier twentieth centuries was not quite that straightforward. For example, the powerful current of Victorian 'medievalism' was radical rather than escapist: a reaction to industrialization and the dreadful treatment of the urban poor. John Ruskin, Charles Kingsley and Thomas Hughes promoted workers' education at the same time as 'muscular' Christianity, sport and patriotism in public schools.[15] Sport was also, of course, seen as character-building for the working classes.

William Morris (1834–1896) was not just a designer of wallpaper and curtain fabrics. The family money came from copper mines, and young Morris was, in his childhood, brought up on a diet of Walter Scott. He was at Oxford with Edward Jones (later better known as the Pre-Raphaelite artist Edward Burne-Jones; 1833–1898), and the two young idealists planned to become radical clergymen – influenced by friends who had done charity work in the Birmingham slums. However, the poetry of Tennyson and Malory also led them into the romantic cult of King Arthur, knightly chivalry and sublimated sex, although they sometimes had problems sticking to Thomas Hughes's credo: 'the crown of all real manliness, of all Christian manliness, is purity'.[16] Some of Burne-Jones's finest stained glass is to be found in Berkshire churches. And across the valley from the White Horse, at Buscot Park, he decorated the Saloon with four gorgeous paintings of the Sleeping Beauty or Briar Rose (1890) in magnificent gilded frames with verses beneath by William Morris, who lived nearby at Kelmscott.

The Medieval Revival also had links with Catholicism. Dr John Henry Newman (1801–1890), the Oxford clergyman who became a Catholic in 1845, published the influential *Apologia pro Vita Sua* ('A Defence of One's Life') twenty years later. In this he wrote, 'First, I mentioned the literary influence of Walter Scott, who turned men's minds in the direction of the middle ages.'[17] Any modern reader, wading through Scott's work, may find this difficult to understand, but Scott's wildly popular medieval fiction struck a chord with generations ignorant of the medieval life of their ancestors, which 'spoke to the emotional and imaginative deficit left by Enlightenment intellectualism'.[18] The ardour and enthusiasm of the Reformation had cooled, leaving a hunger to understand what went before and what had been lost.

As a young man in Marlborough, William Morris seems to have felt a sensual intensity from his experience of landscape – a feeling shared by many poets and painters in the twentieth century. Morris recalled his 'wonder and pleasure' as a boy climbing the Marlborough Downs. 'The Downs' had an almost mesmeric effect, with their vast stretches – 'no end to them almost'. Fiona MacCarthy, Morris's biographer, describes the impact on him of 'the sweep and surge of Wiltshire' – a vision so vital and so intimate it could only be experienced in terms of the erotic: 'intense and overweening love of the very skin and surface of the earth on which man dwells, such as a lover has in the fair flesh of the woman he loves'.[19] Thomas Hughes, I suspect, would have recommended a cold shower.

Morris was also fond of the White Horse. Perhaps it reminded him of his father, whose coat of arms was a horse's head with horseshoes. The abstract, graphic image may also have appealed to his love of heraldry. White Horse Hill held such a magical appeal to Morris that, when he lived at Kelmscott, he made an annual pilgrimage there – even in the year before his death when his health was failing. One of his companions on his trips to the Horse was Philip Webb (1831–1915), the fine Arts and Crafts architect, who had previously designed the Red House at Bexleyheath in southeast London as a home for Morris and his family. When Webb died, his colleagues scattered his ashes 'within an ancient camp on the wind-swept wholesome down about the White Horse at Uffington, as the place was dear to Webb and his old companion Morris'.[20] The great architect-designer of the First World War cemeteries and the Cenotaph in Whitehall, Sir Edwin Lutyens, wrote in praise of Webb that he was the master of the 'right use of materials' whose work had a 'quality of surprise' full of 'freshness and originality'.

The copy of *Letters on Demonology and Witchcraft* by Walter Scott, published in 1831, found during excavation of the round barrow on Uffington Hill in 1993, daubed in red paint with the words 'Demon de Uffing'.

MODERNISTS AND MYSTICS

Critics have been harsh on the visual culture of late Victorian, Edwardian and inter-war Britain, portraying it as backward-looking, parochial, romantic, decorative and conservative – left behind by the Impressionists, abstract artists and sleek modernists on the Continent. The Victoria and Albert Museum's major exhibition in 2006, 'Modernism: Designing a New World, 1914–1939', stuck to the party line. The American curator, Christopher Wilk, when asked why the English contribution to the exhibition was so slight, answered: 'Englishness and modernism were antithetical: Modernism was cosmopolitan – English art was pastoral.'[21]

I admire modernist architecture and design at its best, but the most austere 'less is more' modernists wanted to wipe the slate clean and reject the lumber room of history with its powerful sense of place – the *heimat* ('homeland') beloved by nationalists who had led Europe to disaster. The V&A exhibition failed to reflect the influence of modernism on the English visual artists who, while mindful of great movements abroad, also took the advice of Celia Fiennes and became pilgrims in their own land. Recently, the art historian Alexandra Harris has set the record straight in her book *Romantic Moderns*,[22] in which she unapologetically rescues earlier twentieth-century English artists from the condescension of posterity.

The English poet John Wain was ahead of his time when he explained how Edward Thomas, the great poet of the downlands, writing in 1909 to 1917, captured the spirit and sensibility of the modern world: 'He is perhaps the first, as he is certainly one of the best, of the English modern poets. By "modern" I mean not chic, avant-garde, having the external trappings of international modernism; I mean reflecting accurately those character-istics of the present-day world which mark it off from the world before.'[23] The same could be said of the fine group of artists who brought a modern and international rather than parochial sensibility to their portrayal of the southern English landscape.

Some years ago I headed to England's extreme northwest. My destina-tion was a place that had once been the base for a Roman unit of Gallic cavalry. They knew it as Luguvalium; today we call it Carlisle. The reason for my visit was to see the collection of Roman inscriptions, many from Hadrian's Wall, at the Tullie House Museum. Yet it is not the Roman stones that remain fixed in my memory. Walking through a gallery I was drawn towards a small, rather modest-looking picture. It seemed famil-iar, as well it might. The watercolour was of a distinctive chalk hill, part of Wittenham Clumps – the eastern outlier of the Downs that overlooked another Roman town, Dorchester-on-Thames in south Oxfordshire. I had walked up these wooded hills countless times with Ci, my border collie, and often with groups of students. One of the Clumps is capped by a hill-fort and a group of beech trees. There is a spectacular view along the Vale of the White Horse and across the Thames Valley towards the Chiltern Hills. It is an ideal place to both see and feel six thousand years of history.

Paul Nash (1889–1946) had painted this little watercolour probably in 1913, so it was an early work created before the Great War. The colours are soft and muted: blue-grey, russet and ochre, depicting a land of geometric ploughed fields, blue hills in the background and an opalescent sky. Yet there is a sense of sound, from the wind and the wheeling flocks of rooks, which tack across the sky and glean the fields. Nash's picture conveys the light and space on the Downs, the presence of the absent human beings who made this place. He painted the Clumps many times, and in a letter of September 1911, Nash wrote of his encounter with these 'grey hallowed hills crowned by old trees, Pan-ish places down by the river wonderful to think on, full of strange enchantment ... a beautiful legendary country haunted by old Gods long forgotten'. I am particularly drawn to Nash's phrase 'wonderful to think on'. This is a landscape of imagination that sticks in the mind.[24]

Nash's early images of Wittenham Clumps are subdued yet 'potent and enigmatic', as suggested by literary critic Roger Cardinal, who adds that they 'dramatize the notion that the works of man will in time be repossessed by Nature, a notion which seems somehow consoling rather than disturbing'.[25] This is an attractive idea, although everything in these pictures is man-made: the open downland, the prehistoric earthworks, the hedges of enclosure and the beech copse planted by a fashionable estate owner in the eighteenth century.[26] Even the rooks probably arrived in the past six thousand years after farmers had felled the ancient forest and created an English 'steppe' environment – an environment that also attracted swifts, swallows and skylarks. Nature is present here, but it inhabits a human artefact.

Nash went on to create some of the most powerful images of the First World War. In February 1917 he arrived in France and joined the 15th Battalion of the Hampshire Regiment in the Ypres Salient. By May, he wrote home that everyone was 'sad and sick with longing for the end of this awful unending madness'. Shortly afterwards Nash had a great stroke of luck – he fell into a trench and broke a rib. A week later, while he was away convalescing, many of his colleagues were slaughtered while taking part in an offensive.

After four months, Nash was back on the Front, but now as an official war artist, witnessing the carnage of Passchendaele, which dragged on into winter. He wrote to his wife: 'I have seen the most frightful nightmare of a country.... Unspeakable utterly indescribable.' Nevertheless, he did describe the mud and the shelling: 'striking down horses and mules, annihilating, maiming, maddening; they plunge into the grave which is this land, one huge grave and cast up the poor dead. O it is unspeakable, Godless, hopeless.' Nash says he is no longer an artist but a messenger from the men at the Front to those who want to continue to pursue the war: 'may it burn their lousy souls'. The message was delivered in powerful works like *The Menin Road*, and *We are Making a New World*, with the sun rising over a landscape of shell holes and shattered trees. Ironically, much of the struggle took place over the French downlands and vales, the extension of the quiet chalk hills cut through by the English Channel.

In later life, in another war, Nash would find solace on the Downs, painting mystical images of fantastic trees: of a foreshortened Wittenham Clumps (viewed through binoculars from Boar's Hill, near Oxford), notably *Landscape of the Vernal Equinox* (1944), with a rising moon and setting sun both visible in the sky – a 'landscape of the imagination', as he described it. These paintings are deeply English images that look back to the nineteenth-century landscape painter Samuel Palmer and perhaps beyond, to the diurnal solar and lunar journeys that stimulated the making of the White Horse.

The fine poet of the English downland had less luck than Nash. On Easter Monday, 9 April 1917, Edward Thomas was crouched in an exposed chalk-cut trench just outside Arras. The Battle of Arras, another great push, was due to kick off at 7 a.m. Almost as the whistle blew, Thomas was fatally hit in the chest by a 'pip-squeak' – the harmless-sounding nickname for a 77 mm shell.[27]

Paul Nash, with his brother John (1893–1977), returned to England, where they worked in a studio on the Chilterns, at Chalfont St Peter, and completed some of the most memorable paintings of the war. Like many artists of the time they sought calm and a refuge in the countryside. Paul Nash experimented with surrealism – the dreamlike quality of Italian artist Giorgio de Chirico was particularly influential. His friend, painter Ben Nicholson, and the sculptor Barbara Hepworth developed more abstract forms. In the summer of 1933, attempting to improve his health damaged by the war, Nash went on holiday to the Wiltshire Downs and for the first time visited the prehistoric stone circle of Avebury and the huge pyramid-like mound of Silbury Hill. He wrote to his wife: 'If anything will

Paul Nash in his studio working on *Landscape of the Vernal Equinox* (1944),
his mystical view of the downlands, with the distinctive beech trees of Wittenham Clumps.

Paul Nash's *Equivalents for the Megaliths* (1935): modernism and surrealism
meet the ancient downland landscape, with the distinctive form of
man-made Silbury Hill in the background.

preserve my interest in landscape from a painter's point of view, it will be
this county.'[28]

He was not alone. The endless chalk country of subdued tones and
flashes of luminous white, which spoke of 'the ancientness of Britain',[29]
attracted the likes of artists Graham Sutherland, John Piper and Eric
Ravilious. Aficionados of light and chalk tend, like downland starlings, to
flock together, appreciating: 'When colour's absence gives escape / To the
deeper spirit of the shape'.[30]

This group relished a landscape imbued with humanity rather than one
that overwhelmed mere Man, like the apocalyptic mountains of the earlier
Romantics. Not that Nash often included people or animals in his pictures. His oil painting of 1935, *Equivalents for the Megaliths*, is dominated by
abstract shapes, cylinders and a grid of red lines on a white sheet like graph
paper. Behind are the receding horizons of the downland, in soft colours,
from which projects the terraced mound of Silbury Hill. The picture captures the mystical heritage of the Downs in a startlingly modern way, while
avoiding the familiar imagery of antiquarianism.

In 1937, the art critic Myfanwy Evans (1911–1997) wrote of Nash in her
short-lived magazine *Axis* that he had 'no interest in the past as *past*, but in

the accumulated intenseness of the past as *present*. He disliked archaeology – probably because he felt that the archaeologists who had 'restored' the Avebury stone circle had destroyed its 'awful beauty', its sense of mystery. Certainly, the nationalization of 'heritage' in the twentieth century, the taming of ruins and 'guardianship' of sites by the Ministry of Works would create too many shorn, mown and sterile places with all the romance of a golf course.

Axis was Britain's most avant-garde art magazine in the 1930s, itself a monument to abstraction and to whiteness – it was the start of the white-cube obsession that has dominated modernist galleries to the present day. The style was first showcased in 1936, surprisingly perhaps, in the bastion of rook-racked tradition, Oxford. Ben Nicholson's *White Relief* was abstraction at its purest. In the edition of *Axis* devoted to the exhibition, the editor Myfanwy Evans wrote of 'a passionate belief in the power for good of pure abstract works ... the delicate clarity of one pale line against another, the absence of human and earthly associations, all means to them a positive step to perfection'.[31]

THE UFFINGTON SET: THE PIPERS AND THE BETJEMANS

Paul Nash was sympathetic to such ideas but felt the need to cling to a sense of local identity. Myfanwy Evans would find herself falling into the clutches of the 'experimental antiquarians' when she married John Piper (1903–1992), now most well-known for his theatrical images of churches and castles, but who, in 1936, was creating collages in muted colours, such as *Archaeological Wiltshire*, which showed Avebury's stones set in a curving downland.[32]

Piper was a friend of O. G. S. Crawford, co-author of *Wessex from the Air* (1927), so he was aware that aerial photography was revolutionizing archaeology, and at the same time its flat images were influencing contemporary artists. In *Axis*, John Piper published 'Prehistory from the Air', which placed a 1723 image of Silbury Hill, looking like a great cone, above an aerial photograph in which it appears as a circle. These images were set alongside a painting by Joan Miró of a flat circle, lines and a crescent moon.[33]

Another friend of Piper was Geoffrey Grigson (1905–1985), editor of *New Verse* and promoter of W. H. Auden, who also could not ignore local topography and its small details. His first volume of verse was 'magnetized' by such 'oddments' as:

a white lupin planted
by a shed, a white horse

by a wood, the brown, the green
and off-white of the matt-surface
of the downs[34]

Here is the palette of modernism combined with the idiosyncratic observations of an English allotment. Edward Thomas, holding a handful of earth, said he went to war to fight, literally, for this. Nash, Piper and Co. were also reluctant to let go of the local. Nash did not paint the White Horse, though he drew it for the dust jacket of a book (Pl. xv) and he took black and white photographs of it, close-ups of those enigmatic white lines, pathways to nowhere, as abstract as any modern work. 'Violent foreshortenings', he wrote in an essay called 'Unseen Landscapes' in *Country Life* in 1938, '...more or less indecipherable ... the landscape asserts itself with all the force of its triumphant fusion of natural and artificial design.'

Myfanwy and John Piper became close friends of John Betjeman (1906–1984) – that most English and eccentrically lovable of poets – who moved into Gerard's Farm, Uffington, in 1933 and lived there for twelve years while commuting to London. Eventually his wife Penelope arrived, along with her own white horse, Moti ('a pearl' in Hindi). Penelope seems to have preferred Moti to Betjeman. However, anxious to become pregnant, she observed the local custom of dancing on the eye of the White Horse. The stories about the Horse's fertility-granting powers vary. Some say it takes two people to work. In Penelope's case it was four years before she became pregnant. The Betjeman house in Uffington attracted fashionable poets and artists. Betjeman clearly welcomed the Pipers and seems to have had a crush on Myfanwy: 'Gold Myfanwy blesses us all.'[35]

One of the Betjemans' guests at Gerard's Farm in November 1934 was the brilliant poet and artist David Jones (1895–1974). Jones examined the White Horse up close and wondered how they could 'incise an exact and sweeping line' of such size and 'extraordinary rhythm'. The Horse is commemorated in Jones's great poem *The Anathemata*; it made such an impression on him that years later he kept a photograph of the White Horse on his wall at home.[36]

In his youth, Betjeman tried his best to be a modernist while working on *The Architectural Review*. In this role he met Jack Beddington (1893–1959), the publicity manager of Shell, the oil company. Jack was ex-Rugby and Balliol, and survived the war; he was 'very fat and full of laughter', said Betjeman, 'I used to call him "the old filthy". He liked taking pictures of nude women covered in oil. He didn't like churches one bit.' However, 'old filthy' also had an eye for good artists and commissioned them – Graham

Sutherland, Ben Nicholson, Edward Bawden and Rex Whistler, among many others – to produce Shell posters that promoted motoring into the English countryside, when motoring could still be seen as a pleasure and no one worried about pollution. He also asked Betjeman to edit the new Shell Guides to the counties of Britain and recruit writers and artists. Betjeman asked John Piper to compile the volume on Oxfordshire.

When I was ten years old my classroom in Yorkshire was papered with such Shell posters. I can vividly remember poring over the detail of Wiltshire hill figures, Norfolk churches and Somerset's Glastonbury Tor, usually set in soaring panoramas of unspoilt countryside. It was still a rural fantasy: no one I knew had a car in 1957, and by then the British were an urban people. At the start of the nineteenth century only 17 per cent of the population of England and Wales lived in towns. By the end of the century, in 1891, 54 per cent of the population were town dwellers, many in the hugely expanded industrial conurbations. They were drawn towards jobs, better pay and the opportunities, amenities, entertainment and culture on offer. Their lives would be dominated by the clock, not the passing bells of the parish church, although the rural fantasy still drew them out. Beyond the muck and the money, the hills and fields beckoned.[37]

The English, in particular, remained remarkably attached to the nostalgia of the countryside. Compared with the French and Germans, English First World War poets were obsessed by it. The Shell Oil Company, for commercial reasons, exploited this aspect of British culture, encouraging new car owners to have a day out in the fresh air. Frank Dobson's cheery 1931 poster of the Cerne Abbas Giant – in bright white, red, yellow and blue – was made even more family-friendly by masking the giant's priapic splendour with the shadows of a discreetly passing cloud (Pl. xxiii).

Through advertising, the Shell posters brought modern artists and their vision of the English countryside to a wide audience. The critic Cyril Connolly wrote a review about an exhibition of the Shell posters in which he stated: 'The moral of the landscapes here shown is that it is not the awe-inspiring or exceptional which now seems important but what is most cheerful or genuine in our countryside – England is merry again – farewell romantic caves and peaks, welcome the bracing glories of our clouds, the cirrus and the cumulus, the cold pastoral of the chalk.'[38]

One of the finest artists of 'the cold pastoral of the chalk' was Eric Ravilious (1903–1942), a pupil of Paul Nash's at the Royal College of Art, who did not do work for Shell. Ravilious and his wife, Tirzah Garwood (1908–1951), were both superb wood engravers. Ravilious made use of a distinctive stippling and pattern technique in his paintings. It is particularly

Eric Ravilious's dummy for the cover of a proposed White Horse book. The Westbury hill figure is visible through the window of a railway carriage. The sketch was worked up into the well-known watercolour *Train Landscape* (1939), now in the Aberdeen Art Gallery.

obvious in his image of the Uffington White Horse, which he completed in 1939 and is now in the Tate Gallery in London (Pl. xxii). The Horse is pure white but it does not dominate the picture. The foreground is the swelling, curving downland – with spires of grass, dark splodges and canvas left bare, like exposed chalk. The land resembles the body and pelt of some great, unspecified animal. Its lines take the eye to the Horse, which is disappearing over the skyline and is not completely in view.

Ravilious tackled the Horse because he had been approached by Puffin Picture Books who wished to publish a book for children on hill figures (Pls xx–xxi). In a burst of energy, he painted the Weymouth George III, the Cerne Abbas Giant, the Westbury Horse and the White Horse at Uffington and hoped to do others. The Westbury Horse images are probably the best known: one with a train puffing smoke in the valley below, while in the other, we just catch a glimpse of the Horse through the window of an empty but wonderfully textured railway carriage. There is a mysterious *Mary Celeste* quality to all these images – as if the people had wandered off the set, leaving the horses and giants alone to watch over England.

Unfortunately, in 1939 war loomed, the book was aborted and the hill figures were covered over. Ravilious became a war artist and produced evocative images of ships at sea, submarines and airplanes, all beautifully patterned and calm – a dreamlike phoney war, not the angry, blasted swamp that Nash recorded in the First World War.[39] Kenneth Clark (of *Civilisation* fame) later admitted that he had promoted the War Artists Advisory Committee (WAAC) 'simply to keep artists at work on any pretext and, as far as possible, prevent them from being killed'.

At 05.06 on 2 September 1942, Aircraft V took off from RAF Kaldadarnes in Iceland to search for a missing aircraft. Aircraft V carried a four-man crew – and an artist, Eric Ravilious. The weather turned bad: Aircraft V and the men aboard were never seen again. Paul Nash died in 1946 after another stint as a war artist in another war to end wars. In his final years, he returned to the Long Wittenham landscape and completed his finest works.

CHANGING COUNTIES

In 1972 I was appointed as the archaeologist for Abingdon – a settlement whose origins can be traced back over five thousand years. At that time, Abingdon was in Berkshire, proud that it had once been the county town and still resentful of the usurper, Reading. In 1974 a meddling government decided to mess with the centuries-old county boundaries. Whitehall planned to transfer Abingdon, with its new district The Vale of White Horse and White Horse Hill, into an expanded Oxfordshire. Some people, especially in the southern rump of Berkshire, were not happy: there were mutterings about 'Occupied Berkshire'.

The supporters of Old Berkshire particularly hated the loss of their great icon, the Horse. *The Times* reported efforts to shift the proposed boundary, to incorporate the White Horse back into the new, reduced Berkshire. In response Jacquetta Hawkes, author of *A Land*, wrote, apocalyptically, to the paper 'a small, harmless thing in a world of great and terrible things? Not at all. This disregard of people's feelings, of the power of symbols to give us meaning and identity, is slowly destroying us.' The Abingdon MP, Airey Neave, replied that if Uffington (and the Vale) was moving counties, then the White Horse must also cross over. His constituents would 'violently resent' its removal from their parish. It did not occur to him that the ancient counties might, simply, be left alone. The change went ahead and the Horse meekly crossed into Oxfordshire. Abingdon became the centre for the new Vale of White Horse District Council, looked towards Oxford and turned its back on its old rival Reading.[40]

THE WHITE HORSE AND CONTEMPORARY ART

Since the achievements of the wartime generation of artists, others have continued to be drawn to the downlands and the White Horse. In 1986, Francis Kyle, the London gallerist, brought together about 120 works by British, French, Austrian, American and German artists asked to respond to the landscape of the Ridgeway. The results were fascinating and eclectic[41] – from the aerial views of the White Horse by Paola Nero (American) to the hyper-magical realism of Patrick Malacarnet (French) and the richly textured earthiness of Keith Grant (Yorkshire; Pl. xvi). The book of this fine collection also included a poem by Kevin Crossley-Holland, 'Above the Spring Line: In Celebration of the Ridgeway', which includes the lines:

Overseer of Epona and the fleet horses at Lambourn...
The sarsens like dowdy sheep and dowdy sheep like sarsens.[42]

In 2003 we launched the publication of our White Horse research project in the crowded village hall in Uffington. Among the speakers was Jon Stallworthy (1935–2014), the distinguished promoter of First World War poets and biographer of Wilfred Owen, a work Graham Greene called 'one of the finest biographies of our time'. Jon had come to read from his new long poem 'Skyhorse'. He had taken on board our results, which broadly answered the question: When was the Horse made?

In the poem he tackles the other questions: Who? And why? Each verse adopts the viewpoint of a witness of history, beginning about 1000 BC with a priest, who announces that his sons will whiten the hill with the sign of the horse for the tribes to praise. This simultaneous history brings together, among others, a poet present at the Battle of Ashdown in AD 871 and an eighteenth-century antiquary who, aware of the fashion for the Grand Tour to the Mediterranean, points out the historic interest of the travellers' own homeland, the English landscape itself, and proclaims White Horse Hill as an English Parnassus - the home of the Muses and of Apollo.

The final section, XI, is the most evocative, and probably autobiographical. A 'Wandering Scholar' visits the White Horse for the millennium, the last night of 1999:

Would there be bells? Woolstone church held its tongue
Midnight was zero hour. The Ridgeway air
shuddered under buffeting
flashes and crashes. Star-shells. Very lights.

I might have been dug in on Vimy Ridge
or bunkered on the Golan Heights

I lay down by the horse to watch the show
masque of a murderous century

Stallworthy was a prolific poet and 'Skyhorse' is probably not his finest work, but it is nevertheless an interesting and, at times, vivid one. It was published in a limited edition in 2002 and deserves to be better known, to be read alongside Chesterton by lovers of the White Horse.[43]

The artists attracted to the Horse are a varied bunch. The pop artist Joe Tilson treated the White Horse like a modern piece of graphic design. Anna Dillon is a more traditional landscape artist who, almost obsessively, paints the downland and the Ridgeway, often in bold, stylized bands of colour. Like Nash, she rarely, if ever, includes people. Her images of the White Horse also reproduce aerial views, harking back to the pictures published in *Antiquity*, which allow us to see the hill figure in its, albeit flattened, landscape context (Pl. xxiv). In the 2016 exhibition 'In the Wake of the White Horse' at the Vale and Downland Museum Wantage, Dillon's work was shown alongside that of Chris Hoggett.[44] He is an artist in the mystical tradition of Paul Nash; his Manger is a sleeping horse goddess threatening to stir – a vision also shared with Ravilious (see also page 172).

Tania Kovats's approach is very different. She created *The Museum of the White Horse* in 2007, using a horsebox in which she playfully installed images, drawings, toys, models, artefacts and original artworks relating to the Uffington White Horse and its offspring (Pls xviii–xix). I discovered the 'Museum' parked on a street in Shoreditch, East London, like an abandoned gypsy caravan or the fairground booth of some fortune teller, and a long way from White Horse Hill. Subsequently it travelled to more familiar territory, appearing on the Hill, at the White Horse Show, the Vale and Downland Museum Wantage, and most appropriately, I felt, Newbury racecourse for the Hennessy Gold Cup and the Cheltenham racecourse – to stand near the bronze statue of Best Mate, the greatest local horse of modern times.

The urge to create White Horse figures is still with us in the twenty-first century. When travelling back to England on the Eurostar, the train emerges into daylight at Folkestone. Looking to the right, through the tangle of electrical wires and security fences, it is just possible to catch a glimpse of a white figure set into the green scarp of Cheriton Hill and the appropriately named Horse Hill. This lively hill figure was designed by local artist Charles Newington, inspired by the Uffington Horse, as a millennial landmark. In true British fashion the project ran into planning difficulties. English Nature objected to disturbing the turf and only after a planning enquiry was approval granted and the hill figure completed in 2003. Fortunately, the Horse now benefits from a British virtue – the willingness to volunteer. The Friends of the Folkestone White Horse, founded in 2004, regularly muck out the animal.

I usually disembark from the Eurostar at Ebbsfleet in Kent, a new station and the focal point for a growing community emerging from massive chalk pits. On arriving at the station I had hoped to be met by Mark Wallinger's winning design for a landmark to compete with Antony Gormley's *Angel of the North* – a statue of a gigantic horse thirty-three times life size and 50 m (160 ft) high. Unfortunately, the concept has not reached fruition: its £2 million estimate rose to £15 million – cheap for a premiership footballer, but too much for an Angel of the South. Wallinger's horse project seems to have been aborted – at least for the time being.

A more successful artistic endeavour was Simon Callery's Segsbury Project, a response to the excavation of the hillfort. This was unexpected – a giant cast of the chalk surface of an excavated trench, plan chests full of photographs in stratified drawers and huge white canvases. The work was shown at Great Coxwell Barn, and at the end, or beginning, of England's chalk ridge at Dover Castle.

Of Callery's project, the author Tracy Chevalier wrote: 'His work is open-ended. There are no answers, only unresolved questions, and the joy becomes in the asking.'[45] That just about sums up the pleasure of archaeology, and the pursuit of the White Horse.

AFTERWORD

but the works of man, unless they are of 'now' and of 'this
place' can have no 'forever'

David Jones, 1952

1 JULY 2017

Thankfully, we are back on White Horse Hill. We still fail to see any tumbling lapwings, or the glister of yellowhammers, but an exaltation of skylarks are singing and swifts sweep the scarp. We pass by the black-faced sheep. The upper slopes are now less intensively grazed; purple orchids glow in the turf. From the crest above comes the dull repetitive thud of hammering. People are bent over as if performing some intense ritual. The National Trust has recruited volunteers to repair the Horse. We meet up with the Trust's ranger, Andy Foley, who came here from the Lincolnshire Wolds. People sometimes moan about the Trust as an institution, which tries and sometimes fails to reconcile the impossible, but its guys on the ground are usually popular.

Andy is a phlegmatic countryman. However, get him going and he waxes lyrical: 'This is my world ... the Hill is the jewel in the Trust's crown,' he tells us. But he is worried about the molehills appearing along the Horse's tail and the new parallel scar – an unofficial trackway emerging from the campsite that now lies below the Hill, a scatter of iridescent yellow-orange and green shapes: the local farmer's response to the erratic economy of sheep. Andy doesn't think much of the railway electrification pylons that have recently appeared across the Vale (in 2016), and I have mixed feelings about the vast field of solar panels, now also visible below us. It will take a lot of them to replace Didcot's coal-consuming power station, whose giant cooling towers, now reduced to three, are visible in the distance.

At this time of the morning most of the volunteers are local families, mainly mothers with their children. Perhaps it's a day out for them while their husbands do the weekly shop in the supermarket. Pure chalk nodules are ferried in bags from a nearby quarry hole and then spread over the surface of the Horse. The volunteers pound the lumps into fine powder.

Andy tells me that bankers sometimes come from the City for team-building exercises. I hold my tongue. He was pleased that his boss, Dame Helen Ghosh, turned up to help last year.

This is a sedate affair – no barrels of beer on offer; no rivals from Somerset and Wiltshire happy to beat Berkshire rivals bloody with their staves; no Gypsies in hot pursuit of a cheese or a wheel down the vertiginous slopes of the Manger.

Nowadays there is no scouring pastime on the Hill. There is, though, what Thomas Hughes would have called a 'village veast' – the White Horse Show, held on the August Bank Holiday weekend in fields near to Uffington village. The event was revived in 1972 to raise money for a new village hall, to replace the one paid for by demobbed veterans of the First World War, who selflessly donated the collection made for them by grateful neighbours.

Like the old Pastime, the Show publishes a programme.[1] The 2002 events, over three days, included: heavy horses; a parade of the Old Berks Hunt; White Horse kites; a falconry display; historic motorbikes; the three counties egg-throwing championship; The Adams axemen (lumberjacks from Dorset); a karate display; and Kangaroo Gymnastics. The highlight of the show was a Spitfire fly-past. Most years, sides of Morris Men and military bands feature prominently.

Horses may have disappeared from our streets but they are still popular around here. The 2002 Show announced a Jockey's Gymkhana in aid of the Injured Jockeys' Fund. Visitors were told: 'Everyone knows about Tony McCoy's record-breaking season and that Jim Culloty rode Best Mate to win the Cheltenham Gold Cup – but racing is a dangerous game for jockeys' – and horses, too, they might add. The death of Many Clouds in the Cotswold Chase at Cheltenham in 2017 brought out the most powerful groan I have ever heard from a large crowd. In a titanic struggle with the hot favourite, Thistlecrack, Many Clouds won by a short head, and then collapsed and died. Best Mate, a local horse, was another national hero. He was not a flashy animal, but could, almost effortlessly, change gear and glide through the field to victory. His jumping was immaculate. His bronze statue stands in the nearby village of West Lockinge where he was trained by Henrietta Knight, a drily humorous countrywoman. Best Mate is the only horse whose statue graces the Cheltenham racecourse, having won the Gold Cup three years running (2002–4). He also died in action, racing at Exeter. His ashes are buried by the winning post at Cheltenham.

At the White Horse scouring, I ask volunteers where they have come from. 'Aldershot,' says one lady. 'I read about this in the National Trust newsletter.' An American family, working in international aid, have come from Ethiopia – via Oxford today. The most distinctive character, with an impressive handlebar moustache, is a man named George, from Sonoma County, north of San Francisco. He first came across the White Horse when he saw its image on the cover of the 1982 record *English Settlement* by the band XTC (Swindon's contribution to punk). George tells me he wants a tattoo of the White Horse, but there is a problem – how do you inscribe a white motif on a white skin? He thinks he has a solution: a tattoo that only shows under ultraviolet light. I ask him to email me an image if he manages to pull it off. The volunteers are allotted timed sessions. It is all very disciplined except for the jolly gaggle of dogs: mad Springer Spaniels, hungry Labradors and assorted scruffy terriers.

As the sun begins to go down we head westwards. The sky is sliced with Turner-esque orange streaks; a murmuration of starlings sashays towards the shelter of the trees in the Vale, followed by a gang of rooks. What is a band of rooks called? Is it a 'murder' or an 'unkindness'? They do have a sinister look about them as they wheel into the darkening valley, communally cawing. I check out the name on my iPhone. Apparently, lots of rooks are a 'parliament'. Once these birds would have been an augury, used to read the future.

We follow the road to Ashdown and reach the junction, where a narrow lane heads down into Compton Beauchamp. By the roadside there is a solitary megalith. It isn't a prehistoric one. This is a monument made from a local sarsen stone dedicated to the local dead of the First World War. In the fading light the list of names is just visible: Lovegrove, three men named Luker (were they the sons of one woman, a real band of brothers?), two Timms's. The names are softly eroding after a mere century; some are already so faint that I cannot make them out. These dead lie forever in a foreign field and soon their names will be gone. Will the stone itself become what archaeologists call an 'ancestor artefact' – an object that transmits memory in a non-literate society? The memories do not have to be accurate; people will create new stories. Perhaps King Alfred will claim this stone. Or will the First World War stories outlast people, merge with Waterloo or Agincourt into some mythic Homeric struggle between England and the Continent? Behind us the White Horse is in rude health, vigorous and gleaming in the moonlight, ready to witness another millennium with its large, solitary eye, as we pass by.

NOTES

Introduction (pp. 6–11)
1. Clark, 1940.

Chapter 1:
The Bourn Identity (pp. 12–28)
1. The phrase is from the West Indian poet Derek Walcott's collection of poems *White Egrets*, 2011, London: Faber & Faber.
2. Hughes, 1857.
3. 'The Gypsy', 1915, in Longley (ed.), 2008, pp. 58–9.
4. 'Digging', 1915, in Longley (ed.), 2008, p. 99.
5. In the first issue of the *Wiltshire Archaeological and Natural History Magazine* in 1854, A. E. Smith requested readers to let him know of sightings of the increasingly rare great bustard. He bemoaned the negative impacts of 'modern farming'. The Wiltshire journal is a rare, if welcome, example of a publication that retains the link between natural and cultural history, too often divided by the increasing specialization of academe. The study of ecology and landscape should reunite them.
6. Thomas, 'Rain', 1916, in Longley (ed.), 2008, p. 105.
7. The wealthy Cravens accumulated land in the area. In the eighteenth and nineteenth centuries they were responsible for scouring the White Horse, although hunting seems to have been their favourite activity – at least the men's.
8. Tyack, Bradley and Pevsner, 2010.
9. Hudson, 1900.
10. The military mind continues to obsess about the secrecy of aerial (and now satellite) photography. I tried fruitlessly for a number of years to persuade the Americans to release their routine aerial photography taken in the 1980s – not of military sites in New Mexico, but of Oxfordshire countryside gathered while flying in and out of the US air force base at Upper Heyford. In the same period the Greek government treated all aerial photography as top secret. I had to use German photographs taken in the Second World War to survey a gas pipeline that was to cut through northern Greece and Attica.
11. 'A Strange Story' is referred to in Edward Thomas's *Richard Jefferies* (Thomas, 1909a). Jefferies began work at the *North Wiltshire Herald* aged 17.
12. Miles, 2003.
13. Quoted in Thomas, 1909a (2008 edn, p. 13).
14. For biological data relevant to White Horse Hill, see Allen and Foster, 2015; for the life-ways of beetles, see Jones, 2018.
15. Williams, 1913, p. viii.
16. Adam Thorpe, 'Badger' in 2012, *Voluntary*, London: Jonathan Cape, p. 15.
17. In Modern Welsh the badger is 'broch'.
18. 'The Combe', 1914, in Longley (ed.), 2008, p. 48.

Chapter 2:
Altering the Earth: The Prospect from the Ridgeway (pp. 29–47)
1. The classic work with this title is, of course, Hoskins, 1955. A worthy up-to-date successor is Crane, 2016.
2. Miles, 2016.
3. Parker Pearson, 2012, pp. 119–20.
4. Aubrey, *Monumenta Britannica*, ed. Fowles, 1980.
5. For the history of research in the Avebury area, see Pollard and Reynolds, 2002.
6. For a more detailed description of the henge and the later history of the village, see Pollard and Reynolds, 2002.
7. Wilson, 2015, p. 310.
8. Thomas, 1913.
9. For a more detailed discussion of the place names, topography and references, see Pollard and Reynolds, 2002, pp. 202–9.
10. Wise, 1738.
11. Colt-Hoare, 1821.
12. Steane, 1983.
13. When I was a child at school in the 1950s we chanted and rote-learnt: 12 inches make 1 foot, 3 feet make 1 yard, 22 yards make 1 chain, 10 chains make 1 furlong, 8 furlongs make 1 mile. You see, these things do come in useful.
14. In 1999, RCHME became part of English Heritage. As the new Chief Archaeologist I was privileged to manage the survey teams and help expand the aerial recording programme, known as the National Mapping Programme (NMP). See Bewley, 2001.
15. OS Sheets SU16NW and SU17SW 1:20,000 scale.
16. Bewley, 2001.
17. Fowler, 2000, p. 22.
18. Page and Ditchfield (eds), 1924.
19. Thomas, 1911, p. 28.
20. 'Tall Nettles', 1916, in Longley (ed.), 2008, p. 119.
21. For insights into the work of Edward Thomas I am grateful for Edna Longley's finely edited *Edward Thomas: The Annotated Collected Poems*, 2008, and Andrew Webb's lecture 'Edward Thomas and Poetic Forms', delivered in Oxford, 28 October 2017.
22. 'Good-Night', 1915, in Longley (ed.), 2008, pp. 66–7.
23. A beautifully produced account of the landscape around Blewbury, *A View from the Hill* (Cockrell and Kay (eds), 2006), records the presence of yellowhammers. The holloway from Aston Upthorpe and Aston Tirrold to the Downs is home to blackcaps, the lesser whitethroat, willow warblers and chiffchaff. There is more variety of birds in the gardens of these villages than in the downland landscape, although local people report that swifts and cuckoos have disappeared in recent years.
24. K. Grahame, 'The Romance of the Road', in *Pagan Papers* (E. Mathews & J. Lane, 1893).
25. Hawkes, 1981, p. 86.
26. Macfarlane, Donwood and Richards, 2013, p. 3.
27. Whittle, Healy and Bayliss, 2011.

Chapter 3:
Landmarks and Boundaries (pp. 48–68)

1. Marples, 1949.
2. Petrie, 1926.
3. Whitelock (ed.), 1961 (1965 rev. edn).
4. Ebbsfleet (on the Kent coast, not the station for the high-speed link) has also recently been shown to be the landing site for Julius Caesar's expeditions.
5. Gelling, 1976, *Part 3*, p. 620.
6. See Hooke, 1985, pp. 93–5.
7. *Dun* like *byrig* means 'hill' or 'fortified place' in Old English. The changing languages of the first millennium can cause confusion and certainly tautology. For example, *bre* ('hill' in British Celtic) means the same as *dun* in Old English. As a result, in Leicestershire we have Breedon on the Hill (Hill hill on the hill).
8. These names are described in detail in Gelling, 1976, *Part 3*, pp. 675–8. The name Æscesbyrig means 'the Fort of Aesc'. There are several Old English words for defended places: *dun, burh, bury, byrig*, from which we get the name 'borough'. In the tenth century a number of early towns developed outside monastery gates and were given this name, places such as Peterborough, or after the Norman Conquest the town of Newbury, which was founded where the Lambourn joined the River Kennet. In contrast, the 'bury' name was also applied to prehistoric hillforts, such as Oldbury, an appropriate name for an ancient fortification, and one found in Wiltshire, Gloucestershire and Warwickshire.
9. Gelling, 1976, *Part 3*, pp. 686–9.
10. At Fawler in the Oxfordshire Cotswolds a Romano-British villa with mosaics was found when the River Glyme was diverted to pass under a new railway bridge. The walls of the villa still emerge from the river bank.
11. George Ewart Evans, the local historian of rural history, entitled one of his books *Ask the Fellows Who Cut the Hay*. It's good advice, though their information is not always what you expect. Once, searching for the ruins of a remote West Indian sugar plantation, indicated on a seventeenth-century map, I became so lost in the rain forest that I stopped at a small hamlet and asked the oldest inhabitant if she knew of any plantation ruin. 'No,' she said, 'but I know where there are the stones of an old prison.' Her grandson led me there. It was the plantation I was looking for. But perhaps the old lady was right. All these places had lock-ups to incarcerate slaves.
12. This site was excavated in the early 1970s by Richard Bradley and Anne Ellison. See Bradley and Ellison, 1975.
13. Thoms, 1846, pp. 289–91.
14. In the Public Record Office: IPMC 133/216.
15. Plenderleath, 1874 and 1880.
16. The word *pollus* has been translated as 'foal'. There is no other reference to a second, smaller horse, however, and no trace has been found. It is possible that the phrase *cum pollo suo* means something like 'with its young growth', emphasizing its miraculous appearance from the grass. See Schwyzer, 2004.
17. Woolner, 1965, pp. 31–2.
18. See Hebel (ed.), 1961, p. 284.
19. Hutton, 1994, pp. 214–17.
20. MacCulloch, 2018, p. 227.
21. Earle, 1628, *Micro-Cosmographie, or a Piece of the World Discovered in Essays and Characters,* quoted in Piggott, 1989, p. 16.
22. From Boswell's *Life of Johnson*, Wednesday, 29 April 1778.
23. Stukeley was a pioneer of careful field research. An Anglican parson, in his youth he made valuable records of some of England's outstanding prehistoric sites, but in later life became obsessed with druids. See Piggott, 1985.
24. Defoe, 1725 (1978 edn, p. 51).
25. Wise, 1738.
26. Philalethes Rusticus (aka William Asplin), 1740, *The Impertinence and Imposture of Modern Antiquaries Display'd* (MS in Bodleian Library, Oxford). He refers here to J. Speed's *Historie of Great Britaine* (1611).
27. See Piggott, 1985, p. 142.

Chapter 4:
The Last Pastime (pp. 69–83)

1. The account in this chapter relies mainly on Thomas Hughes's novel *The Scouring of the White Horse*, 1859, including some reported speeches from his text.
2. According to the latest edition of Pevsner's *Berkshire* (Tyack, Bradley and Pevsner, 2010, p. 346).
3. In December 1857 Martin-Atkins was appointed a Fellow of the Society of Antiquaries (FSA) for his efforts.
4. This incident is speculation on the part of the author. Sir Walter Scott was a friend of the Hughes family and a copy of his book *Letters on Demonology and Witchcraft* (2nd ed., 1831) was found during the 1993 excavation of the round barrow on the slope above the White Horse. In the excavation report (Miles et al., 2003) we implied that the book had been buried relatively recently by neo-pagans. I did not agree with this but I was not available to argue the point just before the report went to publication – my own fault. I had argued that Hughes and Atkins might have buried the book themselves.

   My reasons: in recent decades the position of the barrow was difficult to determine (we used geophysics to confirm it). I doubt neo-pagans would have known its location. The small pit had tightly compacted chalk over the book. Assessing the age of a backfilled hole is not an exact science, but to me it certainly did not appear to be recent work. Finally, the book was well preserved, but still had the appearance of having been in the ground for a considerable time.

   Philip Schwyzer has put forward a fascinating, and less subjective, argument in favour of burial in the barrow excavation by Hughes (Schwyzer, 2007, pp. 10–16). He argues that the key to the mystery lies in Scott's third letter in the book: a remarkable tale of barrow digging. In this story the pagan Norse brothers, Asmund and Assueit, swear to be buried together regardless of which of them dies first. So, following Assueit's death, Asmund is interred alive in the same burial mound. A century later a Swedish war-party opens the barrow. No treasure, but ye Gods! Asmund is still alive and covered in gore from fending off his vampire brother. Schwyzer suggests that 'The burial of the *Letters on Demonology* in the soil of an ancient barrow can be read as both a reference to and a re-enactment of this bizarre tale. The gory "Demon de Uffing" suggests a local equivalent of the "evil demon who tenanted (Assueit's) body" [Sir Walter Scott, p. 92], the part of Asmund is performed by the book itself, emerging triumphant before the astonished excavators at the end of its long subterranean ordeal' (2007, pp. 11–12).

The twelfth-century original source for this story is Saxo Grammaticus's *Gesta Danorum*, also the source of another, rather better-known tale full of corpses: that of Amleth, or Hamlet. Both stories were known to the Elizabethans. Thomas Nashe recounted the tale of 'Asuitus and Smundus' in *Pierce Penilesse His Supplication to the Divell* (1592), and, as Schwyzer explains, there is evidence that Shakespeare knew Nashe's work and took details from it for *Hamlet*, and particularly the scene with the jester Yorick in the graveyard. In fact, barrow diggers such as J. Y. Akerman, digging on Salisbury Plain in the 1850s, specifically made the reference.

J. M. Kemble, the author of *The Saxons in England* (1849), the work that did so much to rehabilitate the Anglo-Saxons, was a pioneer of Anglo-Saxon mortuary archaeology (he also belonged to the great dynasty of Shakespearean actors that included his father Charles and sister Fanny). Kemble noted the similarity of funerary urns in Hanover and English cemeteries, concluding in 1856: 'the urns of the "Old Saxon", and those of the "Anglo-Saxon", are in truth identical.... The bones are those whose tongue we speak, whose blood flows in our veins' (quoted in Lucy, 2000).

So Scott, Saxo Grammaticus, Shakespeare, Kemble and the pioneering barrow diggers on White Horse Hill provide us with a virtuous circle that may lead to the burial and discovery of the book.

5. Quoted in Hughes, 1859, pp. 92–3.
6. Quoted in Hughes, 1859, pp. 118- 9.

Chapter 5:
The White Horse: Theories and Speculation (pp. 84–94)

1. Two days ago (as I write), I was in the Dordogne to see the amazing (and expensive) reconstruction of the Lascaux Cave – known as Lascaux IV. Even out of season, in the rainy autumn, its huge car parks were crowded with vehicles. After the school holidays the new nomads, retired French people, arrived in fleets of mobile homes. Lines of shops sold postcards, ice cream and cuddly mammoths. Nearby, at Les Eyzies, a huge new National Museum and Visitor Centre, both impressive Modernist structures, emerge from beneath the overhanging cliffs.
2. Warne, 1866.
3. Greenwell, 1877.
4. Plenderleath, 1892.
5. Piggott, 1983, p. 29.
6. Piggott, 1931, quoted throughout this chapter.
7. For references to Crawford, see Hauser, 2008, pp. 70–71.
8. For Woolner's view and references, see Woolner, 1965 and 1967.
9. The Council for British Archaeology's Countryside Committee had raised this issue following the inadvertent destruction by ploughing of archaeological earthworks on National Trust landholdings.
10. Later he generously gave me his files on the White Horse and the surrounding area. Inside, I found a letter he had written to a colleague at All Souls College that said, 'Who is this Miles? Is he properly educated?' I am not sure about the answer to that one.

Chapter 6:
Light from the Dark (pp. 95–113)

1. James Dyer (1934–2013), the Bedfordshire archaeologist and author of several archaeological guides, subsequently told me that he heard Grimes give a talk at the Council for British Archaeology Group 9 (the South Midlands) annual meeting in the 1950s in which he mentioned the White Horse work.
2. Miles et al., 2003.
3. Quoted in Thomas, 1909a (2008 edn, p. 148).
4. Hughes, 1857 (1989 edn, p. 9).
5. Bell and Lock, 2000.
6. Flannery, 2004, p. 120.
7. J. Rees-Jones and M. Tite, 2003, 'Appendix 1: Optically Stimulated Luminescence (OSL) Dating Results from the White Horse and Linear Ditch', in Miles et al., 2003, pp. 269–71.

Chapter 7:
The Wonder Horse (pp. 114–24)

1. H. M. Evans, 'Wonder and the clinical encounter', *Theoretical Medicine and Bioethics*, 2012, 33(2), pp. 123–36.
2. Ingrams, 1988.
3. A. Einstein, 1936, 'Physics and Reality', *Journal of the Franklin Institute*, vol. 221.
4. Firestein, 2012, p. 10.
5. R. Jefferies, 'The Seasons and the Stars', in *The Old House at Coate*, ed. by S. J. Looker, 1948, London: Lutterworth Press; and R. Jefferies, 1883, *The Story of My Heart: My Autobiography* (2015 edn, Cambridge: Green Books. The stargazing image is reproduced on the book's cover).
6. Cameron, 2016, pp. 340; see also pp. 261 and 336.
7. Thomas, 'But These Things Also', 1915, in Longley (ed.), 2008, p. 67.
8. For example, Flannery, 2001. For a balanced view of the complexity of extinction in which humans may not be the dominant actor, see Mitchell, 2015, pp. 65–7.
9. For wild horses sensitive to warming, see Bendrey, 2012.
10. Suzman, 2017, pp. 135–7.
11. Watts, 2009. Henshilwood and Lombard, 2014.
12. Bahn, 2016.
13. Conard, 2016.

14. Quiles et al., 2016.
15. For a discussion of the theories, see Bahn, 2016, particularly Ch. 11, p. 275; theories include: art for art's sake, hunting magic, the images of shamanistic trances, fertility magic, ancestor myths, etc. Some prefer to avoid the use of the term 'art', as coming from the Western 'art world' and not appropriate to animal depiction in the Palaeolithic and more recent hunter-gatherer societies. See 'Totemism, Animism and the Depiction of Animals', in Ingold, 2000, pp. 111–31.
16. Gell, 1998.

Chapter 8:
Domesticating the Horse (pp. 125–40)

1. MacFadden, 1992.
2. There is a vast literature about horses and humans on the steppes. The most accessible accounts in English with extensive references are: Anthony, 2007; Cunliffe, 2015, an admirably clear account, beautifully illustrated with excellent maps; and Baumer, 2012, also superbly illustrated.
3. This could be a factor in the changing fate of the American horse. Around 13,000 years ago human hunters confronted wild American horses, which were unaccustomed to this new and deadly predator. The horse herds disappeared. On the horse's reintroduction to the Americas after 1493, humans understood domestication and the value of a live horse as an ally. The horses thrived until twentieth-century Americans, motorized and gun-toting, reverted to the hunting ethos. The real feral mustangs of the Plains – there were about two million in 1900 – were being butchered for pet food. In 1971 the last few thousand were granted legal protection. Typically, the current president of the USA is now threatening to remove it: 'Born to be wild, destined to be burgers' in the words of Josh Glancy (*Sunday Times*, 31 December 2017). Like the bison, mustangs almost went the way of the passenger pigeon and still could.

4. For a more detailed study of this, see Anthony, 2007, pp. 193–220.
5. The accumulating evidence supports the interpretation put forward by Anthony, 2007, pp. 216–20.
6. Ewers, 1955.
7. Mitchell, 2015. The same process also happened to the south in the Gran Chaco of Paraguay and Brazil and the grasslands of Chile, Patagonia and Argentina.
8. Usain Bolt, the world's fastest runner, briefly achieved 3.5 hp in his World Record dash of 2009. A fit human can sustain 0.1 hp for a lengthy period. See Stevenson and Wassersug, 1993.
9. For details and references, see Anthony, 2007, and Cunliffe, 2015.
10. For an up-to-date account of the Yamnaya and their genetics, see Reich, 2018, pp. 107–9 and 114–16.
11. For fascinating accounts of the clash of cultures involved in raids to seize women, see Demos, 1996.
12. Rasmussen et al., 2015.
13. Olalde et al., 2018; Cassidy et al., 2016.
14. Anthony, 2009.
15. Matthew 21:7.
16. The Mitanni, in northern Mesopotamia, were well known as charioteers. While the mass of the population spoke a non-Indo-European language, their rulers had Indo-European names. One translates as 'having an attacking chariot'. It seems likely that a group of chariot-riding warriors took control of Mitanni territory in the second millennium BC.
17. Schrader et al., 2018; Heidorn, 1997.
18. Braudel, 2001, p. 18.
19. For Assyrian and Cypriot material, see the catalogue of the British Museum's superb exhibition: Brereton (ed.), 2018.
20. Neer, R. 2012, *Greek Art and Archaeology*, London and New York, Thames & Hudson.

Chapter 9:
A People of Chariots and Horsemen (pp. 141–60)

1. Churchill, 1956, p. 10.
2. Caesar, *The Gallic War*, Book IV, ch. 33.
3. Caesar would spend a large amount of his ill-gotten

gains, plundered from Gaul, in rebuilding Rome's ancient chariot course.
4. There are other horse bones reported from a Neolithic context, but closer examination and, in some cases, radiocarbon dating suggest that they were inserted at a later period. See also Bendrey, 2010.
5. The survival of animal bones in archaeological sites depends upon the chemistry of the soil. On the chalklands of Wessex, alkaline conditions are ideal for preservation. On acidic soils – for example, in parts of northern and western Britain, or in the Lower Thames Valley – bones can virtually disappear.
6. Lawson (ed.), 2000, pp. 101–19.
7. Done, 1991.
8. Allen and Robinson, 1993. For the site in context, see also Lambrick, with Robinson, 2009.
9. Lambrick and Allen, 2004.
10. Not only in European Iron Age society. When the Comanche chief Quannah died, his son said that you could tell that he was a great man because he had given away most of his horses.
11. Collins, 1952–3.
12. Harding, 1972, p. 70.
13. Roadside shrines seem to have been almost universal since roads were invented.
14. Lambrick, with Robinson, 2009, p. 232, fig. 6.19.
15. Harding, D. W.,1972, p. 172, pl. 77.
16. For a clear account of the Late Bronze Age/Iron Age terminology, Hallstatt and La Tène, *see* Cunliffe, 2001, p. 312.
17. *Trésors des princes celtes. Galeries nationales du Grand Palais 20 octobre 1987–15 février 1988* (exhibition catalogue), 1987, Paris: Ministère de la Culture et de la Communication, Editions de la Réunion des Musées Nationaux, pp. 218–31; Müller, 2009.
18. For a useful summary of the Heuneburg and elite burials, see Harding, 2014.
19. Krausse et al., 2017.
20. Horse decoration rarely survives from prehistoric northern Europe, but the bronze 'chamfrein', or pony-cap, from Torrs in southwest Scotland, dating

to about 200 BC, gives us a tantalizing glimpse of what might have been. This strange object was found in the nineteenth century during peat digging and was acquired by Sir Walter Scott. It is thought that the beautiful repoussé decorations on the cap of curvilinear designs and birds' heads is British-made but influenced by continental styles. The cap has two bronze curved horns terminating in duck's heads, but these were added at some unspecified time. Originally the cap held a jaunty crest – a reminder that prehistoric British horses, like Scythian ones, may have dressed in style and perhaps acquired the speed of deer. See Briggs, 2014.

21. G. Argent, 2010, 'Do Clothes Make the Horse: Relationality, Roles and Statuses in Iron Age Inner Asia', *World Archaeology*, 42, pp. 157–74.

22. For a recent and well-illustrated account of the archaeology of the steppes, see Simpson and Pankova, 2017.

23. A hymn possibly written by Emperor Wu about 101 BC, quoted in Piggott, 1992, pp. 66–7. See also Waley, 1955.

24. Fontijn and Fokkens, 2007. For the Aisne/Marne/Moselle burials, see Diepeveen-Jansen, 2007.

25. Human remains are not uncommon in the Iron Age of southern Britain, but they are often fragmentary – for example, odd bones placed in the pits previously used for corn storage. A formal cemetery was recently discovered at Yarnton, north of Oxford, which contained no artefacts to indicate its date. Radiocarbon dating, however, proved it to be Middle Iron Age. Other sites like this may have gone unidentified. Hey, Bayliss and Boyle, 1999.

26. Its meaning is uncertain: one possibility is that it comes from the name of a deity, which translates as the Maker or the Creator.

27. Since radiocarbon dating first came into use in the late 1940s there have been several major advances: the calibration of the

dates to provide a more accurate chronology, and the use of Accelerator Mass Spectrometry (AMS) meaning greater accuracy, more swiftly and cheaply, from small samples. Recently, the use of Bayesian modelling has further increased chronological accuracy.

28. M. Giles, 2012, *A Forged Glamour: Landscape, Identity and Material Culture in the Iron Age*, Oxford, Windgather Press.

29. See *Current Archaeology*, 327, June 2017, pp. 26–31.

30. A. Boyle et al., 'Site D (Ferry Fryston) in the Iron Age and Romano-British Periods' in F. Brown et al. (eds), 2007, *The Archaeology of the A1(M) Darrington to Dishford DBFO Road Scheme*, Lancaster, Lancaster Imprints 12, pp 121–59.

Chapter 10:
The Sun Horse (pp. 161–74)

1. Randsborg, 2009.

2. Renfrew, 2007.

3. The Antikythera Mechanism (second century BC) is the oldest-known astronomical calculator and partly utilizes the Metonic cycle. Meton, a fifth-century BC astronomer in Athens, observed sunrise at the summer solstice over Mount Lycabettus, then the midwinter sunrise over Mount Hymettos.

4. A life-sized solar barge, 44 m (144 ft) long, was buried at the foot of the Great Pyramid of Giza in about 2500 BC.

5. Hutton, 1991.

6. Notably in Green, 1991, which illustrates the Trundholm sun chariot on its cover.

7. Sir James Frazer (1854–1941), the armchair anthropologist, compiled the massive and influential twelve volumes of *The Golden Bough* largely from his study in Trinity College, Cambridge. The abbreviated version, first published in 1922, became a bestseller and influenced artists from T. S. Eliot (*The Waste Land*) to Robert Graves, and Francis Ford Coppola (*Apocalypse Now*).

8. Sutcliff, 1977.

9. T. C. Lethbridge, 1962, *Witches: Investigating an Ancient Religion*,

London: Routledge & Kegan Paul. For a discussion of Tom Lethbridge's work, see Hutton, 1999 (2001 pb edn, p. 274). Lethbridge attempted a survey of the GogMagog figures near Cambridge, but conventional archaeologists saw little merit in his approach.

10. For tribal names, see Rivet and Smith, 1978. Charles Thomas, the distinguished Cornish archaeologist based at the University of Edinburgh in the early 1960s, noted that several northern tribes had 'animal' names that he proposed were clan totems or objects of worship rather than simply animals of economic concern. See Thomas, C., 1961, p. 40.

11. Clark, 1957 (1968 pb edn, p. 135).

12. Unfortunately, we do not have the context of the Basse-Yutz flagons because they were found by road workers in 1927, who deliberately kept quiet about the discovery and sold them to a dealer in England. Now they are in the British Museum. So far the French government has not demanded their return.

13. Renfrew, 2007.

14. Parker Pearson, 2012. This analogous use of anthropological data in archaeology remains contentious. Ironically, some prehistorians draw on evidence from societies thousands of miles and years away from their subjects, while resisting the evidence of the Classical world or medieval Europe.

15. Pollard, 2017.

16. Bradley, 2009, provides references to what is now a massive literature.

17. Reichel-Dolmatoff, 1971.

18. Images on hard rock can survive the ravages of time. Similar, more ephemeral ones may also have been carved into trees, marked on animal hides, woven into textiles or tattooed onto human skin.

19. Bradley, 2006.

20. This idea comes from Kaul, 1998. Bradley suggests this may be a little too 'ingenious'. As the razors are placed in burials perhaps they represent the soul's journey into the afterlife.

21. Mitchell, 2015, fig. 5.11, p. 172.
22. Mitchell, 2015, p. 162.
23. West, 2007.
24. Ibid., p. 203.
25. P. Dillon, 2016, *In the Wake of the White Horse* (exhibition catalogue), Wantage: Vale & Downland Museum.
26. P. Nash, 1938, 'Unseen Landscapes', *Country Life*.
27. Egginton, 2011. Viewshed analysis is a technique commonly used by geographers and available on geographic information systems (GIS) software; it allows the analysis of all points visible from a specific location. For example, it allows you to ask the question: 'Where is the White Horse visible from?' and 'Where is it best visible from?' Or, in this case, 'Could it be placed in a more optimal position for viewers in the Vale?'

Chapter 11:
Changing Horses: Survival in Difficult Times (pp. 175–94)

1. Bryson, 2000.
2. The tribulations of the church at Stanford-in-the-Vale during the Reformation are well documented. See Duffy, 1992, pp. 462, 490 and 547–8.
3. Graham Greene, 'The Explorers'.
4. R. Kipling, *Puck of Pook's Hill*, 1906, London: Macmillan.
5. Eliot, 1957, p. 248.
6. Collard et al., 2006; Lambrick, with Robinson, 2009, pp. 216–17.
7. Waddington et al., 2012.
8. Bowden and McOmish, 1987.
9. Woolf, 1998, p. 206.
10. Creighton, 2000, pp. 122–3.
11. Kamash, Gosden and Lock, 2010.
12. The distinctive shape of a Romano-Celtic temple has recently been seen as a cropmark on aerial photographs 2 km (1¼ miles) to the northeast of Lowbury Hill. Paul Chadwick pers. comm.
13. The limitations of archaeology are reflected in the lack of evidence for the great gatherings of the eighteenth and nineteenth centuries. We know from written evidence that they took place in the hillfort, but we found little trace of them.
14. Green, 1991, provides an excellent, balanced account of solar imagery and the complexities of religions in Gaul and Britain.

Chapter 12:
Strange Meetings: Old Gods and New Gods (pp. 195–217)

1. The 'True Cross' was found by Constantine's mother, St Helen, while on a pilgrimage to Jerusalem. Her archaeological endeavours were aided by the local bishop, Macarius.
2. Lane Fox, 1986 (1988 pb edn, pp. 30–31).
3. In a broader context, the words 'pagan' or 'paganism' are also contentious. Timothy Insoll emphasizes: 'The overall terms of African traditional religion/ religions was developed, rightly, as a counter to demeaning labels such as "paganism", "fetishism", "animism" or "magic" which were formerly applied to describe religious practices in Africa.' Some might regard this as political correctness, but the term 'pagan' does lump together many complex and sophisticated belief systems as primitivism in opposition to Christianity. In the early Anglo-Saxon context, Martin Carver (Professor of Archaeology at the University of York, now retired, who directed the major research project at Sutton Hoo) would prefer to avoid the word 'pagan', but he is not keen on the words 'traditional' or 'religion' either, which makes life difficult. Insoll, 2004.
4. Hirst and Rahtz, 1996.
5. The Germanic people who came into Britain included Angles, Saxons and Jutes – so the terminology varies. To the Romans, Germania included north Germany, Jutland and parts of the Netherlands. Bede was himself an Angle and as a result of his influence we now refer to Anglo-Saxons, who were united under King Alfred. See Manco, 2018, pp. 29, 32, 48, 54, 91 and 137. A recent major study (see Bayliss and Hines (eds), 2013) has clarified the dates of the earlier Anglo-Saxon period, analysing the vast amount of funerary data. For further comment and implications for Christianization, see Scull, 2015.
6. Hamerow, 2002 and 2012.
7. Leeds, 1923; final report, Leeds, 1947.
8. Benson and Miles, 1974.
9. 'Gewisse' is from the Old English adjective *gewis*, meaning 'reliable', though Blair suggests they were 'a strong-arm gang controlling weaker neighbours by brute force'. See Blair, 1994, p. 37.
10. See *The Fall of Phaeton*, Wedgwood blue and white jasperware tablet, *c.* 1780 by George Stubbs (1724–1806), National Museums Liverpool, Lady Lever Art Gallery.
11. Booth et al., 2007, pp. 300–2.
12. Woolner, 1967.
13. The southern royal houses followed the example of Northumbria in adopting Woden. Later Germanic aristocrats, both in Britain and on the Continent, added the classical heroes of Troy to their genealogy.
14. Schwyzer, 2007, p. 40.
15. A. L. Klinck, 2001, *The Old English Elegies: A Critical Edition and Genre Study*, Montreal: McGill-Queen's University Press, pp. 13–16.
16. Fern, 2010.
17. Williams, 2001, p. 204.
18. Fern, 2010, p. 134.
19. See Webster, 1999a, 1999b and 2012; Abels, 2009.
20. 'Fabricius' means in Latin something like 'the Maker', so the name may have reminded the translators of Weland, the skilled metalworker. Smyth, 1995, p. 569.
21. Smyth, 1995, p. 535.
22. Fern, 2010.
23. Gelling, 1974, *Part 2*, p. 361.
24. An image that is also repeated in *Beowulf* line 2213.
25. See Wilson, D., 1992, pp. 28–33 for a more detailed discussion.
26. Bayliss and Hines (eds), 2013.
27. Blair, 1994, pp. 46–7.
28. Hills, 2015. Boyle et al., 1998 and 2011.
29. The gold was not pure and probably came from melted-down coins. The sources of garnet and amethyst could be Afghanistan, via Constantinople. Cowries originated in the Red Sea and ivory from North Africa. These probably came through

Francia and up the Thames from Kent. The beaver tooth was less 'pagan' than wolves' teeth.

30. Hutton, 2010.
31. Amethyst rings are still worn today by Christian bishops. For the Romans, wine-coloured amethyst was a cure for hangovers.
32. Semple, 2011.
33. Bladbean ('blood-beam') in east Kent was possibly where cattle were sacrificed, as the first missionaries reported to Pope Gregory.
34. Blair, 1994, p. 206.
35. Blair, 2018.
36. There were exceptions. The Englishman Aelfsige of Faringdon was a minor landholder before the Conquest. He seems to have ingratiated himself with William and acquired large estates in north Berkshire, the Thames Valley and the Cotswolds.
37. Quoted in Munby, 1996.
38. Munby, 1996.
39. Jenkins, 1999, p. 552.
40. Page and Ditchfield (eds), 1924.

Chapter 13:
Reinventing the Nation's Past
(pp. 218–39)

1. Amusingly, as I write (September 2018) there is a BBC2 TV programme announcing the big historical news: 'Arthur could be a myth'.
2. Hay, 1952, p. 159. Schwzyer, 2004.
3. Earlier sources make no mention of Arthur at Glastonbury. In 1184 a great fire had swept through the abbey and the monks urgently needed to restore their fortunes. Canterbury had also experienced a destructive fire in 1174, only four years after the murder of Thomas Becket, their archbishop. His cult generated a new flow of pilgrims and wealth. No other abbey had claimed Arthur. The 'discovery' of Arthur's grave also suited the English monarchy as it gave the lie to the rebellious Welsh myth of a British king in-waiting, asleep beneath a hill. The past was past. Arthur was dead and here were his gigantic, battle-scarred bones to prove it. For a detailed account, see Rahtz, 1993.

4. MacCulloch, 2016.
5. Sweet, 2004, p. 120.
6. The astrologer John Dee had popularized the term 'The British Empire' in 1575, before even the United Kingdom existed. Speed's impressive frontispiece announces the title in Latin: *Theatrum Imperii Magnae Britanniae*. Standing in the theatrical alcoves are the ancestors – a semi-naked, long-haired 'Britaine', a 'Romane', a Saxon, a Dane and a Norman. The atlas was printed in London in Pope's Head Alley, at 'ye signe of ye White Horse'.
7. Chandler, 1993.
8. The name 'Chipping' refers to a market, as in Chipping Norton and Chipping Camden.
9. Morris (ed.), 1984.
10. Schwyzer, 2004, p. 39.
11. Quoted in Sweet, 2004, p. 189.
12. Wise, 1738.
13. Antiquarianism was a 'manly' pursuit. Ladies, according to one antiquarian, would find reading county histories insuperably irksome. An exception in the eighteenth century was Elizabeth Elstob, a Saxonist, praised for her 'masculine abilities'. Another was Anna Stukeley who wrote to her father in 1758 observing the similarity between the White Horse and images on British coins (see p. 68). See Sweet, 2004, pp. 69–79.
14. Quoted in Francis Wise, 'Postscript to a Letter to Dr Mead', Bodleian Library, Goth Berks 3; the original is a Harleian MS in the British Museum.
15. In 1771, Whitaker published his *History of Manchester*.
16. Camden's 1586 edition of *Britannia* sited the Battle of Ethandune at Edington, near Westbury, Wiltshire. Somerset's Edington continued to claim the battlefield.
17. See Hutton, 1994. Henry Bourne's *Antiquitates Vulgares* (1725) provided a guide for the gentry – what activities were U and non-U.
18. For details of the Uffington Enclosure Award, see Parsons and Millikin, 2014.
19. Ibid., p. 15.

20. See Edwards, 2005, pp. 102–3 and n. 100.
21. Edwards, 2005.
22. Ibid.
23. During the Napoleonic Wars in 1809, in *Genius of the Thames* the patriotic poet Thomas Love Peacock contrasted the 'polluted, blood-stained Seine' with the Thames: 'Where peace, with freedom hand-in-hand / Walks forth along the sparkling strand, / And cheerful toil, and glowing health, / Proclaim a patriot nation's wealth.' This was written scarcely fifty years before the 'Great Stink 'of 1858.
24. Schama, 1995, where this event is described.
25. List compiled from the work of Marples, 1949, and Schwyzer, 2004.
26. The horse was, prosaically, originally named 'Potatoes'. The groom labelled his corn bin 'Potoooooooo', which Abingdon found amusing and registered the name as 'Pot8os'.
27. McGrath, 2016, pp. 80–81.
28. Ibid., p. 36.
29. Colley, 1989.
30. A painting of 1778 by Benjamin West has the Protestant William of Orange mounted on a white horse at the Battle of the Boyne, the victory over the Roman Catholics still celebrated by Ulster marching bands today.
31. Hughes, 1859, p. 71.
32. Edwards, 2005.
33. After the 1870s, the proportion of Britons living in towns and cities increased even more rapidly.
34. The corruption and unfairness of the parliamentary system was typified by the 'rotten boroughs'. One such – Old Sarum, the site of a hillfort and a ruined castle on the Downs above Salisbury – had one vote and returned two MPs. In contrast, the whole county of Lancashire, which included greater Manchester with a million inhabitants, also returned two MPs and only landowners could vote for them. In 1830, the Duke of Wellington, as prime minister, declared that the system was perfect and could not be improved. The 'mob' stormed his house.

35. Chartism was the mass movement for civil rights in Britain. The 1842 Petition, known as the 'Leviathan Petition', was signed by over three million people – about one-third of the adult population and three and a half times the size of the electorate in the general elections of 1841. Stuck together, the paper petitions were about 10 km (6 miles) long. See Chase, 2007, and Howe, 2014.

36. Kingsley can be admired as a forward-thinking reformer, sympathetic to workers and children, or reviled as a self-proclaimed racist. Westward Ho! (named after the novel) is the only place name in England with an exclamation mark. Nearby there is a statue to Kingsley. Should we celebrate it, demolish it or accept it? Ah! The complications of history.

37. Akerman, 1846. Thoms was still arguing for the Saxon origins of the Horse. Akerman's 'letter' was a response: see Thoms, 1846.

38. Lubbock said that if he had called it a 'National Holiday' his bill would have failed. It passed by identifying it with the need for banks to close for administrative reasons.

39. Quoted in MacDougall, 1982, p. 97.

40. Parker, 2007.

Chapter 14:
Into the Modern World (pp. 240–62)

1. The Newbury District Field Club visited the site in 1871 and reported that the Earl of Craven was considering a scouring in that or the following year. Still nothing happened. See report of 'The Excursion to White Horse Hill 6th June 1871', *Transactions of the Newbury District Field Club*, I, 1871, pp. 148–51.

2. *The Times*, 10 June 1871.

3. The booklet (Anon, *White Horse Hill and its Surroundings: Issued in Commemoration of the Unveiling of a Statue of Alfred the Great at Wantage by H.R.H. The Prince of Wales, July 14th 1877*, Wantage, 1877) is described in Edwards, 2005, p. 117 and n. 198, p. 127.

4. Plenderleath, 1880.

5. Marples, 1949 (1981 edn, p. 65).

6. Christian Thomsen was the first curator (1816–65) of the National Museum of Denmark. He famously organized the collection on the basis of the Three Age System (Stone, Bronze and Iron) and promoted it through the museum's 1836 guidebook. His colleague and successor at the museum, Jens Jacob Worsaae, published, at the young age of 22, *Danmark's Oldtid* (1843) – published in Oxford in 1849 as *The Primeval Antiquities of Denmark*. Worsaae was arguably the first professional archaeologist, setting out the need for scientific standards of excavation and the involvement of the public. As Denmark's Inspector General of Antiquities he pioneered investigation, conservation and popularization.

7. Daniel, 1967, pp. 92–7.

8. Private member's bills can be easily disposed of by government, opposition or even cussed individual Members of Parliament – for example, they can simply be talked out and so run out of the time allotted for their presentation in the House of Commons. I had the job of shepherding the National Heritage Bill 2002 (a private member's bill put forward by Baroness Anelay) through Parliament with all-party (and government) support. So no problem perhaps? Not so – I heard on the grapevine that a Labour MP intended to talk it out. I spoke to some of his friends, then tracked him down in his parliamentary lair. I explained the bill's importance and the time and effort that had gone into it. 'Oh, I've nothing against your bill,' the MP said. 'I was going to talk it out to prevent the finance bill, which is coming up next, from getting to the floor of the Commons. I'll tell you what. I'll stop two minutes short and leave time for a vote.' This he did and Baroness Anelay's bill was duly passed. For the first time English Heritage could legally deal with the maritime heritage of the nation's own waters – an

omission caused by the poor drafting of an earlier (1983) Act. It's an odd way to do business.

9. Thurley, 2013 (2014 edn, p. 41), who describes the struggle for the legal protection of ancient monuments and historic buildings. For a more detailed account of the 1882 Act and its slow gestation and implementation, see Chippindale, 1983.

10. Newman, 1997, p. 30.

11. Alexander, 2007. Eliot was more generous to Chesterton in his 1936 obituary of the man, see Alexander, 2007 (2017 edn, p. 195).

12. Nevertheless, Father Brown was made into a good 1954 film starring Alec Guinness as the eponymous hero and Peter Finch as the arch-villain Flambeau. Typically, Father Brown attempts to get Flambeau to see the error of his ways. Redemption is always possible. A television series also began in 2013 starring Mark Williams, which presents a sympathetic if shambolic hero; it is still being screened in 2018.

13. Quoted in Michael Alexander's superb, wide-ranging study of modern attitudes to medievalism: Alexander, 2007 (2017 edn, p. 203).

14. Chesterton, 1911. All quotes are from the 7th edn, 1925.

15. When I was a child in the Calder Valley, the steam engines that powered the textile mills were given names. Across the road I used to visit 'Mary Ellen'. In Hebden Bridge there was a mill boiler named 'Thomas Hughes' in honour of the workers' champion. Lovers of school stories do not always appreciate this aspect of the man.

16. Hughes, 1889 edn, p. 184.

17. J. H. Newman, 1864, *Apologia pro Vita Sua*, London (1994 edn, London: Penguin Books, p. 99), quoted in Alexander, 2007 (2017 edn, pp. 93–4 and n. 26, p. 253).

18. Alexander, 2007 (2017 edn).

19. MacCarthy, 1994.

20. Ibid.

21. Wilk (ed.), 2006.

22. Harris, 2010.

23. Wain, 1977, p. 253.

24. In recent years, the hill has also yielded an increasing amount

of archaeological information. It contains a prehistoric settlement, which lies outside the hillfort, and a complex of Romano-British ritual and burial sites. See Allen et al., 2010.

25. Cardinal, 1989.

26. The owner was Lady Dunch – hence the pair of rounded hills are known locally as 'Mother Dunch's buttocks'. Antiquaries invented the name 'the Sinodun Hills'.

27. Wilson, 2015, p. 413. I believe that this was the same day that my grandfather James Leo Graham lost his leg, 8 km (5 miles) to the north, in the attack on Vimy Ridge with the Canadians. It is also recorded in Uffington that local men died at Arras in April 1917.

28. Nash letters quoted in Haycock, 2002, pp. 71–5.

29. The words of Ann Wroe in her beautiful book Six Facets of Light, 2016.

30. Vita Sackville-West, The Land, 1926, London: Heinemann.

31. For references to Axis magazine, see Harris, 2010, pp. 15 and 20–25.

32. In the 1990s, I was a member of the Oxford Diocesan Advisory Committee. Of the proposals brought to us for permission to be installed in local churches, outstanding by a long way was the little jewel of a stained glass window for Iffley Church, designed by the late John Piper. It was the most gorgeous blue, with bursts of red. A cockerel (with a speech bubble) announced 'Christus natus est!' (Christ is born!); below, an owl hooted 'ubi? ubi?' (Where? Where?). This was the opposite of pure abstraction: rich, amusing and thoughtful, and joyfully celebrating the part nature and animals play in the world.

33. J. Piper, 1937, 'Prehistory from the Air', Axis, 8, pp. 4–8.

34. Grigson, 1939, p. 54.

35. Wilson, 2006 (2007 edn, pp. 103–12).

36. Dilworth, 2017, p. 171.

37. I have the Cambridgeshire poster by John Nash on my study wall. Swallowtail butterflies flutter in the foreground over the milk parsley growing in Wicken Fen, and the silvery line of a drainage dyke carries the eye to Ely Cathedral, misty blue in the distance, silhouetted against the huge fenland sky.

38. Connolly, 1934.

39. For the work of Ravilious, see Russell, 2015, and Friend, 2017.

40. As a result of the change, my job was transferred into the new Oxfordshire Archaeological Unit. I was reminded of these events by Matthew Engel's fascinating book: Engel, 2015, pp. 398–9.

41. Harris, 2010, p. 30.

42. Ingrams, 1988, p. 74.

43. Stallworthy, 2002. The poem is also included in his 2004 collection, Body Language, Manchester: Carcanet Press.

44. See P. Dillon, 2016, In the Wake of the White Horse (exhibition catalogue), Wantage: Vale & Downland Museum.

45. Chevalier, 2003.

Afterword (pp. 263–65)

1. For the history of the modern show, see Tilling, 2007.

BIBLIOGRAPHY

Abels, R., 2009, 'What has Weland to do with Christ? The Franks Casket and the Acculturation of Christianity in Early Anglo-Saxon England', *Speculum*, 84, pp. 549–82

Akerman, J. Y., 1846, 'Letter to William J. Thoms', *Archaeologia*, 31, pp. 297–8

Alexander, M., 2007, *Medievalism: The Middle Ages in Modern England*, New Haven: Yale University Press (2017 rev. pb edn)

Allen, R., and Foster, A. P., 2015, 'The National Trust Nature Conservation Evaluation, White Horse Hill, Oxfordshire' (unpublished)

Allen, T. G., and Robinson, M. A., 1993, *The Prehistoric Landscape and Iron Age Enclosed Settlement at Mingies Ditch, Hardwick-with-Yelford, Oxon*, Thames Valley Landscapes Monograph: The Windrush Valley, vol. 2, Oxford: Oxford Archaeology

Allen, T., et al., 2010, *Castle Hill and its Landscape: Archaeological Investigations at the Wittenhams, Oxfordshire*, Oxford Archaeology Monograph 9, Oxford: Oxford Archaeology

Anthony, D. W., 2007, *The Horse, the Wheel and Language: How Bronze-Age Riders from the Eurasian Steppes Shaped the Modern World*, Princeton: Princeton University Press

Anthony, D. W., 2009, 'The Sintashta Genesis: The Roles of Climate Change, Warfare, and Long-Distance Trade', in B. Hanks and K. Linduff (eds), *Social Complexity in Prehistoric Eurasia: Monuments, Metals and Mobility*, Cambridge: Cambridge University Press, pp. 47–73

Aubrey, J., *Monumenta Britannica: or a Miscellany of British Antiquities*, ed. John Fowles, 1980, Sherborne: Dorset Publishing Company

Bahn, P. G., 2016, *Images of the Ice Age*, Oxford: Oxford University Press

Baumer, C., 2012, *The History of Central Asia: The Age of the Steppe Warriors*, vol. 1, London: I. B. Tauris

Bayliss, A., and Hines, J. (eds), 2013, *Anglo-Saxon Graves and Grave Goods of the 6th and 7th Centuries AD: A Chronological Framework*, Society for Medieval Archaeology Monograph

33, Leeds: Society for Medieval Archaeology

Bede, *A History of the English Church and People*, tr. L. Sherley-Price, 1955, London: Penguin (1986 edn)

Bell, T., and Lock, G., 2000, 'Topographical and Cultural Influences on Walking the Ridgeway in Later Prehistoric Times', in Lock (ed.), 2000, pp. 85–100

Bendrey, R., 2010, 'The Horse', in T. O'Connor and N. Sykes (eds), *Extinctions and Invasions: A Social History of British Fauna*, Oxford: Windgather Press, pp. 10–16

Bendrey, R., 2012, 'From Wild Horses to Domestic Horses: A European Perspective', *World Archaeology*, 44 (1), pp. 135–57

Benson, D., and Miles, D., 1974, 'Cropmarks near the Sutton Courtenay Saxon Site', *Antiquity*, 48, pp. 223–6

Bewley, B., 2001, 'Understanding England's Historic Landscapes: An Aerial Perspective', *Landscapes*, 2 (1), pp. 74–84

Blair, J., 1994, *Anglo-Saxon Oxfordshire*, Stroud: Sutton

Blair, J., 2018, *Building Anglo-Saxon England*, Princeton: Princeton University Press

Booth, P., et al., 2007, *The Thames Through Time: The Archaeology of the Gravel Terraces of the Upper and Middle Thames: The Early Historical Period: AD 1–1000*, Thames Valley Landscapes Monograph 27, Oxford: Oxford Archaeology

Botha, R., and Knight, C. (eds), 2009, *The Cradle of Language*, vol. 2, Oxford: Oxford University Press

Bowden, M., and McOmish, D., 1987, 'The Required Barrier', *Scottish Archaeological Review*, 4, pp. 76–84

Boyle, A., et al., 1998, *The Anglo-Saxon Cemetery at Butler's Field, Lechlade, Gloucestershire: Volume 1*, Thames Valley Landscapes Monograph 10, Oxford: Oxford Archaeology

Boyle, A., et al., 2011, *The Anglo-Saxon Cemetery at Butler's Field, Lechlade, Gloucestershire: Volume 2*, Thames Valley Landscapes Monograph 33, Oxford: Oxford Archaeology

Bradley, R., 2006, 'Danish Razors and Swedish Rocks: Cosmology and the Bronze Age Landscape', *Antiquity*, 80 (308), pp. 372–89

Bradley, R., 2009, *Image and Audience: Rethinking Prehistoric Art*, Oxford: Oxford University Press

Bradley, R., and Ellison, A., 1975, *Rams Hill: A Bronze Age Defended Enclosure and Its Landscape*, BAR British Series 19, Oxford: British Archaeological Reports

Braudel, F., 2001, *The Mediterranean in the Ancient World*, London: Allen Lane

Brereton, G. (ed.), 2018, *I Am Ashurbanipal: King of the World, King of Assyria*, London: Thames & Hudson and The British Museum

Briggs, C. S., 2014, 'The Torrs Chamfrein or Head-piece: Restoring "A very curious relic of antiquity"', in C. Gosden, S. Crawford and K. Ulmschneider (eds), *Celtic Art in Europe: Making Connections, Essays in Honour of Vincent Megaw on his 80th Birthday*, Oxford: Oxbow Books, pp. 341–55

Bryson, B., 2000, Introduction to The Countryside Agency, *The English Landscape*, London: Profile Books

Caesar, *The Gallic War*, trs. H. J. Edwards, 1917, Loeb Classical Library 72, Cambridge, MA: Harvard University Press

Cameron, R., 2016, *Slugs and Snails*, The New Naturalist Library 133, London: William Collins

Cardinal, R., 1989, *The Landscape Vision of Paul Nash*, London: Reaktion Books

Carver, M., Sanmark, A., and Semple, S. (eds), 2010, *Signals of Belief in Early England: Anglo-Saxon Paganism Revisited*, Oxford: Oxbow Books

Cassidy, L. M., et al., 2016, 'Neolithic and Bronze Age Migration to Ireland and Establishment of the Insular Atlantic Genome', *Proceedings of the National Academy of Sciences of the USA*, 113, pp. 368–73

Chandler, J., 1993, *John Leland's Itinerary: Travels in Tudor England*, Stroud: Sutton Publishing

Chase, M., 2007, *Chartism: A New History*, Manchester: Manchester University Press

Chesterton, G. K., 1911, *The Ballad of the White Horse*, London: Methuen (7th edn, 1925)

Chevalier, T., 2003, 'Responding to Segsbury', in P. Bonaventura (ed.), *Segsbury Project: Simon Callery*, Oxford: Ruskin School of Art, pp. 38–40

Chippindale, C., 1983, 'The Making of the First Ancient Monuments Act, 1882, and Its Administration under General Pitt-Rivers', *Journal of the British Archaeological Association*, 136, pp. 1–55

Churchill, W. S., 1956, *A History of the English-Speaking Peoples Volume 1: The Birth of Britain*, London: Cassell and Co.

Clark, G., 1940, *Prehistoric England*, London: Batsford

Clark, G., 1957, *Archaeology and Society*, London: Methuen (1968 pb edn)

Cockrell, P., and Kay, S. (eds), 2006, *A View from the Hill*, Blewbury: Blewbury Village Society

Collard, M., et al., 2006, 'Ironworking in the Bronze Age? Evidence from a 10th Century BC Settlement at Hartshill Copse, Upper Bucklebury, West Berkshire', *Proceedings of the Prehistoric Society*, 72, pp. 367–422

Colley, L., 1989, 'Radical Patriotism in Eighteenth-Century England', in Samuel (ed.), 1989, pp. 169–87

Colley, L., 2010, 'Little Englander Histories', *London Review of Books*, 32 (14), pp. 12–14

Collins, A. E. P., 1952–3, 'Excavations on Blewburton Hill 1948–49', *Berkshire Archaeological Journal*, 53, pp. 21–64

Colt-Hoare, Sir R., 1821, *The Ancient History of North Wiltshire*, London

Conard, N. J., 2016, *The Vogelherd Horse and the Origins of Art*, Tübingen: University of Tübingen

Connolly, C., 1934, 'The New Medici', *The Architectural Review*, 71

Crane, N., 2016, *The Making of the British Landscape*, London: Weidenfeld & Nicolson

Creighton, J., 2000, *Coins and Power in Late Iron Age Britain*, Cambridge: Cambridge University Press

Cunliffe, B., 2001, *Facing the Ocean: The Atlantic and Its Peoples, 8000 BC–AD 1500*, Oxford: Oxford University Press

Cunliffe, B., 2015, *By Steppe, Desert, and Ocean: The Birth of Eurasia*, Oxford: Oxford University Press

Daniel, G., 1967, *The Origins and Growth of Archaeology*, Harmondsworth: Penguin

Daniels, S., 1994, *Fields of Vision: Landscape Imagery and National Identity in England and the United States*, Cambridge: Polity Press

Davis, L. B., and Reeve, B. O. K. (eds), 1990, *Hunters of the Recent Past*, London: Unwin Hyman

Defoe, D., 1725, *A Tour through the Whole Island of Great Britain* (1978 Penguin Classics edn, London: Penguin)

Demos, J., 1996, *The Unredeemed Captive: A Family Story from Early America*, London: Papermac

Diepeveen-Jansen, M., 2007, 'Early La Tène Burial Practices and Social (Re)Constructions in the Marne–Moselle Region', in Haselgrove and Pope (eds), 2007, pp. 374–89

Dilworth, T., 2017, *David Jones: Engraver, Soldier, Painter, Poet*, London: Jonathan Cape

Done, G., 1991, 'The Animal Bone', in Needham, 1991, pp. 327–42

Duffy, E., 1992, *The Stripping of the Altars: Traditional Religion in England, 1400–1580*, New Haven: Yale University Press

Edwards, B., 2005, 'The Scouring of the White Horse Country', *Wiltshire Archaeological and Natural History Magazine*, 98, pp. 90–127

Egginton, A., 2011, 'The Landscape Context of Chalk Geoglyphs in Southern England', unpublished MSc dissertation, University of Southampton

Eliot, T. S., 1957, *On Poetry and Poets*, London: Faber & Faber

Engel, M., 2015, *Engel's England*, London: Profile Books

Ewers, J. C., 1955, *The Horse in Blackfoot Indian Culture, with Comparative Material from Other Western Tribes*, Washington: Smithsonian Institution Bureau of American Ethnology

Fern, C., 2010, 'Horses in Mind', in Carver, Sanmark and Semple (eds), 2010, pp. 128–57

Firestein, S., 2012, *Ignorance: How It Drives Science*, Oxford: Oxford University Press

Flannery, T., 2001, *The Eternal Frontier: An Ecological History of North America and Its Peoples*, London: William Heinemann

Flannery, T., 2004, *Country*, Melbourne: Text Publishing

Fontijn, D., and Fokkens, H., 2007, 'The Emergence of Early Iron Age "Chieftains' Graves" in the Southern Netherlands: Reconsidering Transformations in Burial and Depositional Practices', in Haselgrove and Pope (eds), 2007, pp. 354–73

Fowler, P. J., 2000, *Landscape Plotted and Pieced: Landscape History and Local Archaeology in Fyfield and Overton, Wiltshire*, London: Society of Antiquaries of London

Friend, A., 2017, *Ravilious & Co: The Pattern of Friendship*, London: Thames & Hudson

Gell, A., 1998, *Art and Agency: An Anthropological Theory*, Oxford: Clarendon Press

Gelling, M., 1973, 1974, 1976, *The Place-Names of Berkshire: Parts 1, 2, 3*, English Place-Name Society, Vols XLIX, L, LI, Cambridge: Cambridge University Press

Gelling, P., and Davidson, H. E., 1969, *The Chariot of the Sun and Other Rites and Symbols of the Northern Bronze Age*, London: J. M. Dent

Green, M., 1991, *The Sun-Gods of Ancient Europe*, London: Batsford

Greenwell, W., 1877, *British Barrows: A Record of the Examination of Sepulchral Mounds in Various Parts of England*, Oxford: Clarendon Press

Grigson, G., 1939, *Several Observations*, London: Cresset Press

Hamerow, H., 2002, *Early Medieval Settlements: The Archaeology of Rural Communities in North-West Europe 400–900*, Oxford: Oxford University Press

Hamerow, H., 2012, *Rural Settlements and Society in Anglo-Saxon England*, Oxford: Oxford University Press

Hamerow, H., Hinton, D., and Crawford, S. (eds), 2011, *The Oxford Handbook of Anglo-Saxon Archaeology*, Oxford: Oxford University Press

Harding, A. F., 2014, 'The Later Prehistory of Central and Northern Europe', in Renfrew and Bahn (eds), 2014, *Vol. 3*, pp. 1912–36

Harding, D. W., 1972, *The Iron Age in the Upper Thames Basin*, Oxford: Clarendon Press

Harris, A., 2010, *Romantic Moderns: English Writers, Artists and the Imagination from Virginia Woolf to John Piper*, London: Thames & Hudson

Haselgrove, C., and Pope, R. (eds), 2007, *The Earlier Iron Age in Britain and the Near Continent*, Oxford: Oxbow Books

Hauser, K., 2008, *Bloody Old Britain: O. G. S. Crawford and the Archaeology of Modern Life*, London: Granta Books

Hawkes, J., 1951, *A Land*, London: Cresset Press (1978 edn, Newton Abbot: David & Charles)

Hawkes, J., 1981, *A Guide to the Prehistoric and Roman Monuments in England and Wales*, London: Chatto & Windus

Hawkes, J., and Mills, S. (eds), 1999, *Northumbria's Golden Age*, Stroud: Sutton Publishing

Hay, D., 1952, *Polydore Vergil: Renaissance Historian and Man of Letters*, Oxford: Clarendon Press

Haycock, D. B., 2002, *British Artists: Paul Nash*, London: Tate Publishing

Heaney, S., 1966, *Death of a Naturalist*, London: Faber & Faber

Hebel, J. W. (ed.), 1961, *The Works of Michael Drayton*, vol. 4, Oxford: Basil Blackwell

Heidorn, L. A., 1997, 'The Horses of Kush', *Journal of Near Eastern Studies*, 56 (2), pp. 105–14

Henshilwood, C. S., and Lombard, M., 2014, 'Becoming Human: Archaeology of the Sub-Saharan Middle Stone Age', in Renfrew and Bahn (eds), 2014, *Vol. 1*, pp. 106–30

Hey, G., 2004, *Yarnton: Saxon and Medieval Settlement and Landscape: Results of Excavations 1990–96*, Thames Valley Landscapes Monograph 20, Oxford: Oxford Archaeology

Hey, G., Bayliss, A., and Boyle, A., 1999, 'Iron Age Inhumation Burials at Yarnton, Oxfordshire', *Antiquity*, 73, pp. 551–62

Hills, C., 2015, 'Work Boxes or Reliquaries? Small Copper-Alloy Containers in Seventh-Century Anglo-Saxon Graves', in Ruhmann and Brieske (eds), 2015, pp. 51–62

Hirst, S., and Rahtz, P., 1996, 'Liddington Castle and the Battle of Badon: Excavations and Research 1976', *The Archaeological Journal*, 153, pp. 1–59

Hooke, D., 1985, *The Anglo-Saxon Landscape: The Kingdom of the Hwicce*, Manchester: Manchester University Press

Hoskins, W. G., 1955, *The Making of the English Landscape*, London: Hodder & Stoughton

Howe, C., 2014, *Halifax 1842: A Year of Crisis*, London: Breviary Stuff Publications

Hudson, W. H., 1900, *Nature in Downland*, London: Longmans, Green & Co. (2008 edn, Dodo Press)

Hughes, T., 1857, *Tom Brown's School Days*, Cambridge: MacMillan & Co. (1989 Oxford World's Classics illus. edn, Oxford: Oxford University Press)

Hughes, T., 1859, *The Scouring of the White Horse*, Cambridge: MacMillan & Co.

Hughes, T., 1889 edn, *Tom Brown at Oxford*, London: MacMillan & Co.

Hughes, T., 1984, *What Is the Truth? A Farmyard Fable for the Young*, London: Faber & Faber

Hutton, R., 1991, *The Pagan Religions of the Ancient British Isles: Their Nature and Legacy*, Oxford: Blackwell (1993 pb edn)

Hutton, R., 1994, *The Rise and Fall of Merry England: The Ritual Year 1400–1700*, Oxford: Oxford University Press

Hutton, R., 1999, *The Triumph of the Moon: A History of Modern Pagan Witchcraft*, Oxford: Oxford University Press (2001 pb edn)

Hutton, R., 2010, 'Afterword', in Carver, Sanmark and Semple (eds), 2010, pp. 201–6

Hyland, A., 1990, *Equus: The Horse in the Roman World*, London: Batsford

Ingold, T., 2000, *The Perception of the Environment: Essays on Livelihood, Dwelling and Skill*, London: Routledge

Ingrams, R., 1988, *The Ridgeway: Europe's Oldest Road*, Oxford: Phaidon

Insoll, T., 2004, *Archaeology, Ritual, Religion*, London: Routledge

Jenkins, S., 1999, *England's Thousand Best Churches*, London: Penguin

Jones, D., 1952, *The Anathemata*, London: Faber & Faber

Jones, R., 2018, *Beetles*, The New Naturalist Library 136, London: William Collins

Kamash, Z., Gosden, C., and Lock, G., 2010, 'Continuity and Religious Practices in Roman Britain: The Case of the Rural Religious Complex at Marcham/Frilford, Oxfordshire', *Britannia*, 41, pp. 95–125

Kaul, F., 1998, *Ships on Bronzes: A Study in Bronze Age Religion and Iconography*, Copenhagen: National Museum of Denmark

Kehoe, T. E., 1990, 'Corralling: Evidence from Upper Palaeolithic Cave Art', in Davis and Reeve (eds), 1990, pp. 34–46

Krausse, D., et al., 2017, 'The "Keltenblock" Project: Discovery and Excavation of a Rich Hallstatt Grave at the Heuneburg, Germany', *Antiquity*, 91, pp. 108–23

Kühn, H., 1972, foreword to A. P. Okladnikow, *Der Hirsche mit dem goldenen Geweih* Wiesbaden, quoted in Baumer, C., 2012

Lambrick, G. H., and Allen, T. G., 2004, *Gravelly Guy, Stanton Harcourt, Oxfordshire: The Development of a Prehistoric and Romano-British Community*, Thames Valley Landscapes Monograph 21, Oxford: Oxford Archaeology

Lambrick, G., with Robinson, M., 2009, *The Thames Through Time: The Archaeology of the Gravel Terraces of the Upper and Middle Thames: The Thames Valley in Late Prehistory: 1500 BC – AD 50*, Thames Valley Landscapes Monograph 29, Oxford: Oxford Archaeology

Lane Fox, R., 1986, *Pagans and Christians in the Mediterranean World from the Second Century AD to the Conversion of Constantine*, London: Viking (1988 pb edn, London: Penguin)

Lawson, A. J. (ed.), 2000, *Potterne 1982–5: Animal Husbandry in Later Prehistoric Wiltshire*, Wessex Archaeology Report 17, Salisbury: Trust for Wessex Archaeology

Leeds, E. T., 1923, 'A Saxon Village near Sutton Courtenay, Berkshire', *Archaeologia*, 73, pp. 147–92

Leeds, E. T., 1947, 'A Saxon Village at Sutton Courtenay, Berkshire: Third Report', *Archaeologia*, 92, pp. 79–93

Levick, P., 2015, *Later Prehistoric and Roman Landscapes on the Berkshire Downs*, BAR British Series 612, Oxford: British Archaeological Reports

Lock, G. (ed.), 2000, *Beyond the Map: Archaeological and Spatial Technologies*, Amsterdam: IOS Press

Longley, E. (ed.), 2008, *Edward Thomas: The Annotated Collected Poems*, Tarset: Bloodaxe Books

Lucy, S., 2000, *The Anglo-Saxon Way of Death*, Stroud: Sutton Publishing

MacCarthy, F., 1994, *William Morris: A Life for Our Time*, London: Faber & Faber

MacCulloch, D., 2016, *All Things Made New: Writings on the Reformation*, London: Allen Lane, pp. 94–117

MacCulloch, D., 2018, *Thomas Cromwell: A Life*, London: Allen Lane

MacDougall, H. A., 1982, *Racial Myth in English History: Trojans, Teutons, and Anglo-Saxons*, Montreal & Hanover, New Hampshire: Harvest House & University Press of New England

MacFadden, B. J., 1992, *Fossil Horses: Systematics, Paleobiology, and Evolution of the Family Equidae*, Cambridge: Cambridge University Press

Macfarlane, R., Donwood, S., and Richards, D., 2013, *Holloway*, London: Faber & Faber

McGrath, C., 2016, *Mr Darley's Arabian: High Life, Low Life, Sporting Life: A History of Racing in Twenty-Five Horses*, London: John Murray

Manco, J., 2018, *The Origins of the Anglo-Saxons: Decoding the Ancestry of the English*, London: Thames & Hudson

Marples, M., 1949, *White Horses and Other Hill Figures*, London: Country Life (1981 edn, Stroud: Sutton Publishing)

Mellor, D., 1987, *A Paradise Lost: The Neo-Romantic Imagination in Britain 1935–1955*, London: Lund Humphries and Barbican Art Gallery

Miles, D., 2003, 'An Archaeologist on the Ridgeway', in P. Bonaventura (ed.), *Segsbury Project: Simon Callery*, Oxford: Ruskin School of Art, pp. 53–61

Miles, D., et al., 2003, *Uffington White Horse and Its Landscape: Investigations at White Horse Hill Uffington, 1989–95, and Tower Hill Ashbury, 1993–4*, Thames Valley Landscapes Monograph 18, Oxford: Oxford Archaeology

Miles, D., 2016, *The Tale of the Axe: How the Neolithic Revolution Transformed Britain*, London: Thames & Hudson

Mitchell, P., 2015, *Horse Nations: The Worldwide Impact of the Horse on Indigenous Societies Post-1492*, Oxford: Oxford University Press

Morris, C. (ed.), 1984, *The Illustrated Journeys of Celia Fiennes circa 1682 – circa 1712*, London: Macdonald & Co.

Müller, F., 2009, *Art of the Celts: 700 BC to AD 700*, Historisches Museum Berne, and Brussels: Mercatorfonds

Munby, J., 1996, *Great Coxwell Barn, Oxon* (National Trust guide), Swindon: National Trust

Needham, S. P., 1991, *Excavation and Salvage at Runnymede Bridge 1978: The Late Bronze Age Waterfront Site*, London: British Museum Press

Newman, P., 1997, *Lost Gods of Albion: The Chalk Hill-Figures of Britain*, Stroud: Sutton Publishing

Olalde, I., et al., 2018, 'The Beaker Phenomenon and the Genomic Transformation of Northwest Europe', *Nature*, 555, pp. 190–6

Page, W., and Ditchfield, P. H. (eds), 1924, *A History of the County of Berkshire: Volume 4*, Victoria County History

Parker, J., 2007, '*England's Darling*': *The Victorian Cult of Alfred the Great*, Manchester: Manchester University Press

Parker Pearson, M., 2012, *Stonehenge: Exploring the Greatest Stone Age Mystery*, London: Simon & Schuster

Parsons, A., and Millikin, S., 2014, *Landscape Reinvented: The Uffington Enclosure Award 1778*, Uffington Museum Trust

Petrie, Sir W. F., 1926, *The Hill Figures of England*, London: Royal Anthropological Institute

Piggott, S., 1931, 'The Uffington White Horse', *Antiquity*, 5 (17), pp. 37–46

Piggott, S., 1983, 'Archaeological Retrospect 5', *Antiquity*, 57, pp. 28–37

Piggott, S., 1985, *William Stukeley: An Eighteenth-Century Antiquary*, London: Thames & Hudson

Piggott, S., 1989, *Ancient Britons and the Antiquarian Imagination*, London: Thames & Hudson

Piggott, S., 1992, *Wagon, Chariot and Carriage: Symbol and Status in the History of Transport*, London: Thames & Hudson

Plenderleath, W. C., 1874, 'On the White Horses of Wiltshire and Its Neighbourhood', *Wiltshire Archaeological Magazine*, pp. 12–30

Plenderleath, W. C., 1880, 'The White Horses of Wiltshire', *The North Wiltshire Church Magazine*

Plenderleath, W. C., 1892 (2nd edn), *The White Horses of the West of England*, London: Allen & Storr

Pollard, J., 2017, 'The Uffington White Horse Geoglyph as Sun-horse', *Antiquity*, 91 (356), pp. 406–20

Pollard, J., and Reynolds, A., 2002, *Avebury: The Biography of a Landscape*, Stroud: Tempus

Price, N. (ed.), 2001, *The Archaeology of Shamanism*, London: Routledge

Quiles, A. H., et al., 2016, 'A High Precision Chronological Model for the Decorated Upper Palaeolithic Cave of Chauvet-Pont d'Arc, Ardèche, France', *Proceedings of the National Academy of Sciences of the USA*, 113, pp. 4670–5

Rahtz, P., 1993, *Glastonbury*, London: Batsford and English Heritage

Randsborg, K., 2009, *The Anatomy of Denmark: Archaeology and History from the Ice Age to the Present*, London: Bloomsbury

Rasmussen, S., et al., 2015, 'Early Divergent Strains of *Yersinia pestis* in Eurasia 5,000 Years Ago', *Cell*, 163, pp. 571–82

Raulff, U., 2017, *Farewell to the Horse: The Final Century of Our Relationship*, London: Allen Lane

Reich, D., 2018, *Who We Are and How We Got Here: Ancient DNA and the New Science of the Human Past*, Oxford: Oxford University Press

Reichel-Dolmatoff, G., 1971, *Amazonian Cosmos: The Sexual and Religious Symbolism of the Turkano Indians*, Chicago: University of Chicago Press

Renfrew, C., 2007, *Prehistory: The Making of the Human Mind*, London: Weidenfeld & Nicolson

Renfrew, C., and Bahn, P. (eds), 2014, *The Cambridge World Prehistory, Volume 1: Africa, South and Southeast Asia and the Pacific*, Cambridge: Cambridge University Press

Renfrew, C., and Bahn, P. (eds), 2014, *The Cambridge World Prehistory, Volume 3: West and Central Asia and Europe*, Cambridge: Cambridge University Press

Rivet, A. L. F., and Smith, C., 1978, *The Place-Names of Roman Britain*, London: Batsford

Rowlands, M., 1993, 'The Role of Memory in the Transmission

of Culture', *World Archaeology* 25 (2), pp. 141–51

Ruhmann, C., and Brieske, V. (eds), 2015, *Dying Gods: Religious Beliefs in Northern and Eastern Europe in the Time of Christianisation*, Neue Studien zur Sachsenforschung 5, Hannover: Die Publishing Company

Russell, J., 2015, *Ravilious*, London: Philip Wilson Publishers

Samuel, R. (ed.), 1989, *Patriotism: The Making and Unmaking of British National Identity, Volume 1: History and Politics*, London: Routledge

Schama, S., 1995, *Landscape and Memory*, London: Harper Collins

Schrader, S., et al., 2018, 'Symbolic Equids and Kushite State Formation: A Horse Burial at Tombos', *Antiquity*, 92 (362), pp. 383–97

Schwyzer, P., 1999. 'The Scouring of the White Horse: Archaeology, Identity and "Heritage"', *Representations*, 65, pp. 42–62

Schwyzer, P., 2004, *Literature, Nationalism and Memory in Early Modern England and Wales*, Cambridge: Cambridge University Press

Schwyzer, P., 2007, *Archaeologies of English Renaissance Literature*, Oxford: Oxford University Press

Scull, C., 2015, 'Chronology, Burial and Conversion: The Case of England in the 7th Century', in Ruhmann and Brieske (eds), 2015, pp. 73–83

Semple, S., 2011, 'Sacred Spaces and Places in Pre-Christian and Conversion Period Anglo-Saxon England', in Hamerow, Hinton and Crawford (eds), 2011, pp. 742–63

Simpson, S., and Pankova, S., 2017, *Scythians: Warriors of Ancient Siberia*, London: Thames & Hudson and British Museum

Smyth, A. P., 1995, *King Alfred the Great*, Oxford: Oxford University Press

Stallworthy, J., 2002, *The Skyhorse*, Oxford: Thumbscrew Press

Steane, J., 1983, 'How Old is the Berkshire Ridgeway', *Antiquity*, 57, pp. 103–8

Stevenson, R. D., and Wassersug, R. J., 1993, 'Horsepower from a Horse', *Nature*, 364 (6434), p. 195

Sutcliff, R., 1977, *Sun Horse, Moon Horse*, London: The Bodley Head

Suzman, J., 2017, *Affluence Without Abundance: The Disappearing World of the Bushmen*, New York: Bloomsbury

Sweet, R., 2004, *Antiquaries: The Discovery of the Past in Eighteenth-Century Britain*, London: Hambledon & London

Thomas, C., 1961, 'The Animal Art of the Scottish Iron Age and Its Origins', *The Archaeological Journal*, 118, pp. 14–64

Thomas, E., 1909a, *Richard Jefferies: His Life and Work*, London: Hutchinson (2008 edn, London: Faber & Faber)

Thomas, E., 1909b, *The South Country* (1932 Everyman edn, London: Dent)

Thomas, E., 1911, *Maurice Maeterlinck*, London: Methuen & Co.

Thomas, E., 1913, *The Icknield Way*, London: Constable & Co.

Thoms, W. J., 1846, 'Some Observations on the White Horse of Berkshire', *Archaeologia*, 31, pp. 289–96

Thurley, S., 2013, *Men from the Ministry: How Britain Saved Its Heritage*, New Haven: Yale University Press (2014 pb edn)

Tilling, B. J., 2007, *The White Horse Show: A Village Charity*, London: Athena Press

Tyack, G., Bradley, S., and Pevsner, N., 2010, *Berkshire*, Pevsner Architectural Guides: Buildings of England, New Haven: Yale University Press

Vansittart, P., 1981, *The Death of Robin Hood*, London: Peter Owen

Waddington, C., et al., 2012, 'Excavations at Fin Cop, Derbyshire: An Iron Age Hillfort in Conflict?', *The Archaeological Journal*, 169, pp. 159–236

Wain, J., 1977, *Professing Poetry*, London: Macmillan

Waley, A., 1955, 'The Heavenly Horses of Ferghana: A New View', *History Today*, 5 (2), pp. 95–103

Warne, C., 1866, *The Celtic Tumuli of Dorset*, London: John Russell Smith

Watts, I., 2009, 'Red Ochre, Body Painting, and Language: Interpreting the Blombos Ochre', in Botha and Knight (eds), 2009, pp. 62–93

Webster, L., 1999a, 'The Iconographic Programme of the Franks Casket', in Hawkes and Mills (eds), 1999, pp. 227–46

Webster, L., 1999b, 'The Franks Casket', in M. Lapidge, J. Blair and S. Keynes (eds), *The Blackwell Encyclopaedia of Anglo-Saxon England*, Oxford: Blackwell, pp. 194–5

Webster, L., 2012, *The Franks Casket*, London: British Museum Press

West, M. L., 2007, *Indo-European Poetry and Myth*, Oxford: Oxford University Press

Whitelock, D. (ed.), with D. C. Douglas and S. I. Tucker, 1961, *The Anglo-Saxon Chronicle: A Revised Translation*, London: Eyre & Spottiswoode (1965 rev. edn)

Whittle, A., Healy, F., and Bayliss, A., 2011, *Gathering Time: Dating the Early Neolithic Enclosures of Southern Britain and Ireland, Volume 1*, Oxford: Oxbow Books

Wilk, C. (ed), 2006, *Modernism: Designing a New World 1914–1939*, London: V&A Publications

Williams, A., 1913, *Villages of the White Horse*, London: Duckworth & Co.

Williams, H., 2001, 'An Ideology of Transformation: Cremation Rites and Animal Sacrifice in Early Anglo-Saxon England', in Price (ed.), 2001, pp. 193–212

Wilson, A. N., 2006, *Betjeman*, London: Arrow Books (2007 pb edn)

Wilson, D., 1992, *Anglo-Saxon Paganism*, London: Routledge

Wilson, J. M., 2015, *Edward Thomas, From Adlestrop to Arras: A Biography*, London: Bloomsbury

Wise, F., 1738, *A Letter to Dr Mead, Concerning Some Antiquities in Berkshire, particularly shewing that the White Horse, which gives name to the Vale, is a monument of the West Saxons, made in memory of a great victory obtained over the Danes AD 871*, Oxford: Printed for Thomas Wood at the University Printing-House

Woolf, G., 1998, *Becoming Roman: The Origins of Provincial Civilization in Gaul*, Cambridge: Cambridge University Press

Woolner, D., 1965, 'The White Horse, Uffington', *Transactions of the Newbury District Field Club*, 11 (3), pp. 27–44

Woolner, D., 1967, 'New Light on the White Horse', *Folklore*, 78, pp. 90–111

Wroe, A., 2016, *Six Facets of Light*, London: Jonathan Cape

SOURCES OF ILLUSTRATIONS

ACKNOWLEDGMENTS

First I must thank the members of the team of Oxford archaeologists who contributed to the White Horse project and its publication, notably: Richard Bailey, Alistair Barclay, Anne Marie Cromarty Angela Boyle, Phillipa Bradley, Anne Dodd, Chris Gosden, Alan Hardy, Gary Lock, Mark Robinson, and especially Simon Palmer, who supervised the excavation of the Horse itself. Julie Rees-Jones and Mike Tite of the Research Laboratory for Art History and Archaeology coordinated the pioneering OSL dating.

Hill figures have not always been in fashion among academic archaeologists, so Paul Newman and Rodney Castleden deserve recognition for keeping the flame alight. I have also learnt a great deal about prehistoric, Romano-British and later religious belief from the work of Miranda Aldhouse-Green, Ronald Hutton and Josh Pollard, who developed the idea of the prehistoric sky-horse. For the early modern and political history I have drawn on the writings of Brian Edwards and Philip Schwyzer, to whom I am grateful. For help with the literary and artistic sources I must also thank Adam Thorpe and Anna Dillon. Peter Fowler has been a constant fount of wisdom about English and French landscapes since he gave me my first proper job in archaeology in 1970.

In the Uffington area Sharon Smith, Karen Picher, Sandra Millikin and Anthony Parsons have assisted with local history and Eric Penser with hospitality and information about local land-use, farming and horse-training. The hosts and patrons of the White Horse public house in Woolstone provided good beer, warm fires and anecdotes.

I am grateful to the staff of the National Trust and English Heritage, particularly the late Keith Blaxhall and Andy Foley, the successive dedicated wardens of White Horse Hill.

An author depends upon the assistance of enthusiastic librarians: in my case at the Bodleian and Ashmolean libraries, Oxford, the British Library and the London Library, the librarians at English Heritage and the Local History Library, Newbury.

At Thames & Hudson Colin Ridler and then Ben Hayes commissioned this book and provided unfailing support. Joanna Murray and Sarah Vernon-Hunt had the unenviable task of editing, polishing and pruning the text, both with an amazing facility for detail. Karolina Prymaka designed the book and Poppy David oversaw its production. Pauline Hubner tracked down pictures with the tenacity of a blood hound.

Most of all my love and thanks to Gwyn Miles without whose dogged support this book would still be an incoherent pile of paper.

INDEX